STAR WARS
TALES OF THE
JEDI
Dark Lords of the Sith

DARK HORSE COMICS®

STAR

TALES

JE

Dark Lords

WARS

OF THE

DI

of the Sith

Introduction

For over a thousand generations the Jedi Knights were the guardians of peace and justice in the Old Republic.

—Obi-Wan Kenobi

When George Lucas wrote those stirring words, he called into being millions of untold stories, spanning more than 25,000 years of *Star Wars* history.

Kevin J. Anderson and I are grateful to have been allowed to tell some of these stories, with the assistance of the fine artists who have brought their diverse styles to *Tales of the Jedi*.

Tales of the Jedi began with a two-page-a-month, black-and-white comic which the artist Chris Gossett and I created for the Dark Horse Comics *Insider* beginning in early 1992. These pages, which can be found collected and colored in the *Tales of the Jedi* Volume One paperback, tell the story of a Jedi Master named Arca and his three apprentices, the brothers Ulic

and Cay Qel-Droma, and the Twi'lek Jedi, Tott Doneeta.

My idea was to begin simply, in close-up to the lives of a few Jedi, during a time four thousand years before the birth of Luke Skywalker. As Chris would develop the look of the people and worlds and technologies of that time, we would spin our story outward, eventually, we hoped, touching on events of a Galaxy-spanning nature.

Ultimately, we knew, the story would recount events revealed by the Jedi Holocron to Leia Organa Solo in the text pages of *Star Wars: Dark Empire*. I had conceived these events as an example of what might happen to Leia's brother, Luke. The Holocron told Leia that there once was a great and honored Jedi named Ulic Qel-Droma, who, like Luke Skywalker, had tried to conquer the dark side of the Force by learning its secrets. Ulic had been seduced by the dark side, eventually becoming a political genius who drew the Galaxy into a massive military conflict. Now Chris and I, together with the artists Janine Johnston, David Roach, Mike Barreiro, Tony Akins, Denis Rodier, Suzanne Bourdages,

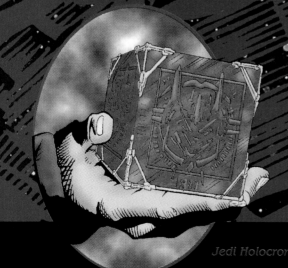

Jedi Holocron

Pamela Rambo, and Dave Dorman were fleshing out the Holocron's tale with images and stories of Ulic and other Jedi Knights and Masters.

Enter Kevin J. Anderson. Kevin and I were in consultation on the continuity of his Jedi Academy novels, trying to achieve a fit with my *Dark Empire* story line. Kevin had a character named Exar Kun, a Dark Lord of the Sith whose spirit had been imprisoned for millennia in an ancient temple of the moon Yavin Four.

"Wouldn't it be great," we said, "if we connected the historical Exar Kun to Ulic Qel-Droma's story in *Tales of the Jedi*?" In a fit of mutual enthusiasm, we constructed a massive proposal for a 12-issue comic-book series to be called *Dark Lords of the Sith*. Our proposal called for major revelations about the history of the *Star Wars* galaxy: we would reveal exactly who the Sith people were, including their arcane mysteries and powers and their ongoing conflict with the Jedi and the Galactic Republic. And we would recount events surrounding the lineage of the infamous Dark-Lords, those fallen Jedi who ruled the Sith using the powers of the dark side of the Force. (Darth Vader, you will remember, was a Dark Lord of the Sith.)

When Lucasfilm approved our proposal, we set to work with editor Dan Thorsland to put it all on paper.

As I look at what we accomplished, I feel a sense of pride. I also see how things didn't turn out as we envisioned. Partway through the project, due to unlucky circumstance, we lost our penciller, Chris Gossett, whose talent for imagining the look and feel of the *Star Wars* universe is, in my opinion, comparable to the work of the artists who designed the *Star Wars* films. Fortunately, penciller Art Wetherell was there to help us carry on. Inker Jordi Ensign, colorist Pamela Rambo, cover artist Hugh Fleming, and letterer Willie Schubert were with us from start to finish.

My thanks to all of them and to Kevin J. Anderson for many delightful hours "mindstorming" *Star Wars* ideas. My special thanks to George Lucas for giving us free rein with his creations and to the avid *Star Wars* fans who have helped keep the spirit of *Star Wars* burning brightly for the past eighteen years.

It is our fervent hope you'll enjoy this brief glimpse into the past of the *Star Wars* galaxy — and the history of the great order of Jedi Knights.

May the Force be with you!

—Tom Veitch

script **Tom Veitch &**
Kevin J. Anderson

pencils **Chris Gossett &**
Art Wetherell

inks **Mike Barreiro &**
Jordi Ensign

cover art **Hugh Fleming**

lettering **Willie Schubert**

coloring **Pamela Rambo**

publisher
Mike Richardson

series editors
Dan Thorsland &
Ryder Windham

collection editor
Lynn Adair

collection designer
Scott Tice

collection design manager
Brian Gogolin

special thanks to
Lucy Autrey Wilson &
Allan Kausch
at Lucasfilm Licensing

STAR WARS® TALES OF THE JEDI™ - DARK LORDS OF THE SITH

This book collects issues one through six of the Dark Horse comic-book series
Star Wars: Tales of the Jedi - Dark Lords of the Sith.

Published by
Dark Horse Comics, Inc.
10956 SE Main Street
Milwaukie, OR 97222

February 1996
First edition
ISBN:1-56971-095-3

10 9 8 7 6 5 4 3

Printed in Canada

For a thousand generations young Jedi Knights
have dedicated their lives to preserving
harmony and justice throughout the Galactic
Republic.

Four millennia before the birth of Luke Skywalker,
the brothers Ulic and Cay Qel-Droma were two who
took up the Jedi way. Together with the Twi'lek Tott
Doneeta they apprenticed to the wise Jedi Master Arca
of Arkania.

Another student of the Force was Nomi Sunrider, who
chose to become a Jedi Knight after the tragic death of her
Jedi husband, Andur. Nomi and her daughter Vima were
taught by the great beast-Jedi, Master Thon of Ambria.

These renowned Jedi, and others equally as valiant, became
enmeshed in dramatic and harrowing events surrounding the
reappearance of the dark teachings of the Sith, an ancient race
of magicians long thought extinct.

Four hundred years before Arca and Thon, a dark Jedi named
Freedon Nadd introduced the suppressed Sith teachings to the
planet Onderon. Nadd's dark-side powers took hold on the
isolated world, and flourished unchecked until Master Arca brought
together a band of Jedi to root them out.

Now Freedon Nadd's living spirit has managed to confound the great
old Jedi. On Onderon, under Arca's very nose, Nadd has instructed two
young aristocrats, Satal Keto and Aleema, heirs to the throne of the
Empress Teta System. Satal and Aleema have returned to their
homeworld as powerful initiates of the Sith way.

Elsewhere, other events are unfolding that will affect the future of the
Galaxy: On the planet Dantooine, a proud Jedi named Exar Kun steals his
Master's holocron, curious to learn more about the legendary fallen Jedi
Knights who were known as the Dark Lords of the Sith.

The Holocron speaks . . .

"Time and again, throughout the eons, the power of the dark side of the Force has advanced with the fury of a storm, sweeping up star system after star system. Only in great conflagration were the forces of the dark side defeated..."

"The dark side has come before, and it will come again. Do **not** underestimate its power. That is why I have devoted my life to teaching Jedi Knights, to strengthen the light side against the tide of darkness that is sure to come."

Vodo-Siosk Baas, Jedi Master

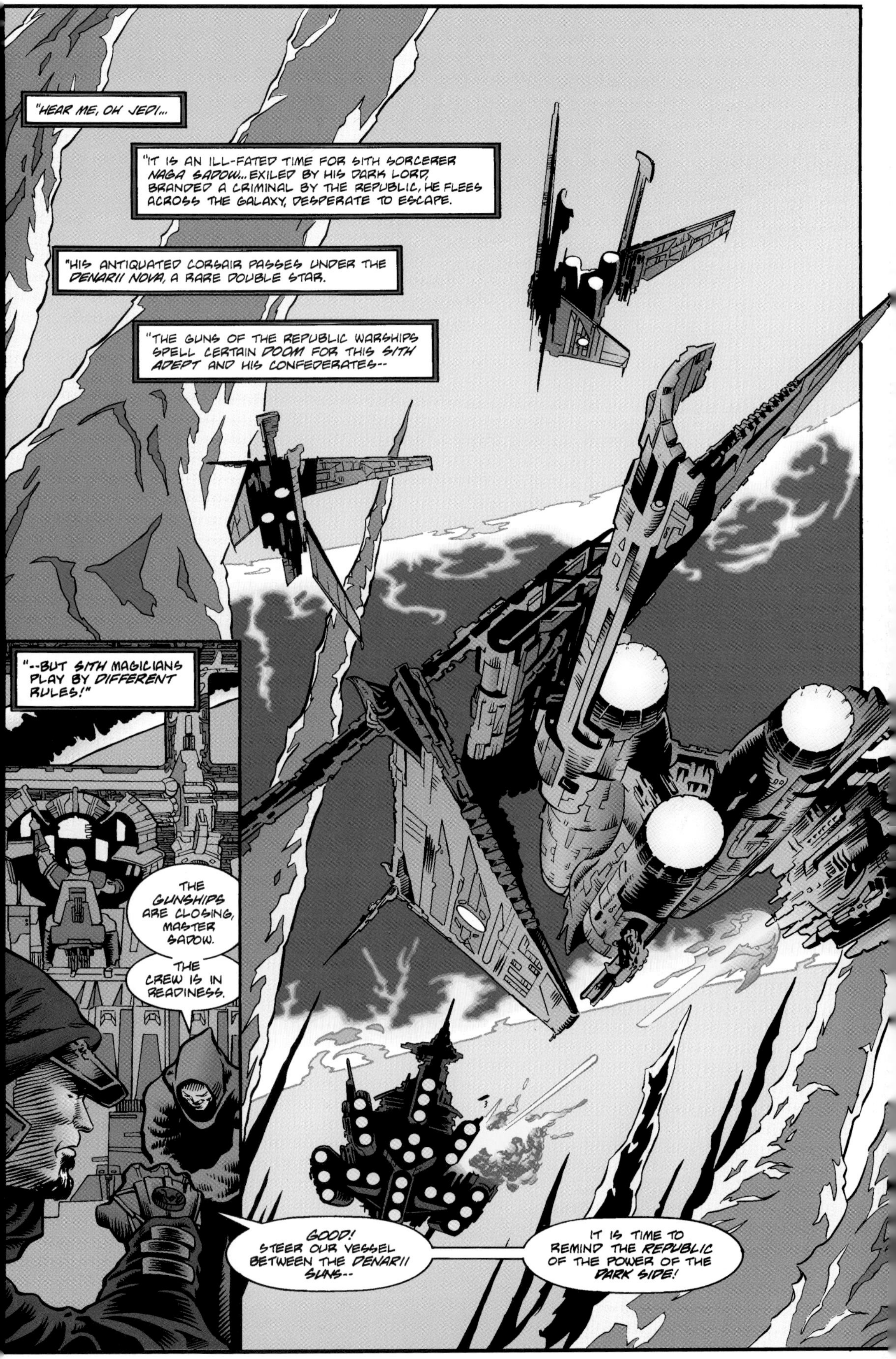
"HEAR ME, OH JEDI...
"IT IS AN ILL-FATED TIME FOR SITH SORCERER NAGA SADOW... EXILED BY HIS DARK LORD, BRANDED A CRIMINAL BY THE REPUBLIC, HE FLEES ACROSS THE GALAXY, DESPERATE TO ESCAPE.
"HIS ANTIQUATED CORSAIR PASSES UNDER THE DENARII NOVA, A RARE DOUBLE STAR.
"THE GUNS OF THE REPUBLIC WARSHIPS SPELL CERTAIN DOOM FOR THIS SITH ADEPT AND HIS CONFEDERATES--
"--BUT SITH MAGICIANS PLAY BY DIFFERENT RULES!"
THE GUNSHIPS ARE CLOSING, MASTER SADOW.
THE CREW IS IN READINESS.
GOOD! STEER OUR VESSEL BETWEEN THE DENARII SUNS--
IT IS TIME TO REMIND THE REPUBLIC OF THE POWER OF THE DARK SIDE!

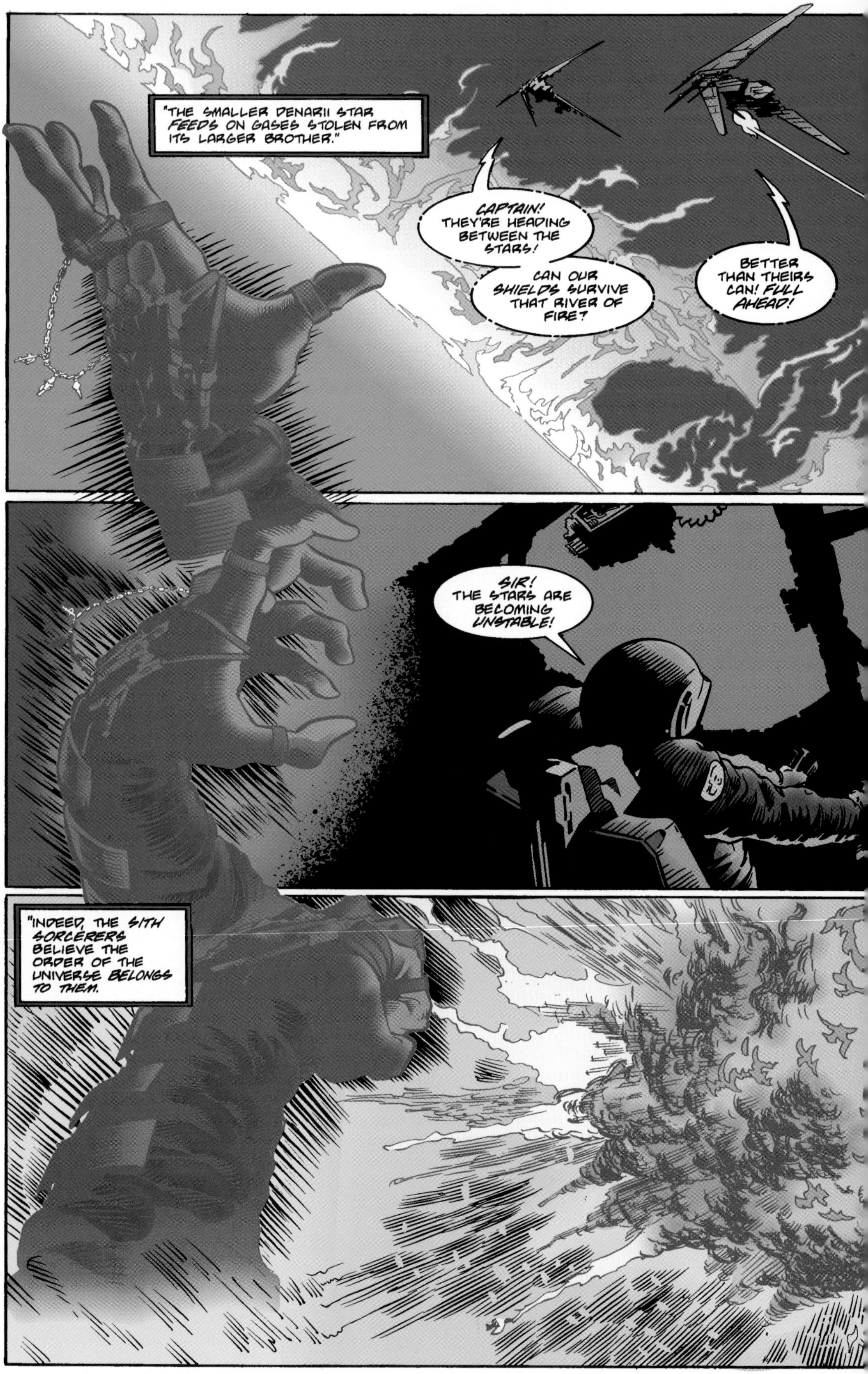
"THE SMALLER DENARII STAR FEEDS ON GASES STOLEN FROM ITS LARGER BROTHER."
CAPTAIN! THEY'RE HEADING BETWEEN THE STARS!
CAN OUR SHIELDS SURVIVE THAT RIVER OF FIRE?
BETTER THAN THEIRS CAN! FULL AHEAD!
SIR! THE STARS ARE BECOMING UNSTABLE!
"INDEED, THE SITH SORCERERS BELIEVE THE ORDER OF THE UNIVERSE BELONGS TO THEM.

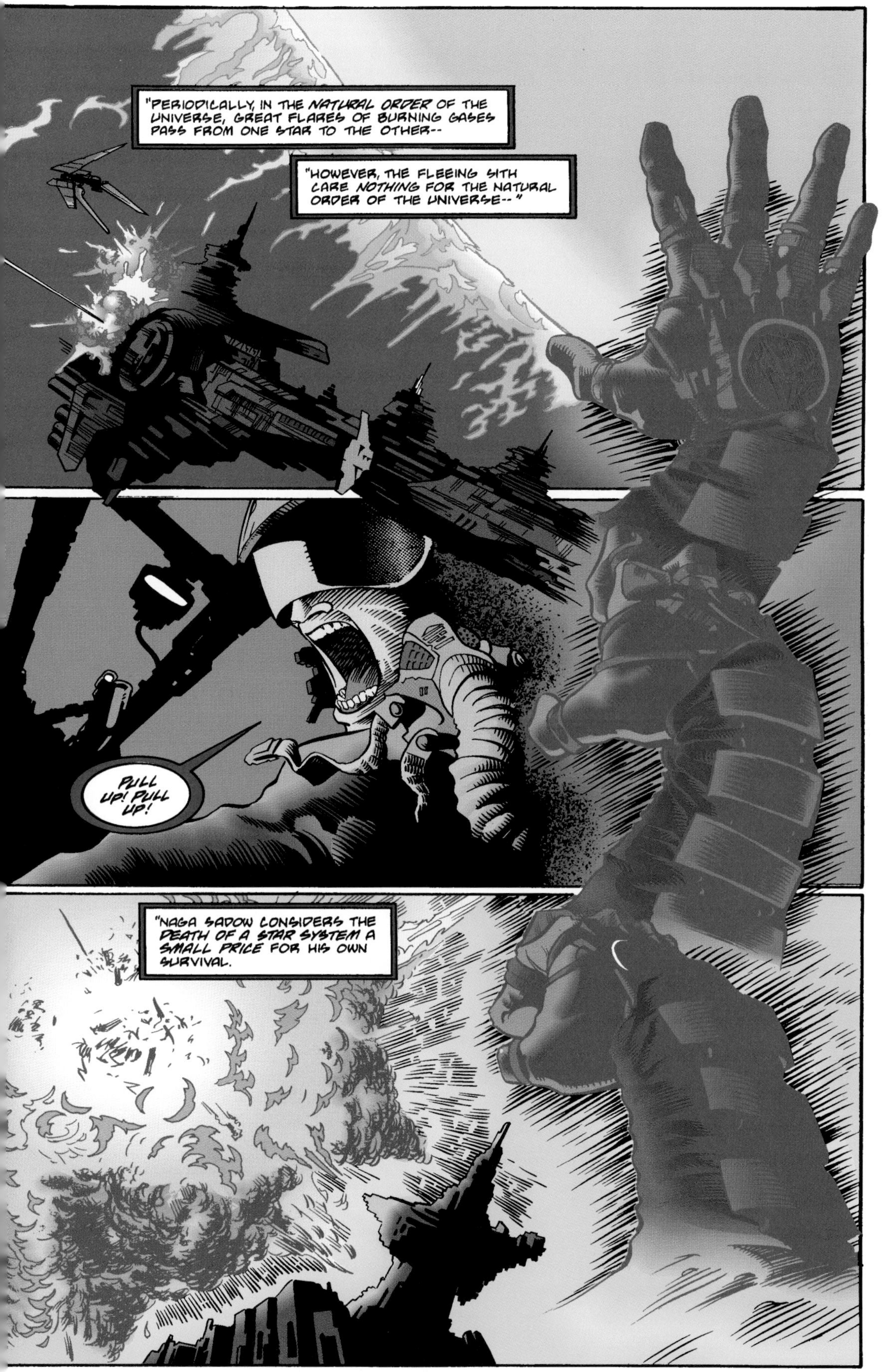
"PERIODICALLY, IN THE NATURAL ORDER OF THE UNIVERSE, GREAT FLARES OF BURNING GASES PASS FROM ONE STAR TO THE OTHER--
"HOWEVER, THE FLEEING SITH CARE NOTHING FOR THE NATURAL ORDER OF THE UNIVERSE--"
PULL UP! PULL UP!
"NAGA SADOW CONSIDERS THE DEATH OF A STAR SYSTEM A SMALL PRICE FOR HIS OWN SURVIVAL.

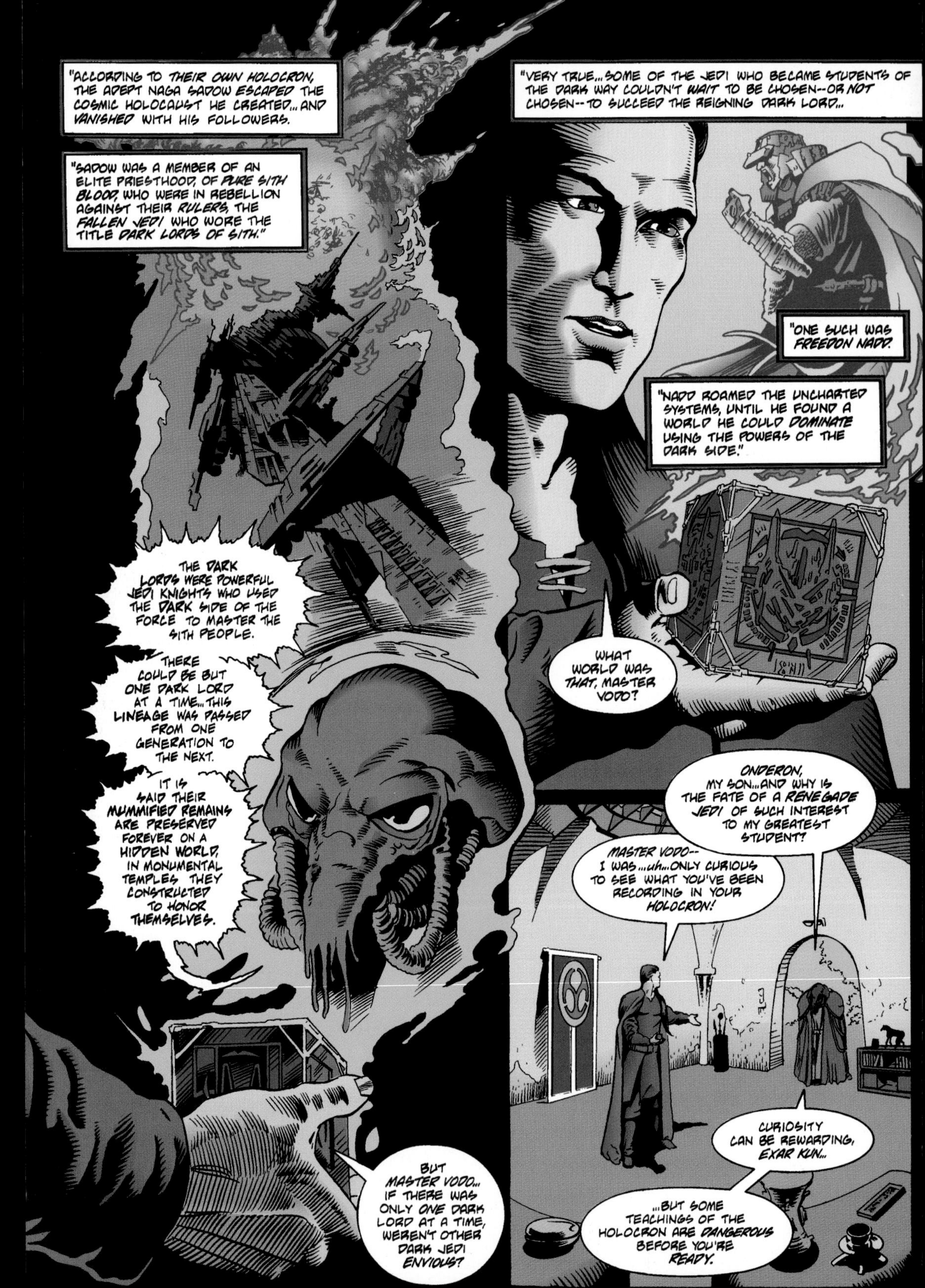

"ACCORDING TO THEIR OWN HOLOCRON, THE ADEPT NAGA SADOW ESCAPED THE COSMIC HOLOCAUST HE CREATED... AND VANISHED WITH HIS FOLLOWERS.
"SADOW WAS A MEMBER OF AN ELITE PRIESTHOOD, OF PURE SITH BLOOD, WHO WERE IN REBELLION AGAINST THEIR RULERS, THE FALLEN JEDI WHO WORE THE TITLE DARK LORDS OF SITH."
THE DARK LORDS WERE POWERFUL JEDI KNIGHTS WHO USED THE DARK SIDE OF THE FORCE TO MASTER THE SITH PEOPLE.
THERE COULD BE BUT ONE DARK LORD AT A TIME... THIS LINEAGE WAS PASSED FROM ONE GENERATION TO THE NEXT.
IT IS SAID THEIR MUMMIFIED REMAINS ARE PRESERVED FOREVER ON A HIDDEN WORLD, IN MONUMENTAL TEMPLES THEY CONSTRUCTED TO HONOR THEMSELVES.
BUT MASTER VODO... IF THERE WAS ONLY ONE DARK LORD AT A TIME, WEREN'T OTHER DARK JEDI ENVIOUS?
"VERY TRUE... SOME OF THE JEDI WHO BECAME STUDENTS OF THE DARK WAY COULDN'T WAIT TO BE CHOSEN--OR NOT CHOSEN--TO SUCCEED THE REIGNING DARK LORD...
"ONE SUCH WAS FREEDON NADD.
"NADD ROAMED THE UNCHARTED SYSTEMS, UNTIL HE FOUND A WORLD HE COULD DOMINATE USING THE POWERS OF THE DARK SIDE."
WHAT WORLD WAS THAT, MASTER VODO?
ONDERON, MY SON... AND WHY IS THE FATE OF A RENEGADE JEDI OF SUCH INTEREST TO MY GREATEST STUDENT?
MASTER VODO-- I WAS... uh... ONLY CURIOUS TO SEE WHAT YOU'VE BEEN RECORDING IN YOUR HOLOCRON!
CURIOSITY CAN BE REWARDING, EXAR KUN...
...BUT SOME TEACHINGS OF THE HOLOCRON ARE DANGEROUS BEFORE YOU'RE READY.

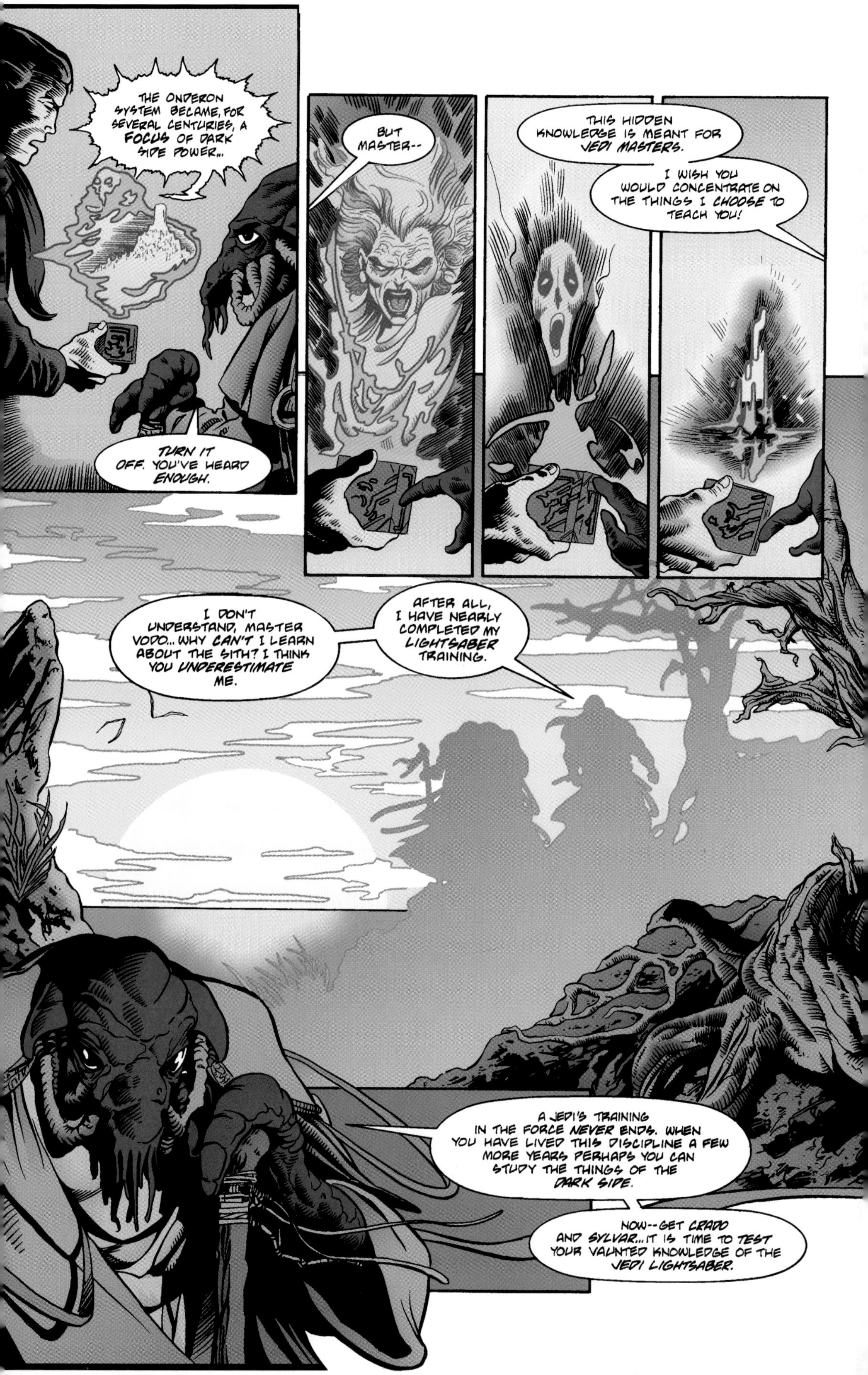
THE ONDERON SYSTEM BECAME, FOR SEVERAL CENTURIES, A FOCUS OF DARK SIDE POWER...
TURN IT OFF. YOU'VE HEARD ENOUGH.
BUT MASTER--
THIS HIDDEN KNOWLEDGE IS MEANT FOR JEDI MASTERS.
I WISH YOU WOULD CONCENTRATE ON THE THINGS I CHOOSE TO TEACH YOU!
I DON'T UNDERSTAND, MASTER VODO... WHY CAN'T I LEARN ABOUT THE SITH? I THINK YOU UNDERESTIMATE ME.
AFTER ALL, I HAVE NEARLY COMPLETED MY LIGHTSABER TRAINING.
A JEDI'S TRAINING IN THE FORCE NEVER ENDS. WHEN YOU HAVE LIVED THIS DISCIPLINE A FEW MORE YEARS PERHAPS YOU CAN STUDY THE THINGS OF THE DARK SIDE.
NOW--GET CRADO AND SYLVAR... IT IS TIME TO TEST YOUR VAUNTED KNOWLEDGE OF THE JEDI LIGHTSABER.

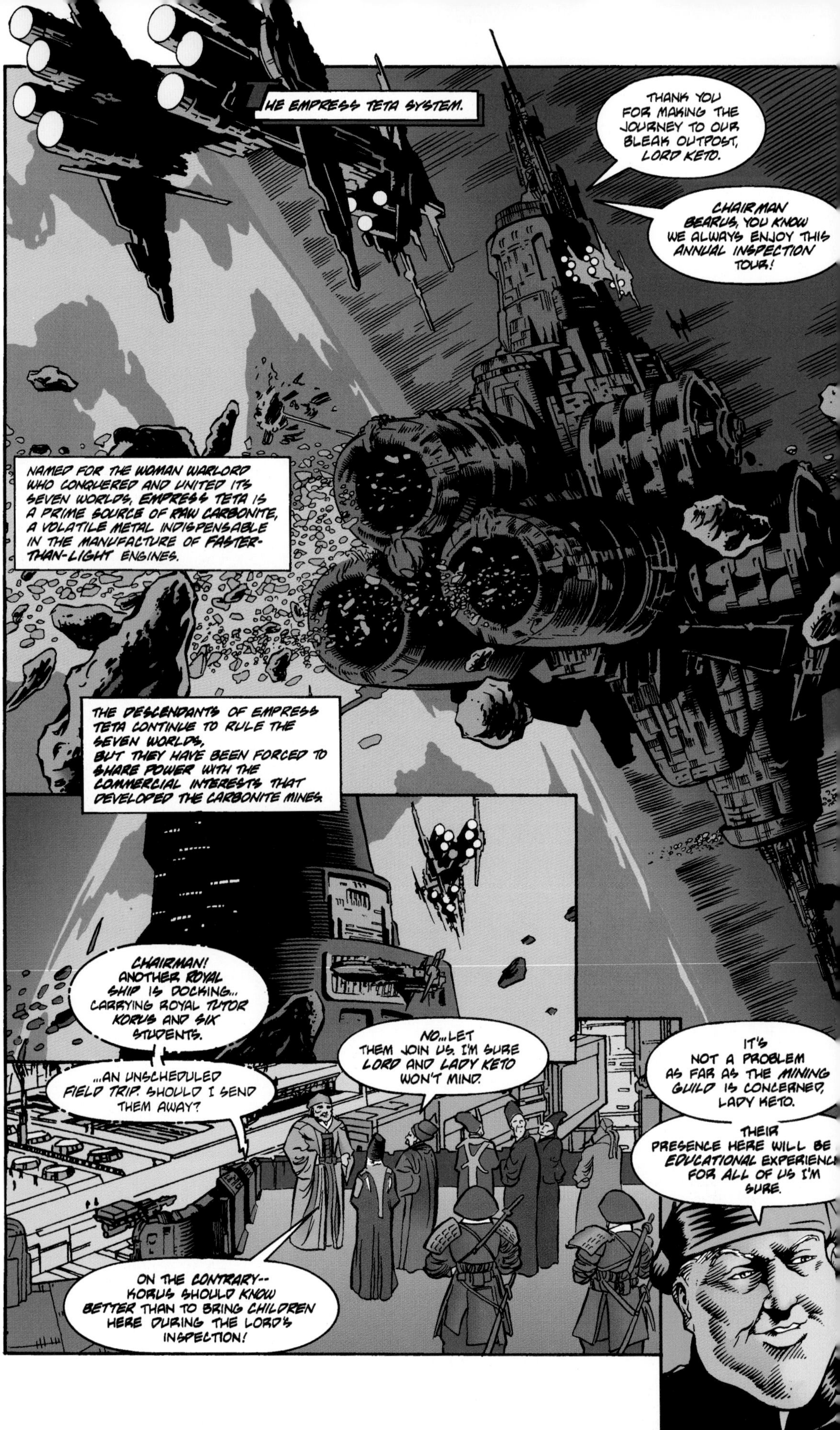

HE EMPRESS TETA SYSTEM.
THANK YOU FOR MAKING THE JOURNEY TO OUR BLEAK OUTPOST, LORD KETO.
CHAIRMAN BEARUS, YOU KNOW WE ALWAYS ENJOY THIS ANNUAL INSPECTION TOUR!
NAMED FOR THE WOMAN WARLORD WHO CONQUERED AND UNITED ITS SEVEN WORLDS, EMPRESS TETA IS A PRIME SOURCE OF RAW CARBONITE, A VOLATILE METAL INDISPENSABLE IN THE MANUFACTURE OF FASTER-THAN-LIGHT ENGINES.
THE DESCENDANTS OF EMPRESS TETA CONTINUE TO RULE THE SEVEN WORLDS, BUT THEY HAVE BEEN FORCED TO SHARE POWER WITH THE COMMERCIAL INTERESTS THAT DEVELOPED THE CARBONITE MINES.
CHAIRMAN! ANOTHER ROYAL SHIP IS DOCKING... CARRYING ROYAL TUTOR KORUS AND SIX STUDENTS.
...AN UNSCHEDULED FIELD TRIP. SHOULD I SEND THEM AWAY?
ON THE CONTRARY-- KORUS SHOULD KNOW BETTER THAN TO BRING CHILDREN HERE DURING THE LORD'S INSPECTION!
NO...LET THEM JOIN US. I'M SURE LORD AND LADY KETO WON'T MIND.
IT'S NOT A PROBLEM AS FAR AS THE MINING GUILD IS CONCERNED, LADY KETO.
THEIR PRESENCE HERE WILL BE EDUCATIONAL EXPERIENC FOR ALL OF US I'M SURE.

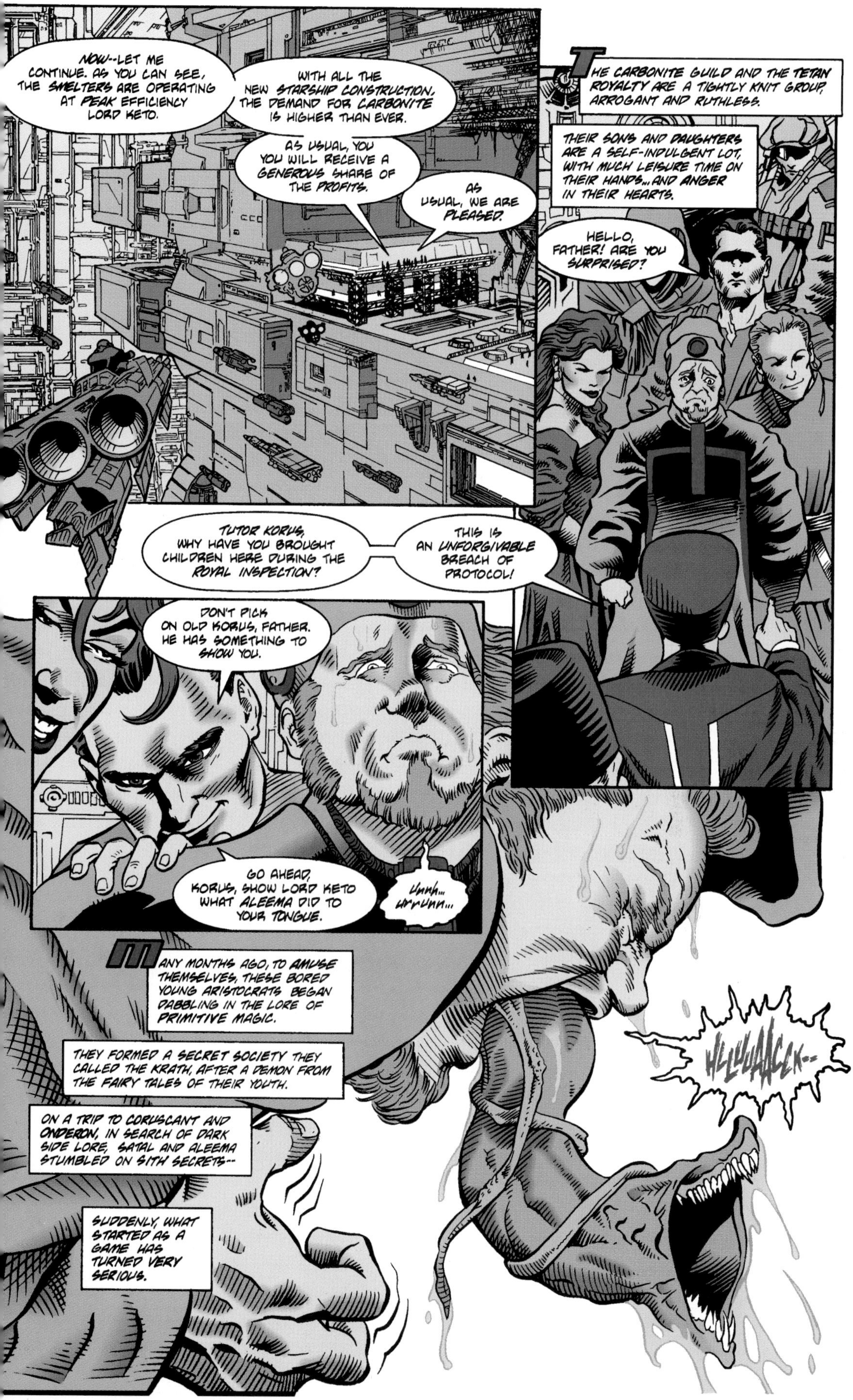
NOW--LET ME CONTINUE. AS YOU CAN SEE, THE SMELTERS ARE OPERATING AT PEAK EFFICIENCY LORD KETO.
WITH ALL THE NEW STARSHIP CONSTRUCTION, THE DEMAND FOR CARBONITE IS HIGHER THAN EVER.
AS USUAL, YOU YOU WILL RECEIVE A GENEROUS SHARE OF THE PROFITS.
AS USUAL, WE ARE PLEASED.
THE CARBONITE GUILD AND THE TETAN ROYALTY ARE A TIGHTLY KNIT GROUP, ARROGANT AND RUTHLESS.
THEIR SONS AND DAUGHTERS ARE A SELF-INDULGENT LOT, WITH MUCH LEISURE TIME ON THEIR HANDS... AND ANGER IN THEIR HEARTS.
HELLO, FATHER! ARE YOU SURPRISED?
TUTOR KORUS, WHY HAVE YOU BROUGHT CHILDREN HERE DURING THE ROYAL INSPECTION?
THIS IS AN UNFORGIVABLE BREACH OF PROTOCOL!
DON'T PICK ON OLD KORUS, FATHER. HE HAS SOMETHING TO SHOW YOU.
GO AHEAD, KORUS, SHOW LORD KETO WHAT ALEEMA DID TO YOUR TONGUE.
Unnh... urrunn...
MANY MONTHS AGO, TO AMUSE THEMSELVES, THESE BORED YOUNG ARISTOCRATS BEGAN DABBLING IN THE LORE OF PRIMITIVE MAGIC.
THEY FORMED A SECRET SOCIETY THEY CALLED THE KRATH, AFTER A DEMON FROM THE FAIRY TALES OF THEIR YOUTH.
ON A TRIP TO CORUSCANT AND ONDERON, IN SEARCH OF DARK SIDE LORE, SATAL AND ALEEMA STUMBLED ON SITH SECRETS--
SUDDENLY, WHAT STARTED AS A GAME HAS TURNED VERY SERIOUS.
HLLUUAACCK--

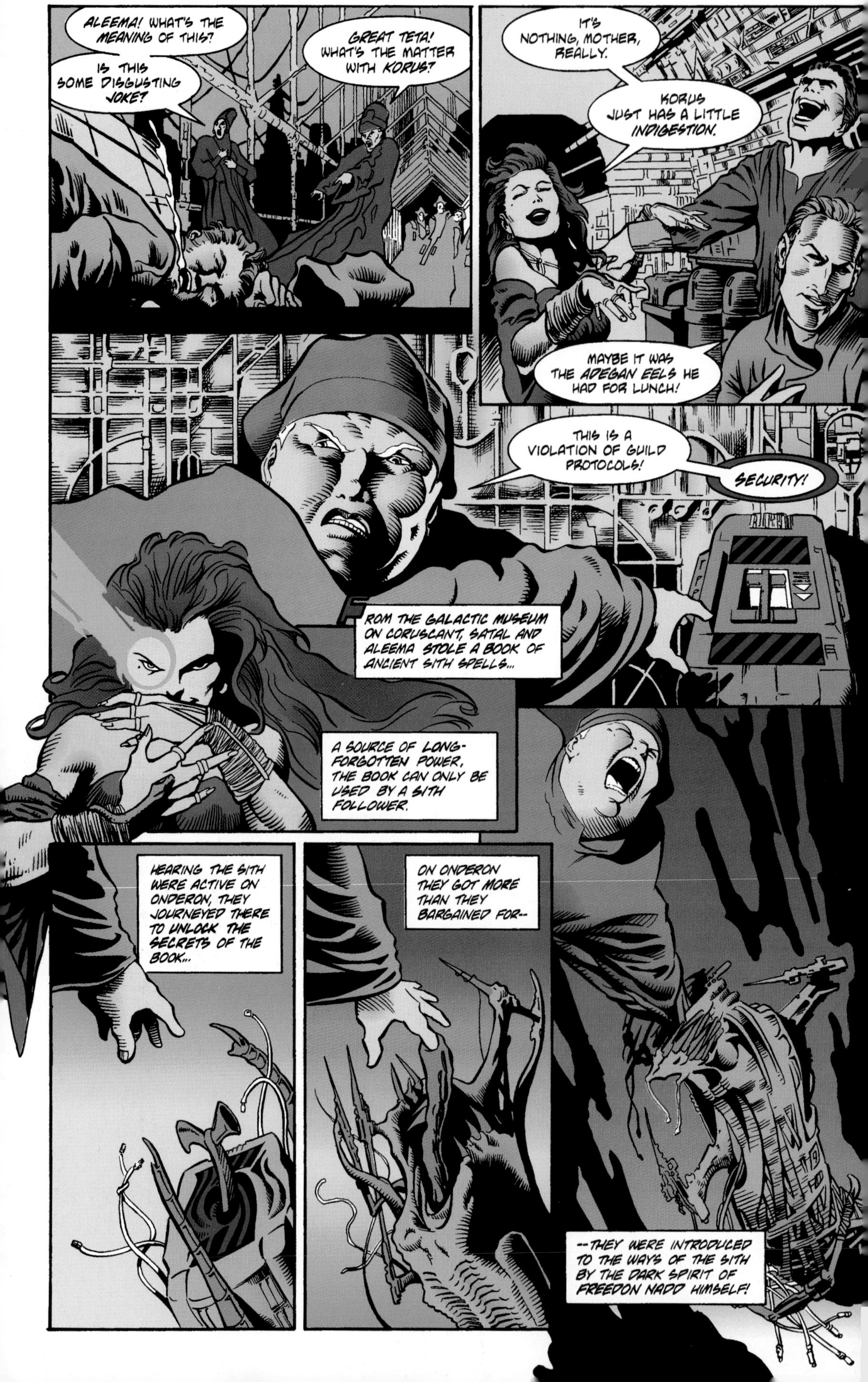
ALEEMA! WHAT'S THE MEANING OF THIS?
IS THIS SOME DISGUSTING JOKE?
GREAT TETA! WHAT'S THE MATTER WITH KORUS?
IT'S NOTHING, MOTHER, REALLY.
KORUS JUST HAS A LITTLE INDIGESTION.
MAYBE IT WAS THE ADEGAN EELS HE HAD FOR LUNCH!
THIS IS A VIOLATION OF GUILD PROTOCOLS!
SECURITY!
FROM THE GALACTIC MUSEUM ON CORUSCANT, SATAL AND ALEEMA STOLE A BOOK OF ANCIENT SITH SPELLS...
A SOURCE OF LONG-FORGOTTEN POWER, THE BOOK CAN ONLY BE USED BY A SITH FOLLOWER.
HEARING THE SITH WERE ACTIVE ON ONDERON, THEY JOURNEYED THERE TO UNLOCK THE SECRETS OF THE BOOK...
ON ONDERON THEY GOT MORE THAN THEY BARGAINED FOR--
--THEY WERE INTRODUCED TO THE WAYS OF THE SITH BY THE DARK SPIRIT OF FREEDON NADD HIMSELF!

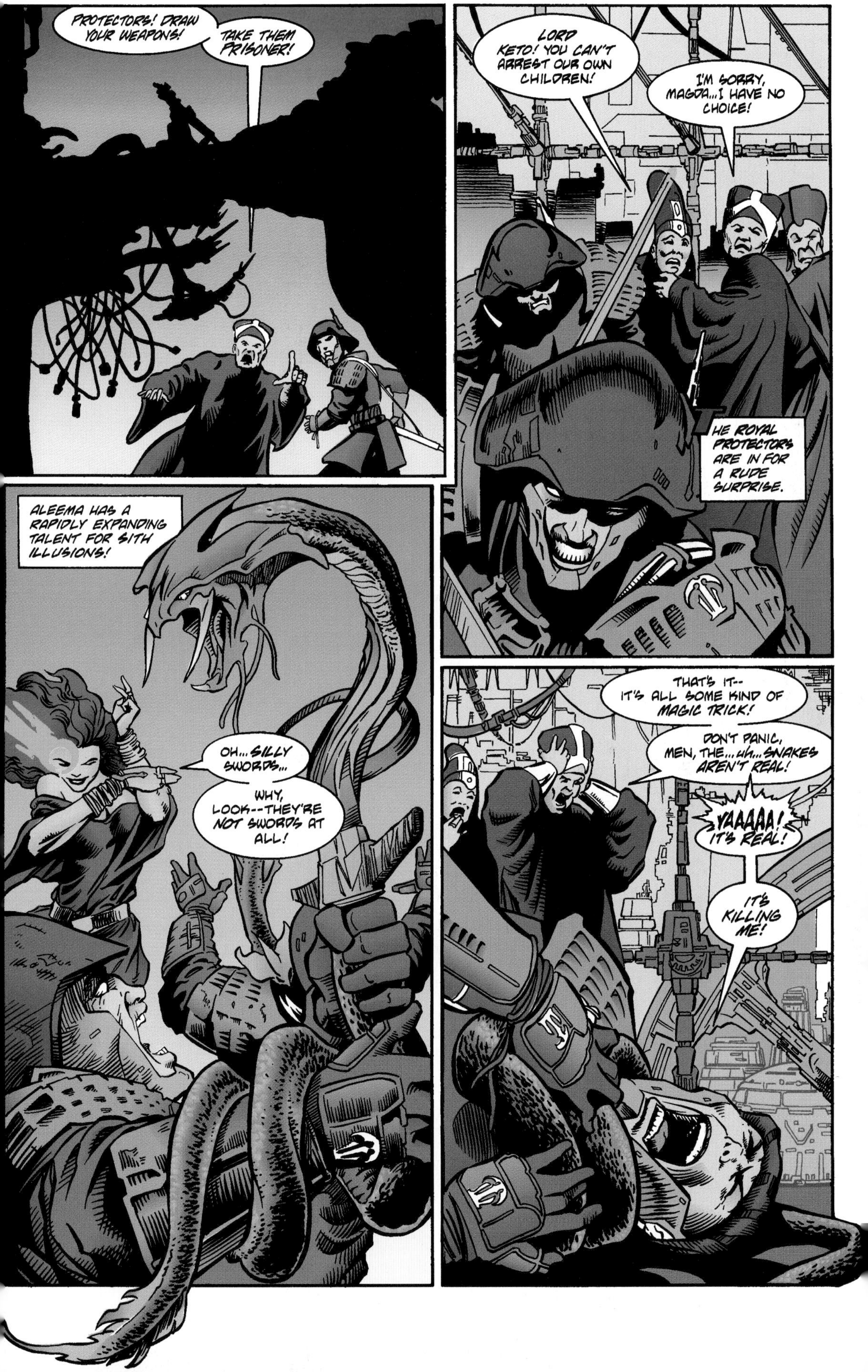
PROTECTORS! DRAW YOUR WEAPONS!
TAKE THEM PRISONER!
LORD KETO! YOU CAN'T ARREST OUR OWN CHILDREN!
I'M SORRY, MAGDA...I HAVE NO CHOICE!
HE ROYAL PROTECTORS ARE IN FOR A RUDE SURPRISE.
ALEEMA HAS A RAPIDLY EXPANDING TALENT FOR SITH ILLUSIONS!
OH... SILLY SWORDS...
WHY, LOOK--THEY'RE NOT SWORDS AT ALL!
THAT'S IT-- IT'S ALL SOME KIND OF MAGIC TRICK!
DON'T PANIC, MEN, THE... UH... SNAKES AREN'T REAL!
YAAAAA! IT'S REAL!
IT'S KILLING ME!

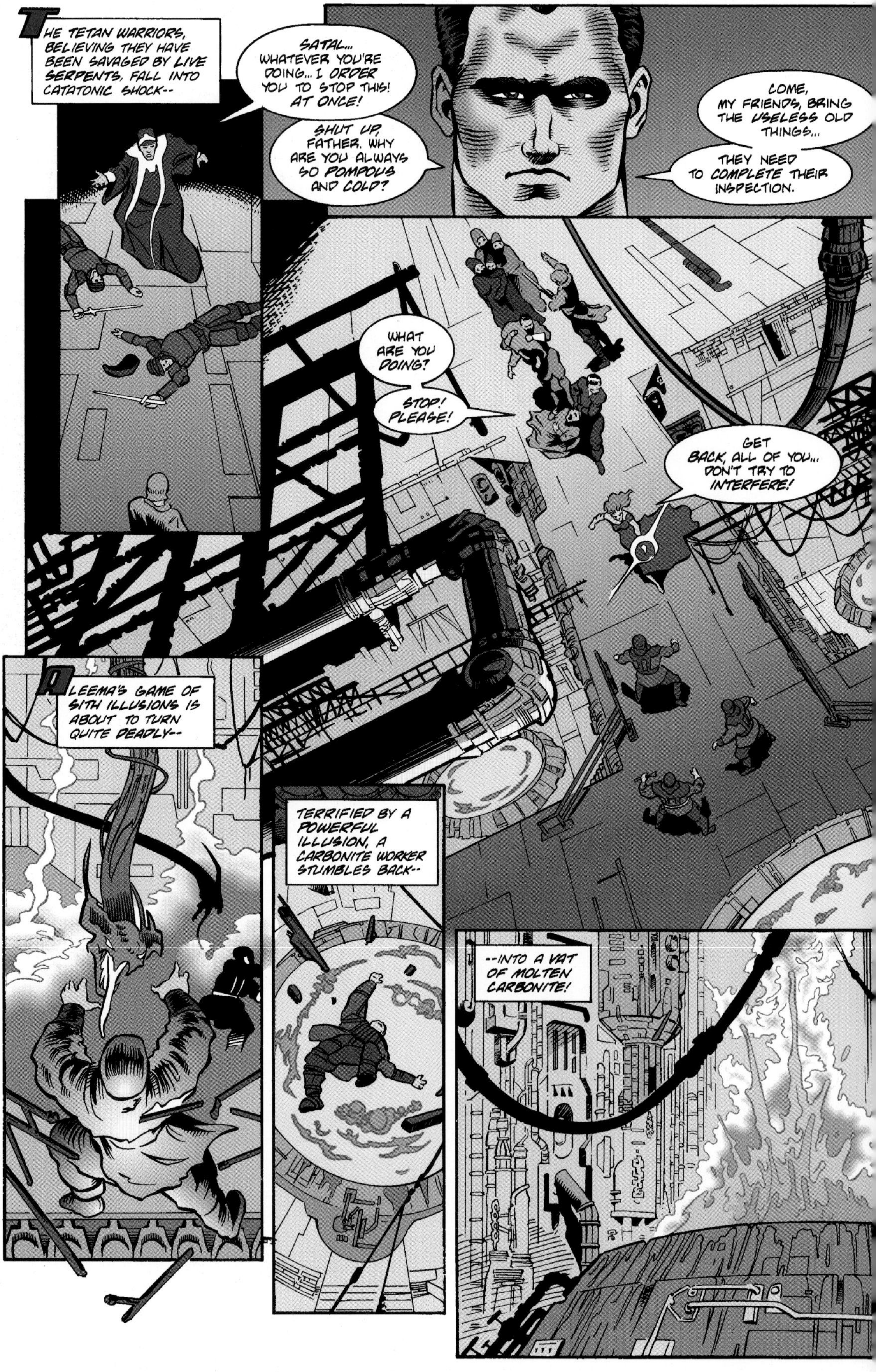
THE TETAN WARRIORS, BELIEVING THEY HAVE BEEN SAVAGED BY LIVE SERPENTS, FALL INTO CATATONIC SHOCK--
SATAL... WHATEVER YOU'RE DOING... I ORDER YOU TO STOP THIS! AT ONCE!
SHUT UP, FATHER. WHY ARE YOU ALWAYS SO POMPOUS AND COLD?
COME, MY FRIENDS, BRING THE USELESS OLD THINGS...
THEY NEED TO COMPLETE THEIR INSPECTION.
WHAT ARE YOU DOING?
STOP! PLEASE!
GET BACK, ALL OF YOU... DON'T TRY TO INTERFERE!
ALEEMA'S GAME OF SITH ILLUSIONS IS ABOUT TO TURN QUITE DEADLY--
TERRIFIED BY A POWERFUL ILLUSION, A CARBONITE WORKER STUMBLES BACK--
--INTO A VAT OF MOLTEN CARBONITE!

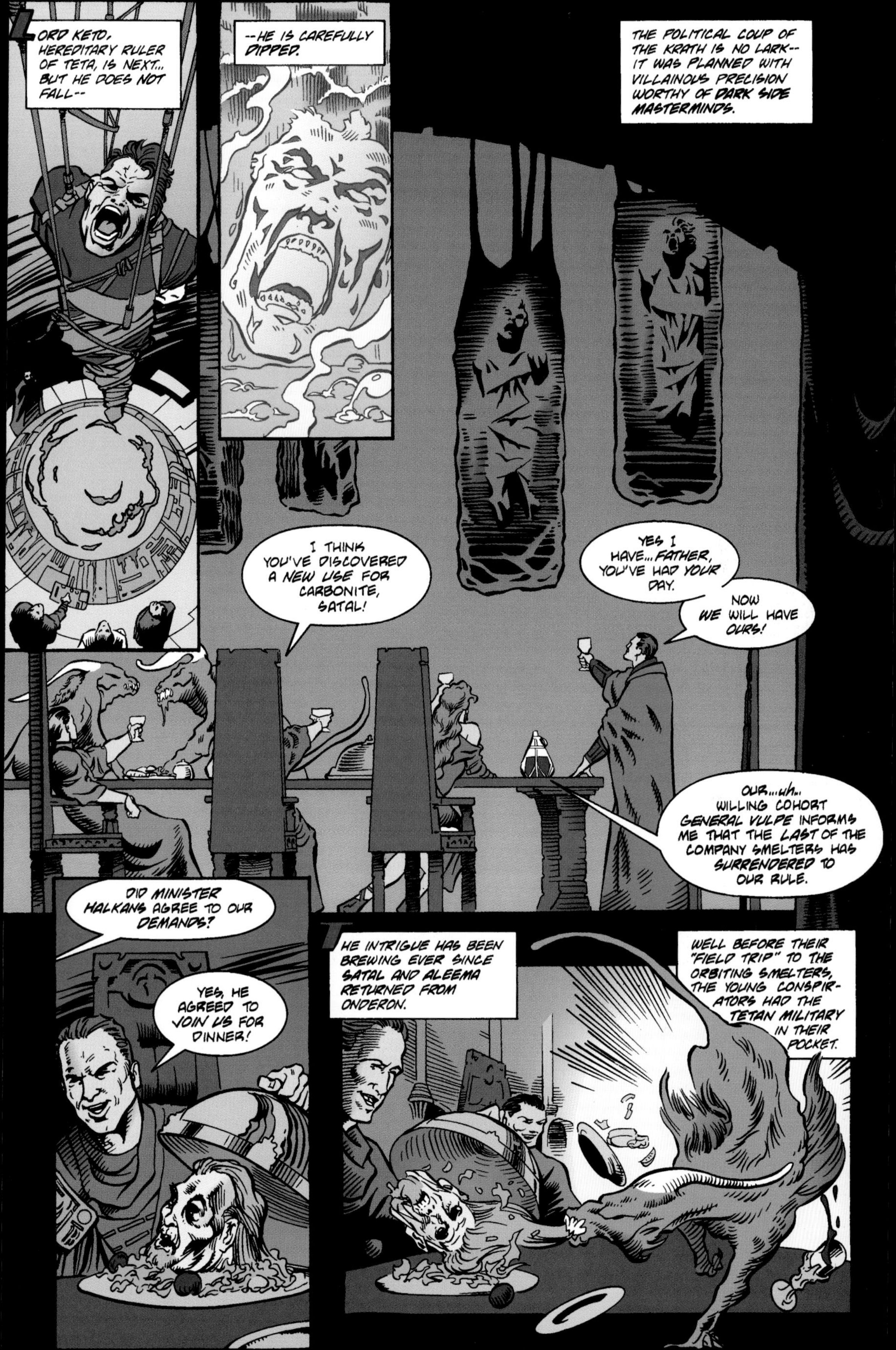
LORD KETO, HEREDITARY RULER OF TETA, IS NEXT... BUT HE DOES NOT FALL--
--HE IS CAREFULLY DIPPED.
THE POLITICAL COUP OF THE KRATH IS NO LARK-- IT WAS PLANNED WITH VILLAINOUS PRECISION WORTHY OF DARK SIDE MASTERMINDS.
I THINK YOU'VE DISCOVERED A NEW USE FOR CARBONITE, SATAL!
YES I HAVE... FATHER, YOU'VE HAD YOUR DAY.
NOW WE WILL HAVE OURS!
OUR...uh... WILLING COHORT GENERAL VULPE INFORMS ME THAT THE LAST OF THE COMPANY SMELTERS HAS SURRENDERED TO OUR RULE.
DID MINISTER HALKANS AGREE TO OUR DEMANDS?
YES, HE AGREED TO JOIN US FOR DINNER!
THE INTRIGUE HAS BEEN BREWING EVER SINCE SATAL AND ALEEMA RETURNED FROM ONDERON.
WELL BEFORE THEIR "FIELD TRIP" TO THE ORBITING SMELTERS, THE YOUNG CONSPIR-ATORS HAD THE TETAN MILITARY IN THEIR POCKET.

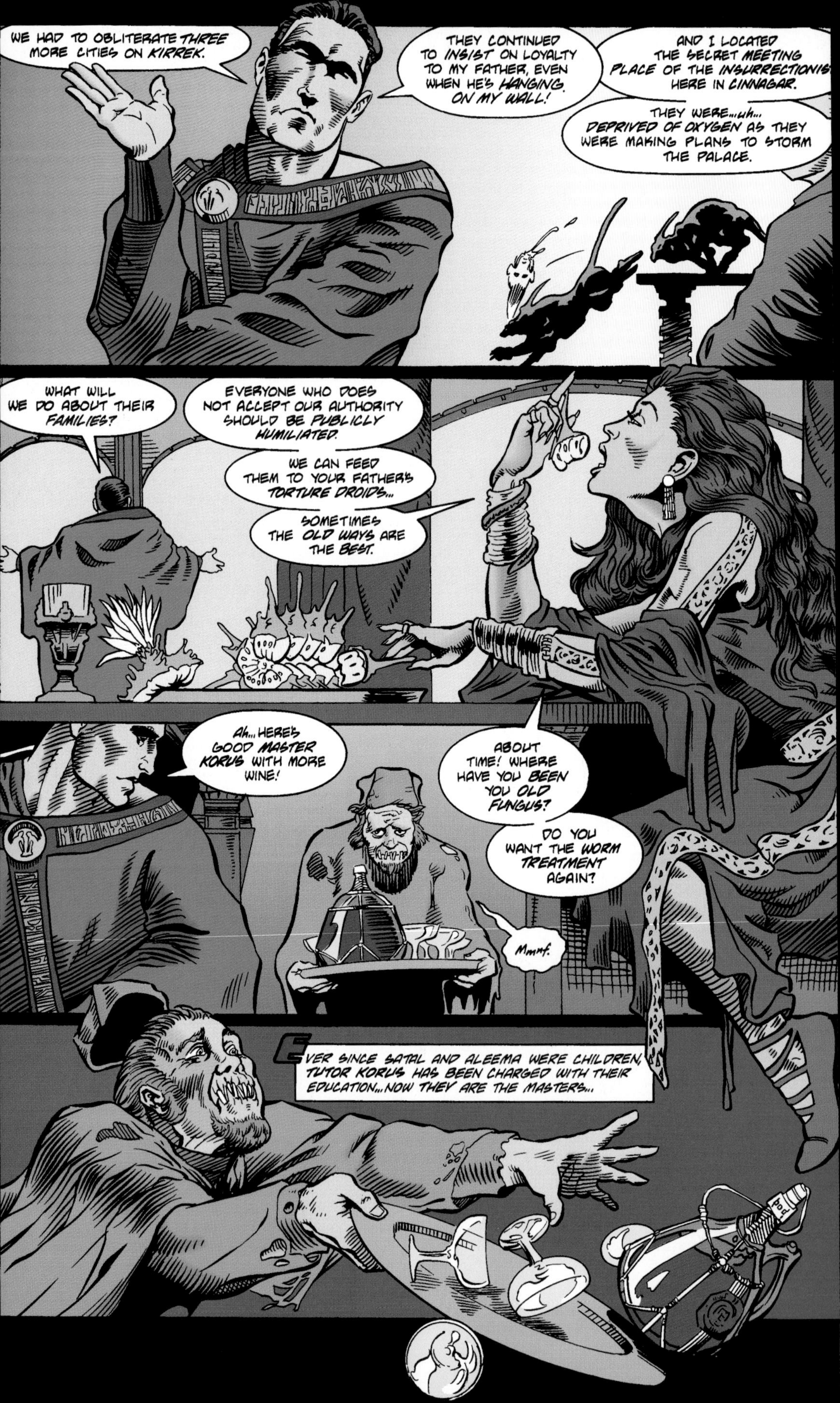
WE HAD TO OBLITERATE THREE MORE CITIES ON KIRREK.
THEY CONTINUED TO INSIST ON LOYALTY TO MY FATHER, EVEN WHEN HE'S HANGING ON MY WALL!
AND I LOCATED THE SECRET MEETING PLACE OF THE INSURRECTIONISTS HERE IN CINNAGAR.
THEY WERE...uh... DEPRIVED OF OXYGEN AS THEY WERE MAKING PLANS TO STORM THE PALACE.
WHAT WILL WE DO ABOUT THEIR FAMILIES?
EVERYONE WHO DOES NOT ACCEPT OUR AUTHORITY SHOULD BE PUBLICLY HUMILIATED.
WE CAN FEED THEM TO YOUR FATHER'S TORTURE DROIDS...
SOMETIMES THE OLD WAYS ARE THE BEST.
Ah... HERE'S GOOD MASTER KORUS WITH MORE WINE!
ABOUT TIME! WHERE HAVE YOU BEEN YOU OLD FUNGUS?
DO YOU WANT THE WORM TREATMENT AGAIN?
Mmmf.
EVER SINCE SATAL AND ALEEMA WERE CHILDREN, TUTOR KORUS HAS BEEN CHARGED WITH THEIR EDUCATION... NOW THEY ARE THE MASTERS...

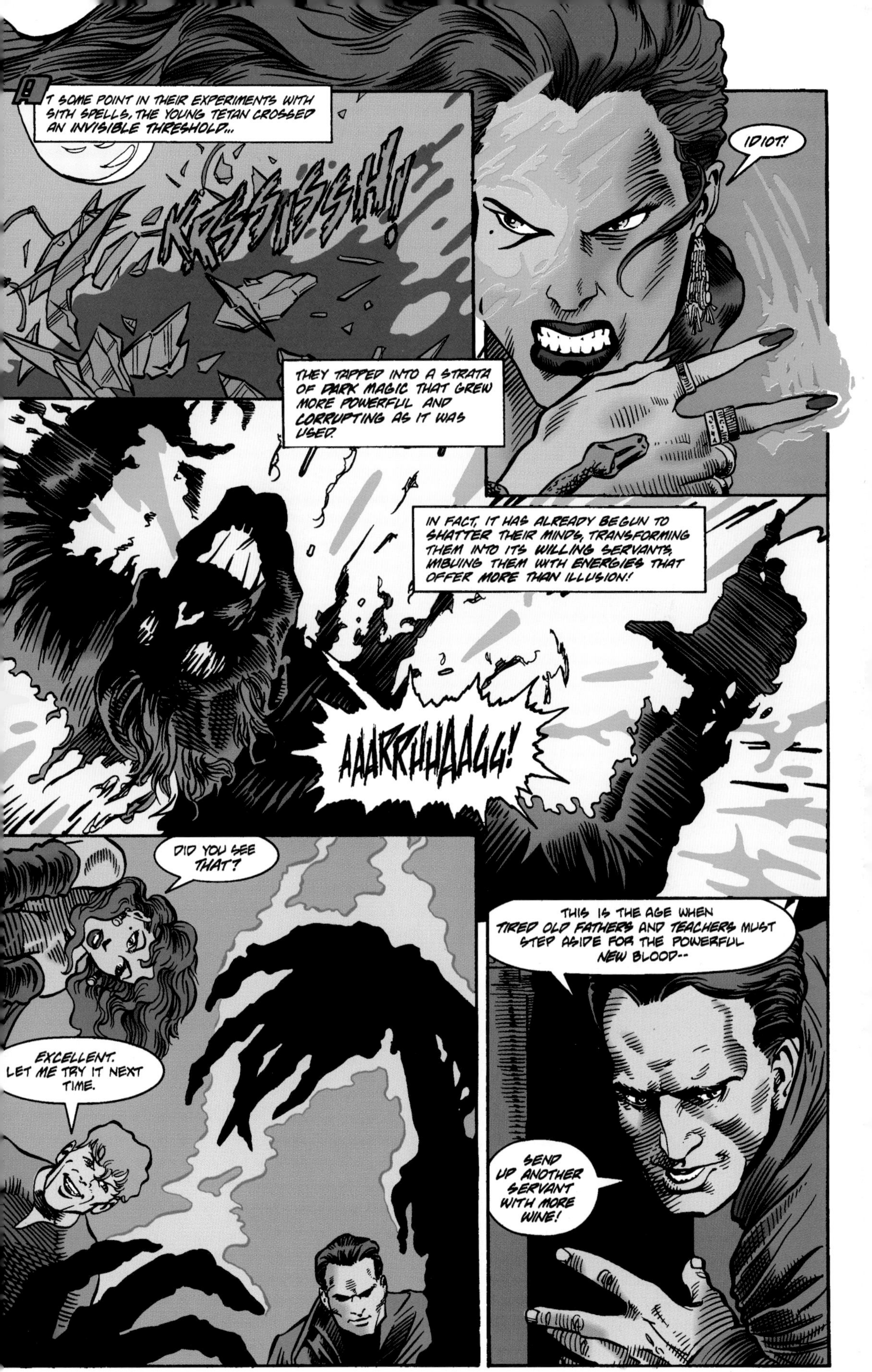
AT SOME POINT IN THEIR EXPERIMENTS WITH SITH SPELLS, THE YOUNG TETAN CROSSED AN INVISIBLE THRESHOLD...
KRSSSSSH!
IDIOT!
THEY TAPPED INTO A STRATA OF DARK MAGIC THAT GREW MORE POWERFUL AND CORRUPTING AS IT WAS USED.
IN FACT, IT HAS ALREADY BEGUN TO SHATTER THEIR MINDS, TRANSFORMING THEM INTO ITS WILLING SERVANTS, IMBUING THEM WITH ENERGIES THAT OFFER MORE THAN ILLUSION!
AAARRHHAAGG!
DID YOU SEE THAT?
EXCELLENT. LET ME TRY IT NEXT TIME.
THIS IS THE AGE WHEN TIRED OLD FATHERS AND TEACHERS MUST STEP ASIDE FOR THE POWERFUL NEW BLOOD--
SEND UP ANOTHER SERVANT WITH MORE WINE!

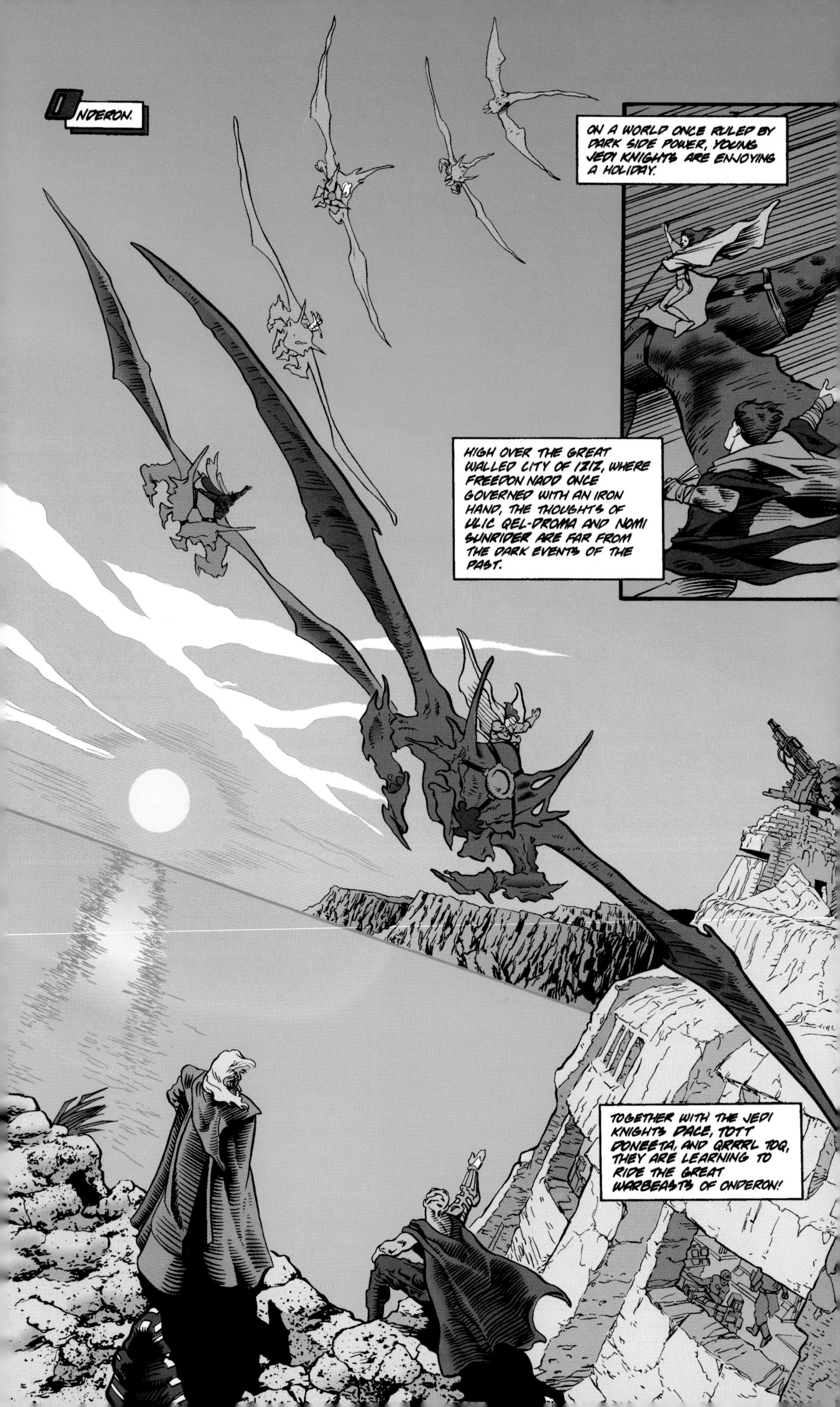
ONDERON.
ON A WORLD ONCE RULED BY DARK SIDE POWER, YOUNG JEDI KNIGHTS ARE ENJOYING A HOLIDAY.
HIGH OVER THE GREAT WALLED CITY OF IZIZ, WHERE FREEDON NADD ONCE GOVERNED WITH AN IRON HAND, THE THOUGHTS OF ULIC QEL-DROMA AND NOMI SUNRIDER ARE FAR FROM THE DARK EVENTS OF THE PAST.
TOGETHER WITH THE JEDI KNIGHTS DACE, TOTT DONEETA, AND QRRRL TOQ, THEY ARE LEARNING TO RIDE THE GREAT WARBEASTS OF ONDERON!

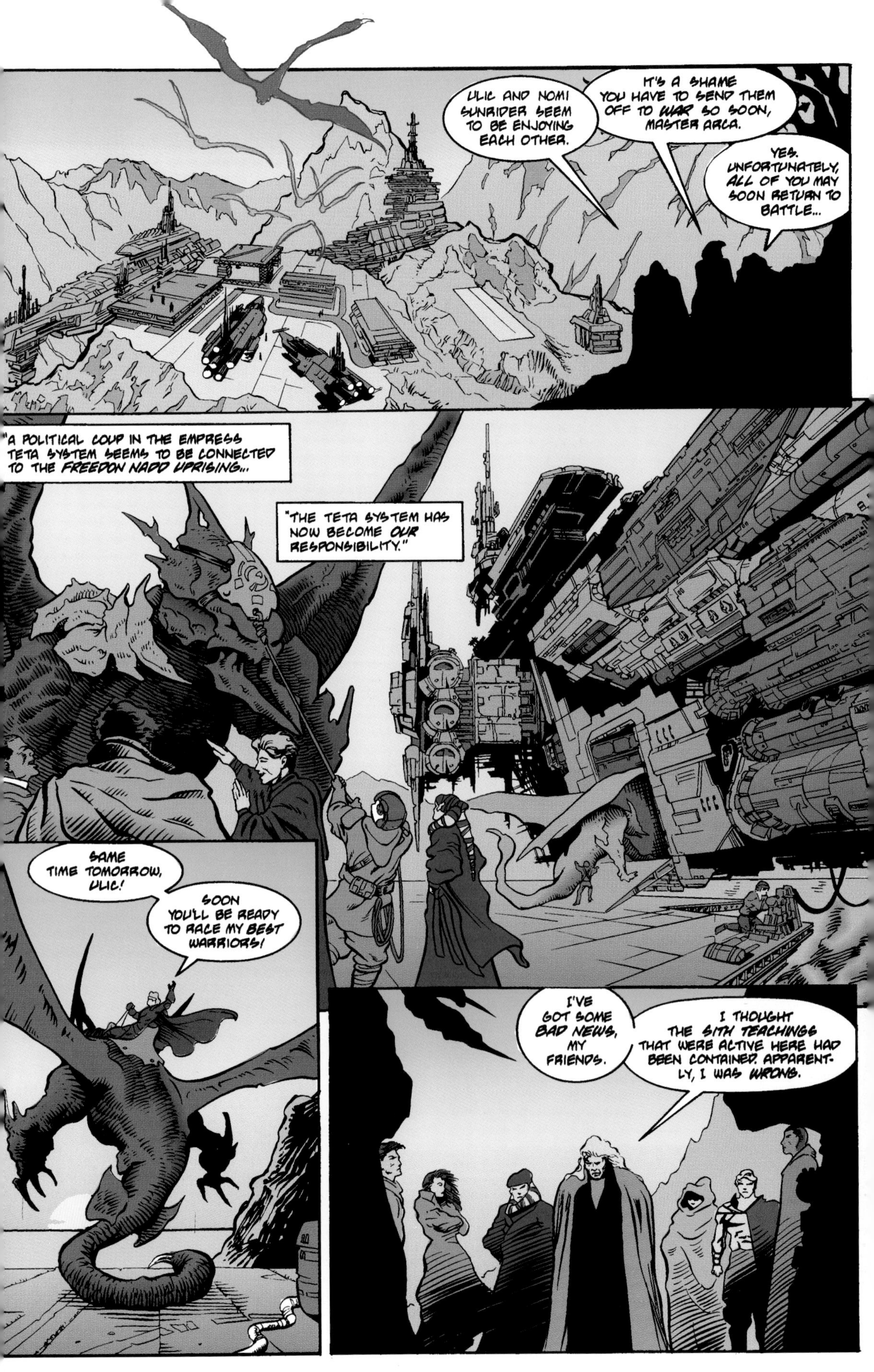
ULIC AND NOMI SUNRIDER SEEM TO BE ENJOYING EACH OTHER.
IT'S A SHAME YOU HAVE TO SEND THEM OFF TO WAR SO SOON, MASTER ARCA.
YES. UNFORTUNATELY, ALL OF YOU MAY SOON RETURN TO BATTLE...
"A POLITICAL COUP IN THE EMPRESS TETA SYSTEM SEEMS TO BE CONNECTED TO THE FREEDON NADD UPRISING...
"THE TETA SYSTEM HAS NOW BECOME OUR RESPONSIBILITY."
SAME TIME TOMORROW, ULIC!
SOON YOU'LL BE READY TO RACE MY BEST WARRIORS!
I'VE GOT SOME BAD NEWS, MY FRIENDS.
I THOUGHT THE SITH TEACHINGS THAT WERE ACTIVE HERE HAD BEEN CONTAINED. APPARENTLY, I WAS WRONG.

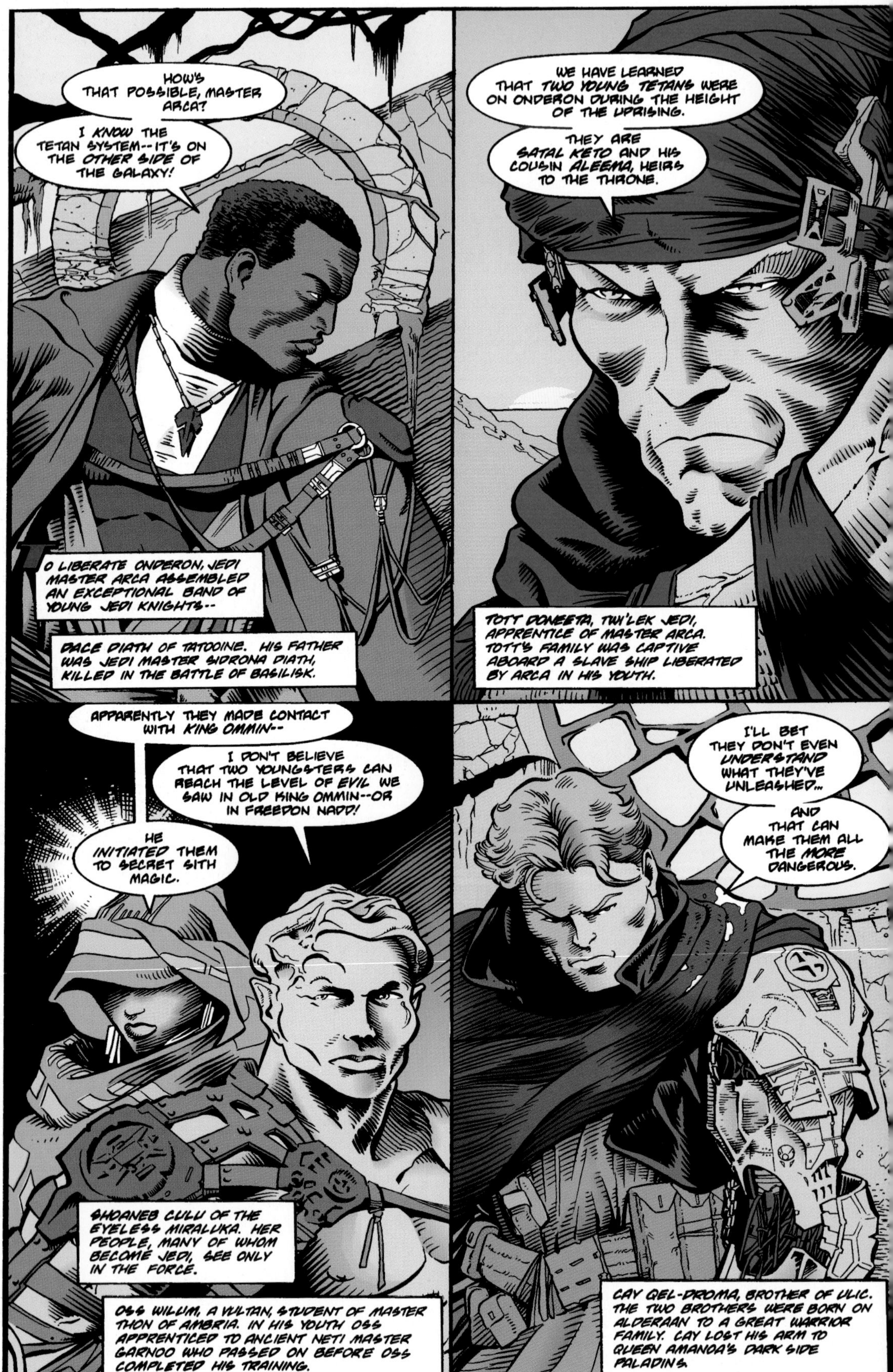
HOW'S THAT POSSIBLE, MASTER ARCA?
I KNOW THE TETAN SYSTEM--IT'S ON THE OTHER SIDE OF THE GALAXY!
TO LIBERATE ONDERON, JEDI MASTER ARCA ASSEMBLED AN EXCEPTIONAL BAND OF YOUNG JEDI KNIGHTS--
DACE DIATH OF TATOOINE. HIS FATHER WAS JEDI MASTER SIDRONA DIATH, KILLED IN THE BATTLE OF BASILISK.
WE HAVE LEARNED THAT TWO YOUNG TETANS WERE ON ONDERON DURING THE HEIGHT OF THE UPRISING.
THEY ARE SATAL KETO AND HIS COUSIN ALEEMA, HEIRS TO THE THRONE.
TOTT DONEETA, TWI'LEK JEDI, APPRENTICE OF MASTER ARCA. TOTT'S FAMILY WAS CAPTIVE ABOARD A SLAVE SHIP LIBERATED BY ARCA IN HIS YOUTH.
APPARENTLY THEY MADE CONTACT WITH KING OMMIN--
HE INITIATED THEM TO SECRET SITH MAGIC.
I DON'T BELIEVE THAT TWO YOUNGSTERS CAN REACH THE LEVEL OF EVIL WE SAW IN OLD KING OMMIN--OR IN FREEDON NADD!
SHOANEB CULU OF THE EYELESS MIRALUKA. HER PEOPLE, MANY OF WHOM BECOME JEDI, SEE ONLY IN THE FORCE.
OSS WILUM, A VULTAN, STUDENT OF MASTER THON OF AMBRIA. IN HIS YOUTH OSS APPRENTICED TO ANCIENT NETI MASTER GARNOO WHO PASSED ON BEFORE OSS COMPLETED HIS TRAINING.
I'LL BET THEY DON'T EVEN UNDERSTAND WHAT THEY'VE UNLEASHED...
AND THAT CAN MAKE THEM ALL THE MORE DANGEROUS.
CAY QEL-DROMA, BROTHER OF ULIC. THE TWO BROTHERS WERE BORN ON ALDERAAN TO A GREAT WARRIOR FAMILY. CAY LOST HIS ARM TO QUEEN AMANOA'S DARK SIDE PALADINS.

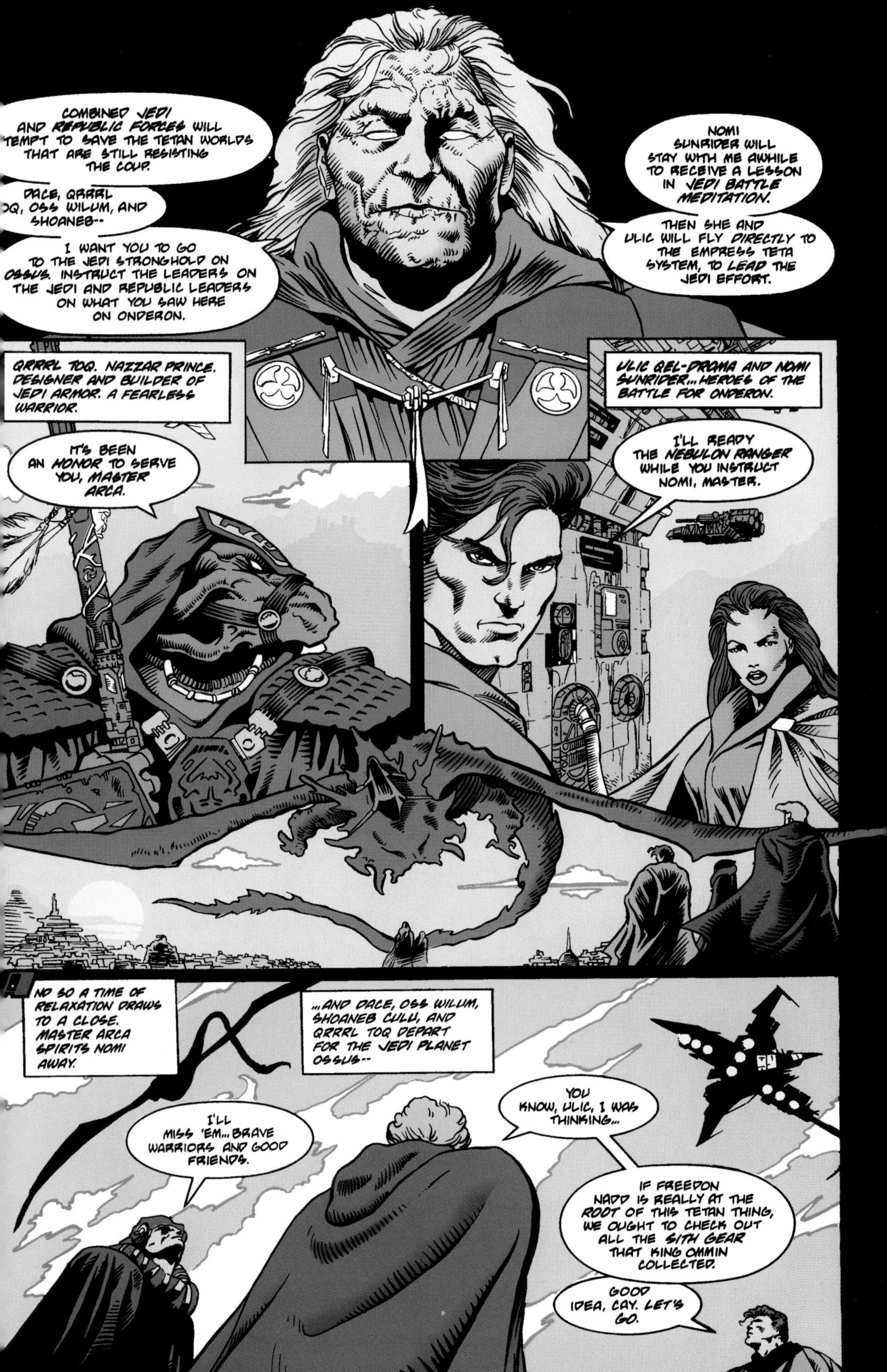
COMBINED JEDI AND REPUBLIC FORCES WILL TEMPT TO SAVE THE TETAN WORLDS THAT ARE STILL RESISTING THE COUP.
DACE, QRRRL OQ, OSS WILUM, AND SHOANEB--
I WANT YOU TO GO TO THE JEDI STRONGHOLD ON OSSUS. INSTRUCT THE LEADERS ON THE JEDI AND REPUBLIC LEADERS ON WHAT YOU SAW HERE ON ONDERON.
NOMI SUNRIDER WILL STAY WITH ME AWHILE TO RECEIVE A LESSON IN JEDI BATTLE MEDITATION.
THEN SHE AND ULIC WILL FLY DIRECTLY TO THE EMPRESS TETA SYSTEM, TO LEAD THE JEDI EFFORT.
QRRRL TOQ. NAZZAR PRINCE. DESIGNER AND BUILDER OF JEDI ARMOR. A FEARLESS WARRIOR.
IT'S BEEN AN HONOR TO SERVE YOU, MASTER ARCA.
ULIC QEL-DROMA AND NOMI SUNRIDER... HEROES OF THE BATTLE FOR ONDERON.
I'LL READY THE NEBULON RANGER WHILE YOU INSTRUCT NOMI, MASTER.
ND SO A TIME OF RELAXATION DRAWS TO A CLOSE. MASTER ARCA SPIRITS NOMI AWAY.
...AND DACE, OSS WILUM, SHOANEB CULU, AND QRRRL TOQ DEPART FOR THE JEDI PLANET OSSUS--
I'LL MISS 'EM... BRAVE WARRIORS AND GOOD FRIENDS.
YOU KNOW, ULIC, I WAS THINKING...
IF FREEDON NADD IS REALLY AT THE ROOT OF THIS TETAN THING, WE OUGHT TO CHECK OUT ALL THE SITH GEAR THAT KING OMMIN COLLECTED.
GOOD IDEA, CAY. LET'S GO.

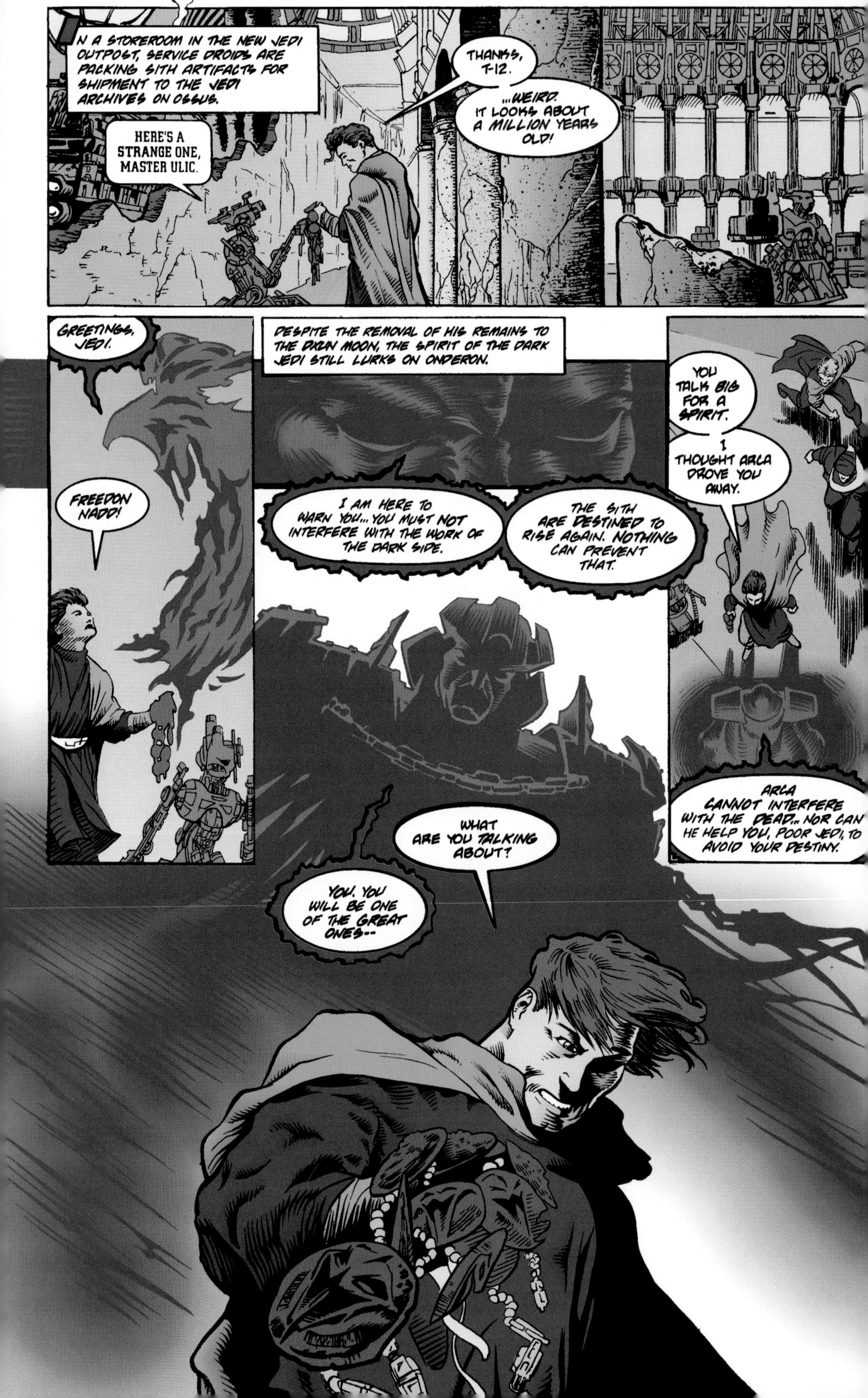
N A STOREROOM IN THE NEW JEDI OUTPOST, SERVICE DROIDS ARE PACKING SITH ARTIFACTS FOR SHIPMENT TO THE JEDI ARCHIVES ON OSSUS.
HERE'S A STRANGE ONE, MASTER ULIC.
THANKS, T-12.
...WEIRD. IT LOOKS ABOUT A MILLION YEARS OLD!
GREETINGS, JEDI.
FREEDON NADD!
DESPITE THE REMOVAL OF HIS REMAINS TO THE DXUN MOON, THE SPIRIT OF THE DARK JEDI STILL LURKS ON ONDERON.
I AM HERE TO WARN YOU... YOU MUST NOT INTERFERE WITH THE WORK OF THE DARK SIDE.
THE SITH ARE DESTINED TO RISE AGAIN. NOTHING CAN PREVENT THAT.
YOU TALK BIG FOR A SPIRIT.
I THOUGHT ARCA DROVE YOU AWAY.
ARCA CANNOT INTERFERE WITH THE DEAD... NOR CAN HE HELP YOU, POOR JEDI, TO AVOID YOUR DESTINY.
WHAT ARE YOU TALKING ABOUT?
YOU. YOU WILL BE ONE OF THE GREAT ONES--

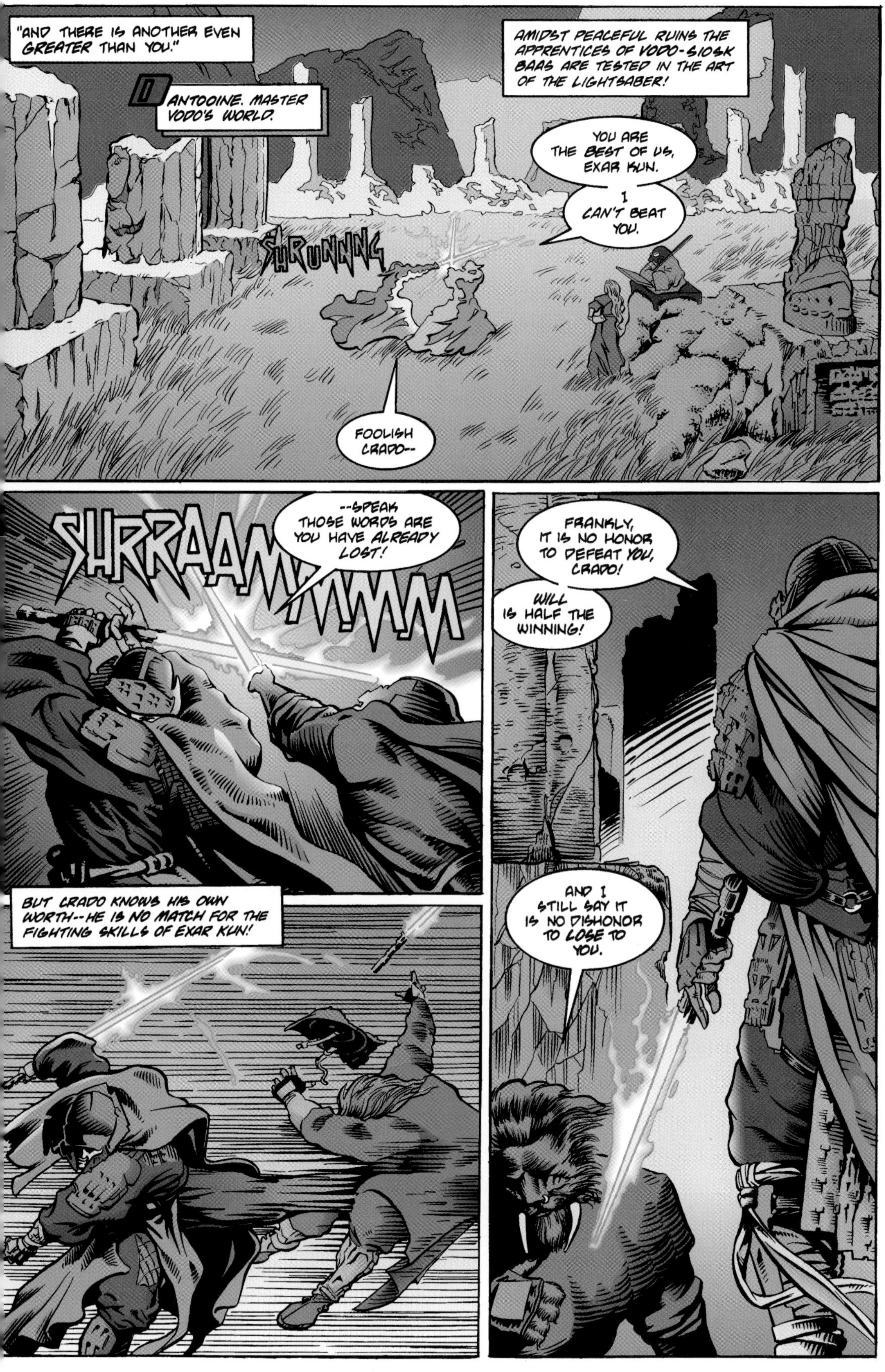
"AND THERE IS ANOTHER EVEN GREATER THAN YOU."
ANTOOINE. MASTER VODO'S WORLD.
AMIDST PEACEFUL RUINS THE APPRENTICES OF VODO-SIOSK BAAS ARE TESTED IN THE ART OF THE LIGHTSABER!
YOU ARE THE BEST OF US, EXAR KUN.
I CAN'T BEAT YOU.
SHRUNNNG
FOOLISH CRADO--
SHRRAAMMMMM
--SPEAK THOSE WORDS ARE YOU HAVE ALREADY LOST!
FRANKLY, IT IS NO HONOR TO DEFEAT YOU, CRADO!
WILL IS HALF THE WINNING!
BUT CRADO KNOWS HIS OWN WORTH--HE IS NO MATCH FOR THE FIGHTING SKILLS OF EXAR KUN!
AND I STILL SAY IT IS NO DISHONOR TO LOSE TO YOU.

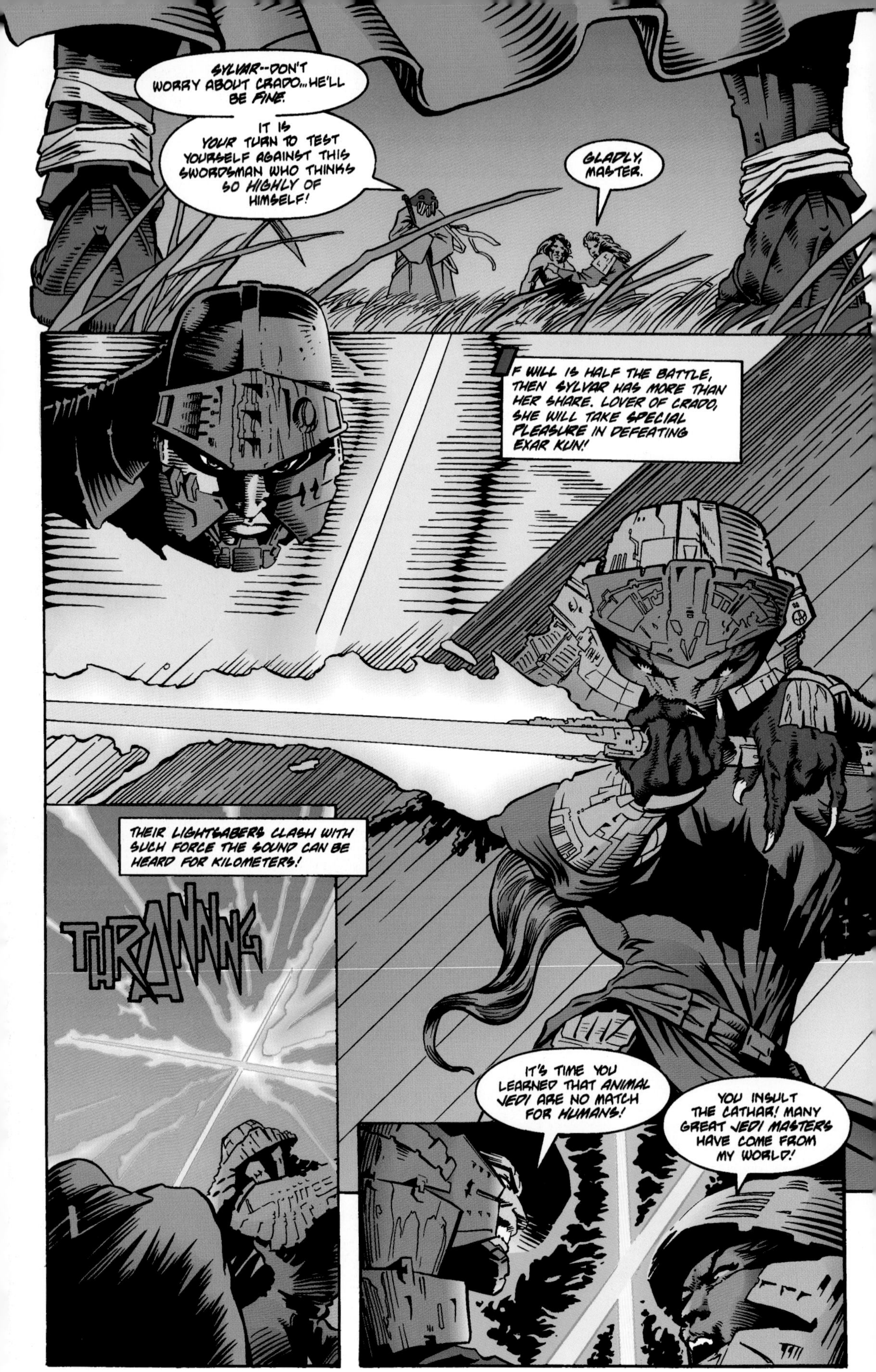
SYLVAR--DON'T WORRY ABOUT CRADO... HE'LL BE FINE.
IT IS YOUR TURN TO TEST YOURSELF AGAINST THIS SWORDSMAN WHO THINKS SO HIGHLY OF HIMSELF!
GLADLY, MASTER.
IF WILL IS HALF THE BATTLE, THEN SYLVAR HAS MORE THAN HER SHARE. LOVER OF CRADO, SHE WILL TAKE SPECIAL PLEASURE IN DEFEATING EXAR KUN!
THEIR LIGHTSABERS CLASH WITH SUCH FORCE THE SOUND CAN BE HEARD FOR KILOMETERS!
THRANNNG
IT'S TIME YOU LEARNED THAT ANIMAL JEDI ARE NO MATCH FOR HUMANS!
YOU INSULT THE CATHAR! MANY GREAT JEDI MASTERS HAVE COME FROM MY WORLD!

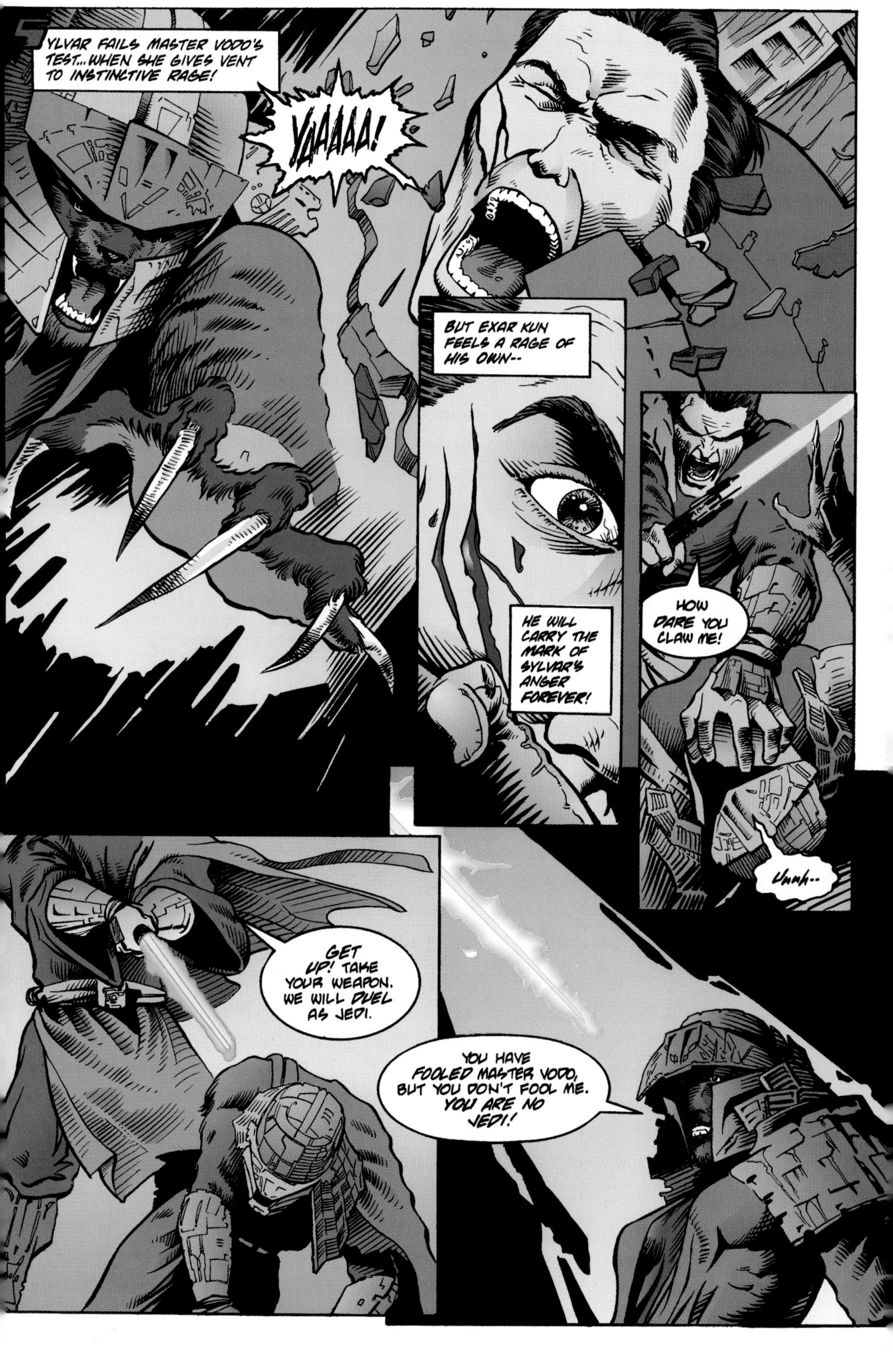
SYLVAR FAILS MASTER VODO'S TEST... WHEN SHE GIVES VENT TO INSTINCTIVE RAGE!
YAAAAA!
BUT EXAR KUN FEELS A RAGE OF HIS OWN--
HE WILL CARRY THE MARK OF SYLVAR'S ANGER FOREVER!
HOW DARE YOU CLAW ME!
Unnh..
GET UP! TAKE YOUR WEAPON. WE WILL DUEL AS JEDI.
YOU HAVE FOOLED MASTER VODO, BUT YOU DON'T FOOL ME. YOU ARE NO JEDI!

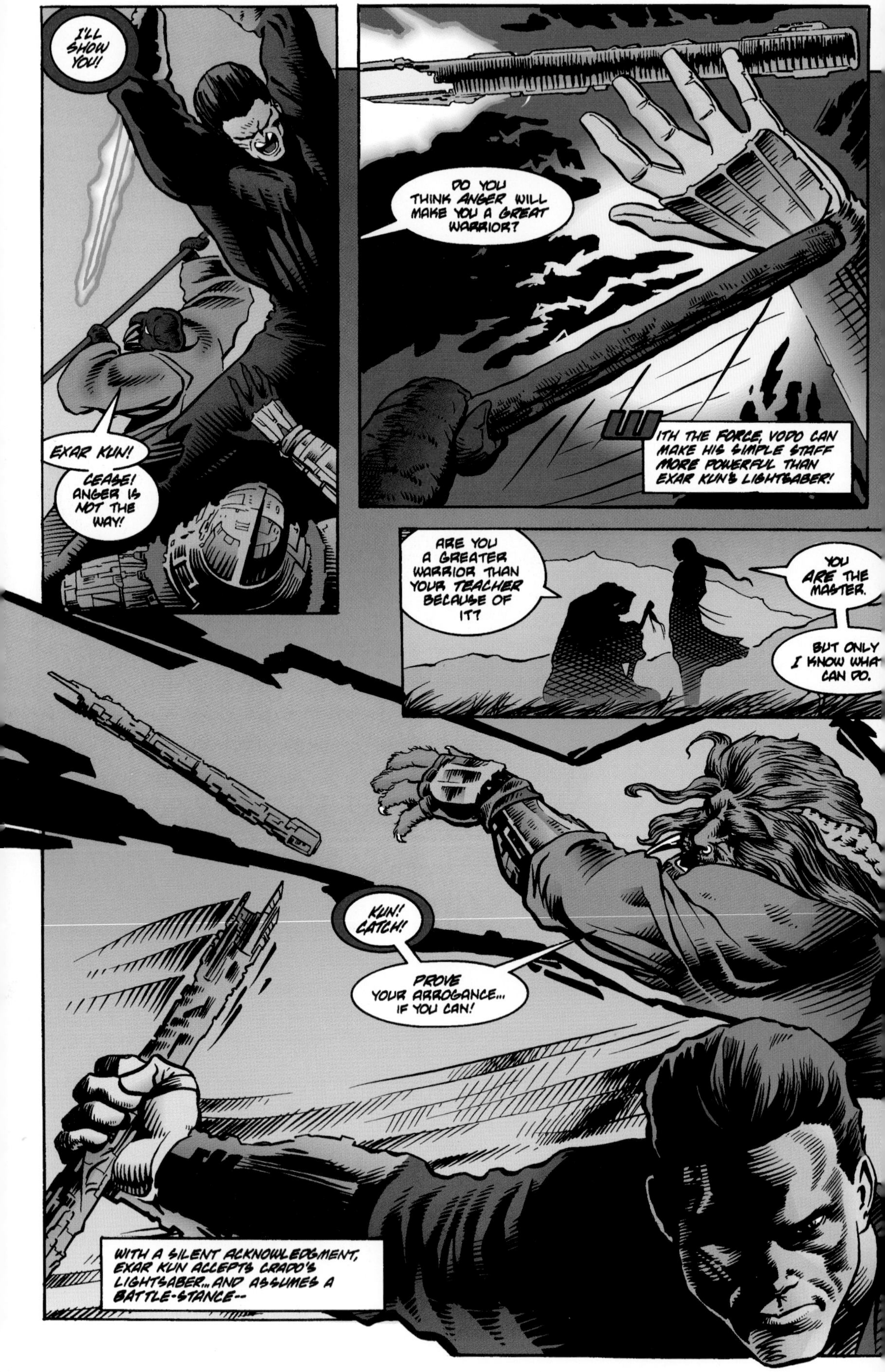
I'LL SHOW YOU!!
EXAR KUN!
CEASE! ANGER IS NOT THE WAY!
DO YOU THINK ANGER WILL MAKE YOU A GREAT WARRIOR?
WITH THE FORCE, VODO CAN MAKE HIS SIMPLE STAFF MORE POWERFUL THAN EXAR KUN'S LIGHTSABER!
ARE YOU A GREATER WARRIOR THAN YOUR TEACHER BECAUSE OF IT?
YOU ARE THE MASTER.
BUT ONLY I KNOW WHA CAN DO.
KUN! CATCH!
PROVE YOUR ARROGANCE... IF YOU CAN!
WITH A SILENT ACKNOWLEDGMENT, EXAR KUN ACCEPTS CRADO'S LIGHTSABER... AND ASSUMES A BATTLE-STANCE--

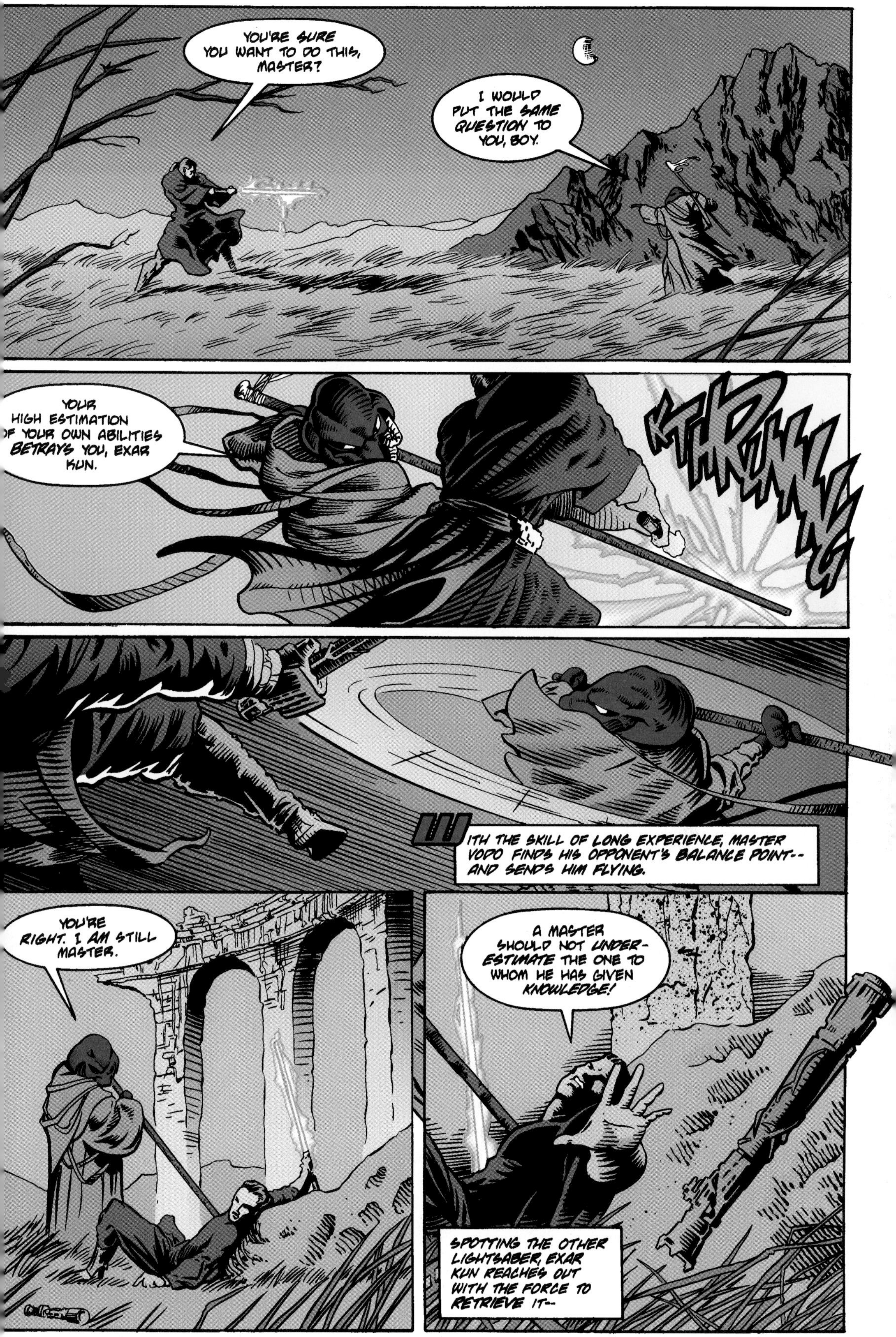
YOU'RE SURE YOU WANT TO DO THIS, MASTER?
I WOULD PUT THE SAME QUESTION TO YOU, BOY.
YOUR HIGH ESTIMATION OF YOUR OWN ABILITIES BETRAYS YOU, EXAR KUN.
K-THRUNNG
WITH THE SKILL OF LONG EXPERIENCE, MASTER VODO FINDS HIS OPPONENT'S BALANCE POINT-- AND SENDS HIM FLYING.
YOU'RE RIGHT. I AM STILL MASTER.
A MASTER SHOULD NOT UNDER-ESTIMATE THE ONE TO WHOM HE HAS GIVEN KNOWLEDGE!
SPOTTING THE OTHER LIGHTSABER, EXAR KUN REACHES OUT WITH THE FORCE TO RETRIEVE IT--

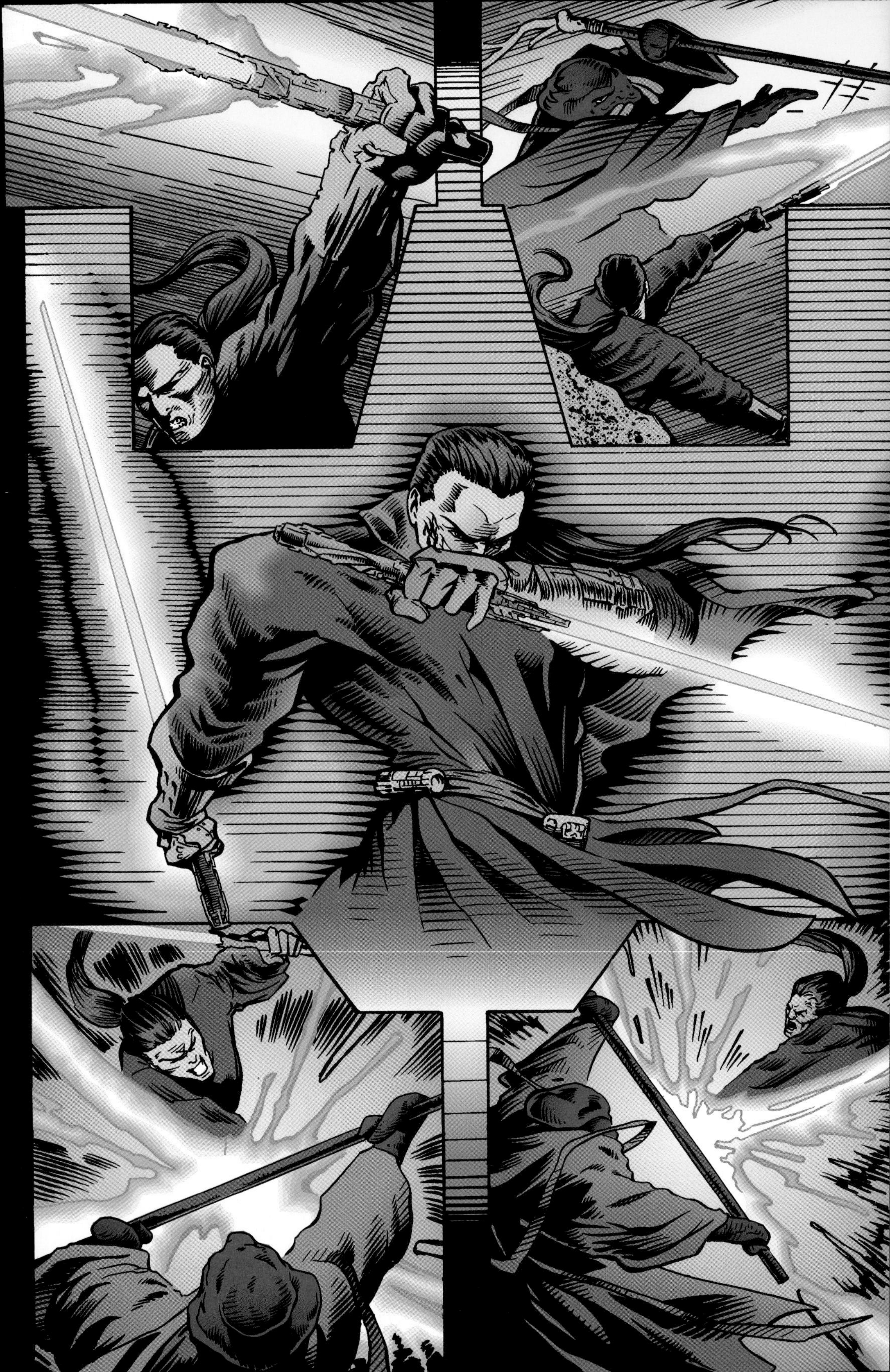

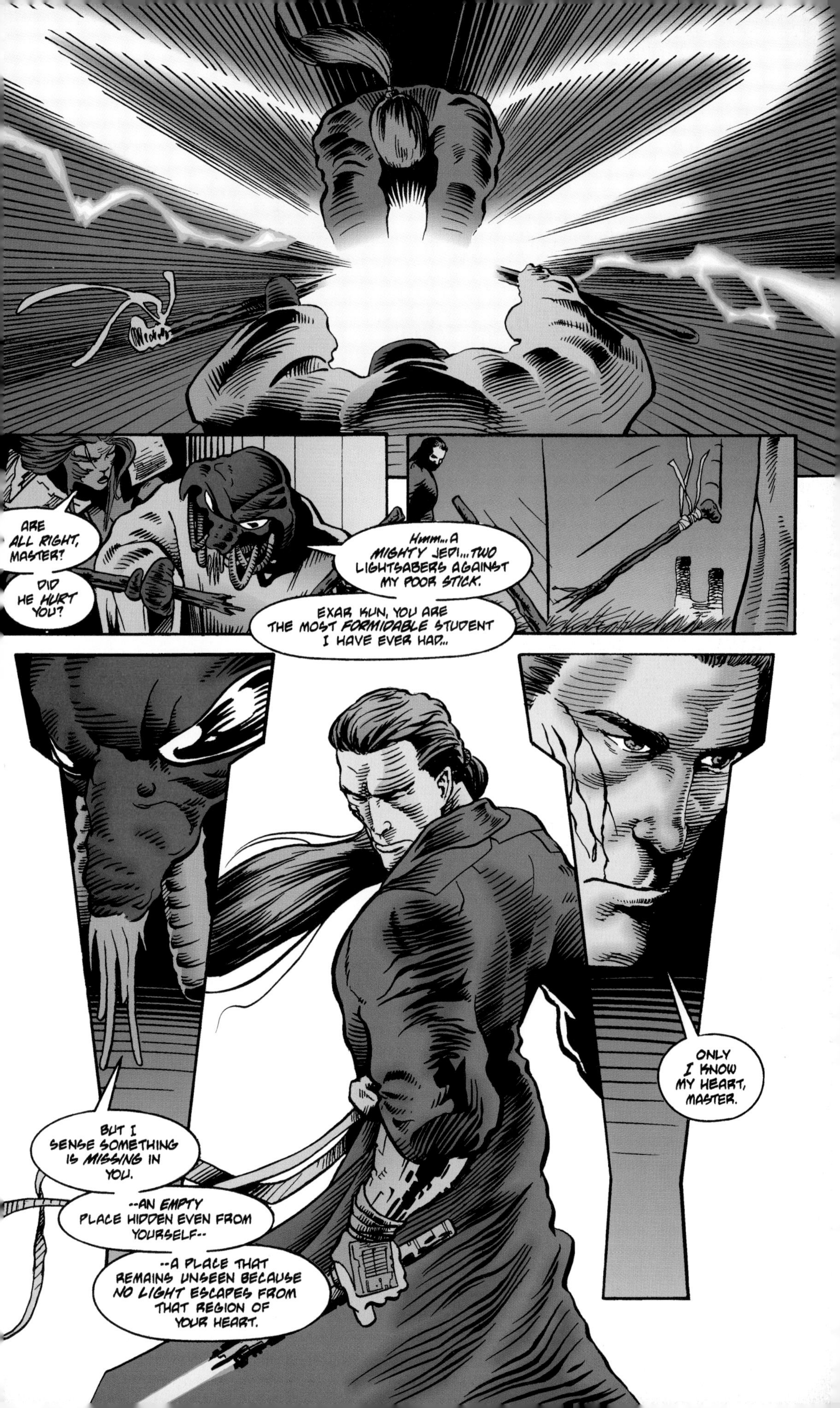
ARE ALL RIGHT, MASTER?
DID HE HURT YOU?
Hmm... A MIGHTY JEDI... TWO LIGHTSABERS AGAINST MY POOR STICK.
EXAR KUN, YOU ARE THE MOST FORMIDABLE STUDENT I HAVE EVER HAD...
BUT I SENSE SOMETHING IS MISSING IN YOU.
--AN EMPTY PLACE HIDDEN EVEN FROM YOURSELF--
--A PLACE THAT REMAINS UNSEEN BECAUSE NO LIGHT ESCAPES FROM THAT REGION OF YOUR HEART.
ONLY I KNOW MY HEART, MASTER.

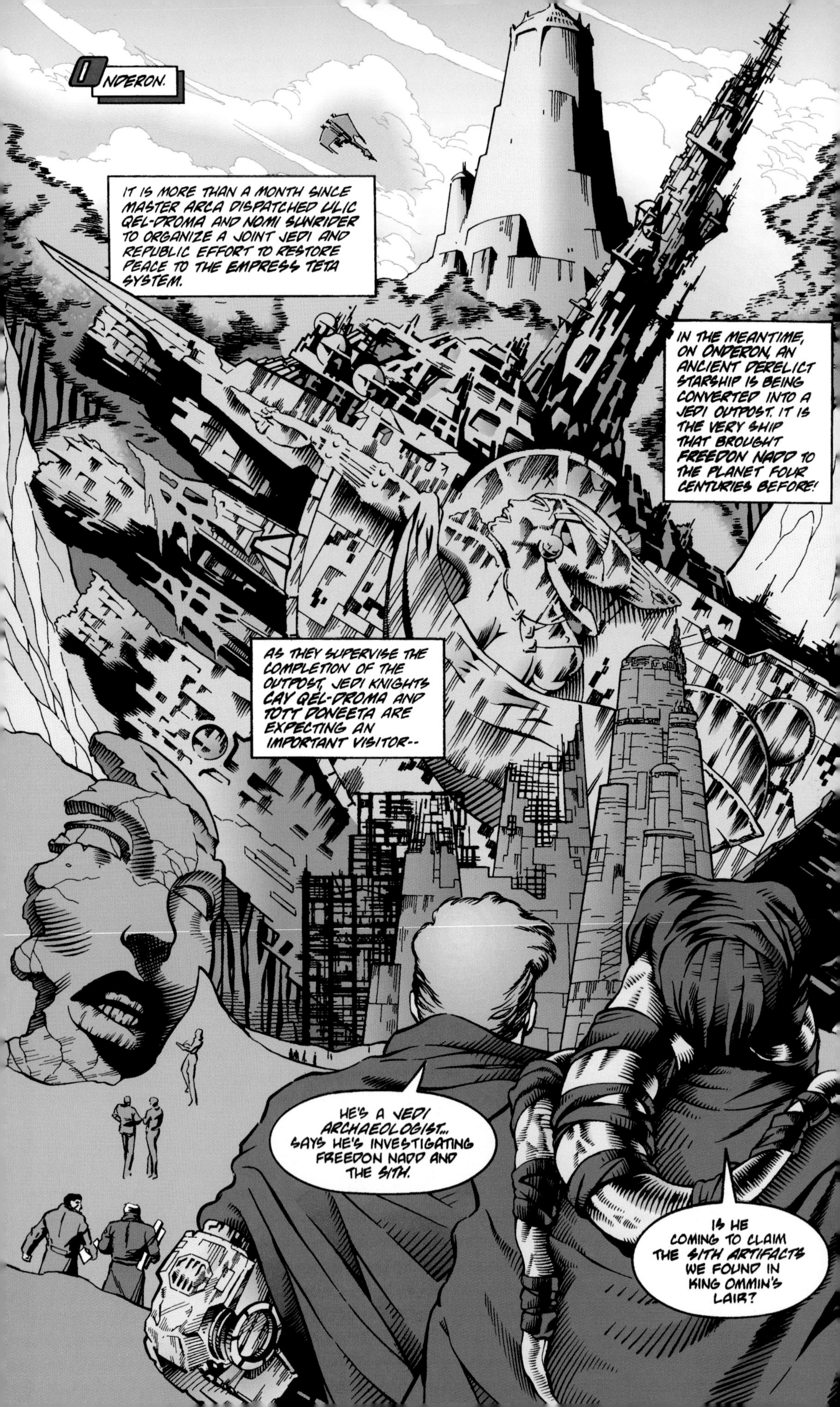
ONDERON.
IT IS MORE THAN A MONTH SINCE MASTER ARCA DISPATCHED ULIC QEL-DROMA AND NOMI SUNRIDER TO ORGANIZE A JOINT JEDI AND REPUBLIC EFFORT TO RESTORE PEACE TO THE EMPRESS TETA SYSTEM.
IN THE MEANTIME, ON ONDERON, AN ANCIENT DERELICT STARSHIP IS BEING CONVERTED INTO A JEDI OUTPOST. IT IS THE VERY SHIP THAT BROUGHT FREEDON NADD TO THE PLANET FOUR CENTURIES BEFORE!
AS THEY SUPERVISE THE COMPLETION OF THE OUTPOST, JEDI KNIGHTS CAY QEL-DROMA AND TOTT DONEETA ARE EXPECTING AN IMPORTANT VISITOR--
HE'S A JEDI ARCHAEOLOGIST... SAYS HE'S INVESTIGATING FREEDON NADD AND THE SITH.
IS HE COMING TO CLAIM THE SITH ARTIFACTS WE FOUND IN KING OMMIN'S LAIR?

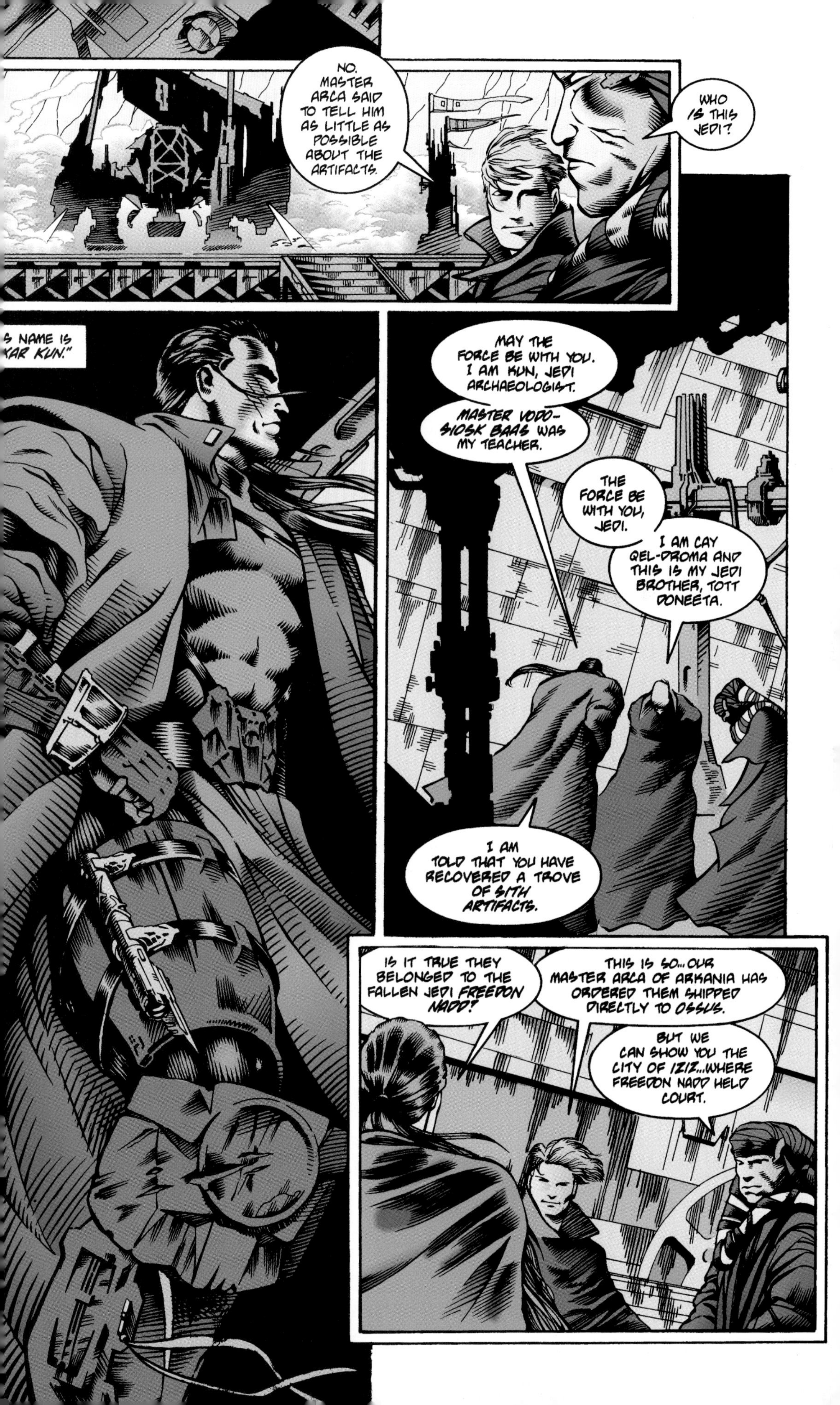

NO. MASTER ARCA SAID TO TELL HIM AS LITTLE AS POSSIBLE ABOUT THE ARTIFACTS.
WHO IS THIS JEDI?
S NAME IS YAR KUN."
MAY THE FORCE BE WITH YOU. I AM KUN, JEDI ARCHAEOLOGIST.
MASTER VODO-SIOSK BAAS WAS MY TEACHER.
THE FORCE BE WITH YOU, JEDI.
I AM CAY QEL-DROMA AND THIS IS MY JEDI BROTHER, TOTT DONEETA.
I AM TOLD THAT YOU HAVE RECOVERED A TROVE OF SITH ARTIFACTS.
IS IT TRUE THEY BELONGED TO THE FALLEN JEDI FREEDON NADD?
THIS IS SO... OUR MASTER ARCA OF ARKANIA HAS ORDERED THEM SHIPPED DIRECTLY TO OSSUS.
BUT WE CAN SHOW YOU THE CITY OF IZIZ... WHERE FREEDON NADD HELD COURT.

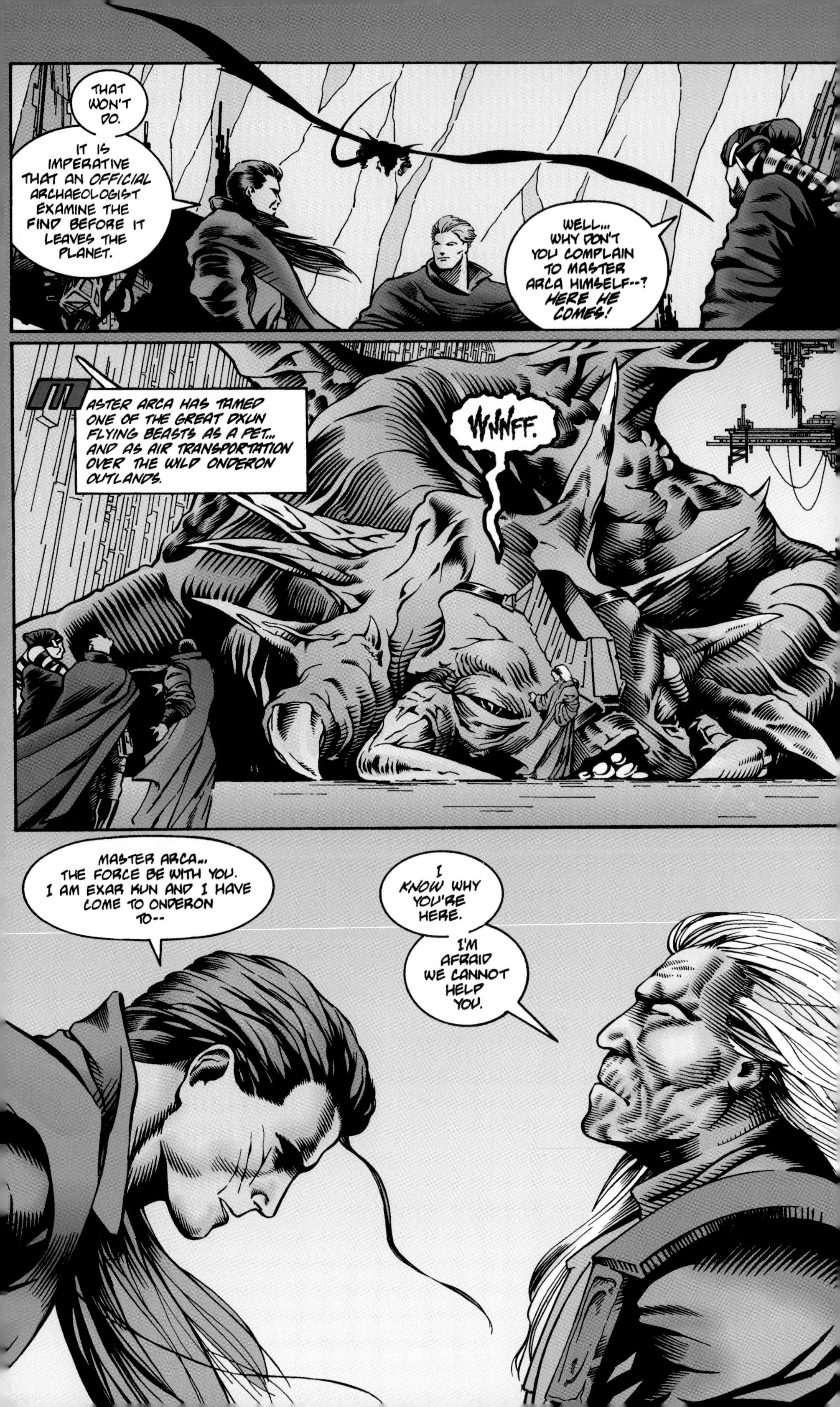

THAT WON'T DO.
IT IS IMPERATIVE THAT AN OFFICIAL ARCHAEOLOGIST EXAMINE THE FIND BEFORE IT LEAVES THE PLANET.
WELL... WHY DON'T YOU COMPLAIN TO MASTER ARCA HIMSELF--? HERE HE COMES!
MASTER ARCA HAS TAMED ONE OF THE GREAT DXUN FLYING BEASTS AS A PET... AND AS AIR TRANSPORTATION OVER THE WILD ONDERON OUTLANDS.
WNNFF.
MASTER ARCA... THE FORCE BE WITH YOU. I AM EXAR KUN AND I HAVE COME TO ONDERON TO--
I KNOW WHY YOU'RE HERE.
I'M AFRAID WE CANNOT HELP YOU.

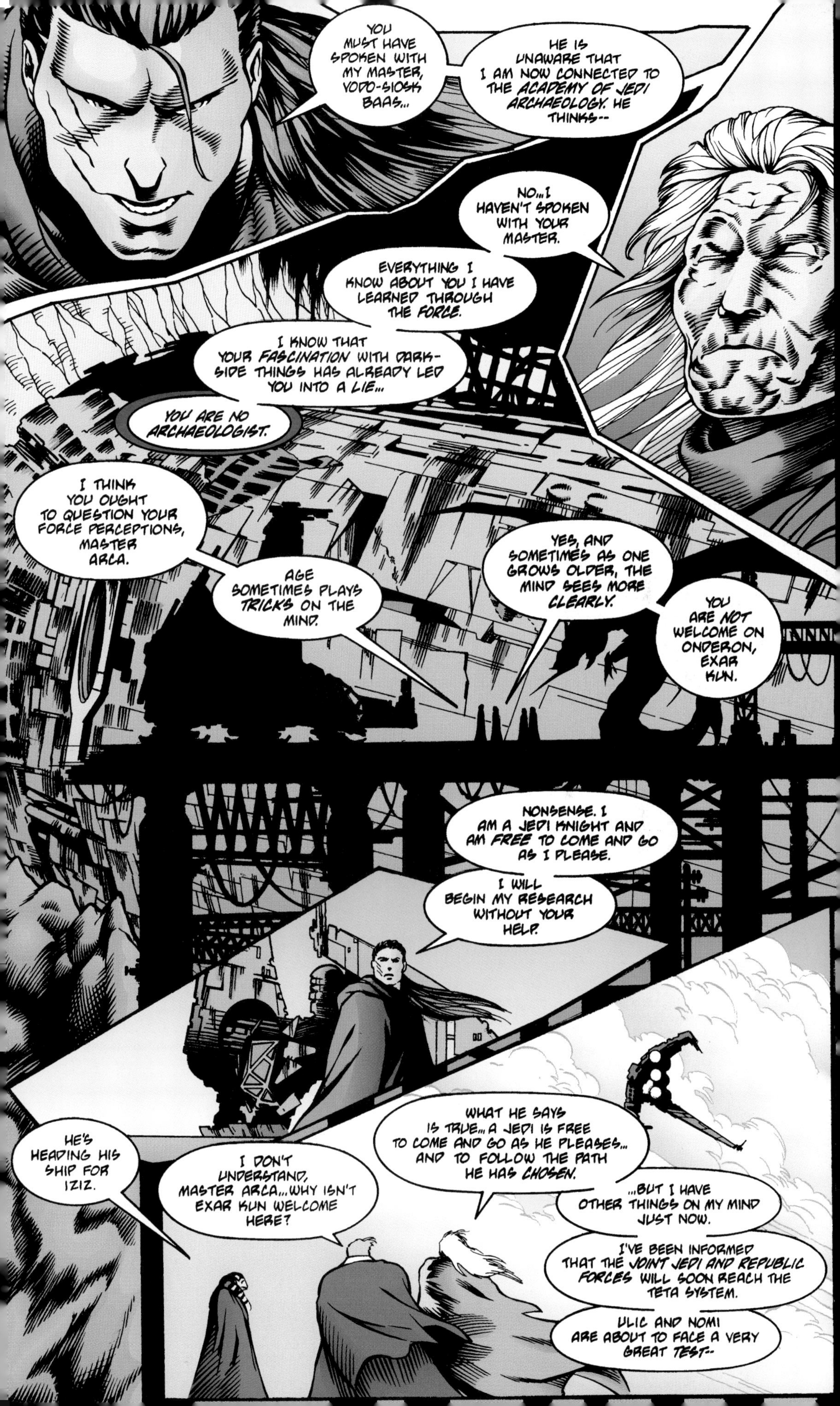
YOU MUST HAVE SPOKEN WITH MY MASTER, VODO-SIOSK BAAS...
HE IS UNAWARE THAT I AM NOW CONNECTED TO THE ACADEMY OF JEDI ARCHAEOLOGY. HE THINKS--
NO...I HAVEN'T SPOKEN WITH YOUR MASTER.
EVERYTHING I KNOW ABOUT YOU I HAVE LEARNED THROUGH THE FORCE.
I KNOW THAT YOUR FASCINATION WITH DARK-SIDE THINGS HAS ALREADY LED YOU INTO A LIE...
YOU ARE NO ARCHAEOLOGIST.
I THINK YOU OUGHT TO QUESTION YOUR FORCE PERCEPTIONS, MASTER ARCA.
AGE SOMETIMES PLAYS TRICKS ON THE MIND.
YES, AND SOMETIMES AS ONE GROWS OLDER, THE MIND SEES MORE CLEARLY.
YOU ARE NOT WELCOME ON ONDERON, EXAR KUN.
NONSENSE. I AM A JEDI KNIGHT AND AM FREE TO COME AND GO AS I PLEASE.
I WILL BEGIN MY RESEARCH WITHOUT YOUR HELP.
HE'S HEADING HIS SHIP FOR IZIZ.
I DON'T UNDERSTAND, MASTER ARCA...WHY ISN'T EXAR KUN WELCOME HERE?
WHAT HE SAYS IS TRUE... A JEDI IS FREE TO COME AND GO AS HE PLEASES... AND TO FOLLOW THE PATH HE HAS CHOSEN.
...BUT I HAVE OTHER THINGS ON MY MIND JUST NOW.
I'VE BEEN INFORMED THAT THE JOINT JEDI AND REPUBLIC FORCES WILL SOON REACH THE TETA SYSTEM.
ULIC AND NOMI ARE ABOUT TO FACE A VERY GREAT TEST--

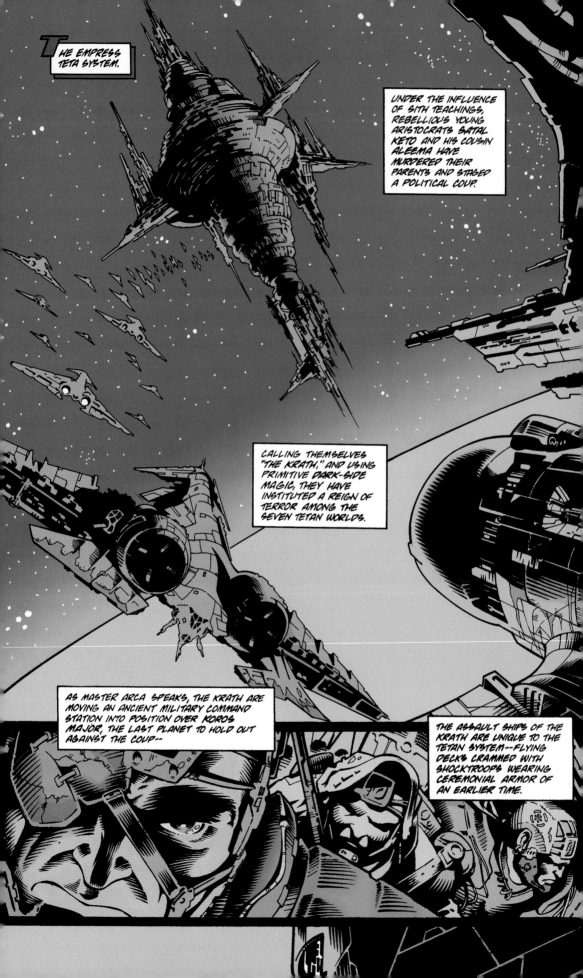

THE EMPRESS TETA SYSTEM.

UNDER THE INFLUENCE OF SITH TEACHINGS, REBELLIOUS YOUNG ARISTOCRATS SATAL KETO AND HIS COUSIN ALEEMA HAVE MURDERED THEIR PARENTS AND STAGED A POLITICAL COUP.

CALLING THEMSELVES "THE KRATH," AND USING PRIMITIVE DARK-SIDE MAGIC, THEY HAVE INSTITUTED A REIGN OF TERROR AMONG THE SEVEN TETAN WORLDS.

AS MASTER ARCA SPEAKS, THE KRATH ARE MOVING AN ANCIENT MILITARY COMMAND STATION INTO POSITION OVER KOROS MAJOR, THE LAST PLANET TO HOLD OUT AGAINST THE COUP--

THE ASSAULT SHIPS OF THE KRATH ARE UNIQUE TO THE TETAN SYSTEM--FLYING DECKS CRAMMED WITH SHOCKTROOPS WEARING CEREMONIAL ARMOR OF AN EARLIER TIME.

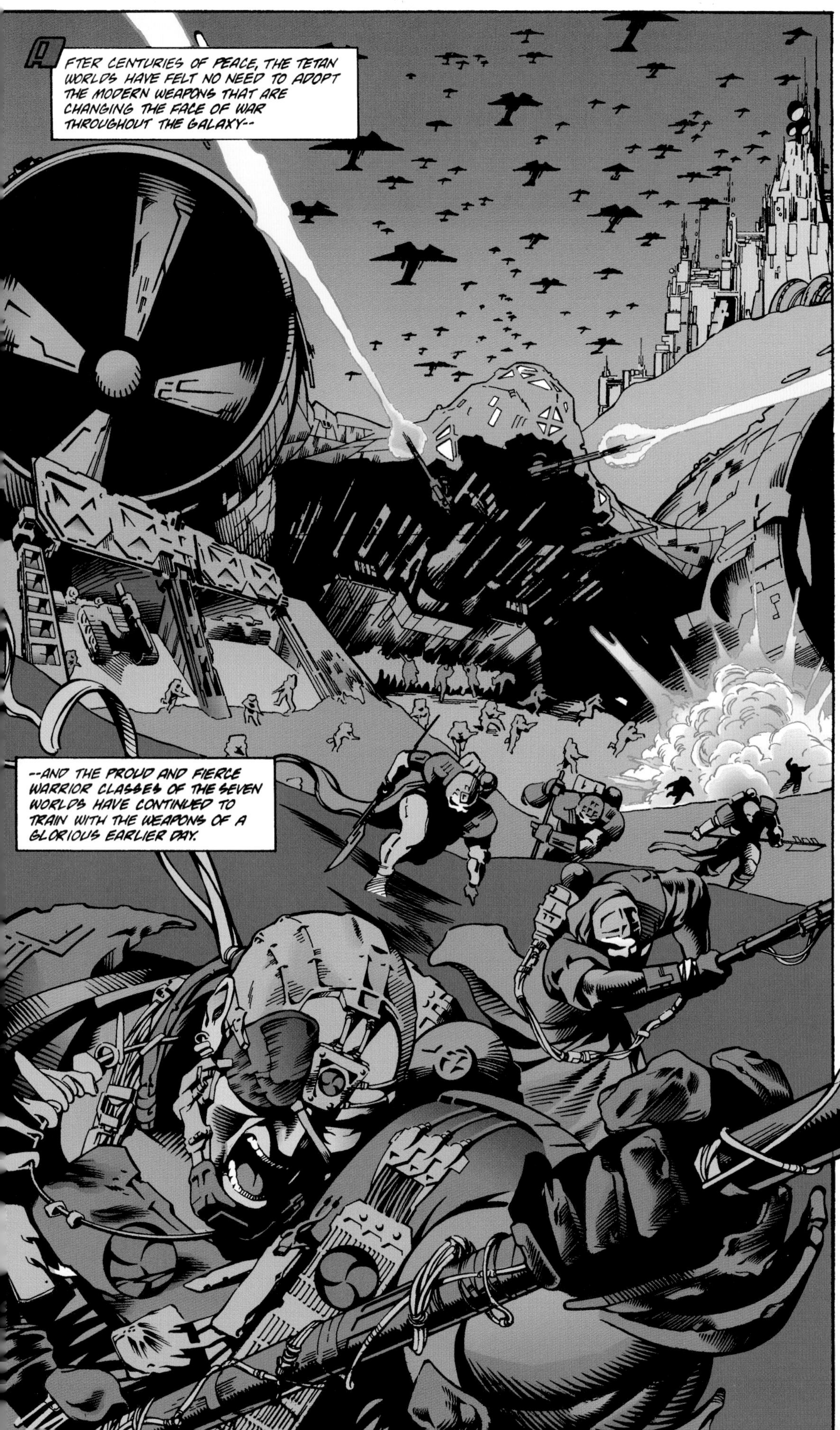
AFTER CENTURIES OF PEACE, THE TETAN WORLDS HAVE FELT NO NEED TO ADOPT THE MODERN WEAPONS THAT ARE CHANGING THE FACE OF WAR THROUGHOUT THE GALAXY--
--AND THE PROUD AND FIERCE WARRIOR CLASSES OF THE SEVEN WORLDS HAVE CONTINUED TO TRAIN WITH THE WEAPONS OF A GLORIOUS EARLIER DAY.

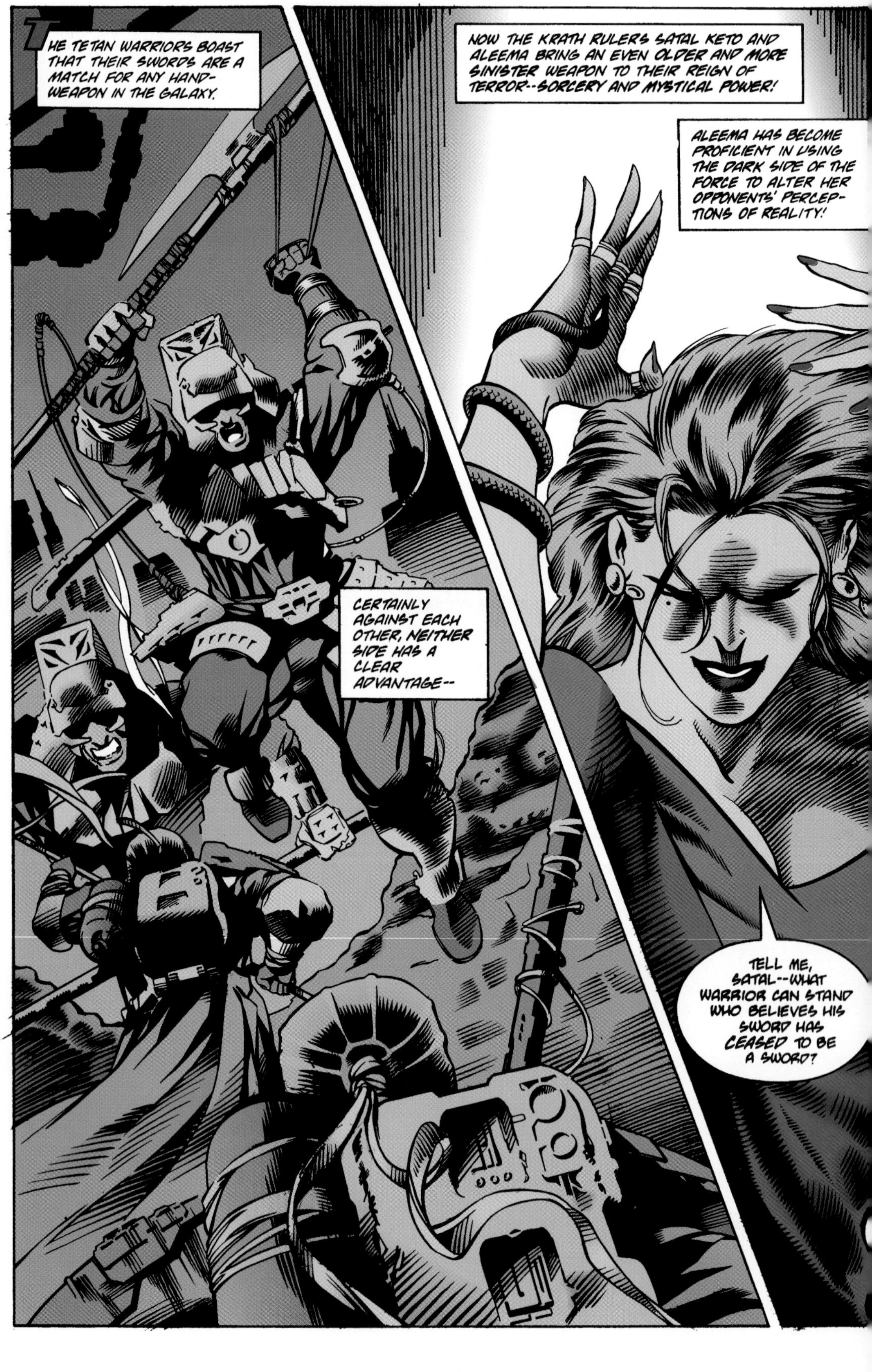
THE TETAN WARRIORS BOAST THAT THEIR SWORDS ARE A MATCH FOR ANY HAND-WEAPON IN THE GALAXY.
CERTAINLY AGAINST EACH OTHER, NEITHER SIDE HAS A CLEAR ADVANTAGE--
NOW THE KRATH RULERS SATAL KETO AND ALEEMA BRING AN EVEN OLDER AND MORE SINISTER WEAPON TO THEIR REIGN OF TERROR--SORCERY AND MYSTICAL POWER!
ALEEMA HAS BECOME PROFICIENT IN USING THE DARK SIDE OF THE FORCE TO ALTER HER OPPONENTS' PERCEPTIONS OF REALITY!
TELL ME, SATAL--WHAT WARRIOR CAN STAND WHO BELIEVES HIS SWORD HAS CEASED TO BE A SWORD?

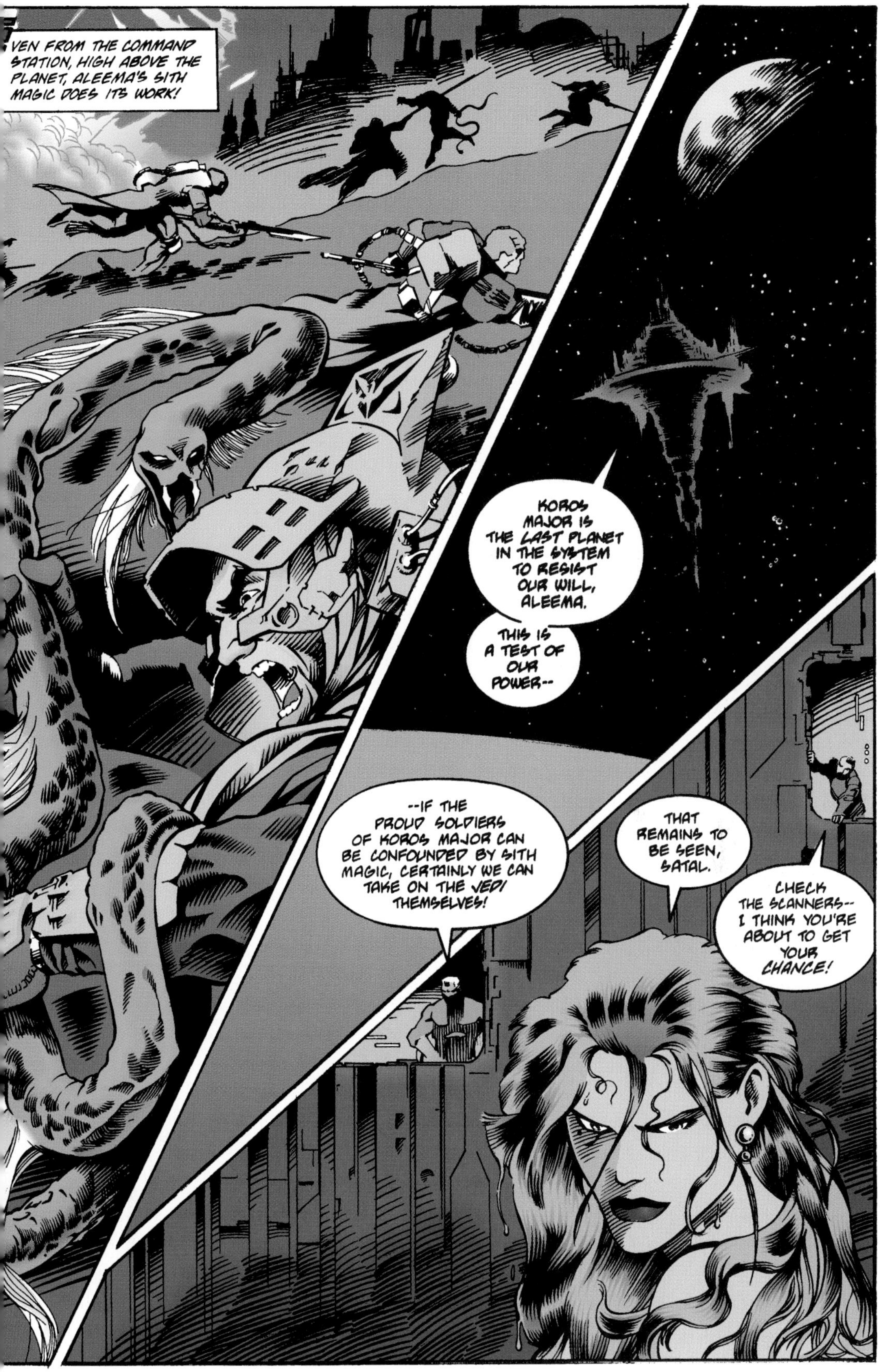
VEN FROM THE COMMAND STATION, HIGH ABOVE THE PLANET, ALEEMA'S SITH MAGIC DOES ITS WORK!
KOROS MAJOR IS THE LAST PLANET IN THE SYSTEM TO RESIST OUR WILL, ALEEMA.
THIS IS A TEST OF OUR POWER--
--IF THE PROUD SOLDIERS OF KOROS MAJOR CAN BE CONFOUNDED BY SITH MAGIC, CERTAINLY WE CAN TAKE ON THE JEDI THEMSELVES!
THAT REMAINS TO BE SEEN, SATAL.
CHECK THE SCANNERS-- I THINK YOU'RE ABOUT TO GET YOUR CHANCE!

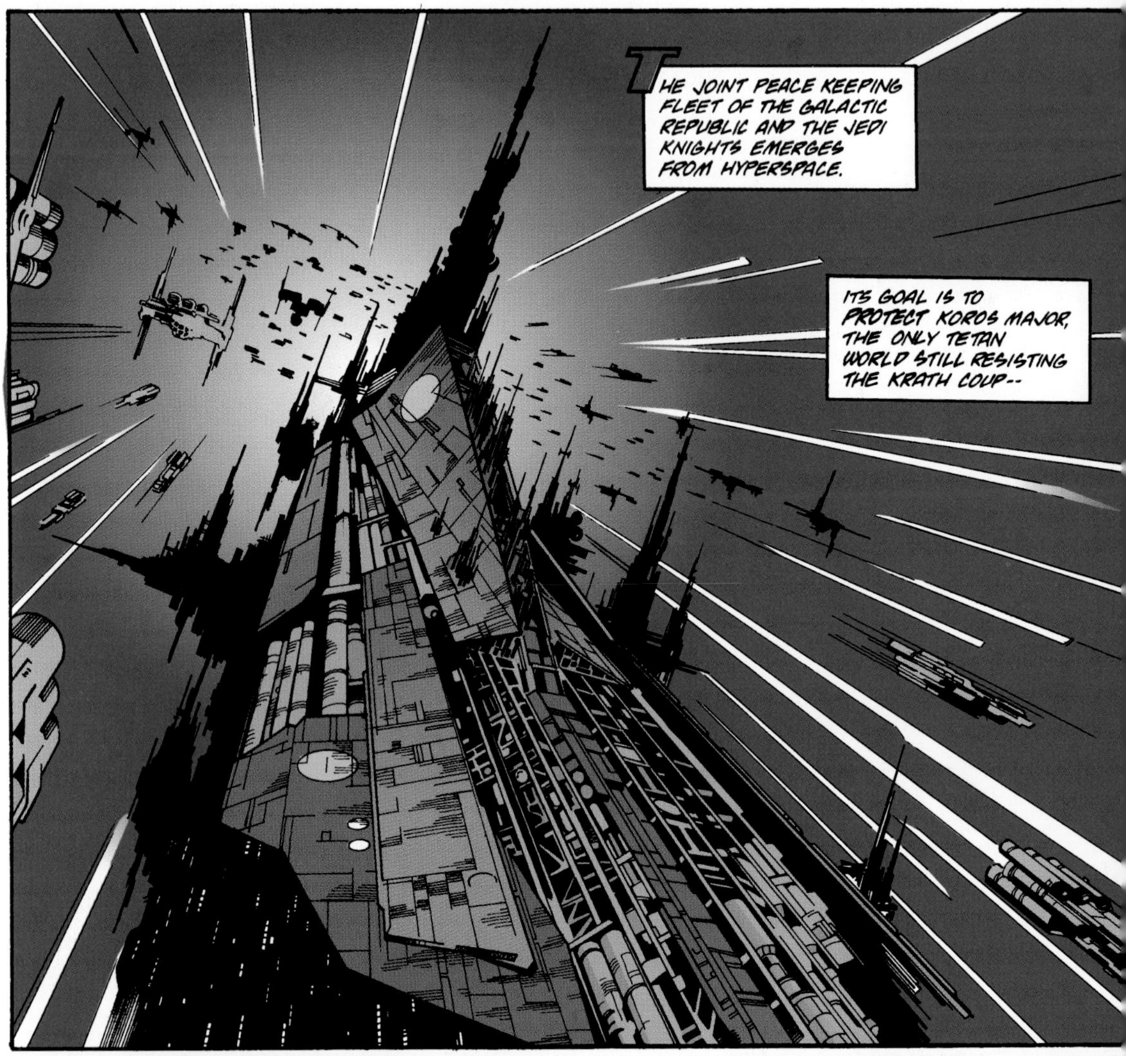
THE JOINT PEACE KEEPING FLEET OF THE GALACTIC REPUBLIC AND THE JEDI KNIGHTS EMERGES FROM HYPERSPACE.
ITS GOAL IS TO PROTECT KOROS MAJOR, THE ONLY TETAN WORLD STILL RESISTING THE KRATH COUP--

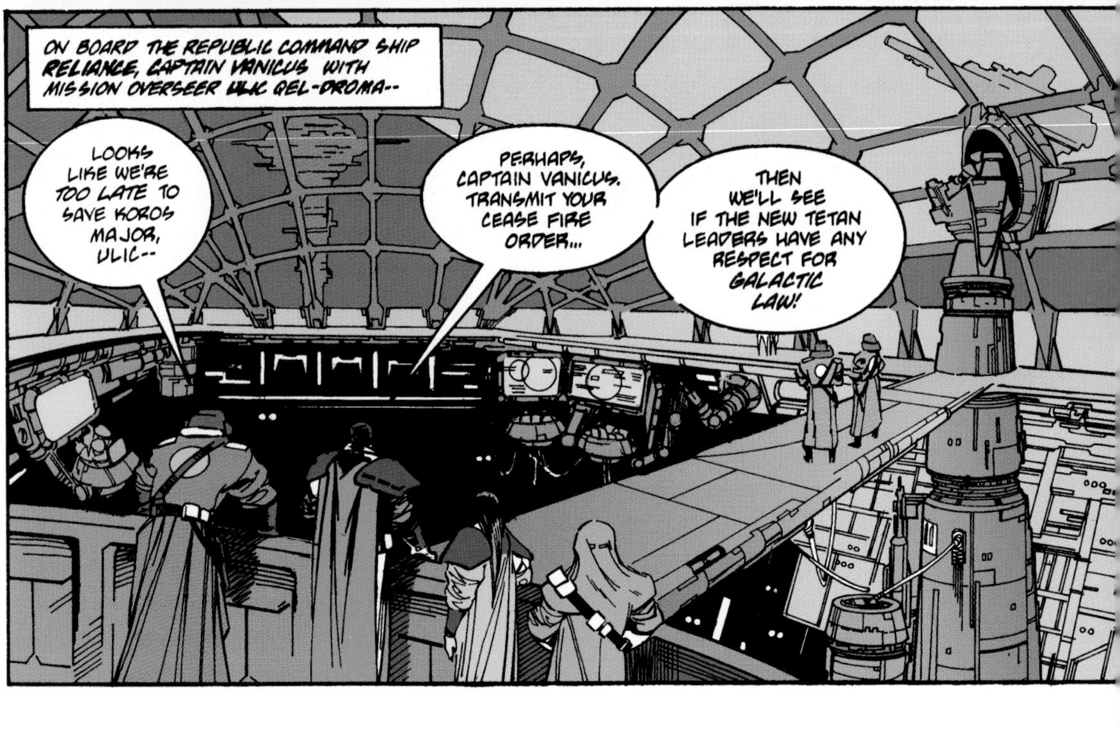
ON BOARD THE REPUBLIC COMMAND SHIP RELIANCE, CAPTAIN VANICUS WITH MISSION OVERSEER ULIC QEL-DROMA--
LOOKS LIKE WE'RE TOO LATE TO SAVE KOROS MAJOR, ULIC--
PERHAPS, CAPTAIN VANICUS. TRANSMIT YOUR CEASE FIRE ORDER...
THEN WE'LL SEE IF THE NEW TETAN LEADERS HAVE ANY RESPECT FOR GALACTIC LAW!

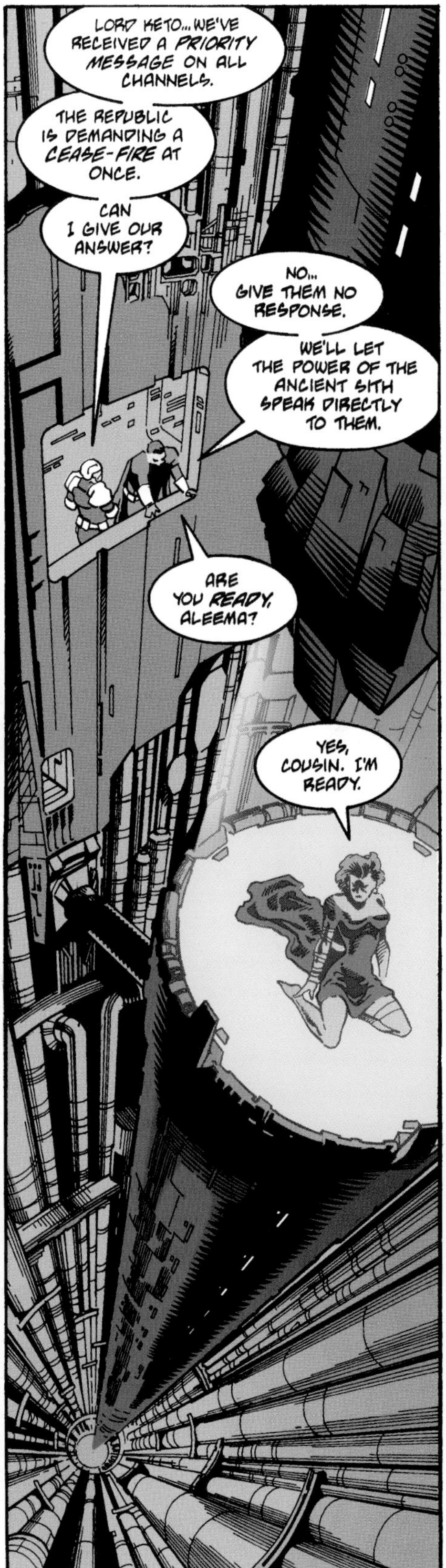
LORD KETO... WE'VE RECEIVED A PRIORITY MESSAGE ON ALL CHANNELS.
THE REPUBLIC IS DEMANDING A CEASE-FIRE AT ONCE.
CAN I GIVE OUR ANSWER?
NO... GIVE THEM NO RESPONSE.
WE'LL LET THE POWER OF THE ANCIENT SITH SPEAK DIRECTLY TO THEM.
ARE YOU READY, ALEEMA?
YES, COUSIN. I'M READY.

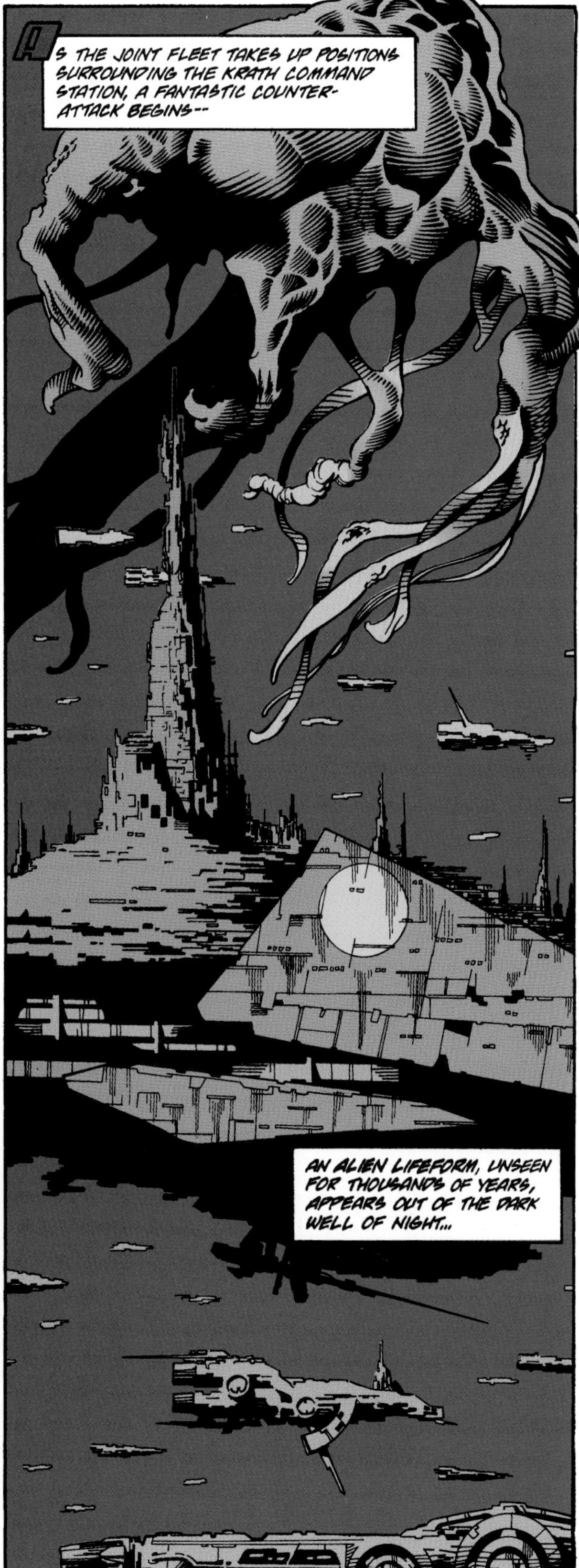
AS THE JOINT FLEET TAKES UP POSITIONS SURROUNDING THE KRATH COMMAND STATION, A FANTASTIC COUNTER-ATTACK BEGINS--
AN ALIEN LIFEFORM, UNSEEN FOR THOUSANDS OF YEARS, APPEARS OUT OF THE DARK WELL OF NIGHT...

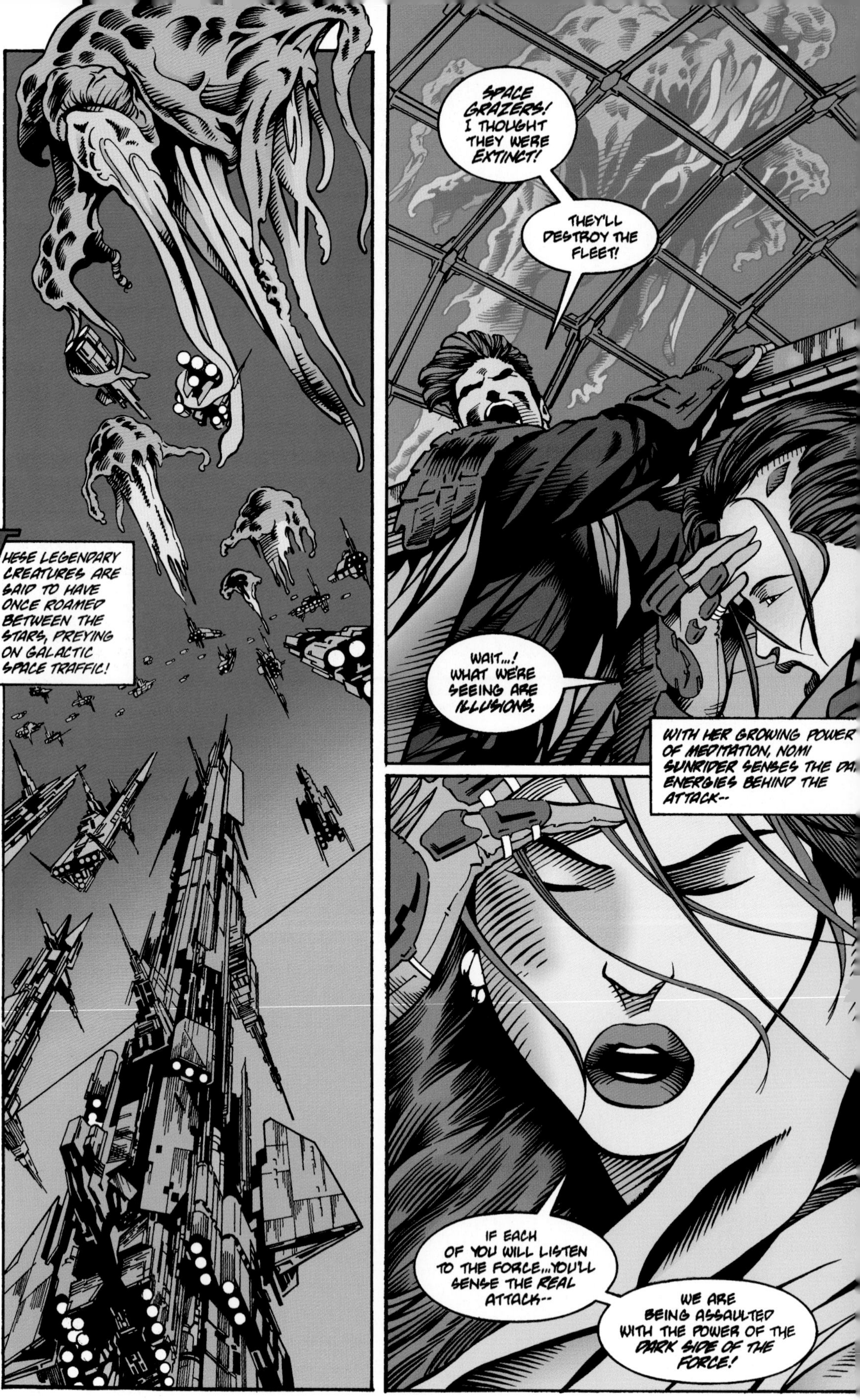
THESE LEGENDARY CREATURES ARE SAID TO HAVE ONCE ROAMED BETWEEN THE STARS, PREYING ON GALACTIC SPACE TRAFFIC!
SPACE GRAZERS! I THOUGHT THEY WERE EXTINCT!
THEY'LL DESTROY THE FLEET!
WAIT...! WHAT WE'RE SEEING ARE ILLUSIONS.
WITH HER GROWING POWER OF MEDITATION, NOMI SUNRIDER SENSES THE DA ENERGIES BEHIND THE ATTACK--
IF EACH OF YOU WILL LISTEN TO THE FORCE...YOU'LL SENSE THE REAL ATTACK--
WE ARE BEING ASSAULTED WITH THE POWER OF THE DARK SIDE OF THE FORCE!

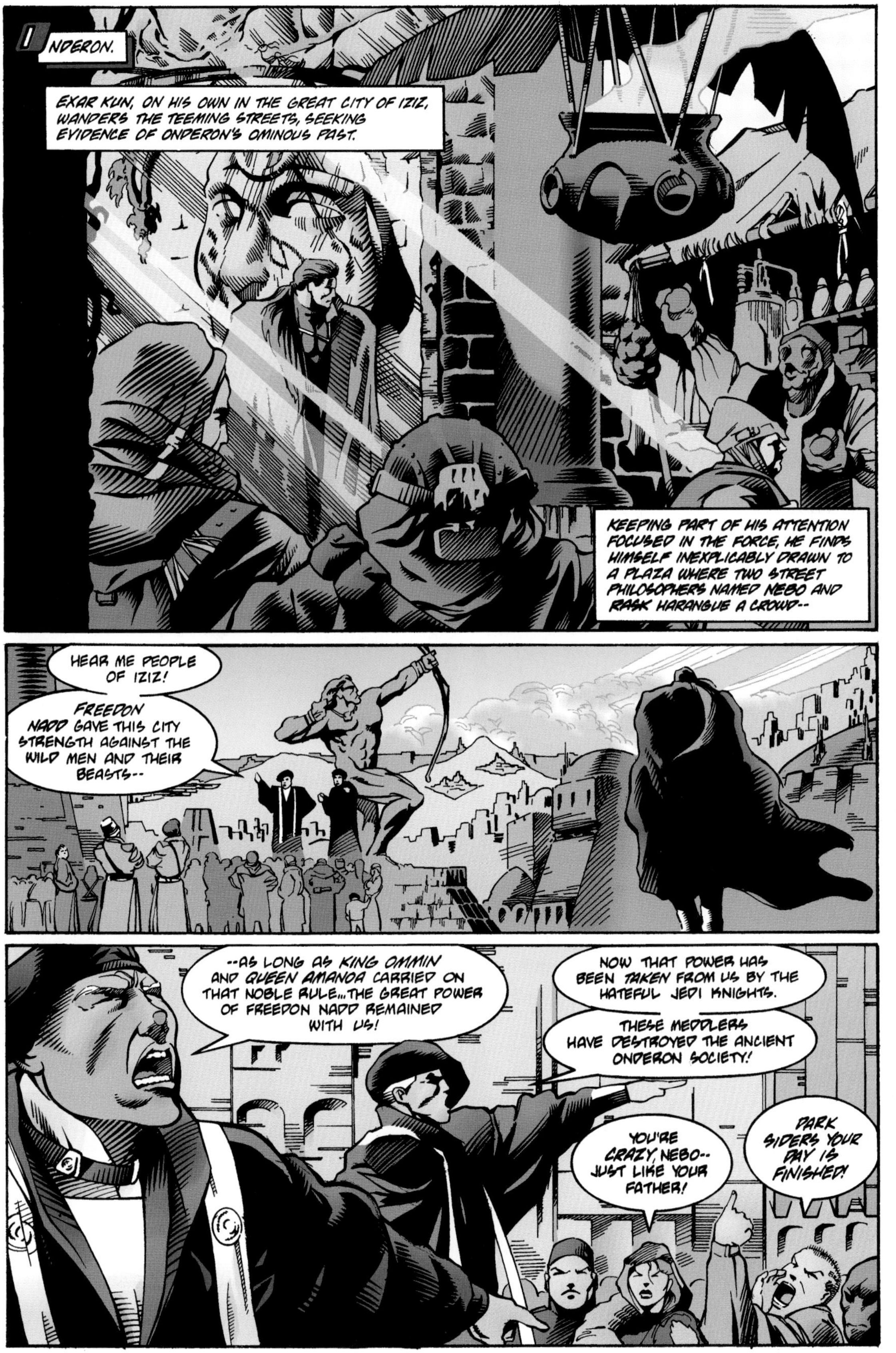
ONDERON.
EXAR KUN, ON HIS OWN IN THE GREAT CITY OF IZIZ, WANDERS THE TEEMING STREETS, SEEKING EVIDENCE OF ONDERON'S OMINOUS PAST.
KEEPING PART OF HIS ATTENTION FOCUSED IN THE FORCE, HE FINDS HIMSELF INEXPLICABLY DRAWN TO A PLAZA WHERE TWO STREET PHILOSOPHERS NAMED NEBO AND RASK HARANGUE A CROWD--
HEAR ME PEOPLE OF IZIZ!
FREEDON NADD GAVE THIS CITY STRENGTH AGAINST THE WILD MEN AND THEIR BEASTS--
--AS LONG AS KING OMMIN AND QUEEN AMANOA CARRIED ON THAT NOBLE RULE... THE GREAT POWER OF FREEDON NADD REMAINED WITH US!
NOW THAT POWER HAS BEEN TAKEN FROM US BY THE HATEFUL JEDI KNIGHTS.
THESE MEDDLERS HAVE DESTROYED THE ANCIENT ONDERON SOCIETY!
YOU'RE CRAZY, NEBO-- JUST LIKE YOUR FATHER!
DARK SIDERS YOUR DAY IS FINISHED!

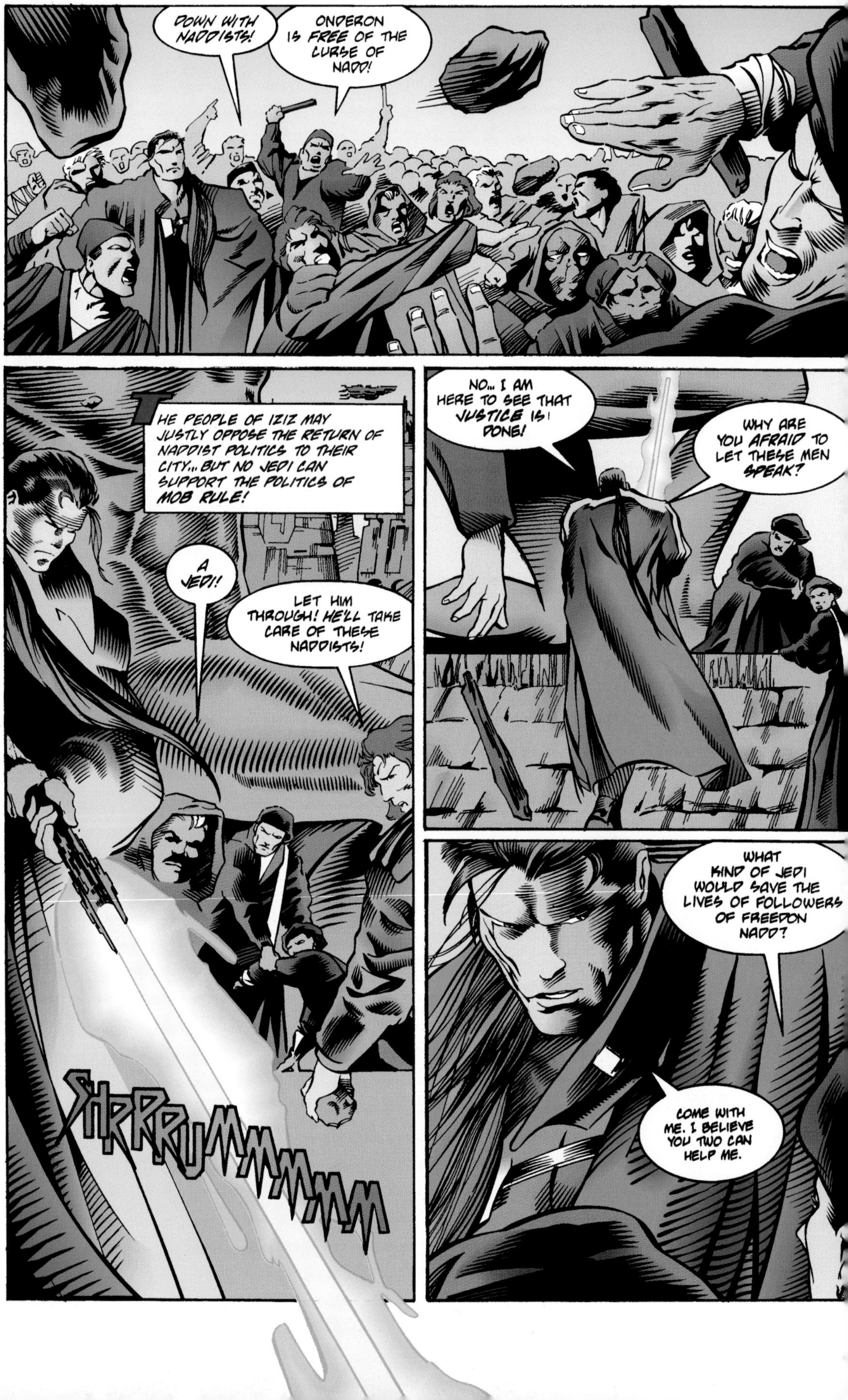
DOWN WITH NADDISTS!
ONDERON IS FREE OF THE CURSE OF NADD!
THE PEOPLE OF IZIZ MAY JUSTLY OPPOSE THE RETURN OF NADDIST POLITICS TO THEIR CITY... BUT NO JEDI CAN SUPPORT THE POLITICS OF MOB RULE!
A JEDI!
LET HIM THROUGH! HE'LL TAKE CARE OF THESE NADDISTS!
SHRRRUMMMMMMM
NO... I AM HERE TO SEE THAT JUSTICE IS DONE!
WHY ARE YOU AFRAID TO LET THESE MEN SPEAK?
WHAT KIND OF JEDI WOULD SAVE THE LIVES OF FOLLOWERS OF FREEDON NADD?
COME WITH ME. I BELIEVE YOU TWO CAN HELP ME.

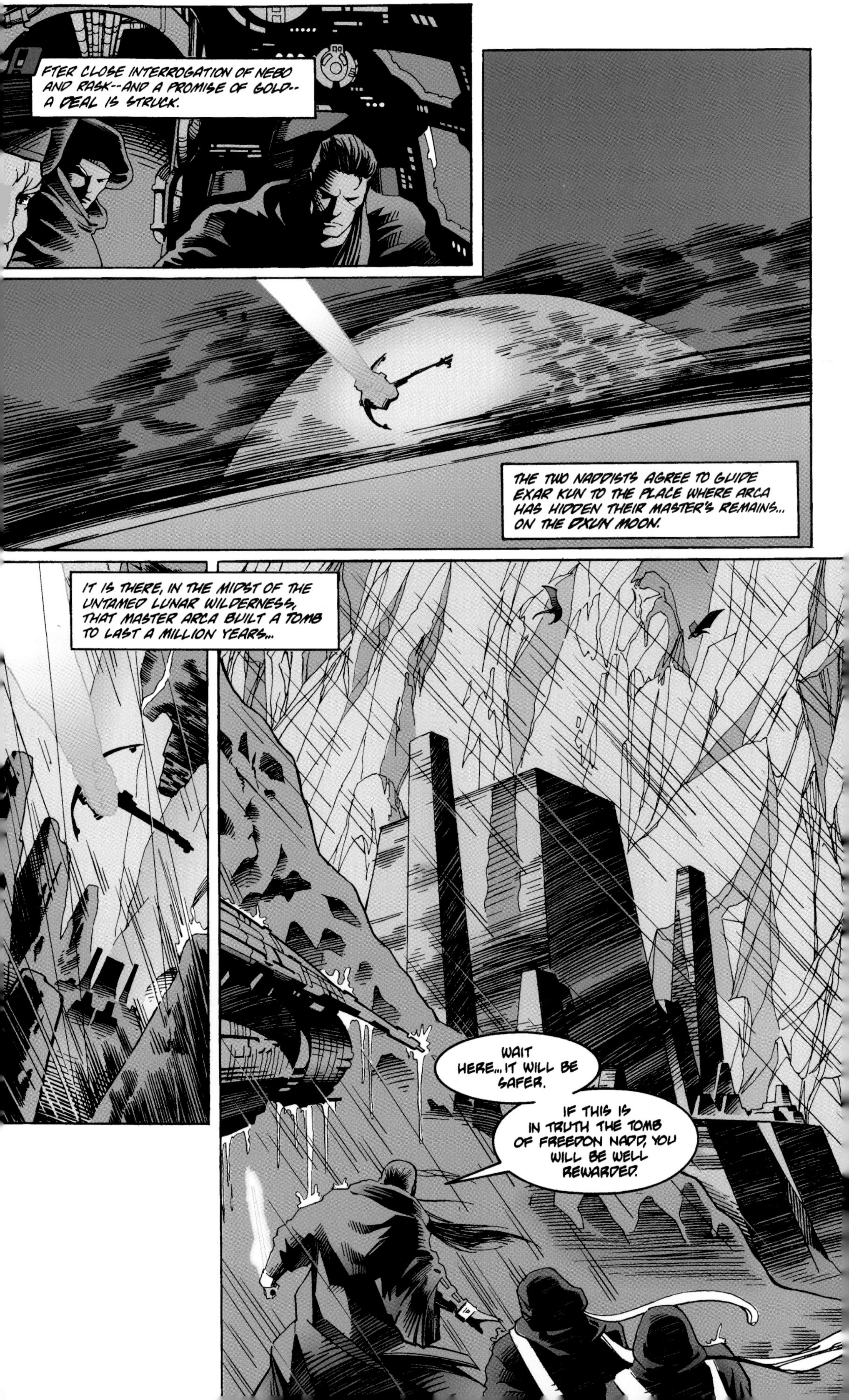
FTER CLOSE INTERROGATION OF NEBO AND RASK--AND A PROMISE OF GOLD--A DEAL IS STRUCK.
THE TWO NADDISTS AGREE TO GUIDE EXAR KUN TO THE PLACE WHERE ARCA HAS HIDDEN THEIR MASTER'S REMAINS... ON THE DXUN MOON.
IT IS THERE, IN THE MIDST OF THE UNTAMED LUNAR WILDERNESS, THAT MASTER ARCA BUILT A TOMB TO LAST A MILLION YEARS...
WAIT HERE... IT WILL BE SAFER.
IF THIS IS IN TRUTH THE TOMB OF FREEDON NADD, YOU WILL BE WELL REWARDED.

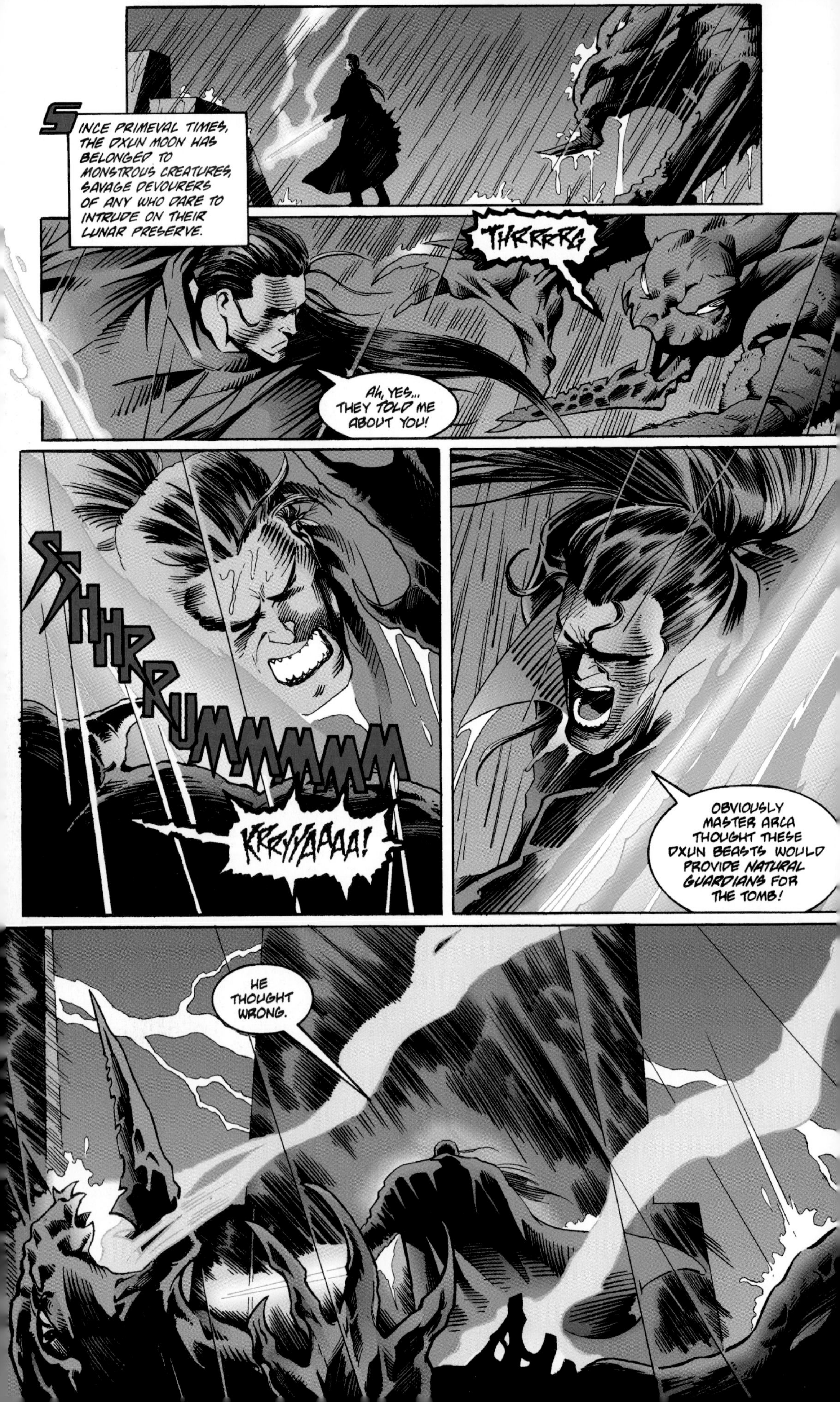
SINCE PRIMEVAL TIMES, THE DXUN MOON HAS BELONGED TO MONSTROUS CREATURES, SAVAGE DEVOURERS OF ANY WHO DARE TO INTRUDE ON THEIR LUNAR PRESERVE.
THRRRRG
AH, YES... THEY TOLD ME ABOUT YOU!
SHHRRUMMMMMM
KRRYYAAAA!
OBVIOUSLY MASTER ARCA THOUGHT THESE DXUN BEASTS WOULD PROVIDE NATURAL GUARDIANS FOR THE TOMB!
HE THOUGHT WRONG.

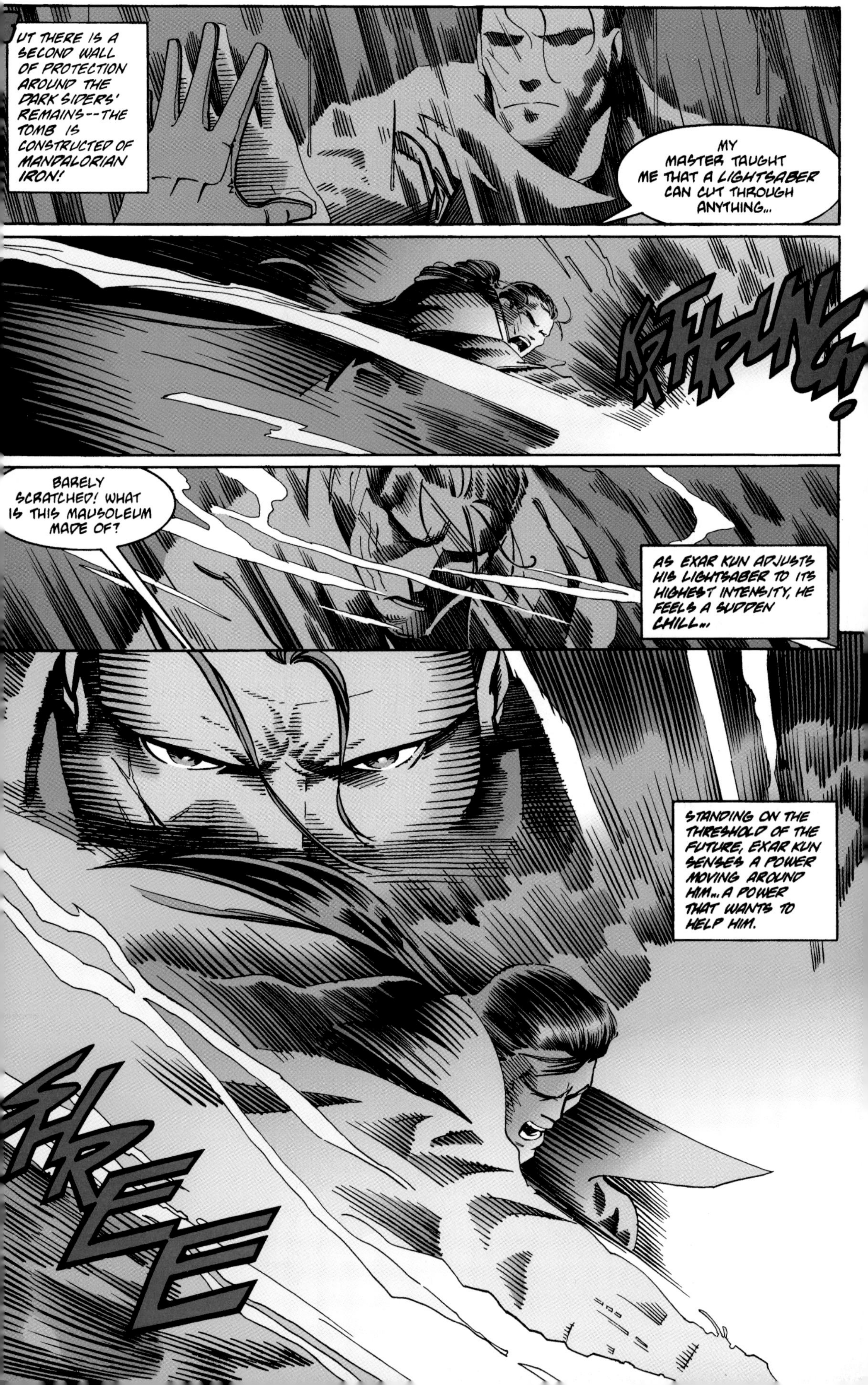
UT THERE IS A SECOND WALL OF PROTECTION AROUND THE DARK SIDERS' REMAINS--THE TOMB IS CONSTRUCTED OF MANDALORIAN IRON!
MY MASTER TAUGHT ME THAT A LIGHTSABER CAN CUT THROUGH ANYTHING...
KRTHRUNG!
BARELY SCRATCHED! WHAT IS THIS MAUSOLEUM MADE OF?
AS EXAR KUN ADJUSTS HIS LIGHTSABER TO ITS HIGHEST INTENSITY, HE FEELS A SUDDEN CHILL...
STANDING ON THE THRESHOLD OF THE FUTURE, EXAR KUN SENSES A POWER MOVING AROUND HIM... A POWER THAT WANTS TO HELP HIM.
SHREEE

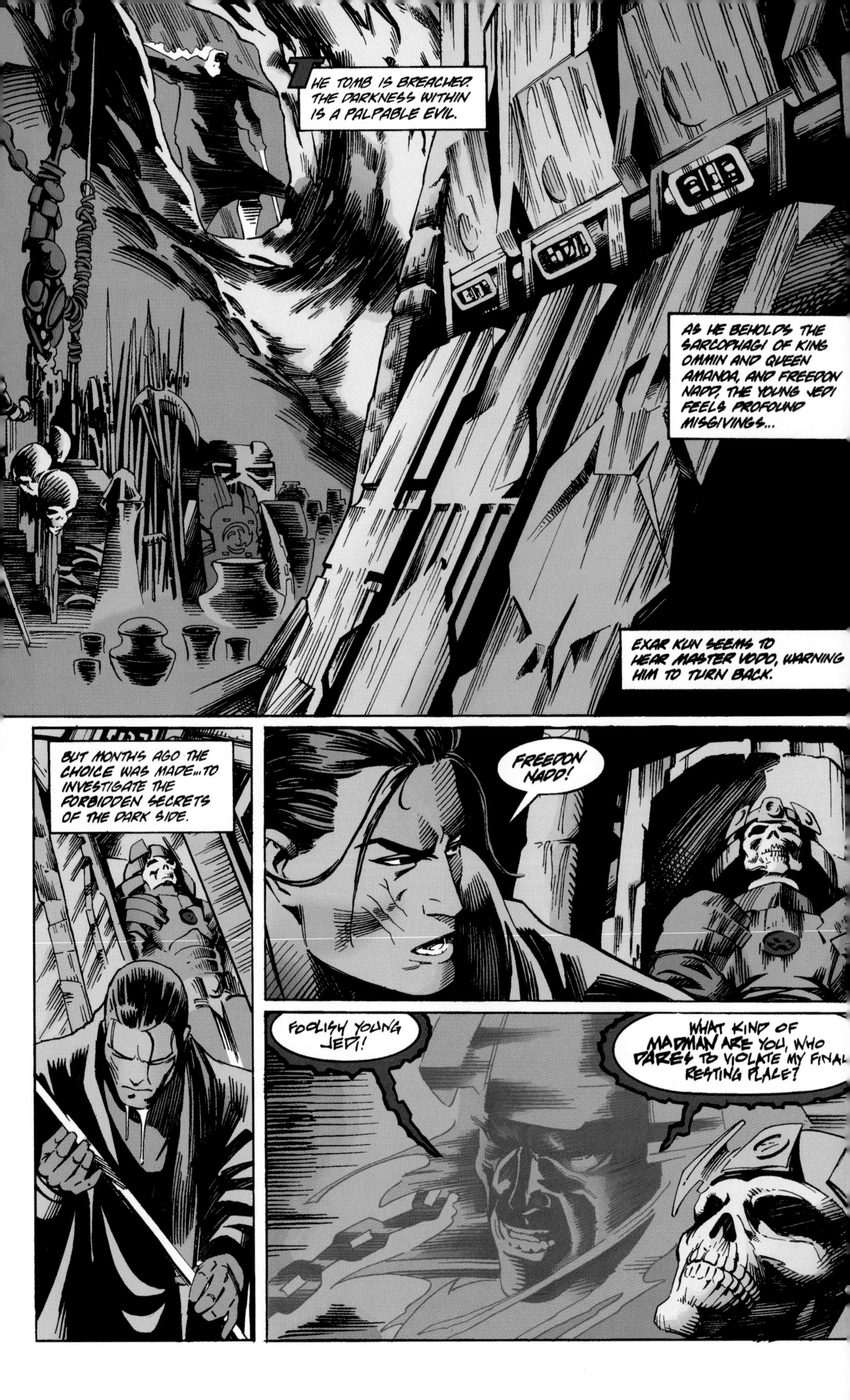
THE TOMB IS BREACHED. THE DARKNESS WITHIN IS A PALPABLE EVIL.
AS HE BEHOLDS THE SARCOPHAGI OF KING OMMIN AND QUEEN AMANDA, AND FREEDON NADD, THE YOUNG JEDI FEELS PROFOUND MISGIVINGS...
EXAR KUN SEEMS TO HEAR MASTER VODO, WARNING HIM TO TURN BACK.
BUT MONTHS AGO THE CHOICE WAS MADE...TO INVESTIGATE THE FORBIDDEN SECRETS OF THE DARK SIDE.
FREEDON NADD!
FOOLISH YOUNG JEDI!
WHAT KIND OF MADMAN ARE YOU, WHO DARES TO VIOLATE MY FINAL RESTING PLACE?

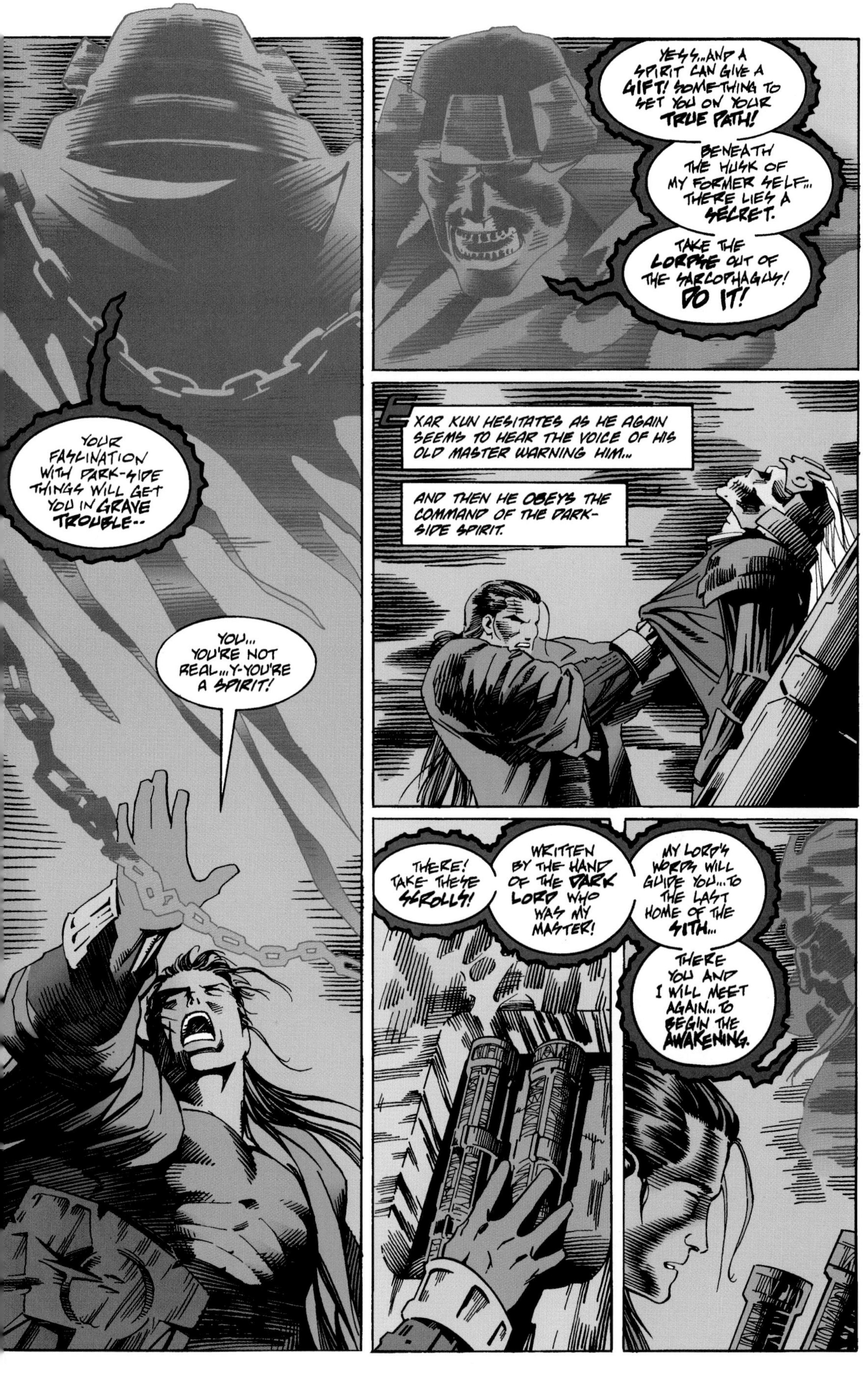
YOUR FASCINATION WITH DARK-SIDE THINGS WILL GET YOU IN GRAVE TROUBLE--
YOU... YOU'RE NOT REAL... Y-YOU'RE A SPIRIT!
YESS...AND A SPIRIT CAN GIVE A GIFT! SOMETHING TO SET YOU ON YOUR TRUE PATH!
BENEATH THE HUSK OF MY FORMER SELF... THERE LIES A SECRET.
TAKE THE CORPSE OUT OF THE SARCOPHAGUS! DO IT!
EXAR KUN HESITATES AS HE AGAIN SEEMS TO HEAR THE VOICE OF HIS OLD MASTER WARNING HIM...
AND THEN HE OBEYS THE COMMAND OF THE DARK-SIDE SPIRIT.
THERE! TAKE THESE SCROLLS!
WRITTEN BY THE HAND OF THE DARK LORD WHO WAS MY MASTER!
MY LORD'S WORDS WILL GUIDE YOU... TO THE LAST HOME OF THE SITH...
THERE YOU AND I WILL MEET AGAIN... TO BEGIN THE AWAKENING.

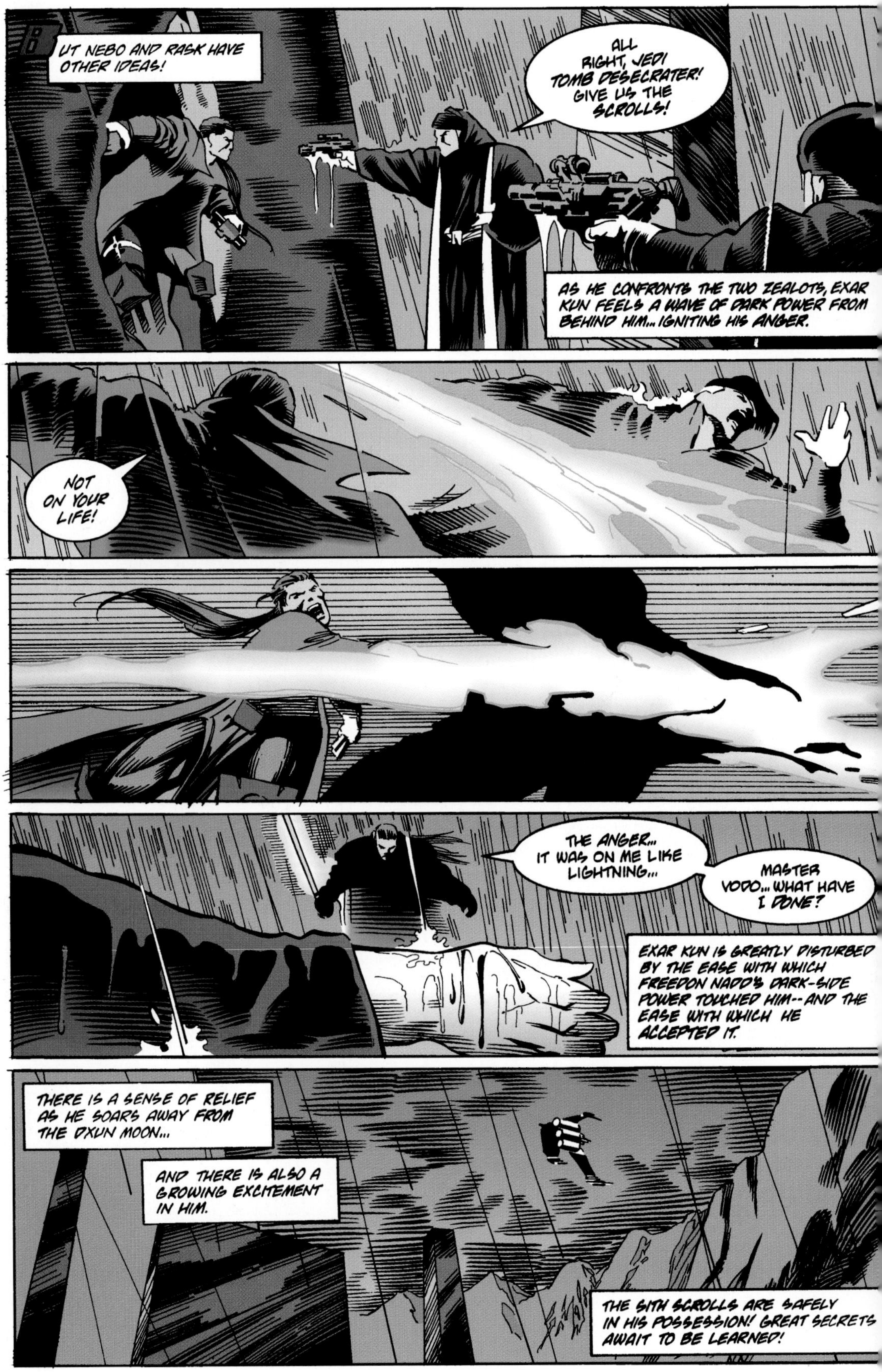
BUT NEBO AND RASK HAVE OTHER IDEAS!
ALL RIGHT, JEDI TOMB DESECRATER! GIVE US THE SCROLLS!
AS HE CONFRONTS THE TWO ZEALOTS, EXAR KUN FEELS A WAVE OF DARK POWER FROM BEHIND HIM... IGNITING HIS ANGER.
NOT ON YOUR LIFE!
THE ANGER... IT WAS ON ME LIKE LIGHTNING...
MASTER VODO... WHAT HAVE I DONE?
EXAR KUN IS GREATLY DISTURBED BY THE EASE WITH WHICH FREEDON NADD'S DARK-SIDE POWER TOUCHED HIM--AND THE EASE WITH WHICH HE ACCEPTED IT.
THERE IS A SENSE OF RELIEF AS HE SOARS AWAY FROM THE DXUN MOON...
AND THERE IS ALSO A GROWING EXCITEMENT IN HIM.
THE SITH SCROLLS ARE SAFELY IN HIS POSSESSION! GREAT SECRETS AWAIT TO BE LEARNED!

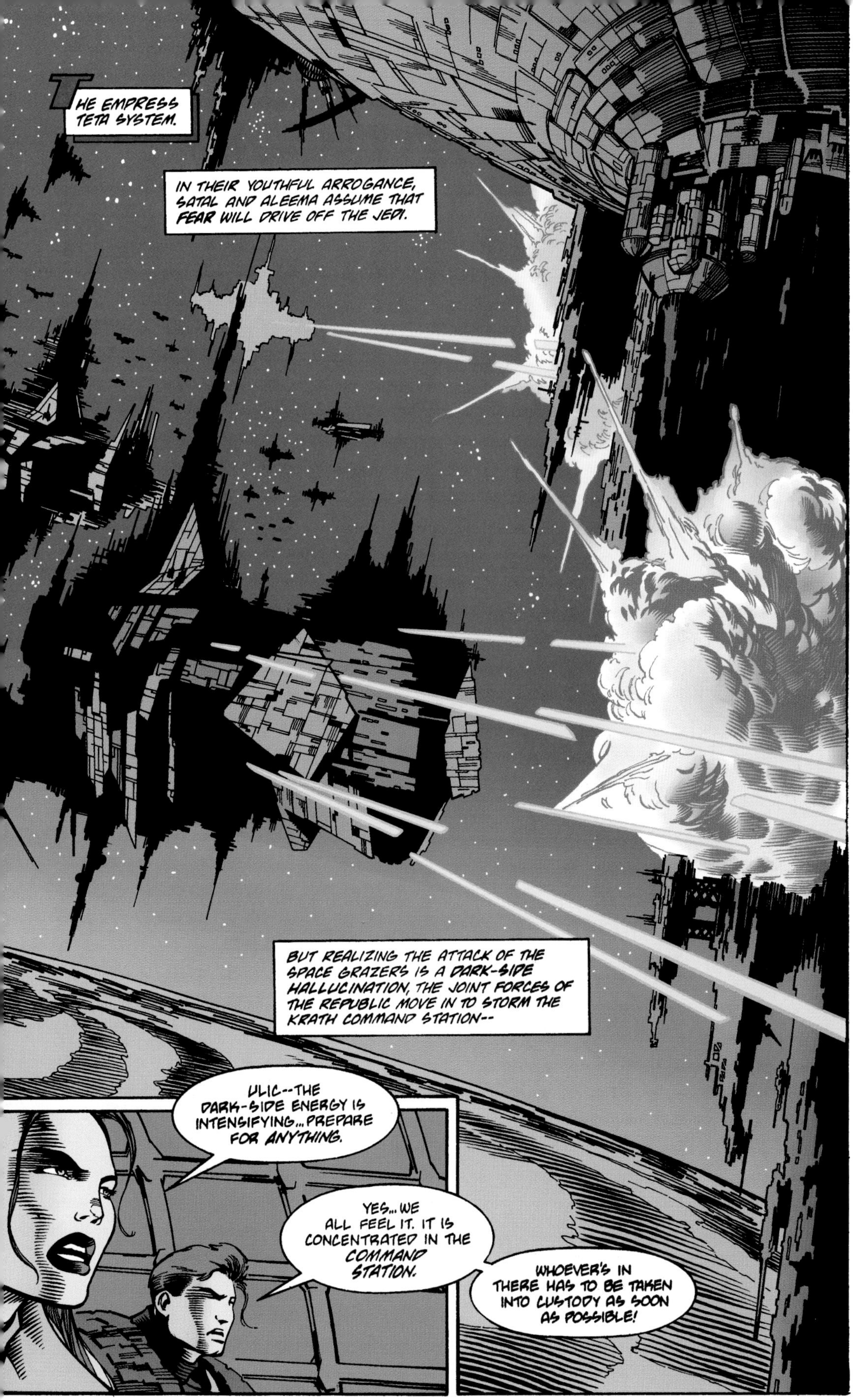
THE EMPRESS TETA SYSTEM.
IN THEIR YOUTHFUL ARROGANCE, SATAL AND ALEEMA ASSUME THAT FEAR WILL DRIVE OFF THE JEDI.
BUT REALIZING THE ATTACK OF THE SPACE GRAZERS IS A DARK-SIDE HALLUCINATION, THE JOINT FORCES OF THE REPUBLIC MOVE IN TO STORM THE KRATH COMMAND STATION--
ULIC--THE DARK-SIDE ENERGY IS INTENSIFYING...PREPARE FOR ANYTHING.
YES... WE ALL FEEL IT. IT IS CONCENTRATED IN THE COMMAND STATION.
WHOEVER'S IN THERE HAS TO BE TAKEN INTO CUSTODY AS SOON AS POSSIBLE!

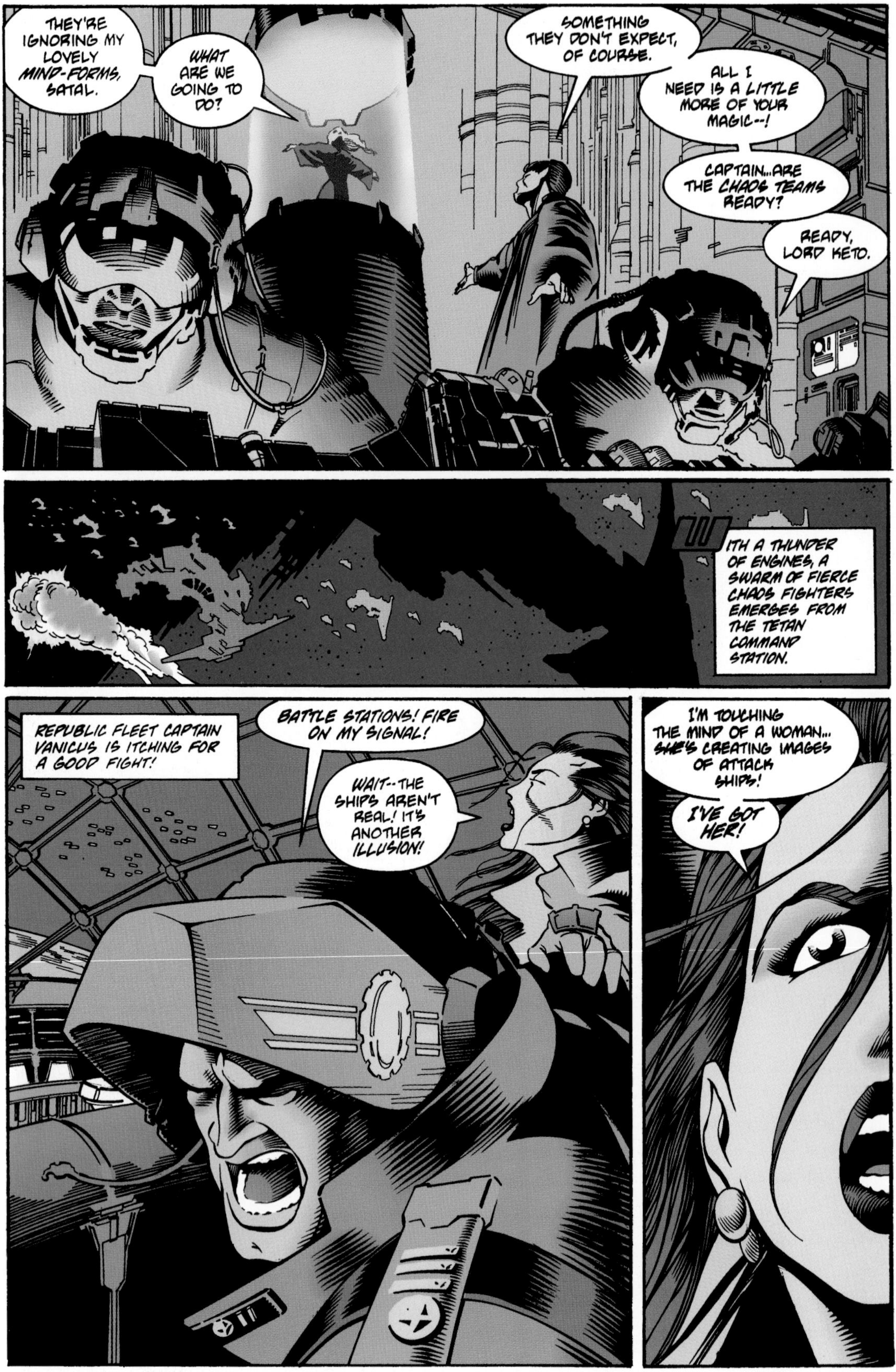
THEY'RE IGNORING MY LOVELY MIND-FORMS, SATAL.
WHAT ARE WE GOING TO DO?
SOMETHING THEY DON'T EXPECT, OF COURSE.
ALL I NEED IS A LITTLE MORE OF YOUR MAGIC--!
CAPTAIN...ARE THE CHAOS TEAMS READY?
READY, LORD KETO.
ITH A THUNDER OF ENGINES, A SWARM OF FIERCE CHAOS FIGHTERS EMERGES FROM THE TETAN COMMAND STATION.
REPUBLIC FLEET CAPTAIN VANICUS IS ITCHING FOR A GOOD FIGHT!
BATTLE STATIONS! FIRE ON MY SIGNAL!
WAIT--THE SHIPS AREN'T REAL! IT'S ANOTHER ILLUSION!
I'M TOUCHING THE MIND OF A WOMAN... SHE'S CREATING IMAGES OF ATTACK SHIPS!
I'VE GOT HER!

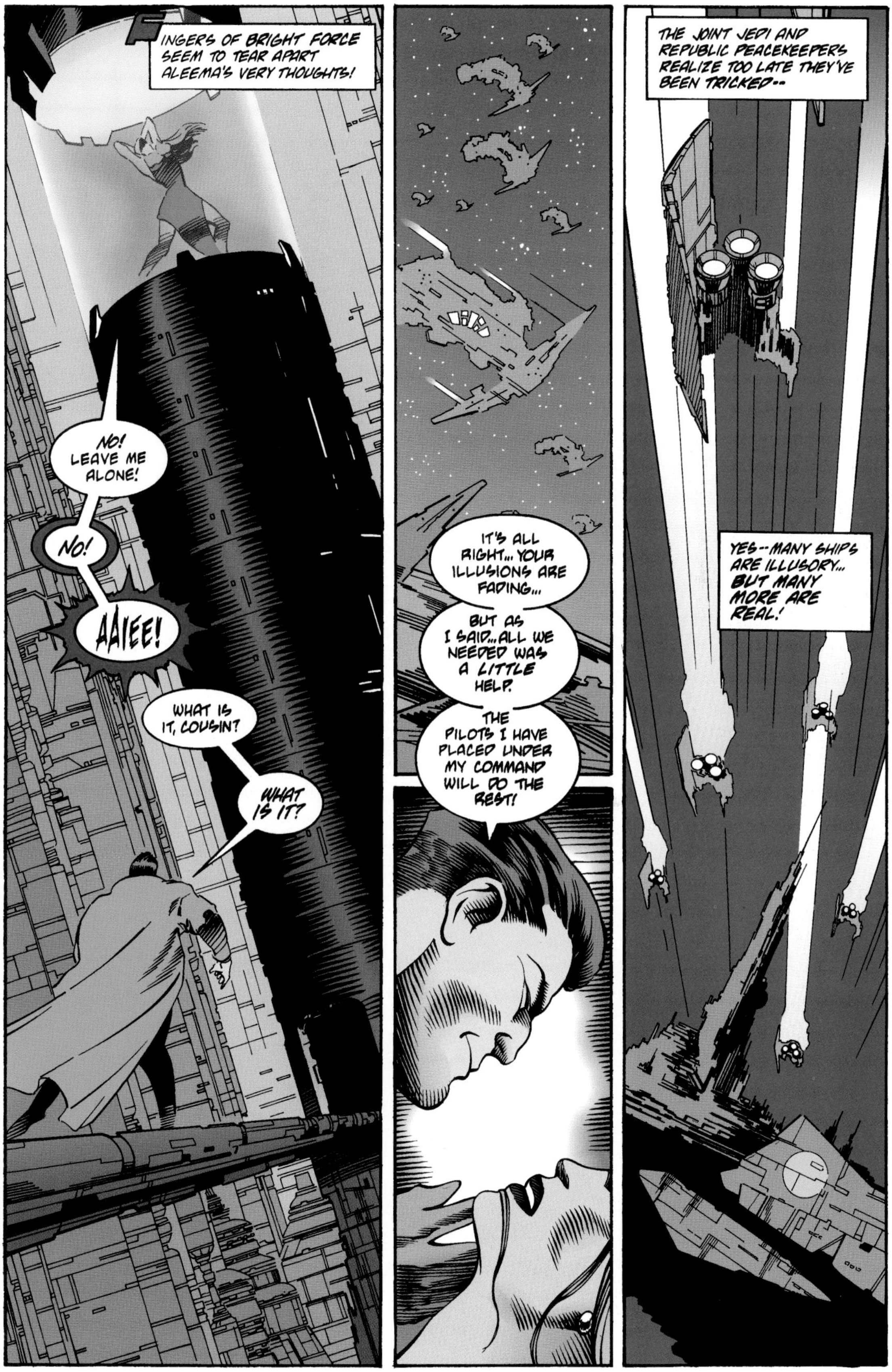

FINGERS OF BRIGHT FORCE SEEM TO TEAR APART ALEEMA'S VERY THOUGHTS!
NO! LEAVE ME ALONE!
NO!
AAIEE!
WHAT IS IT, COUSIN?
WHAT IS IT?
IT'S ALL RIGHT... YOUR ILLUSIONS ARE FADING...
BUT AS I SAID... ALL WE NEEDED WAS A LITTLE HELP.
THE PILOTS I HAVE PLACED UNDER MY COMMAND WILL DO THE REST!
THE JOINT JEDI AND REPUBLIC PEACEKEEPERS REALIZE TOO LATE THEY'VE BEEN TRICKED--
YES--MANY SHIPS ARE ILLUSORY... BUT MANY MORE ARE REAL!

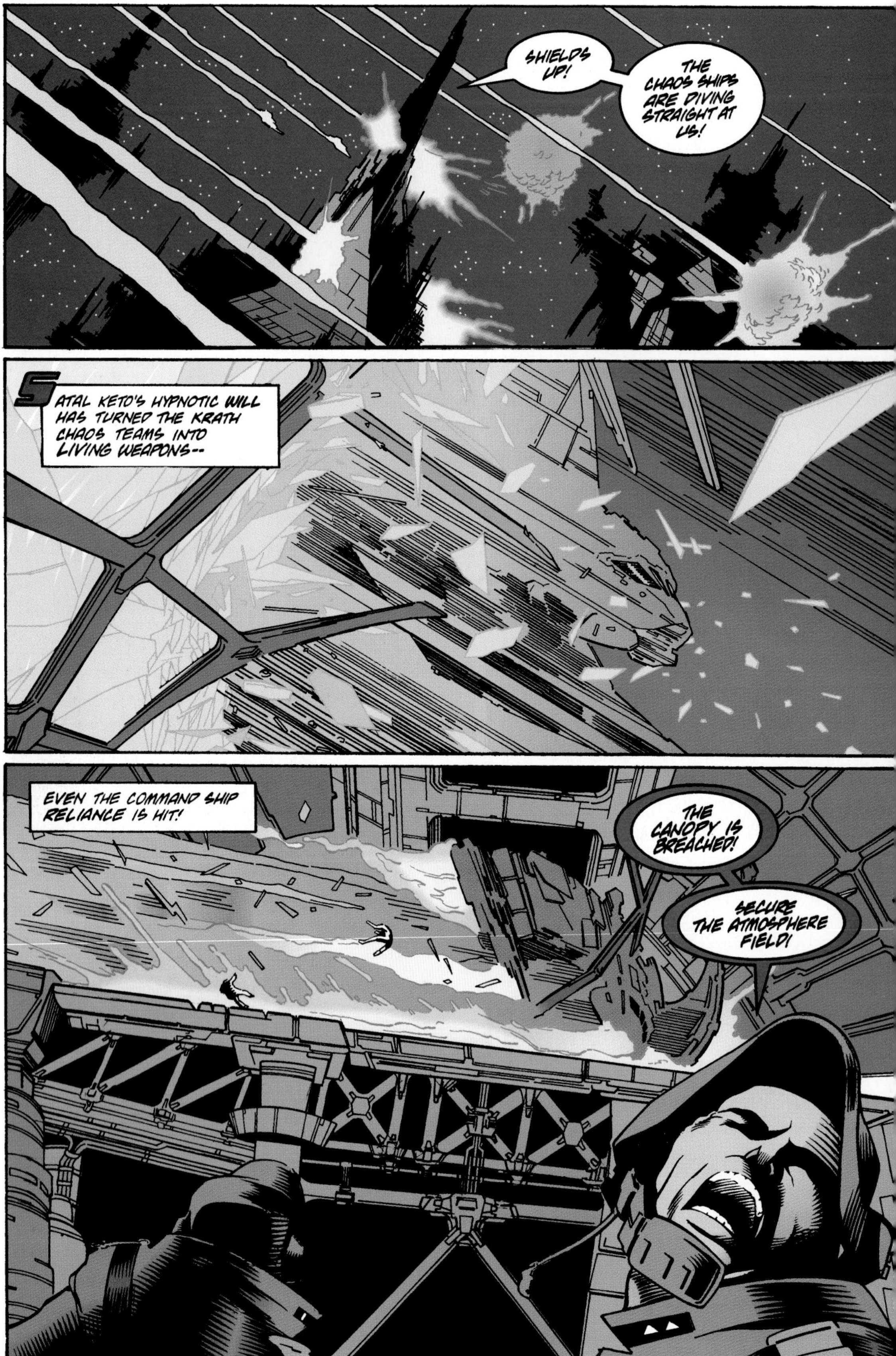
SHIELDS UP!
THE CHAOS SHIPS ARE DIVING STRAIGHT AT US!
SATAL KETO'S HYPNOTIC WILL HAS TURNED THE KRATH CHAOS TEAMS INTO LIVING WEAPONS--
EVEN THE COMMAND SHIP RELIANCE IS HIT!
THE CANOPY IS BREACHED!
SECURE THE ATMOSPHERE FIELD!

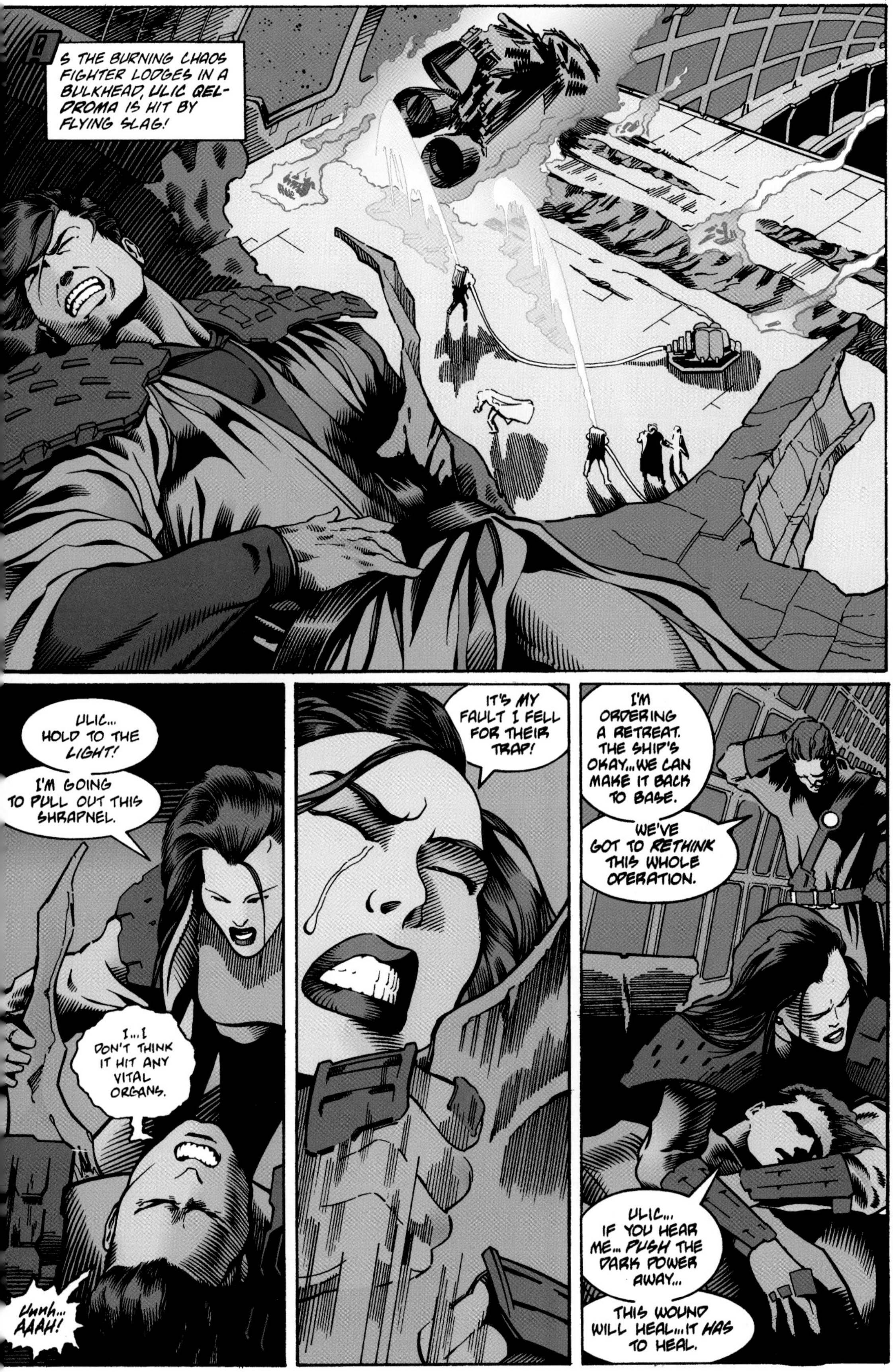

AS THE BURNING CHAOS FIGHTER LODGES IN A BULKHEAD, ULIC QEL-DROMA IS HIT BY FLYING SLAG!
ULIC... HOLD TO THE LIGHT!
I'M GOING TO PULL OUT THIS SHRAPNEL.
I...I DON'T THINK IT HIT ANY VITAL ORGANS.
Unnh... AAAH!
IT'S MY FAULT I FELL FOR THEIR TRAP!
I'M ORDERING A RETREAT. THE SHIP'S OKAY...WE CAN MAKE IT BACK TO BASE.
WE'VE GOT TO RETHINK THIS WHOLE OPERATION.
ULIC... IF YOU HEAR ME... PUSH THE DARK POWER AWAY...
THIS WOUND WILL HEAL...IT HAS TO HEAL.

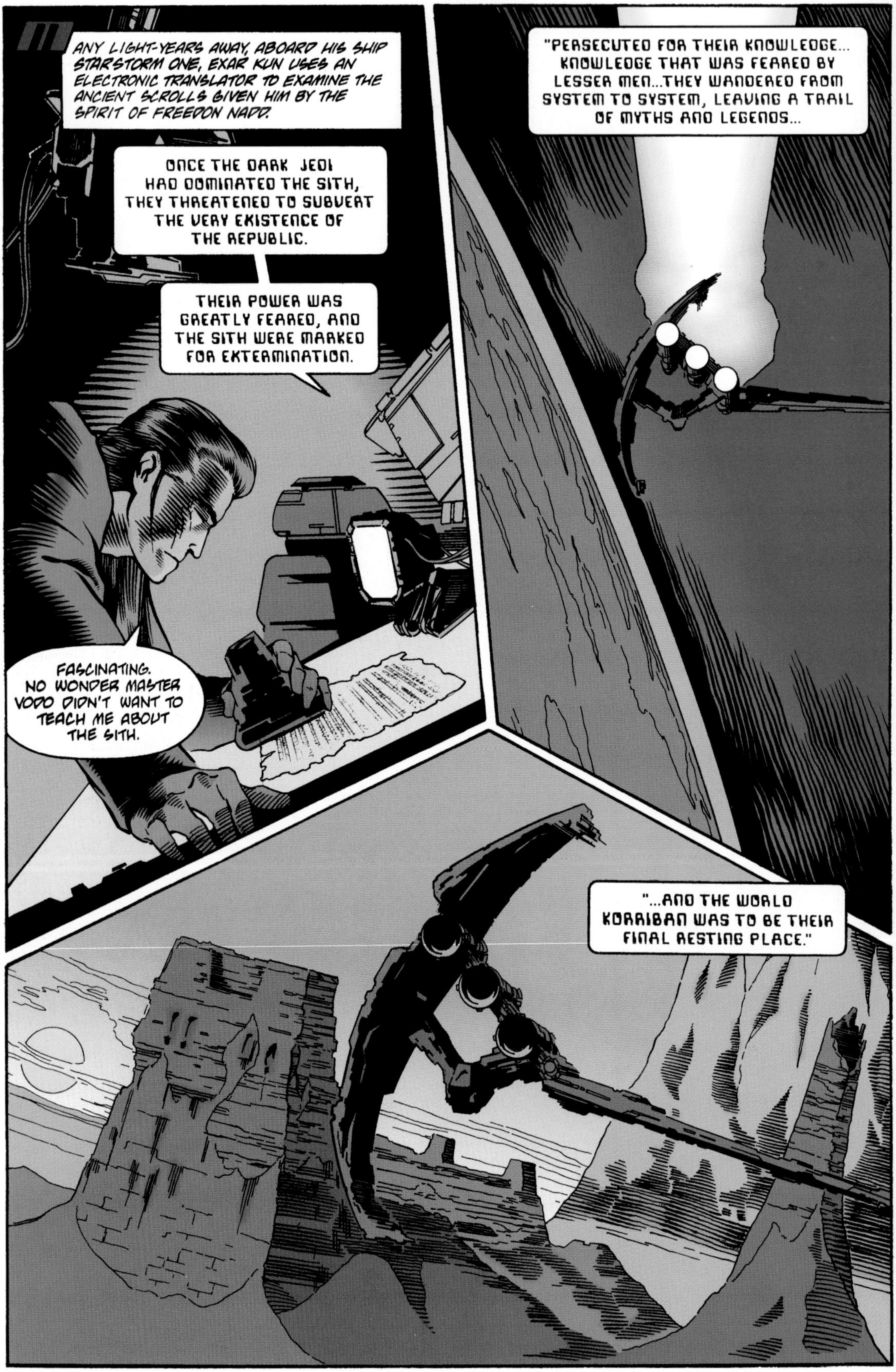
MANY LIGHT-YEARS AWAY, ABOARD HIS SHIP STARSTORM ONE, EXAR KUN USES AN ELECTRONIC TRANSLATOR TO EXAMINE THE ANCIENT SCROLLS GIVEN HIM BY THE SPIRIT OF FREEDON NADD.
ONCE THE DARK JEDI HAD DOMINATED THE SITH, THEY THREATENED TO SUBVERT THE VERY EXISTENCE OF THE REPUBLIC.
THEIR POWER WAS GREATLY FEARED, AND THE SITH WERE MARKED FOR EXTERMINATION.
FASCINATING. NO WONDER MASTER VODO DIDN'T WANT TO TEACH ME ABOUT THE SITH.
"PERSECUTED FOR THEIR KNOWLEDGE... KNOWLEDGE THAT WAS FEARED BY LESSER MEN...THEY WANDERED FROM SYSTEM TO SYSTEM, LEAVING A TRAIL OF MYTHS AND LEGENDS...
"...AND THE WORLD KORRIBAN WAS TO BE THEIR FINAL RESTING PLACE."

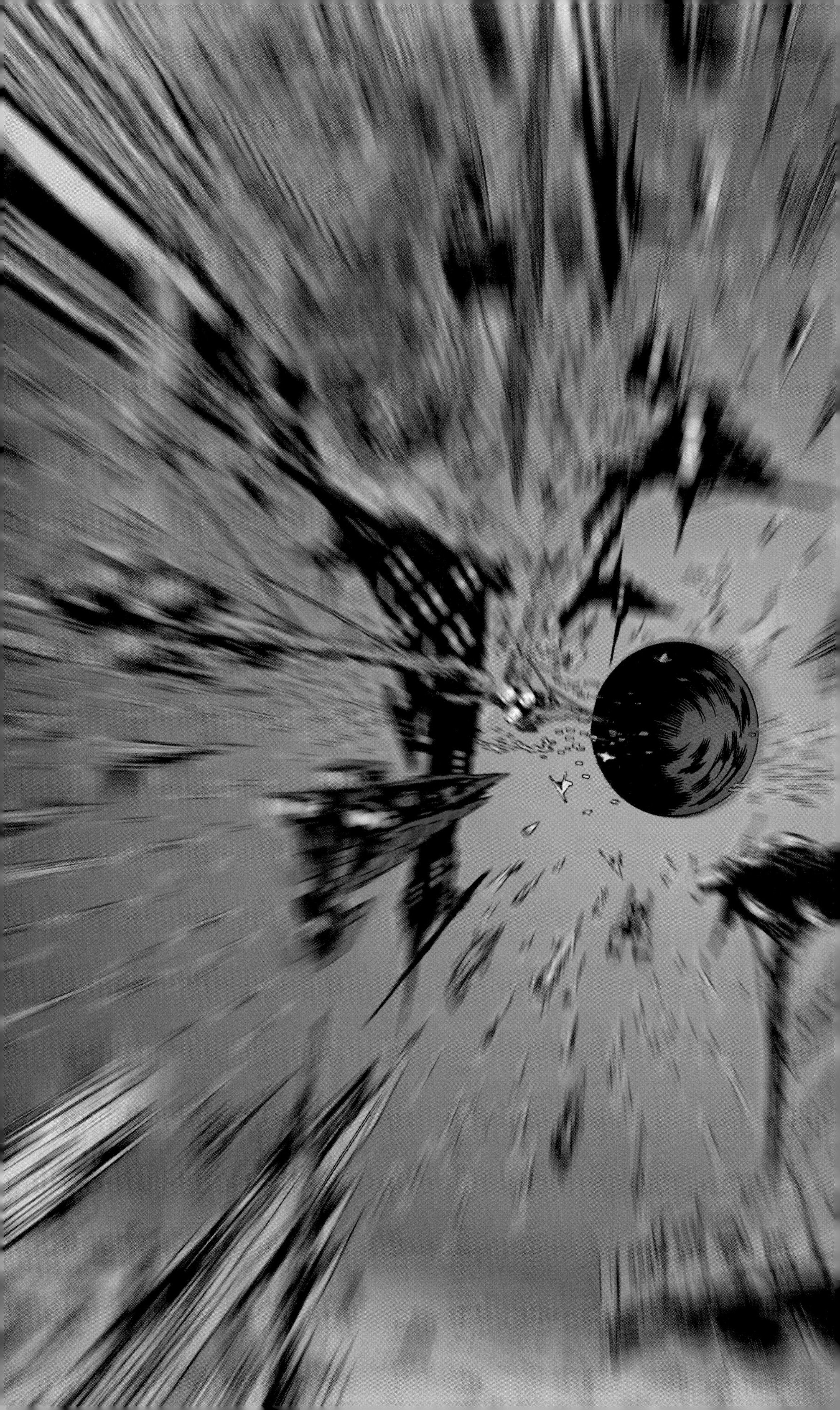

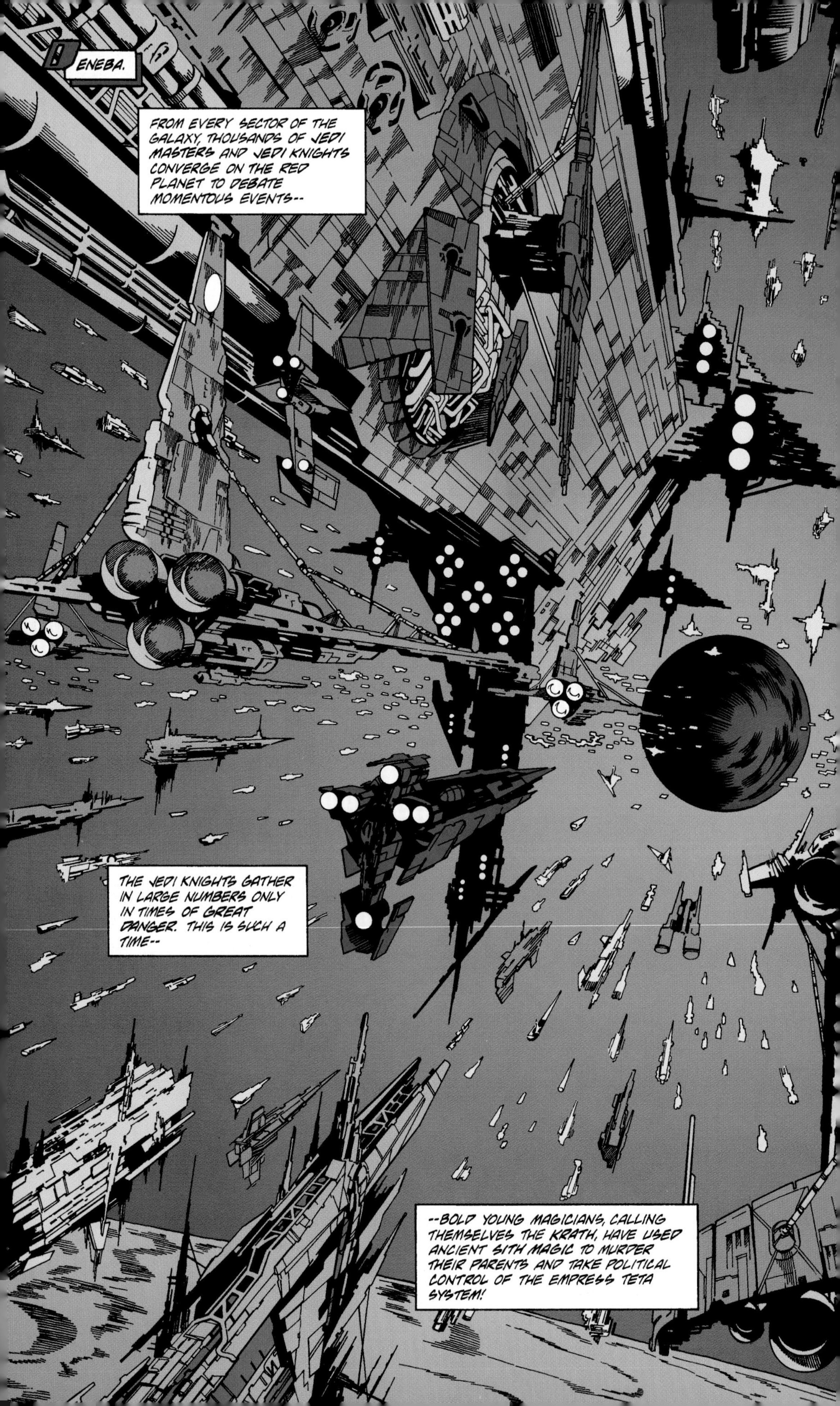
DENEBA.
FROM EVERY SECTOR OF THE GALAXY, THOUSANDS OF JEDI MASTERS AND JEDI KNIGHTS CONVERGE ON THE RED PLANET TO DEBATE MOMENTOUS EVENTS--
THE JEDI KNIGHTS GATHER IN LARGE NUMBERS ONLY IN TIMES OF GREAT DANGER. THIS IS SUCH A TIME--
--BOLD YOUNG MAGICIANS, CALLING THEMSELVES THE KRATH, HAVE USED ANCIENT SITH MAGIC TO MURDER THEIR PARENTS AND TAKE POLITICAL CONTROL OF THE EMPRESS TETA SYSTEM!

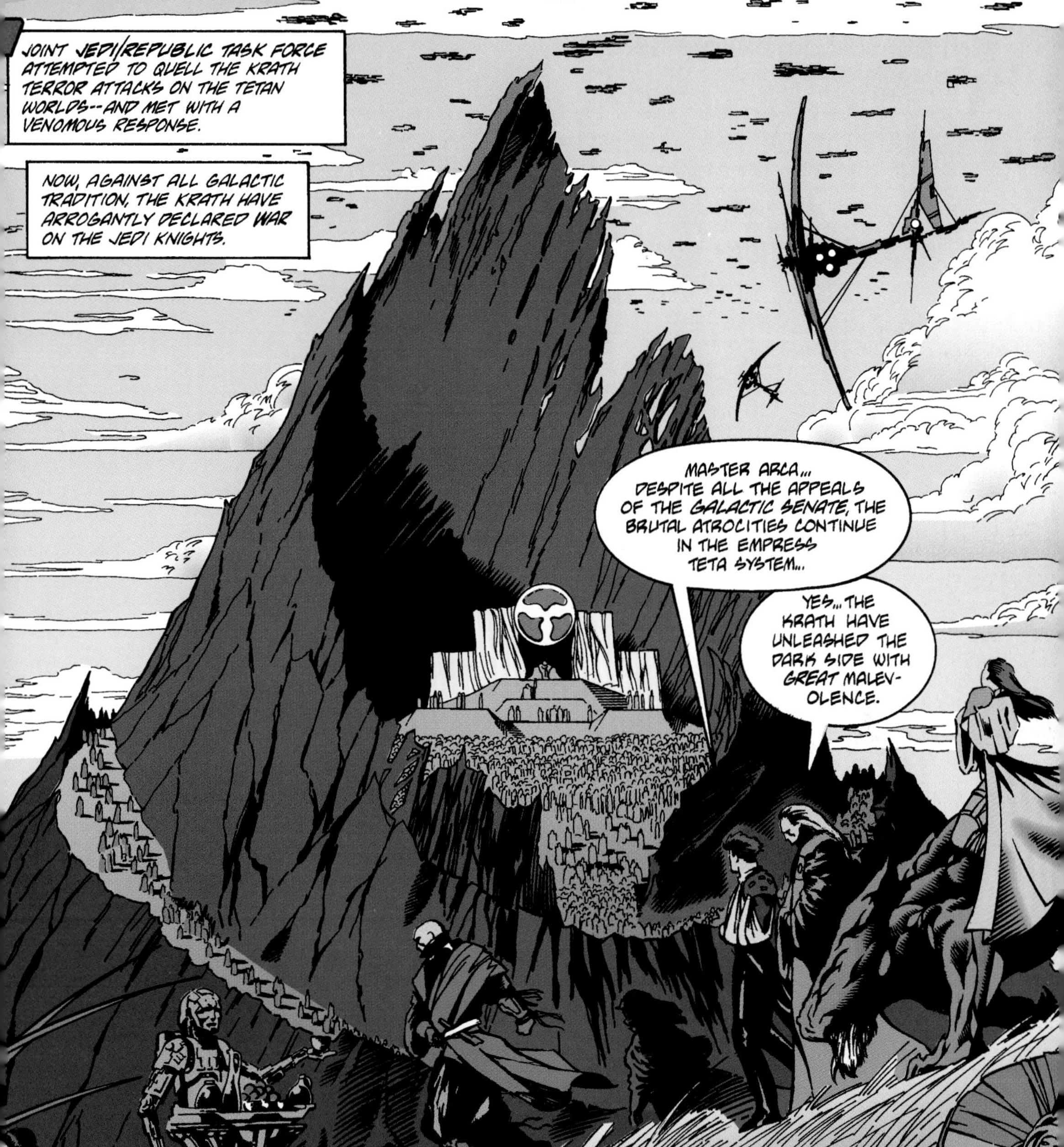
JOINT JEDI/REPUBLIC TASK FORCE ATTEMPTED TO QUELL THE KRATH TERROR ATTACKS ON THE TETAN WORLDS--AND MET WITH A VENOMOUS RESPONSE.
NOW, AGAINST ALL GALACTIC TRADITION, THE KRATH HAVE ARROGANTLY DECLARED WAR ON THE JEDI KNIGHTS.
MASTER ARCA... DESPITE ALL THE APPEALS OF THE GALACTIC SENATE, THE BRUTAL ATROCITIES CONTINUE IN THE EMPRESS TETA SYSTEM...
YES... THE KRATH HAVE UNLEASHED THE DARK SIDE WITH GREAT MALEV-OLENCE.

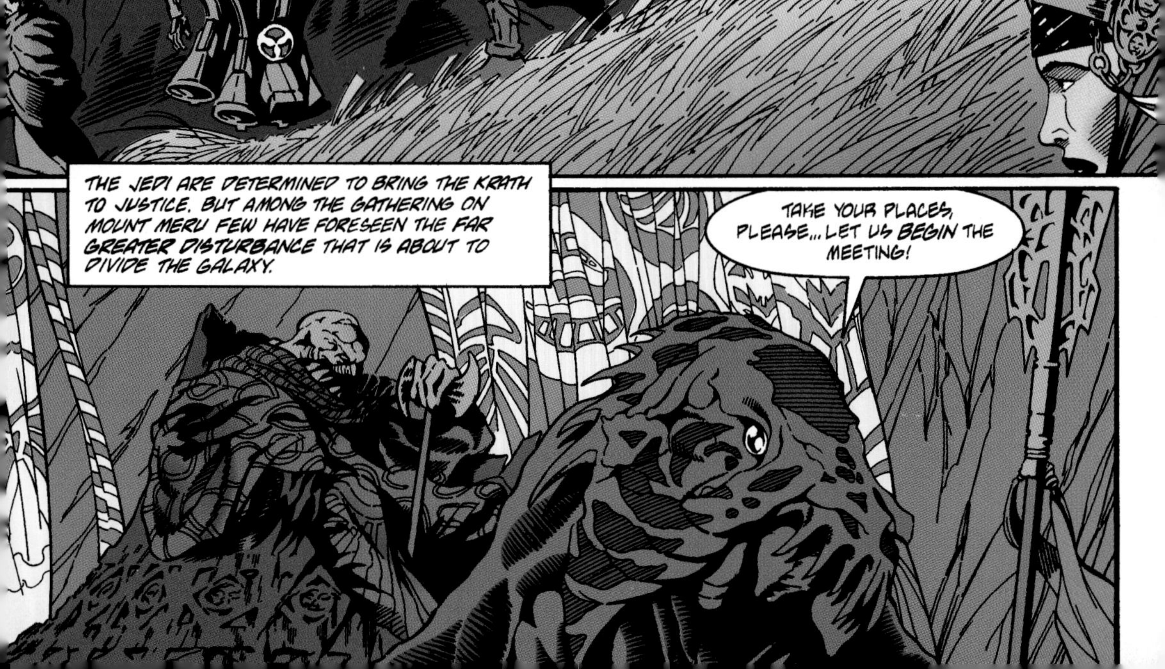
THE JEDI ARE DETERMINED TO BRING THE KRATH TO JUSTICE. BUT AMONG THE GATHERING ON MOUNT MERU FEW HAVE FORESEEN THE FAR GREATER DISTURBANCE THAT IS ABOUT TO DIVIDE THE GALAXY.
TAKE YOUR PLACES, PLEASE... LET US BEGIN THE MEETING!

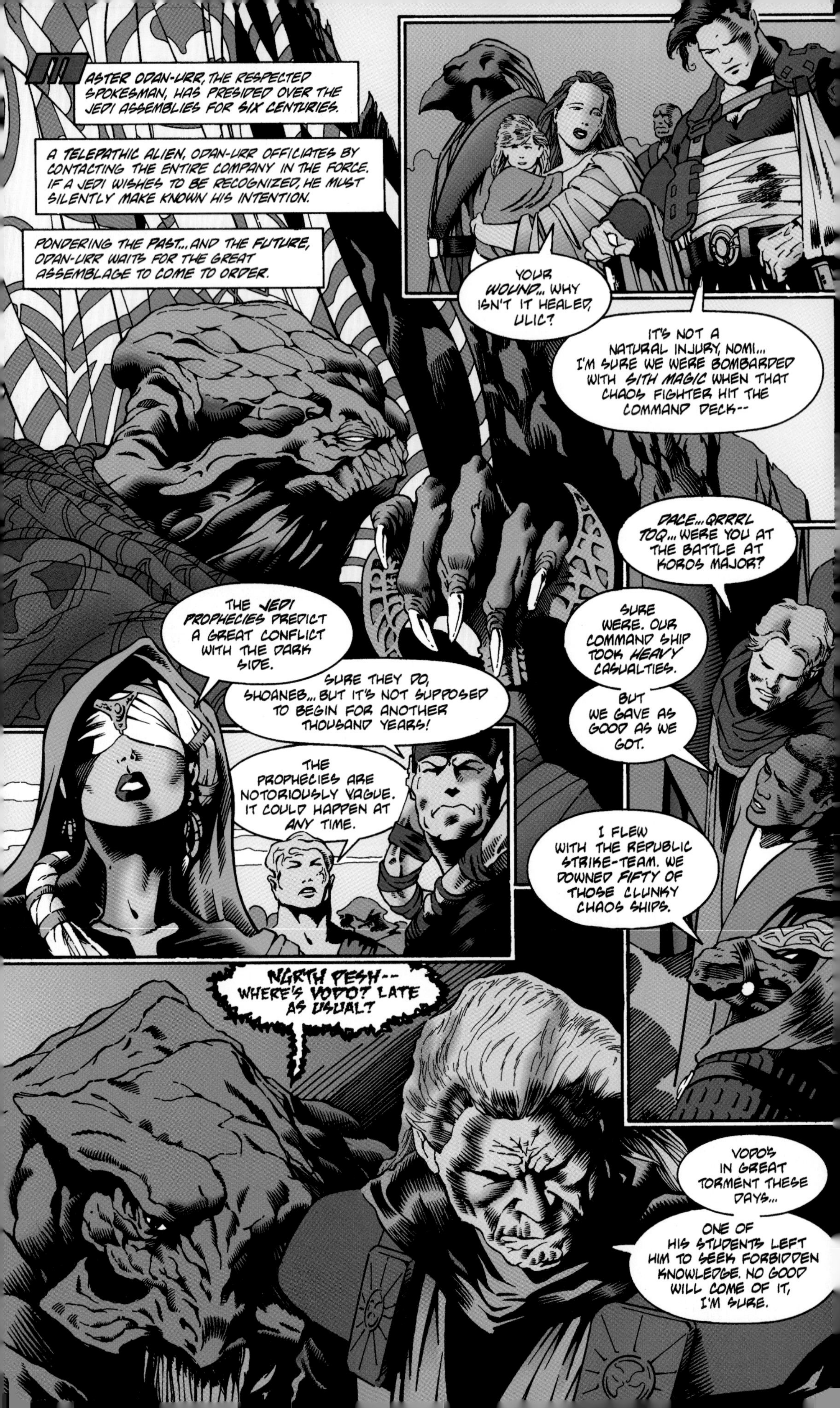
MASTER ODAN-URR, THE RESPECTED SPOKESMAN, HAS PRESIDED OVER THE JEDI ASSEMBLIES FOR SIX CENTURIES.
A TELEPATHIC ALIEN, ODAN-URR OFFICIATES BY CONTACTING THE ENTIRE COMPANY IN THE FORCE. IF A JEDI WISHES TO BE RECOGNIZED, HE MUST SILENTLY MAKE KNOWN HIS INTENTION.
PONDERING THE PAST... AND THE FUTURE, ODAN-URR WAITS FOR THE GREAT ASSEMBLAGE TO COME TO ORDER.
YOUR WOUND... WHY ISN'T IT HEALED, ULIC?
IT'S NOT A NATURAL INJURY, NOMI... I'M SURE WE WERE BOMBARDED WITH SITH MAGIC WHEN THAT CHAOS FIGHTER HIT THE COMMAND DECK--
DACE... QRRRL TOQ... WERE YOU AT THE BATTLE AT KOROS MAJOR?
SURE WERE. OUR COMMAND SHIP TOOK HEAVY CASUALTIES.
BUT WE GAVE AS GOOD AS WE GOT.
I FLEW WITH THE REPUBLIC STRIKE-TEAM. WE DOWNED FIFTY OF THOSE CLUNKY CHAOS SHIPS.
THE JEDI PROPHECIES PREDICT A GREAT CONFLICT WITH THE DARK SIDE.
SURE THEY DO, SHOANEB... BUT IT'S NOT SUPPOSED TO BEGIN FOR ANOTHER THOUSAND YEARS!
THE PROPHECIES ARE NOTORIOUSLY VAGUE. IT COULD HAPPEN AT ANY TIME.
NGRTH PESH-- WHERE'S VODO? LATE AS USUAL?
VODO'S IN GREAT TORMENT THESE DAYS...
ONE OF HIS STUDENTS LEFT HIM TO SEEK FORBIDDEN KNOWLEDGE. NO GOOD WILL COME OF IT, I'M SURE.

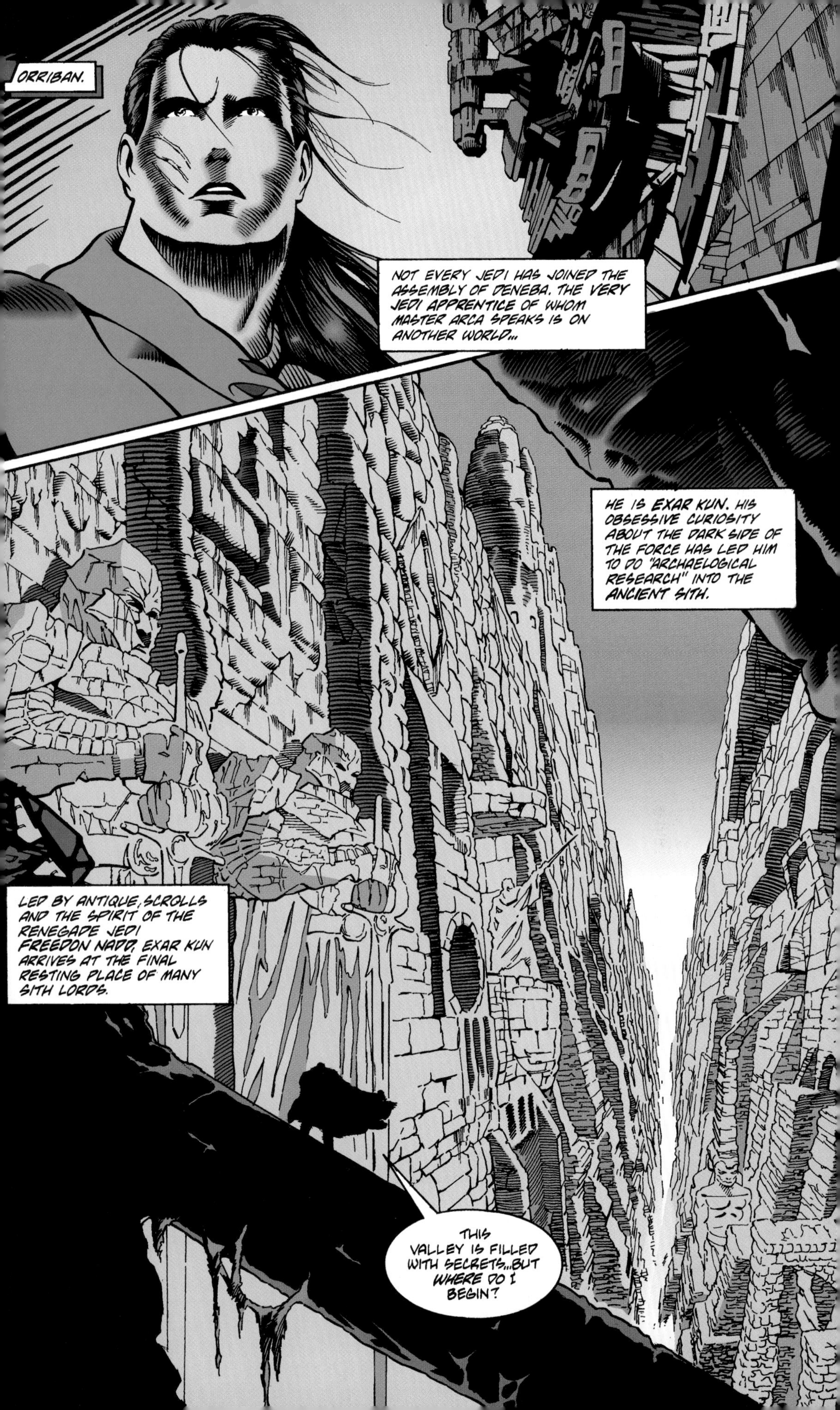
ORRIBAN.
NOT EVERY JEDI HAS JOINED THE ASSEMBLY OF DENEBA. THE VERY JEDI APPRENTICE OF WHOM MASTER ARCA SPEAKS IS ON ANOTHER WORLD...
HE IS EXAR KUN. HIS OBSESSIVE CURIOSITY ABOUT THE DARK SIDE OF THE FORCE HAS LED HIM TO DO "ARCHAELOGICAL RESEARCH" INTO THE ANCIENT SITH.
LED BY ANTIQUE SCROLLS AND THE SPIRIT OF THE RENEGADE JEDI FREEDON NADD, EXAR KUN ARRIVES AT THE FINAL RESTING PLACE OF MANY SITH LORDS.
THIS VALLEY IS FILLED WITH SECRETS...BUT WHERE DO I BEGIN?

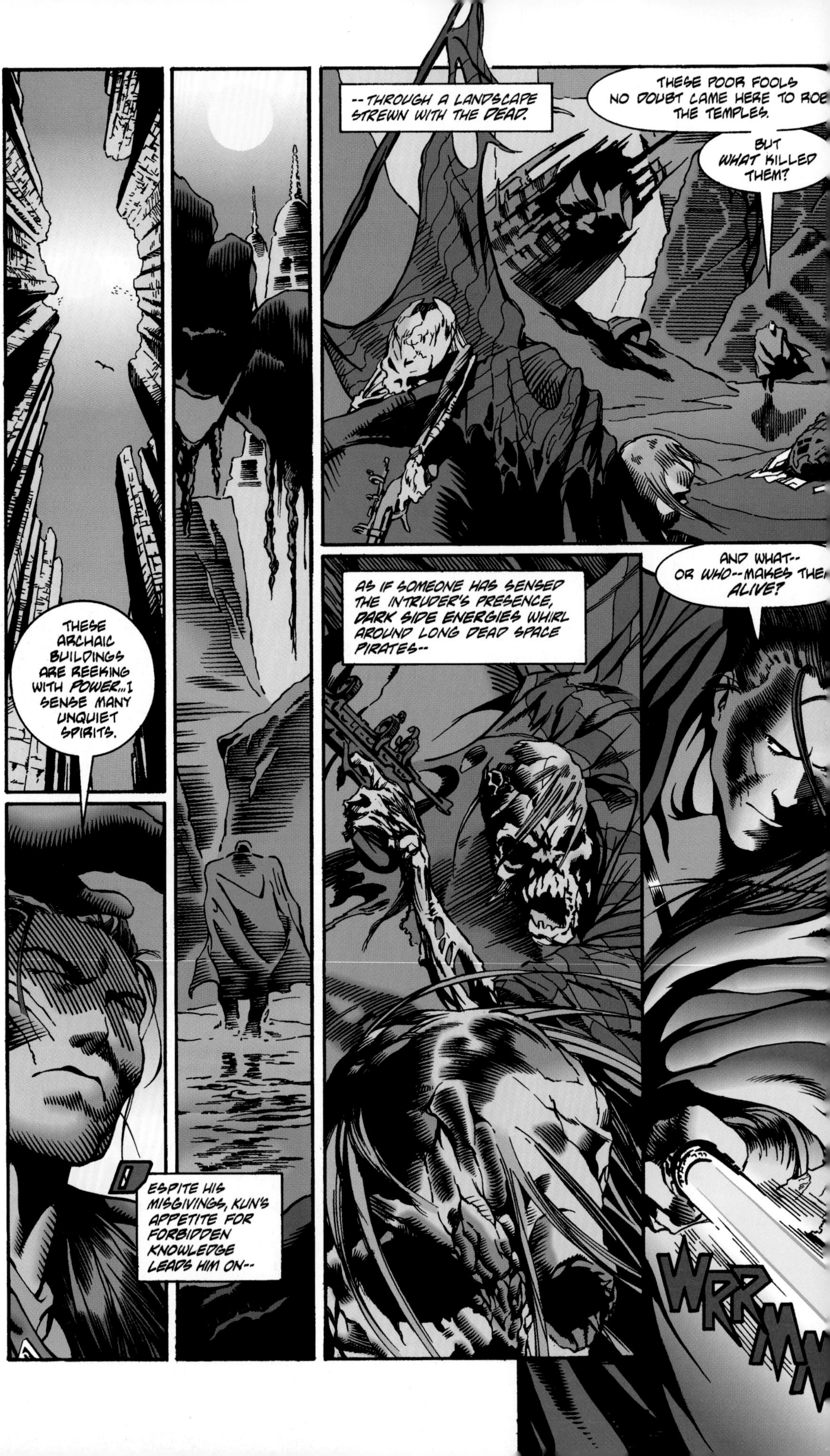
THESE ARCHAIC BUILDINGS ARE REEKING WITH POWER...I SENSE MANY UNQUIET SPIRITS.
DESPITE HIS MISGIVINGS, KUN'S APPETITE FOR FORBIDDEN KNOWLEDGE LEADS HIM ON--
--THROUGH A LANDSCAPE STREWN WITH THE DEAD.
THESE POOR FOOLS NO DOUBT CAME HERE TO RO THE TEMPLES.
BUT WHAT KILLED THEM?
AS IF SOMEONE HAS SENSED THE INTRUDER'S PRESENCE, DARK SIDE ENERGIES WHIRL AROUND LONG DEAD SPACE PIRATES--
AND WHAT--OR WHO--MAKES THE ALIVE?
WRRMM

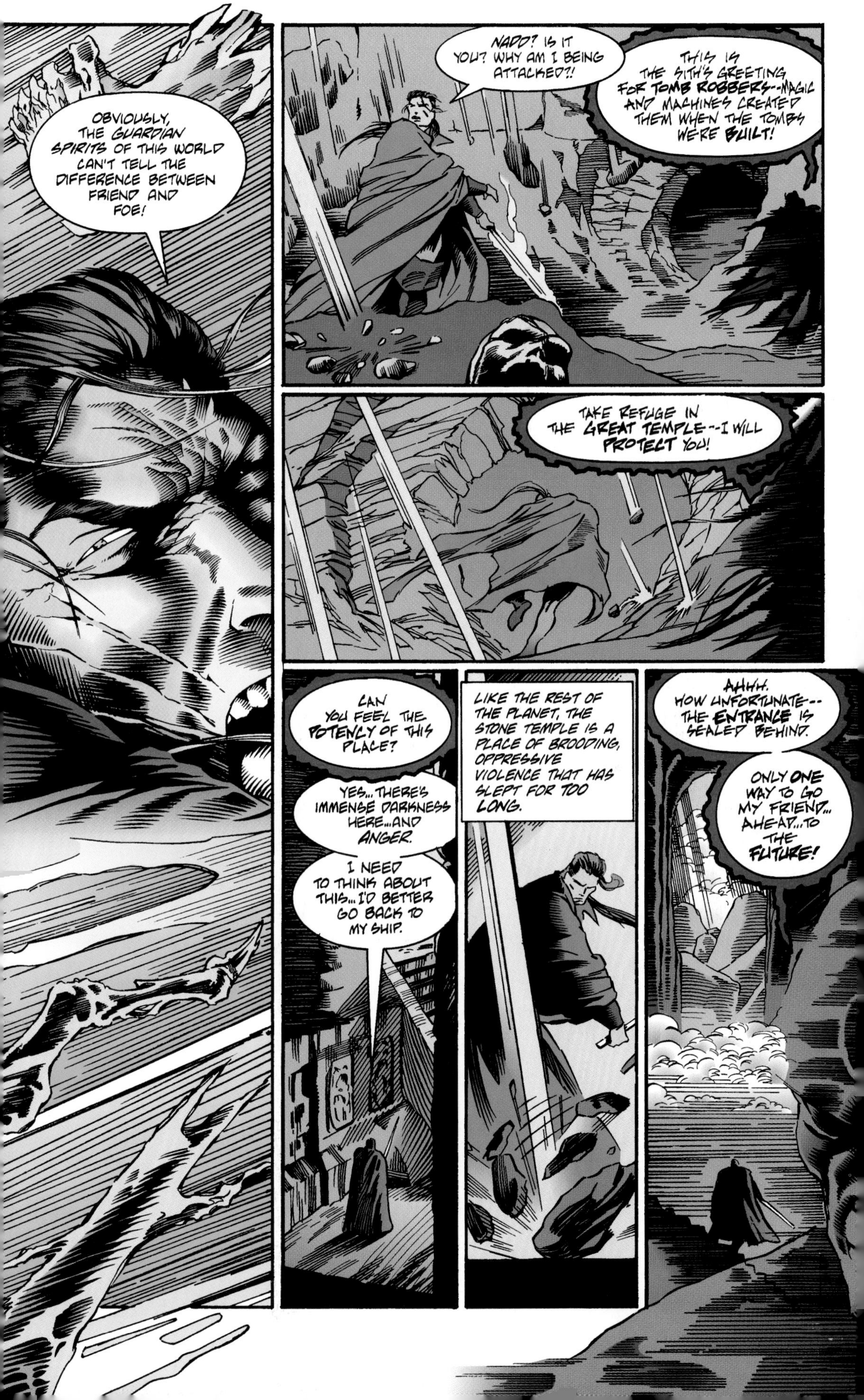
OBVIOUSLY, THE GUARDIAN SPIRITS OF THIS WORLD CAN'T TELL THE DIFFERENCE BETWEEN FRIEND AND FOE!
NADD? IS IT YOU? WHY AM I BEING ATTACKED?!
THIS IS THE SITH'S GREETING FOR TOMB ROBBERS--MAGIC AND MACHINES CREATED THEM WHEN THE TOMBS WERE BUILT!
TAKE REFUGE IN THE GREAT TEMPLE--I WILL PROTECT YOU!
CAN YOU FEEL THE POTENCY OF THIS PLACE?
YES... THERE'S IMMENSE DARKNESS HERE... AND ANGER.
I NEED TO THINK ABOUT THIS... I'D BETTER GO BACK TO MY SHIP.
LIKE THE REST OF THE PLANET, THE STONE TEMPLE IS A PLACE OF BROODING, OPPRESSIVE VIOLENCE THAT HAS SLEPT FOR TOO LONG.
AHHH. HOW UNFORTUNATE-- THE ENTRANCE IS SEALED BEHIND.
ONLY ONE WAY TO GO MY FRIEND... AHEAD... TO THE FUTURE!

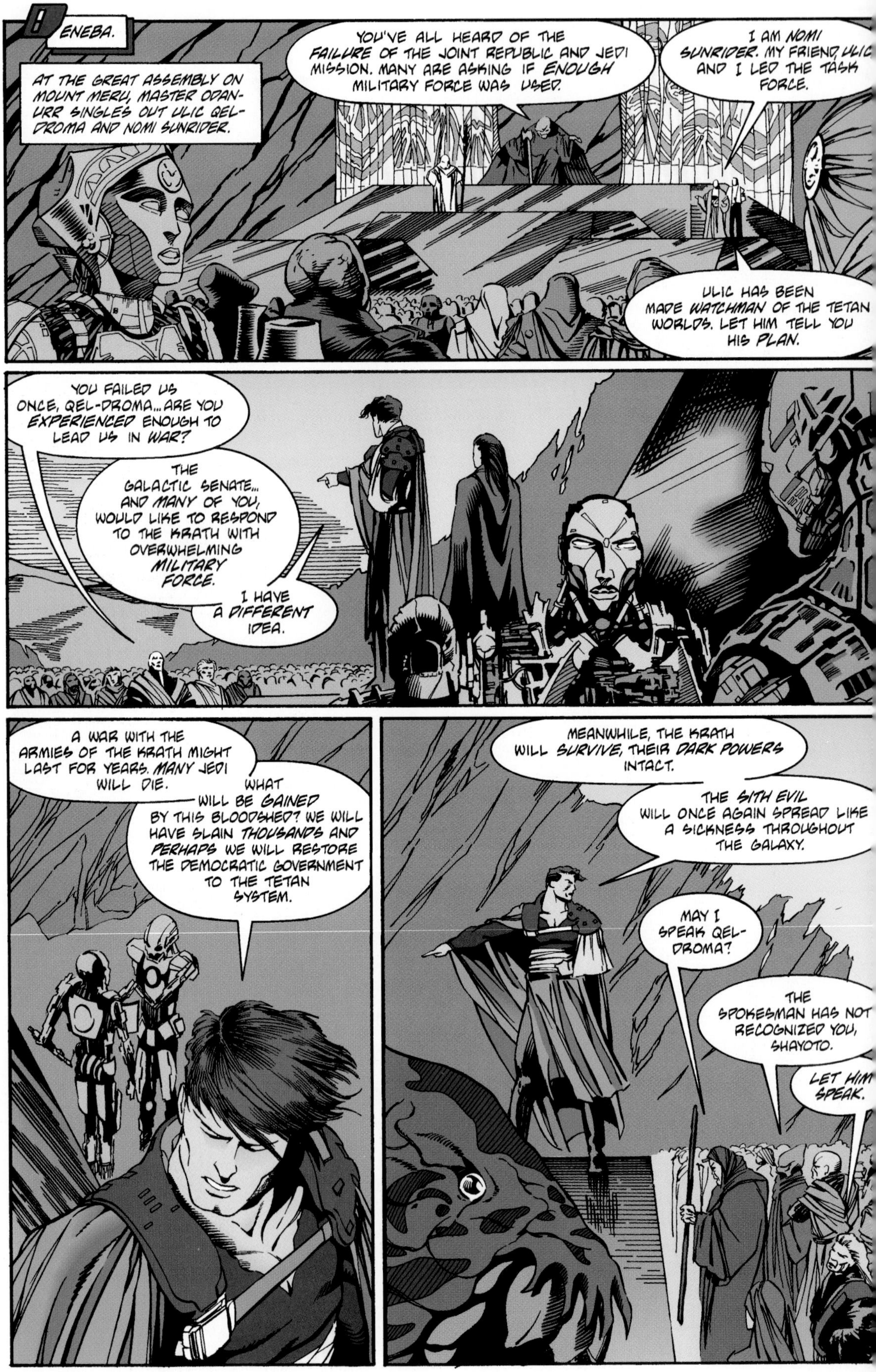
DENEBA.
AT THE GREAT ASSEMBLY ON MOUNT MERU, MASTER ODAN-URR SINGLES OUT ULIC QEL-DROMA AND NOMI SUNRIDER.
YOU'VE ALL HEARD OF THE FAILURE OF THE JOINT REPUBLIC AND JEDI MISSION. MANY ARE ASKING IF ENOUGH MILITARY FORCE WAS USED.
I AM NOMI SUNRIDER. MY FRIEND, ULIC AND I LED THE TASK FORCE.
ULIC HAS BEEN MADE WATCHMAN OF THE TETAN WORLDS. LET HIM TELL YOU HIS PLAN.
YOU FAILED US ONCE, QEL-DROMA... ARE YOU EXPERIENCED ENOUGH TO LEAD US IN WAR?
THE GALACTIC SENATE... AND MANY OF YOU, WOULD LIKE TO RESPOND TO THE KRATH WITH OVERWHELMING MILITARY FORCE.
I HAVE A DIFFERENT IDEA.
A WAR WITH THE ARMIES OF THE KRATH MIGHT LAST FOR YEARS. MANY JEDI WILL DIE.
WHAT WILL BE GAINED BY THIS BLOODSHED? WE WILL HAVE SLAIN THOUSANDS AND PERHAPS WE WILL RESTORE THE DEMOCRATIC GOVERNMENT TO THE TETAN SYSTEM.
MEANWHILE, THE KRATH WILL SURVIVE, THEIR DARK POWERS INTACT.
THE SITH EVIL WILL ONCE AGAIN SPREAD LIKE A SICKNESS THROUGHOUT THE GALAXY.
MAY I SPEAK QEL-DROMA?
THE SPOKESMAN HAS NOT RECOGNIZED YOU, SHAYOTO.
LET HIM SPEAK.

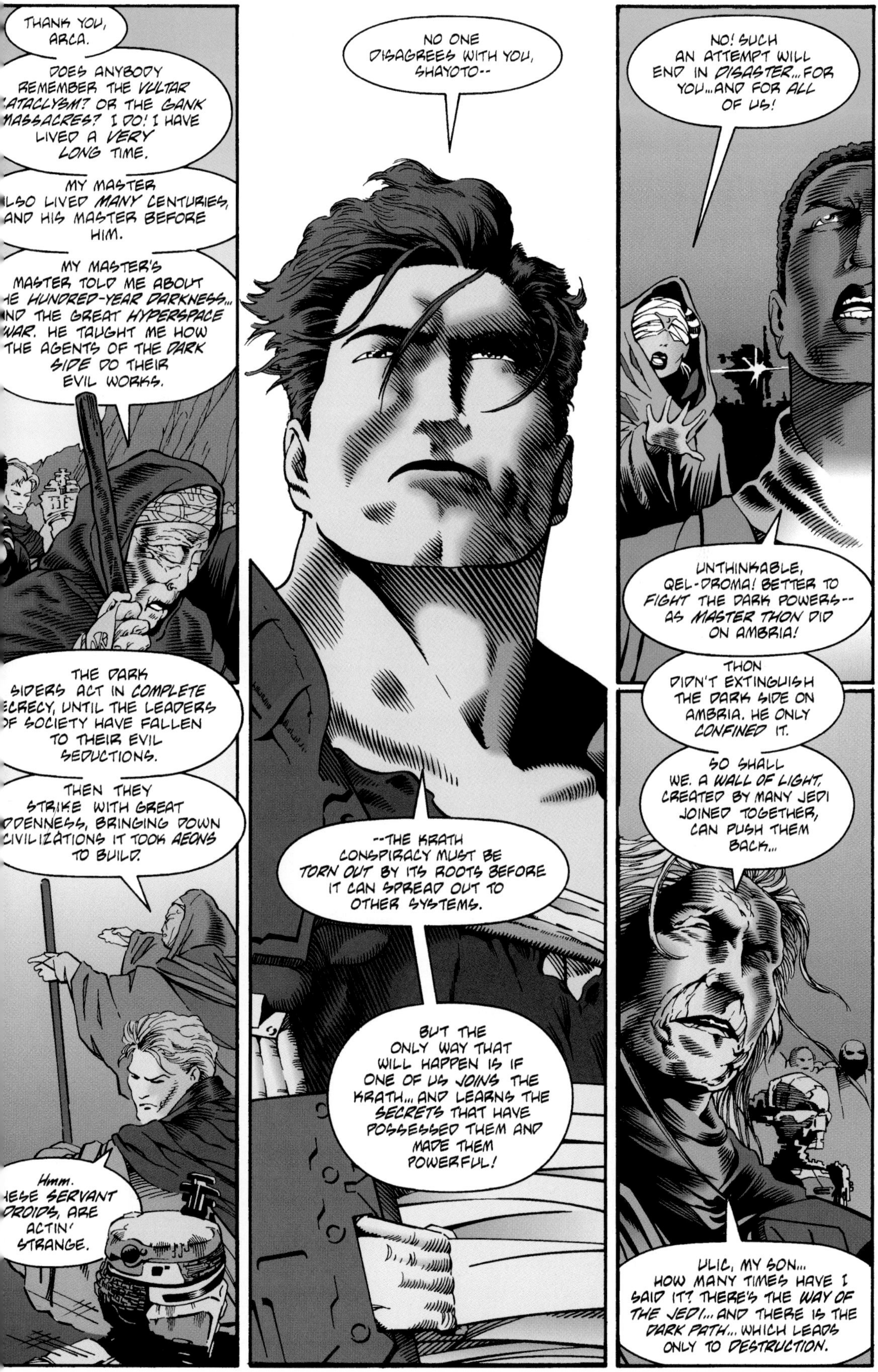
THANK YOU, ARCA.
DOES ANYBODY REMEMBER THE VULTAR CATACLYSM? OR THE GANK MASSACRES? I DO! I HAVE LIVED A VERY LONG TIME.
MY MASTER ALSO LIVED MANY CENTURIES, AND HIS MASTER BEFORE HIM.
MY MASTER'S MASTER TOLD ME ABOUT THE HUNDRED-YEAR DARKNESS... AND THE GREAT HYPERSPACE WAR. HE TAUGHT ME HOW THE AGENTS OF THE DARK SIDE DO THEIR EVIL WORKS.
THE DARK SIDERS ACT IN COMPLETE SECRECY, UNTIL THE LEADERS OF SOCIETY HAVE FALLEN TO THEIR EVIL SEDUCTIONS.
THEN THEY STRIKE WITH GREAT SUDDENNESS, BRINGING DOWN CIVILIZATIONS IT TOOK AEONS TO BUILD.
Hmm. HESE SERVANT ROIDS, ARE ACTIN' STRANGE.
NO ONE DISAGREES WITH YOU, SHAYOTO--
--THE KRATH CONSPIRACY MUST BE TORN OUT BY ITS ROOTS BEFORE IT CAN SPREAD OUT TO OTHER SYSTEMS.
BUT THE ONLY WAY THAT WILL HAPPEN IS IF ONE OF US JOINS THE KRATH... AND LEARNS THE SECRETS THAT HAVE POSSESSED THEM AND MADE THEM POWERFUL!
NO! SUCH AN ATTEMPT WILL END IN DISASTER... FOR YOU... AND FOR ALL OF US!
UNTHINKABLE, QEL-DROMA! BETTER TO FIGHT THE DARK POWERS-- AS MASTER THON DID ON AMBRIA!
THON DIDN'T EXTINGUISH THE DARK SIDE ON AMBRIA. HE ONLY CONFINED IT.
SO SHALL WE. A WALL OF LIGHT, CREATED BY MANY JEDI JOINED TOGETHER, CAN PUSH THEM BACK...
ULIC, MY SON... HOW MANY TIMES HAVE I SAID IT? THERE'S THE WAY OF THE JEDI... AND THERE IS THE DARK PATH... WHICH LEADS ONLY TO DESTRUCTION.

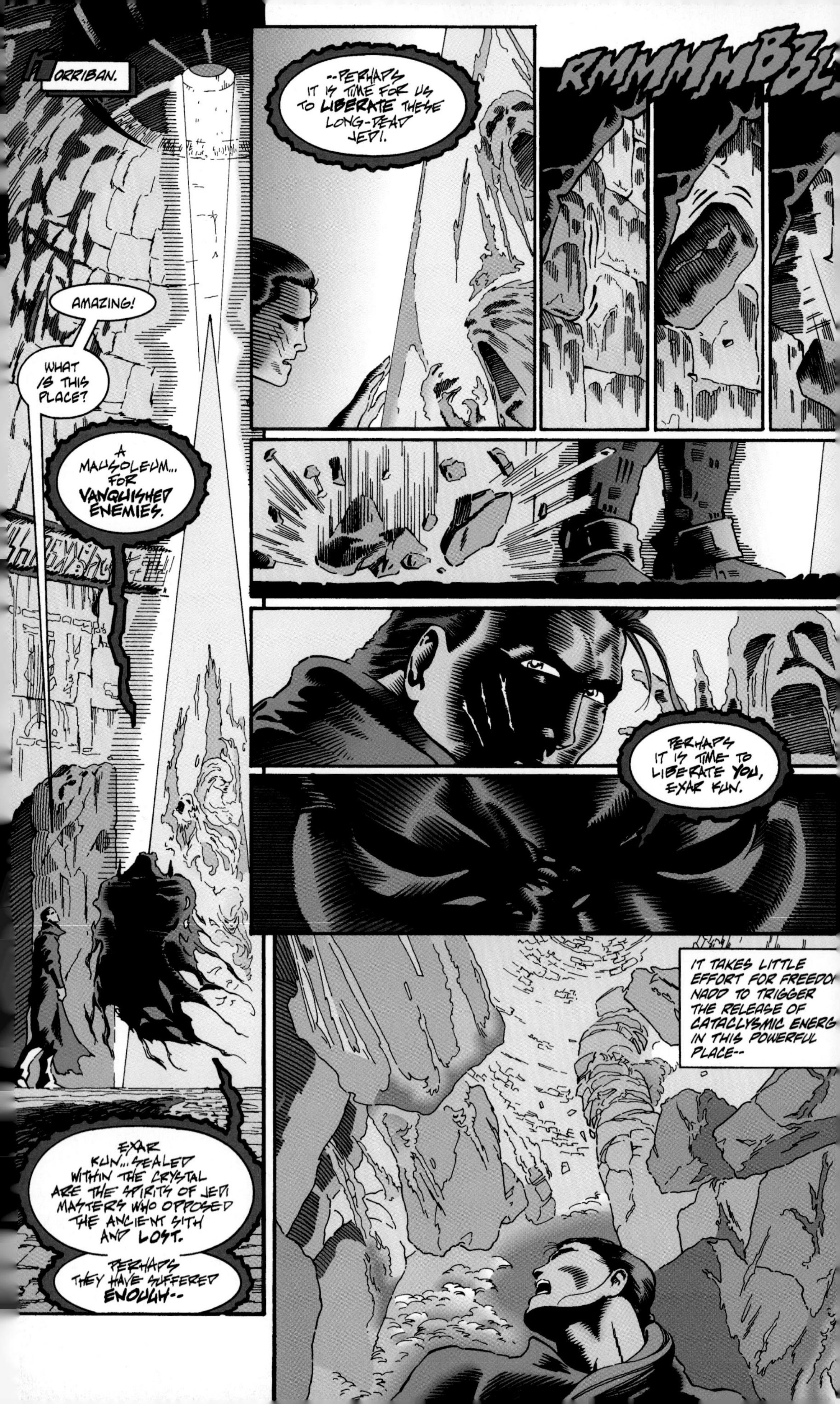
KORRIBAN.
AMAZING!
WHAT IS THIS PLACE?
A MAUSOLEUM... FOR VANQUISHED ENEMIES.
EXAR KUN... SEALED WITHIN THE CRYSTAL ARE THE SPIRITS OF JEDI MASTERS WHO OPPOSED THE ANCIENT SITH AND LOST.
PERHAPS THEY HAVE SUFFERED ENOUGH--
--PERHAPS IT IS TIME FOR US TO LIBERATE THESE LONG-DEAD JEDI.
RMMMMMBBL
PERHAPS IT IS TIME TO LIBERATE YOU, EXAR KUN.
IT TAKES LITTLE EFFORT FOR FREEDO NADD TO TRIGGER THE RELEASE OF CATACLYSMIC ENERG IN THIS POWERFUL PLACE--

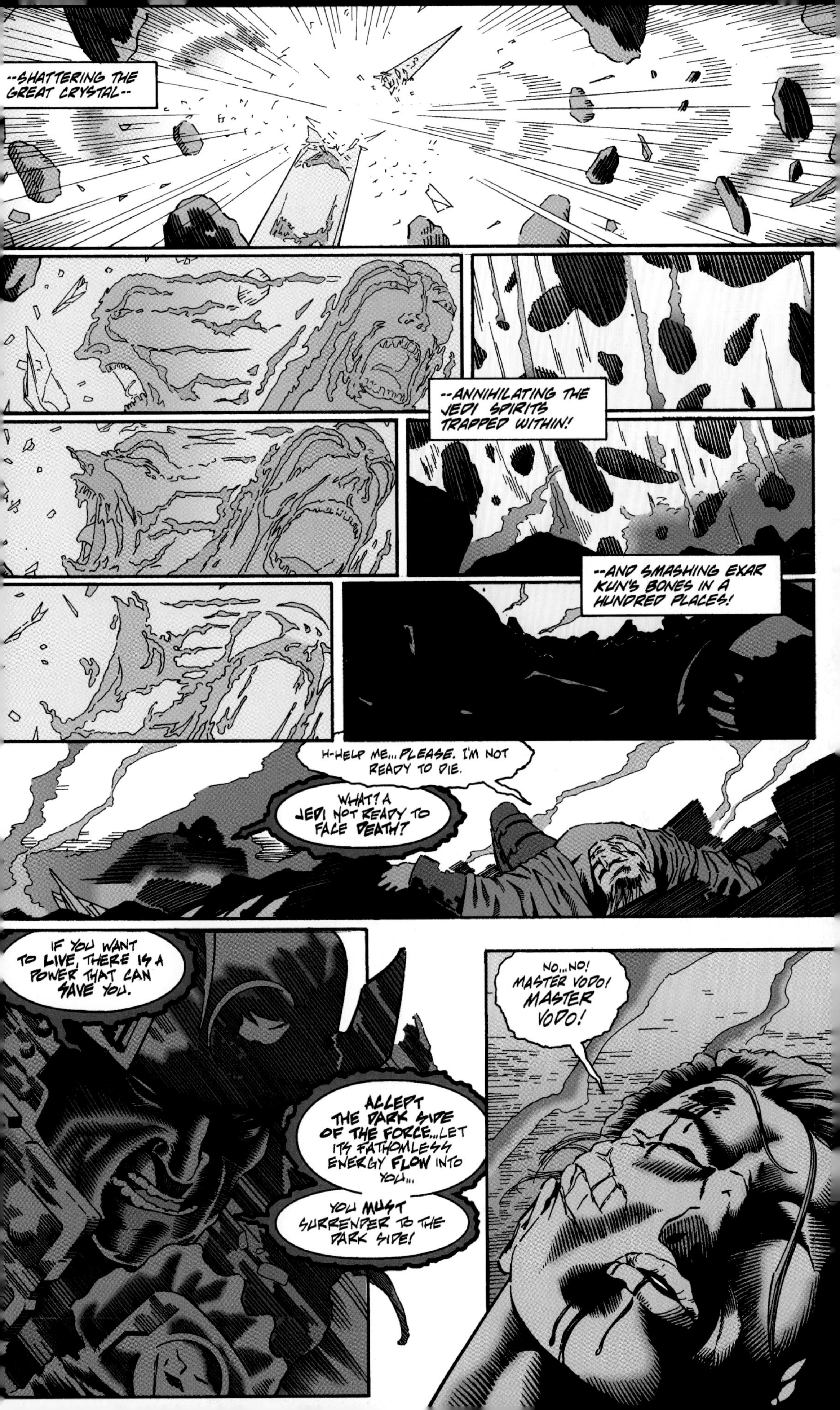
--SHATTERING THE GREAT CRYSTAL--
--ANNIHILATING THE JEDI SPIRITS TRAPPED WITHIN!
--AND SMASHING EXAR KUN'S BONES IN A HUNDRED PLACES!
H-HELP ME... PLEASE. I'M NOT READY TO DIE.
WHAT? A JEDI NOT READY TO FACE DEATH?
IF YOU WANT TO LIVE, THERE IS A POWER THAT CAN SAVE YOU.
ACCEPT THE DARK SIDE OF THE FORCE... LET ITS FATHOMLESS ENERGY FLOW INTO YOU...
YOU MUST SURRENDER TO THE DARK SIDE!
NO... NO! MASTER VODO! MASTER VODO!

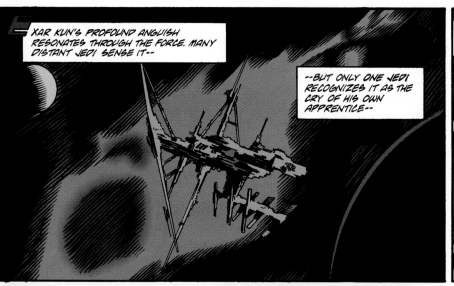

XAR KUN'S PROFOUND ANGUISH RESONATES THROUGH THE FORCE. MANY DISTANT JEDI SENSE IT--

--BUT ONLY ONE JEDI RECOGNIZES IT AS THE CRY OF HIS OWN APPRENTICE--

OH, EXAR... EXAR! IT IS AS PREDICTED! DARKNESS HAS FOUND YOU!

ELSEWHERE ON VODO'S SHIP, HIS CATHAR APPRENTICES ARE ENJOYING THEIR LOVE FOR ONE ANOTHER.

SYLVAR... LET'S MARRY AND RETURN TO CATHAR. WITH THE KNOWLEDGE WE HAVE LEARNED FROM MASTER VODO, WE WILL BECOME RENOWNED AMONG OUR PEOPLE.

I LOVE YOU CRADO... AND I WILL GLADLY BEAR YOUR WHELP... BUT I AM A JEDI FOREVER.

CRADO... SYLVAR... WILL YOU TAKE THE CONTROLS... WE ARE APPROACHING DENEBA.

SOMETHING TERRIBLE HAS HAPPEN TO EXAR KUN... I MUS HELP HIM... IF I CAN.

THE MERU SPACEPORT HAS CLEARED US FOR LANDING, MASTER.

HOW IS IT POSSIBLE TO HELP EXAR AT TH DISTANCE, MASTER!

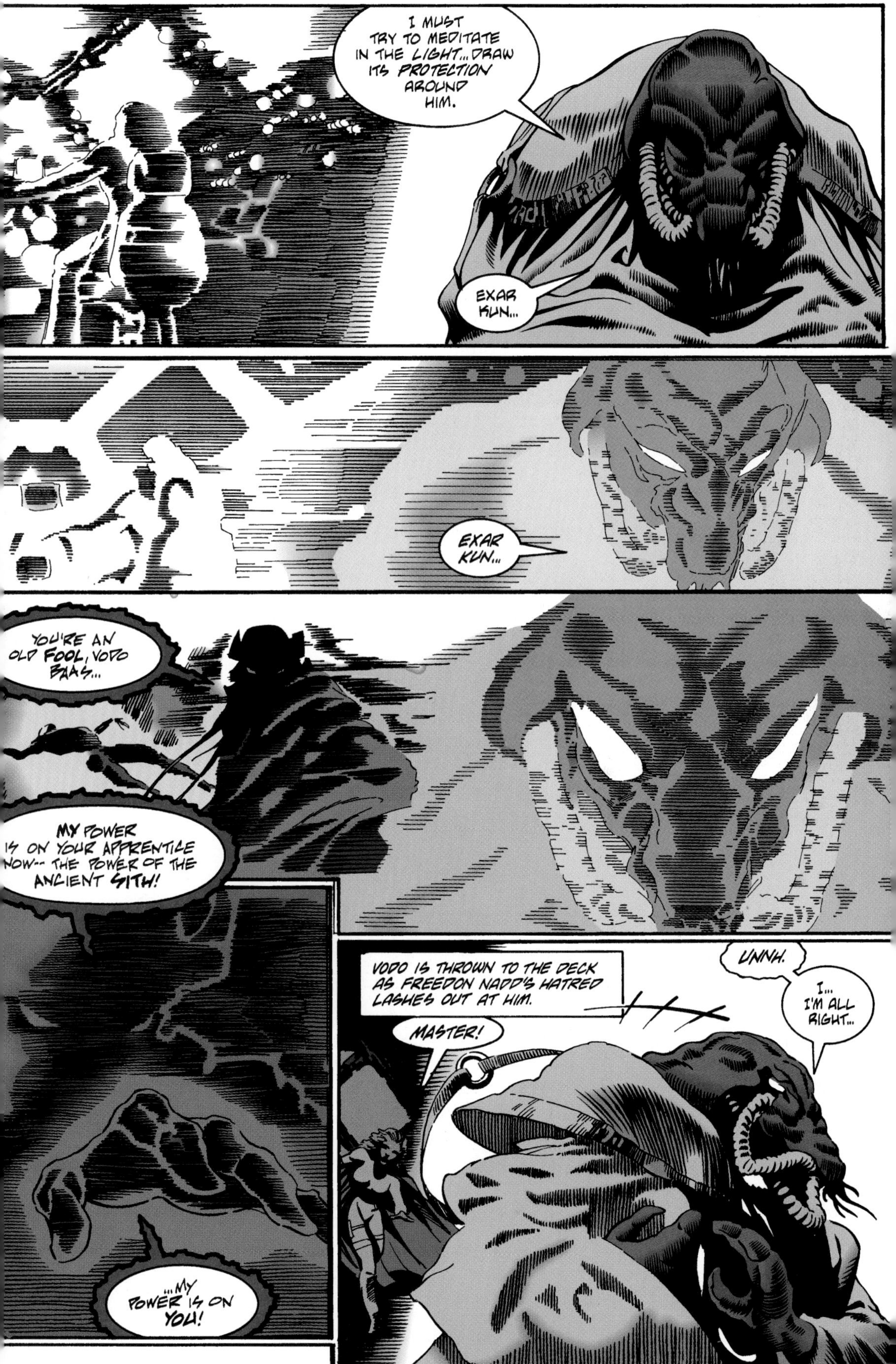
I MUST TRY TO MEDITATE IN THE LIGHT... DRAW ITS PROTECTION AROUND HIM.
EXAR KUN...
EXAR KUN...
YOU'RE AN OLD FOOL, VODO BAAS...
MY POWER IS ON YOUR APPRENTICE NOW-- THE POWER OF THE ANCIENT SITH!
...MY POWER IS ON YOU!
VODO IS THROWN TO THE DECK AS FREEDON NADD'S HATRED LASHES OUT AT HIM.
UNNH.
I... I'M ALL RIGHT...
MASTER!

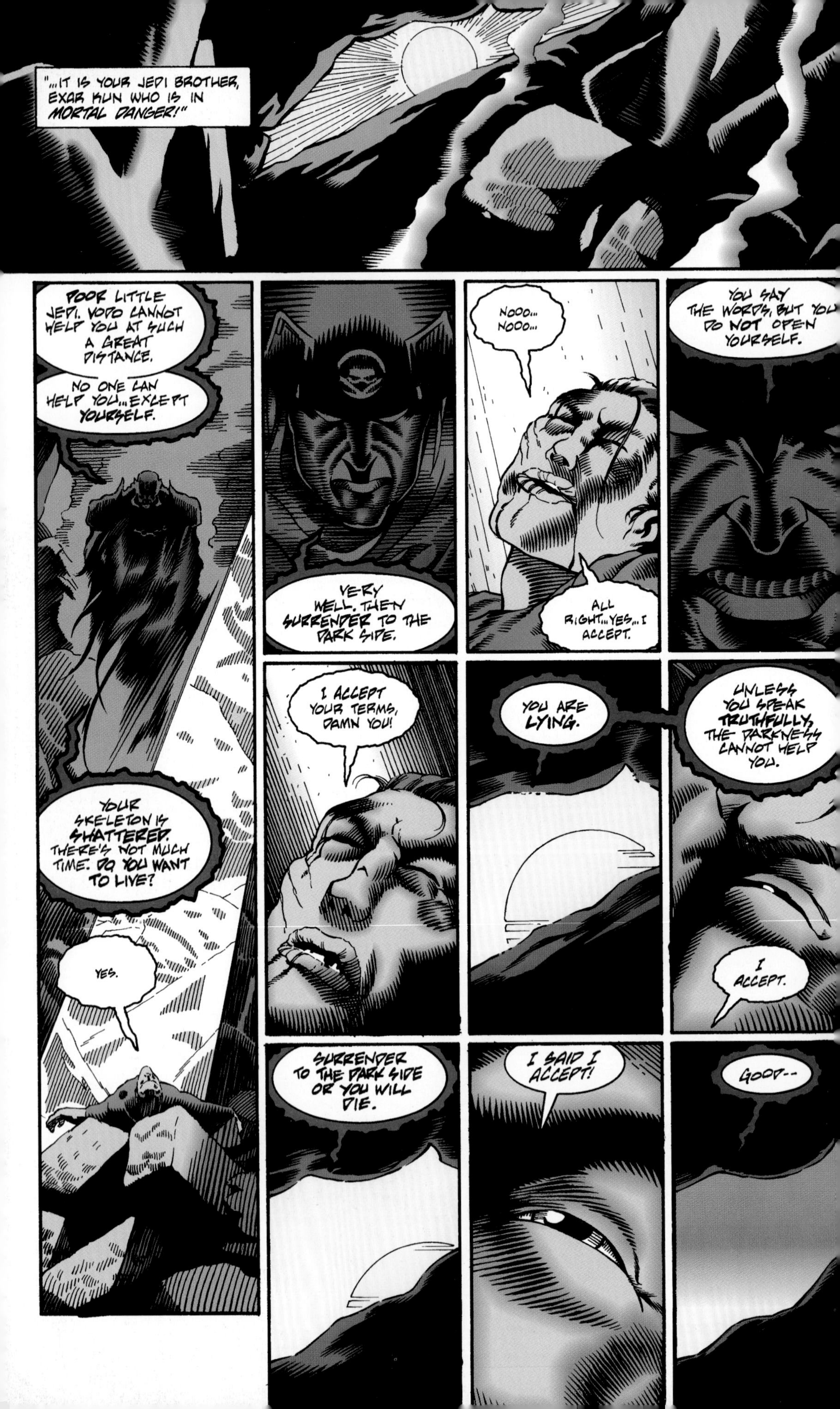
"...IT IS YOUR JEDI BROTHER, EXAR KUN WHO IS IN MORTAL DANGER!"
POOR LITTLE JEDI. VODO CANNOT HELP YOU AT SUCH A GREAT DISTANCE.
NO ONE CAN HELP YOU...EXCEPT YOURSELF.
YOUR SKELETON IS SHATTERED. THERE'S NOT MUCH TIME. DO YOU WANT TO LIVE?
YES.
VERY WELL. THEN SURRENDER TO THE DARK SIDE.
NOOO... NOOO...
ALL RIGHT... YES... I ACCEPT.
YOU SAY THE WORDS, BUT YOU DO NOT OPEN YOURSELF.
I ACCEPT YOUR TERMS, DAMN YOU!
YOU ARE LYING.
UNLESS YOU SPEAK TRUTHFULLY, THE DARKNESS CANNOT HELP YOU.
I ACCEPT.
SURRENDER TO THE DARK SIDE OR YOU WILL DIE.
I SAID I ACCEPT!
GOOD--

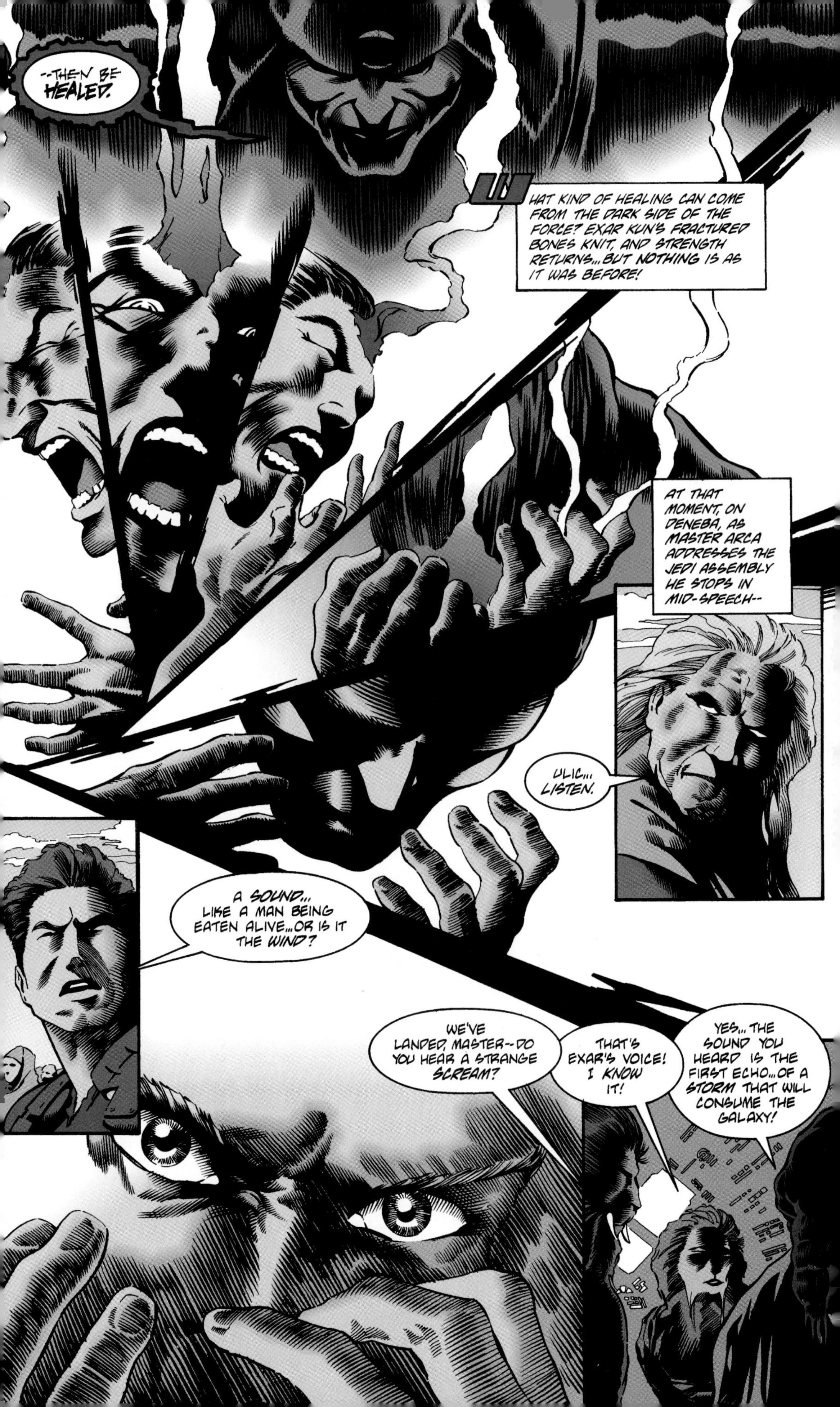
--THEN BE HEALED.
WHAT KIND OF HEALING CAN COME FROM THE DARK SIDE OF THE FORCE? EXAR KUN'S FRACTURED BONES KNIT, AND STRENGTH RETURNS... BUT NOTHING IS AS IT WAS BEFORE!
AT THAT MOMENT, ON DENEBA, AS MASTER ARCA ADDRESSES THE JEDI ASSEMBLY HE STOPS IN MID-SPEECH--
ULIC... LISTEN.
A SOUND... LIKE A MAN BEING EATEN ALIVE... OR IS IT THE WIND?
WE'VE LANDED, MASTER--DO YOU HEAR A STRANGE SCREAM?
THAT'S EXAR'S VOICE! I KNOW IT!
YES... THE SOUND YOU HEARD IS THE FIRST ECHO... OF A STORM THAT WILL CONSUME THE GALAXY!

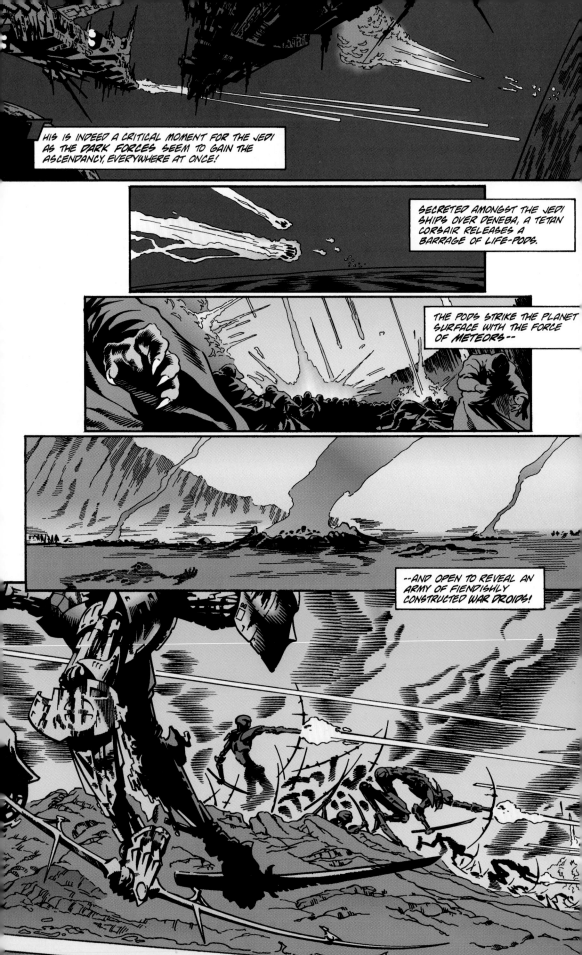

HIS IS INDEED A CRITICAL MOMENT FOR THE JEDI! AS THE DARK FORCES SEEM TO GAIN THE ASCENDANCY, EVERYWHERE AT ONCE!

SECRETED AMONGST THE JEDI SHIPS OVER DENEBA, A TETAN CORSAIR RELEASES A BARRAGE OF LIFE-PODS.

THE PODS STRIKE THE PLANET SURFACE WITH THE FORCE OF METEORS--

--AND OPEN TO REVEAL AN ARMY OF FIENDISHLY CONSTRUCTED WAR DROIDS!

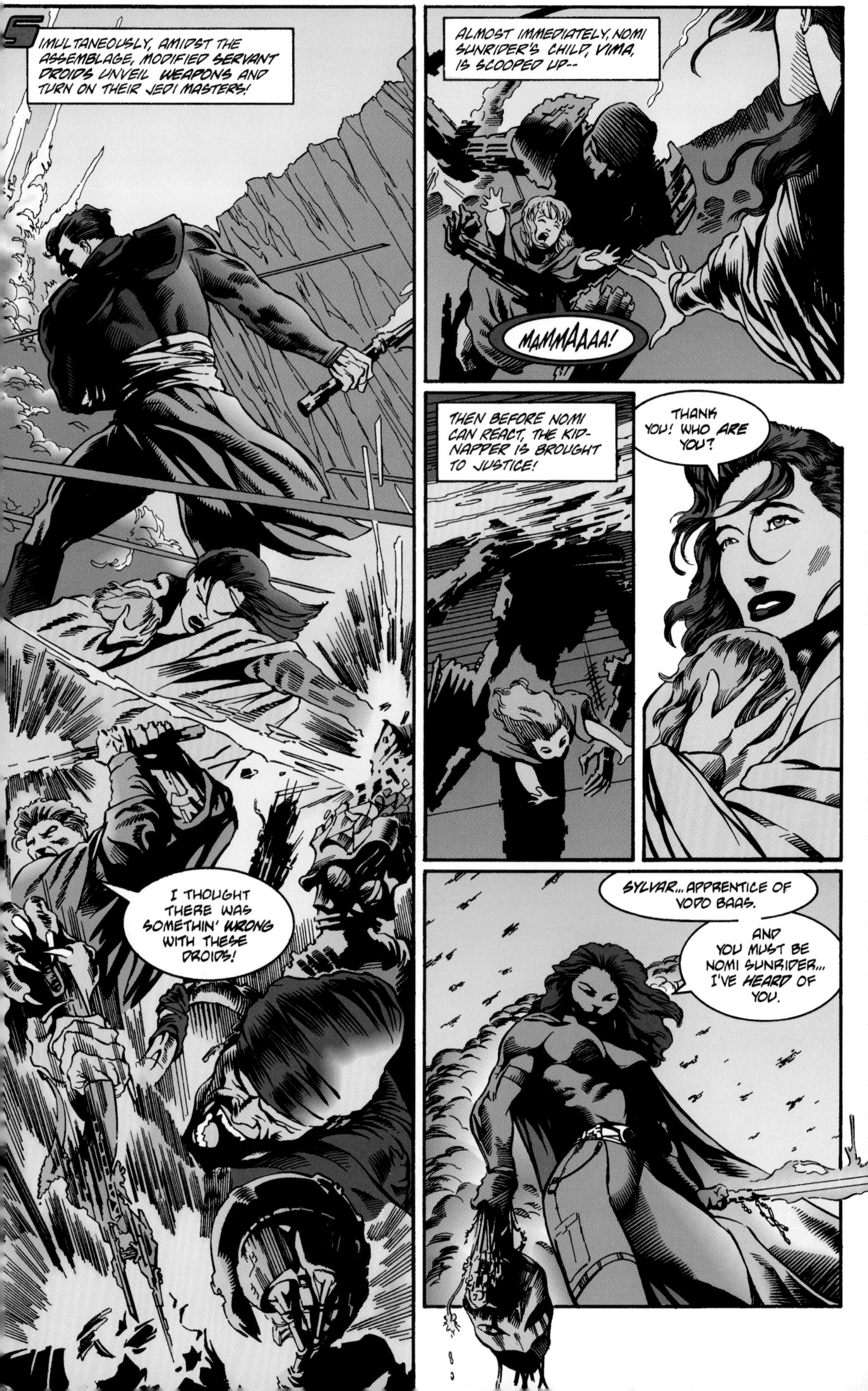
SIMULTANEOUSLY, AMIDST THE ASSEMBLAGE, MODIFIED SERVANT DROIDS UNVEIL WEAPONS AND TURN ON THEIR JEDI MASTERS!
I THOUGHT THERE WAS SOMETHIN' WRONG WITH THESE DROIDS!
ALMOST IMMEDIATELY, NOMI SUNRIDER'S CHILD, VIMA, IS SCOOPED UP--
MAMMAAAA!
THEN BEFORE NOMI CAN REACT, THE KID-NAPPER IS BROUGHT TO JUSTICE!
THANK YOU! WHO ARE YOU?
SYLVAR... APPRENTICE OF VODO BAAS.
AND YOU MUST BE NOMI SUNRIDER... I'VE HEARD OF YOU.

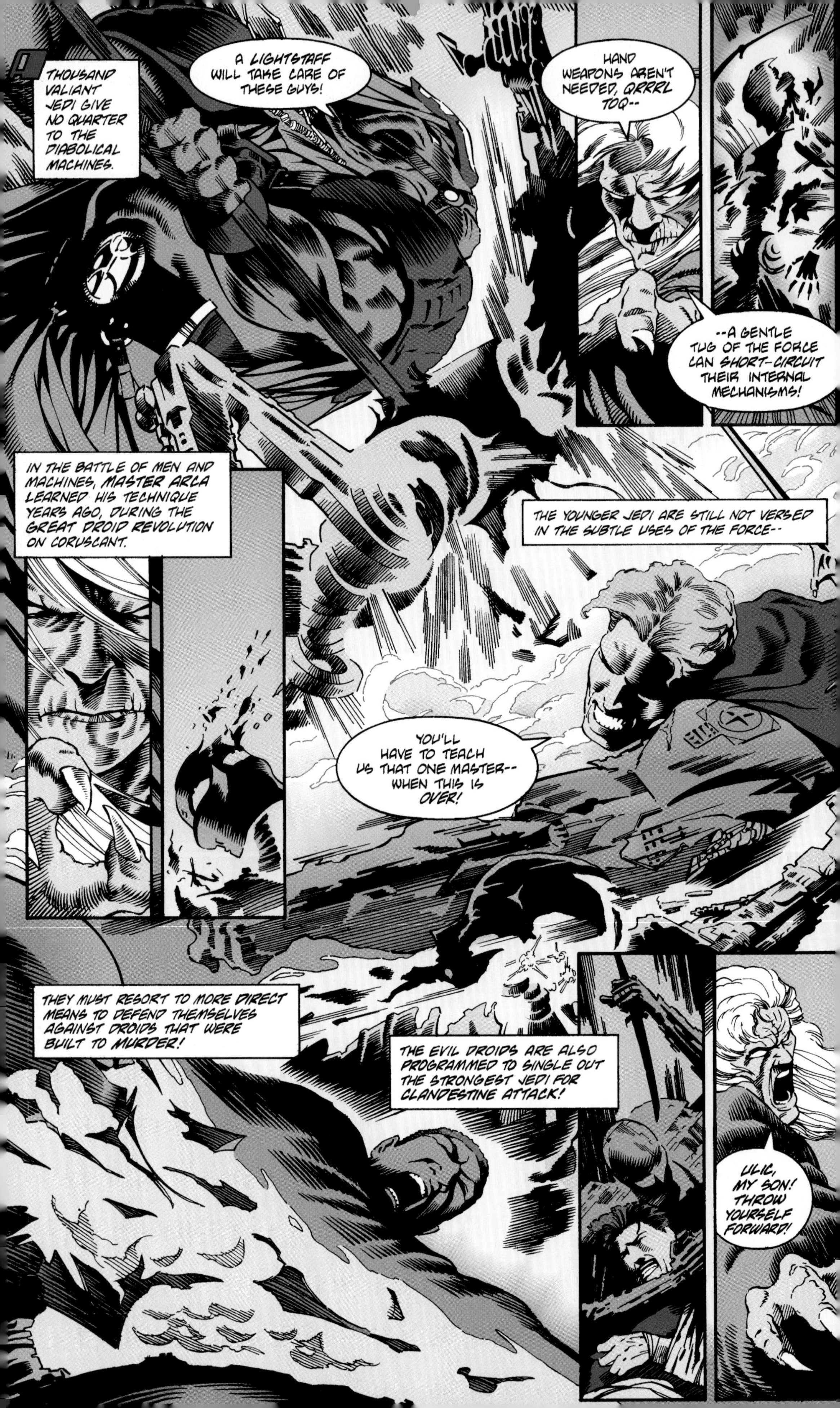
THOUSAND VALIANT JEDI GIVE NO QUARTER TO THE DIABOLICAL MACHINES.
A LIGHTSTAFF WILL TAKE CARE OF THESE GUYS!
HAND WEAPONS AREN'T NEEDED, QRRRL TOQ--
--A GENTLE TUG OF THE FORCE CAN SHORT-CIRCUIT THEIR INTERNAL MECHANISMS!
IN THE BATTLE OF MEN AND MACHINES, MASTER ARCA LEARNED HIS TECHNIQUE YEARS AGO, DURING THE GREAT DROID REVOLUTION ON CORUSCANT.
THE YOUNGER JEDI ARE STILL NOT VERSED IN THE SUBTLE USES OF THE FORCE--
YOU'LL HAVE TO TEACH US THAT ONE MASTER-- WHEN THIS IS OVER!
THEY MUST RESORT TO MORE DIRECT MEANS TO DEFEND THEMSELVES AGAINST DROIDS THAT WERE BUILT TO MURDER!
THE EVIL DROIDS ARE ALSO PROGRAMMED TO SINGLE OUT THE STRONGEST JEDI FOR CLANDESTINE ATTACK!
ULIC, MY SON! THROW YOURSELF FORWARD!

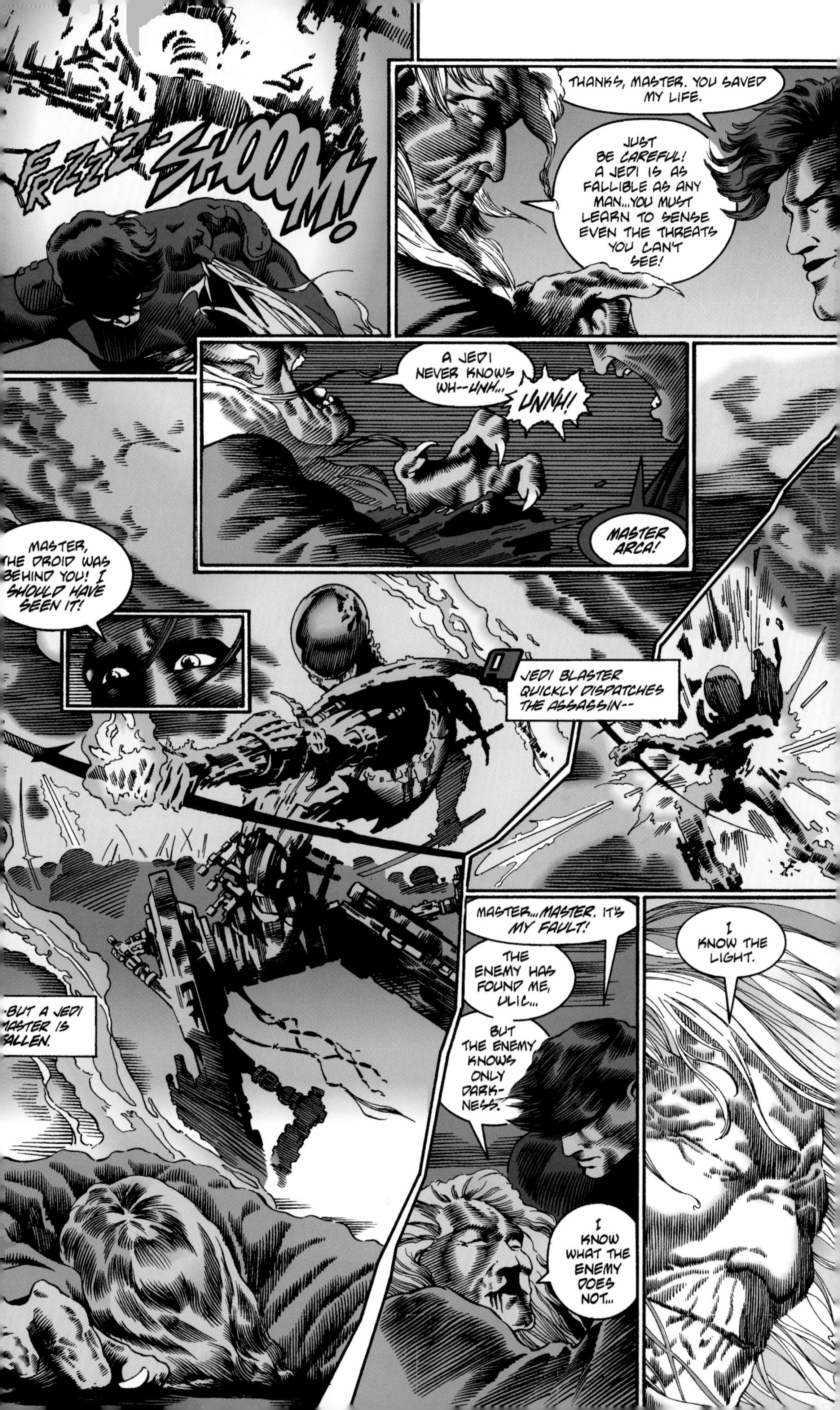
FRZZZ-SHOOOM!
THANKS, MASTER. YOU SAVED MY LIFE.
JUST BE CAREFUL! A JEDI IS AS FALLIBLE AS ANY MAN...YOU MUST LEARN TO SENSE EVEN THE THREATS YOU CAN'T SEE!
A JEDI NEVER KNOWS WH--UNH...
UNNH!
MASTER ARCA!
MASTER, THE DROID WAS BEHIND YOU! I SHOULD HAVE SEEN IT!
JEDI BLASTER QUICKLY DISPATCHES THE ASSASSIN--
--BUT A JEDI MASTER IS FALLEN.
MASTER...MASTER. IT'S MY FAULT!
THE ENEMY HAS FOUND ME, ULIC...
BUT THE ENEMY KNOWS ONLY DARKNESS.
I KNOW WHAT THE ENEMY DOES NOT...
I KNOW THE LIGHT.

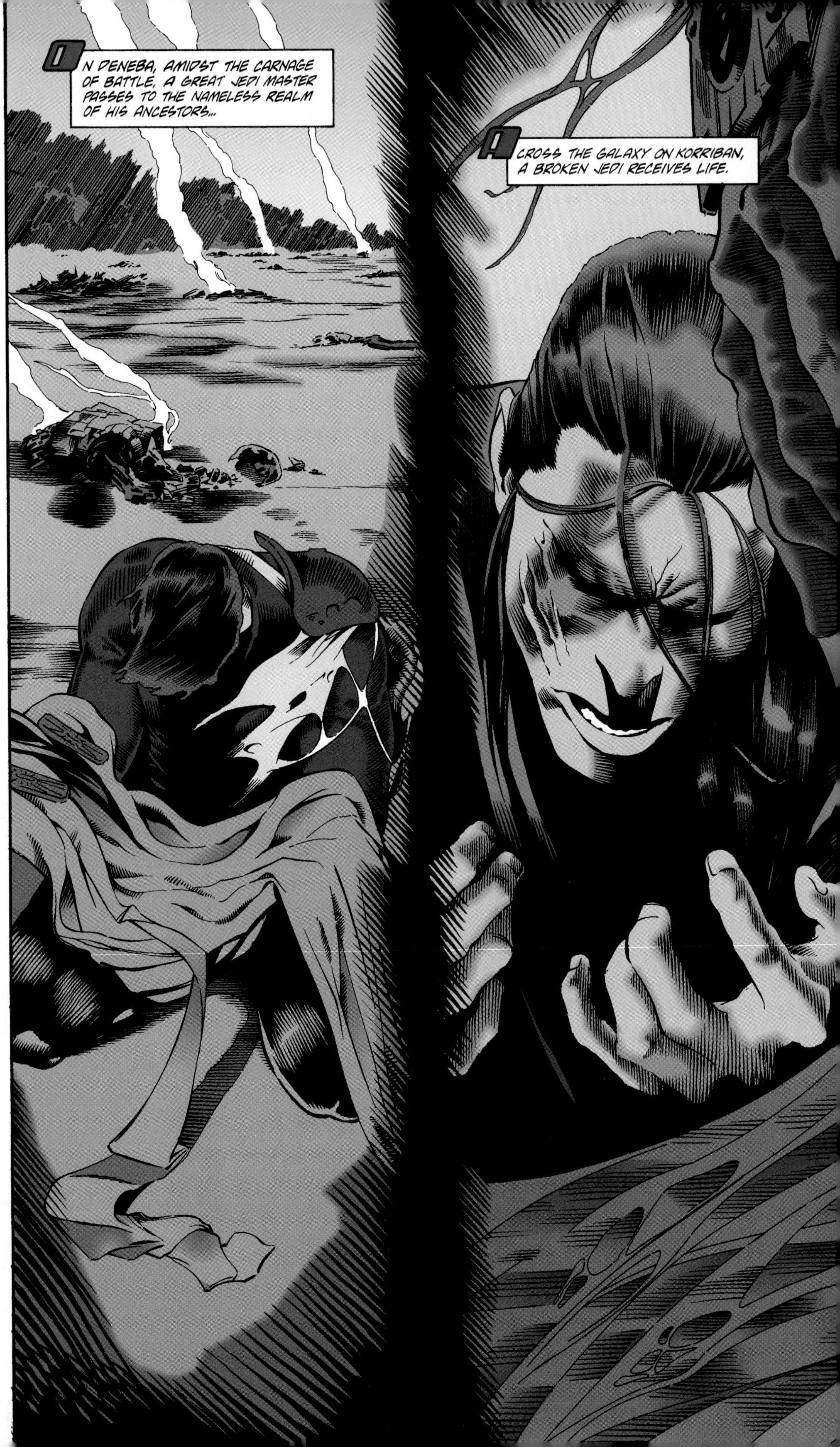
ON DENEBA, AMIDST THE CARNAGE OF BATTLE, A GREAT JEDI MASTER PASSES TO THE NAMELESS REALM OF HIS ANCESTORS...
ACROSS THE GALAXY ON KORRIBAN, A BROKEN JEDI RECEIVES LIFE.

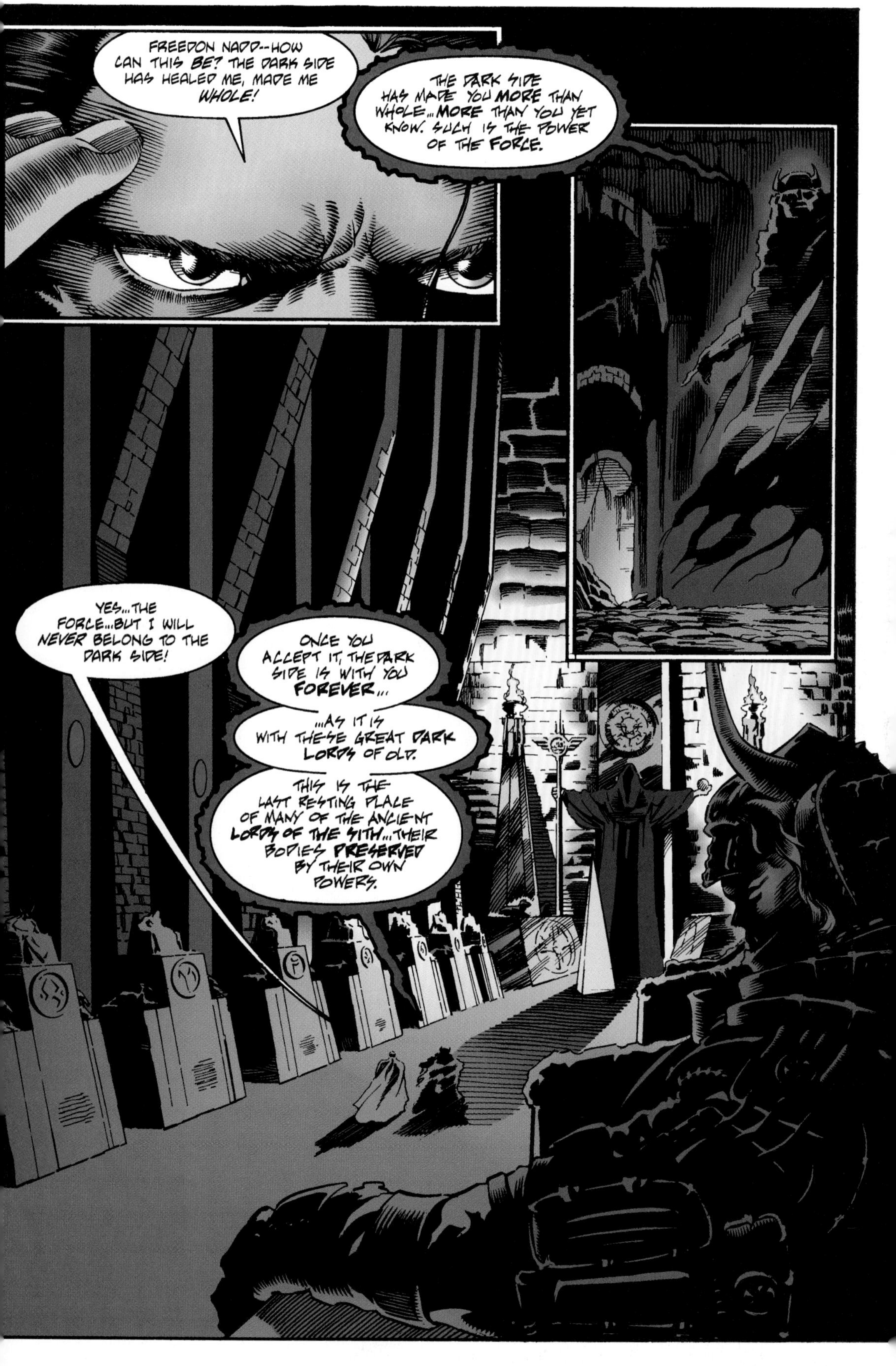
FREEDON NADD--HOW CAN THIS BE? THE DARK SIDE HAS HEALED ME, MADE ME WHOLE!
THE DARK SIDE HAS MADE YOU MORE THAN WHOLE...MORE THAN YOU YET KNOW. SUCH IS THE POWER OF THE FORCE.
YES...THE FORCE...BUT I WILL NEVER BELONG TO THE DARK SIDE!
ONCE YOU ACCEPT IT, THE DARK SIDE IS WITH YOU FOREVER...
...AS IT IS WITH THESE GREAT DARK LORDS OF OLD.
THIS IS THE LAST RESTING PLACE OF MANY OF THE ANCIENT LORDS OF THE SITH...THEIR BODIES PRESERVED BY THEIR OWN POWERS.

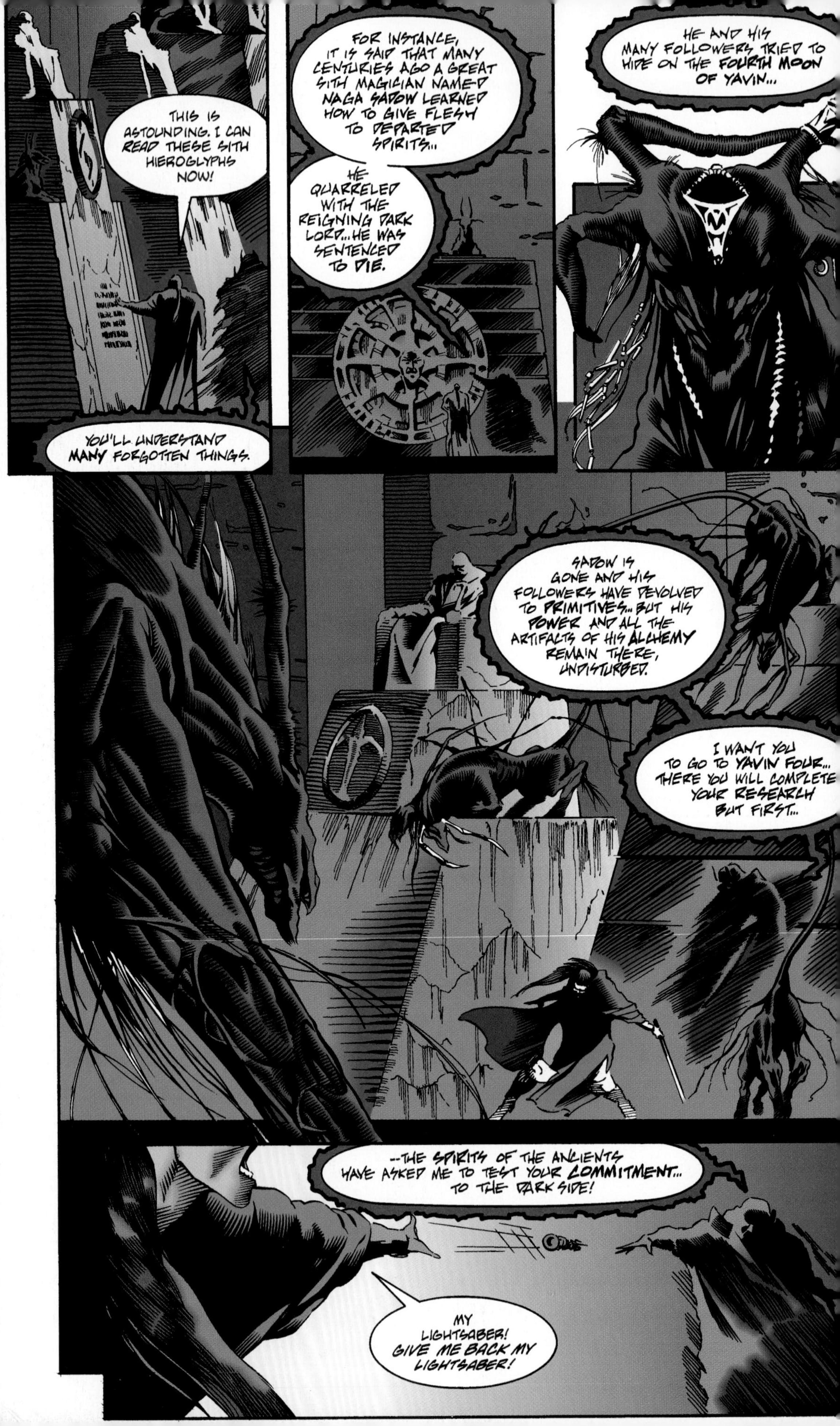
THIS IS ASTOUNDING. I CAN READ THESE SITH HIEROGLYPHS NOW!
YOU'LL UNDERSTAND MANY FORGOTTEN THINGS.
FOR INSTANCE, IT IS SAID THAT MANY CENTURIES AGO A GREAT SITH MAGICIAN NAMED NAGA SADOW LEARNED HOW TO GIVE FLESH TO DEPARTED SPIRITS...
HE QUARRELED WITH THE REIGNING DARK LORD...HE WAS SENTENCED TO DIE.
HE AND HIS MANY FOLLOWERS TRIED TO HIDE ON THE FOURTH MOON OF YAVIN...
SADOW IS GONE AND HIS FOLLOWERS HAVE DEVOLVED TO PRIMITIVES... BUT HIS POWER AND ALL THE ARTIFACTS OF HIS ALCHEMY REMAIN THERE, UNDISTURBED.
I WANT YOU TO GO TO YAVIN FOUR... THERE YOU WILL COMPLETE YOUR RESEARCH BUT FIRST...
--THE SPIRITS OF THE ANCIENTS HAVE ASKED ME TO TEST YOUR COMMITMENT... TO THE DARK SIDE!
MY LIGHTSABER! GIVE ME BACK MY LIGHTSABER!

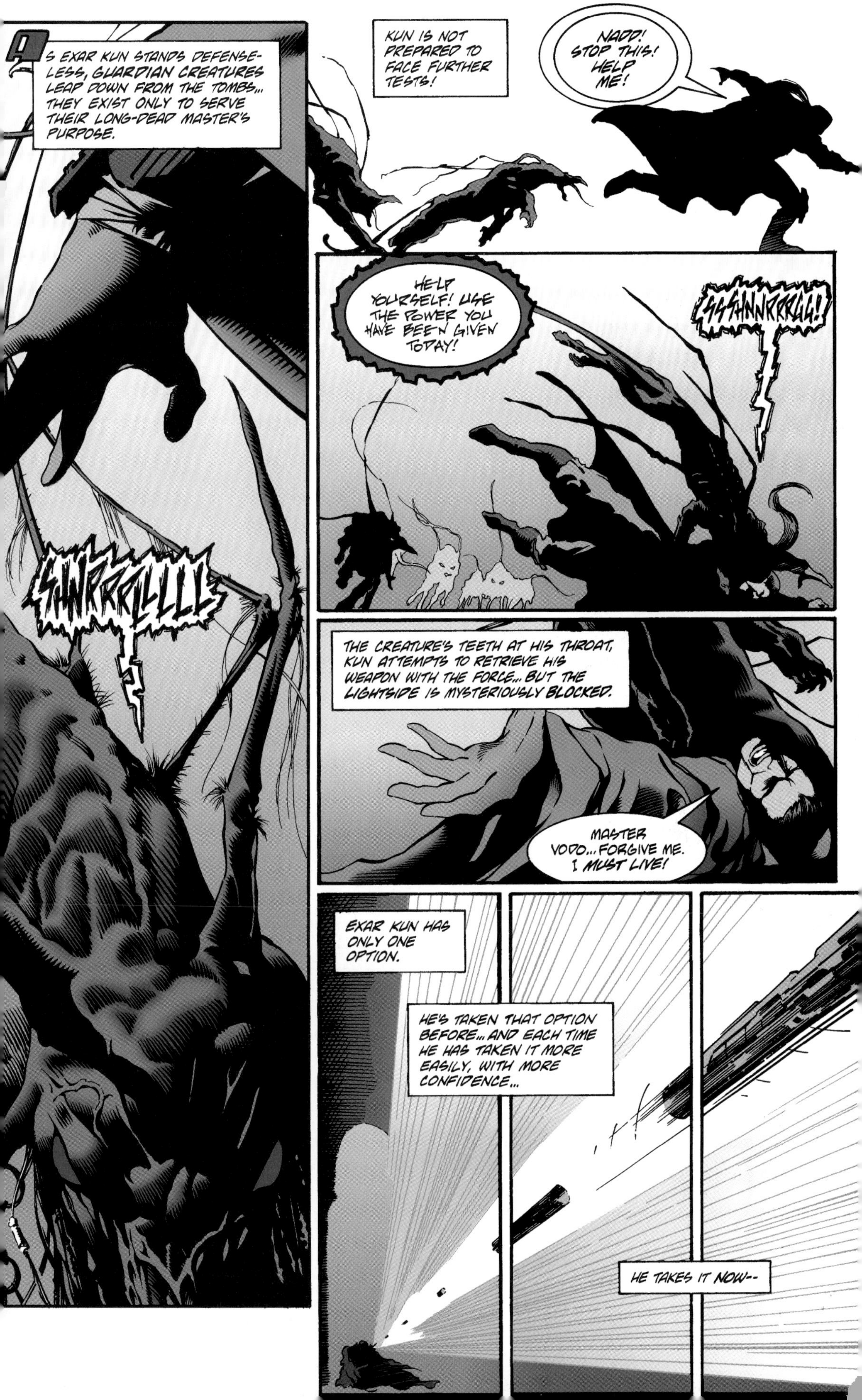
AS EXAR KUN STANDS DEFENSELESS, GUARDIAN CREATURES LEAP DOWN FROM THE TOMBS... THEY EXIST ONLY TO SERVE THEIR LONG-DEAD MASTER'S PURPOSE.
KUN IS NOT PREPARED TO FACE FURTHER TESTS!
NADD! STOP THIS! HELP ME!
SHNRRRILLLLL!
HELP YOURSELF! USE THE POWER YOU HAVE BEEN GIVEN TODAY!
SSSHNNRRRGG!
THE CREATURE'S TEETH AT HIS THROAT, KUN ATTEMPTS TO RETRIEVE HIS WEAPON WITH THE FORCE... BUT THE LIGHTSIDE IS MYSTERIOUSLY BLOCKED.
MASTER VODO... FORGIVE ME. I MUST LIVE!
EXAR KUN HAS ONLY ONE OPTION.
HE'S TAKEN THAT OPTION BEFORE... AND EACH TIME HE HAS TAKEN IT MORE EASILY, WITH MORE CONFIDENCE...
HE TAKES IT NOW--

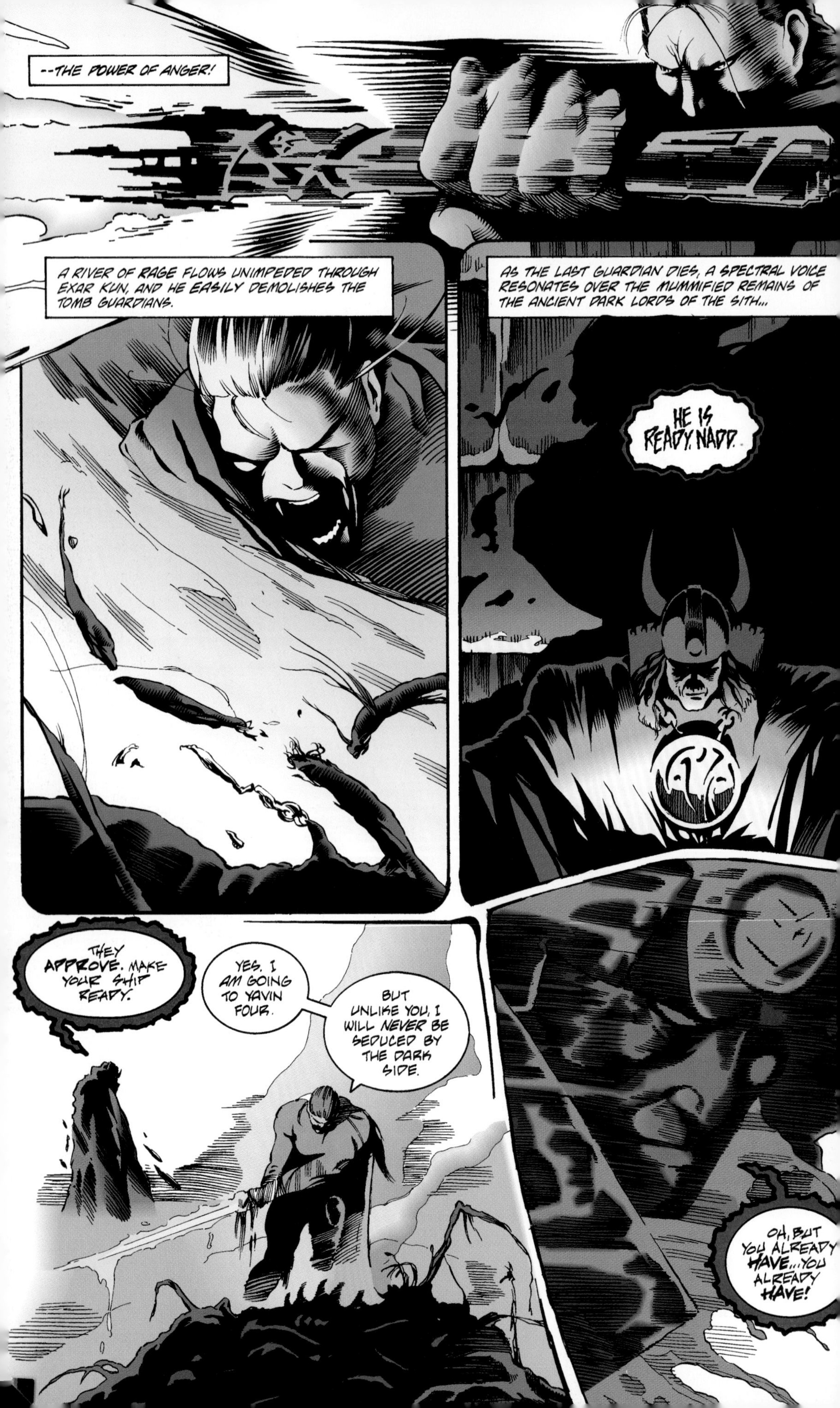
--THE POWER OF ANGER!
A RIVER OF RAGE FLOWS UNIMPEDED THROUGH EXAR KUN, AND HE EASILY DEMOLISHES THE TOMB GUARDIANS.
AS THE LAST GUARDIAN DIES, A SPECTRAL VOICE RESONATES OVER THE MUMMIFIED REMAINS OF THE ANCIENT DARK LORDS OF THE SITH...
HE IS READY, NADD.
THEY APPROVE. MAKE YOUR SHIP READY.
YES. I AM GOING TO YAVIN FOUR.
BUT UNLIKE YOU, I WILL NEVER BE SEDUCED BY THE DARK SIDE.
OH, BUT YOU ALREADY HAVE... YOU ALREADY HAVE!

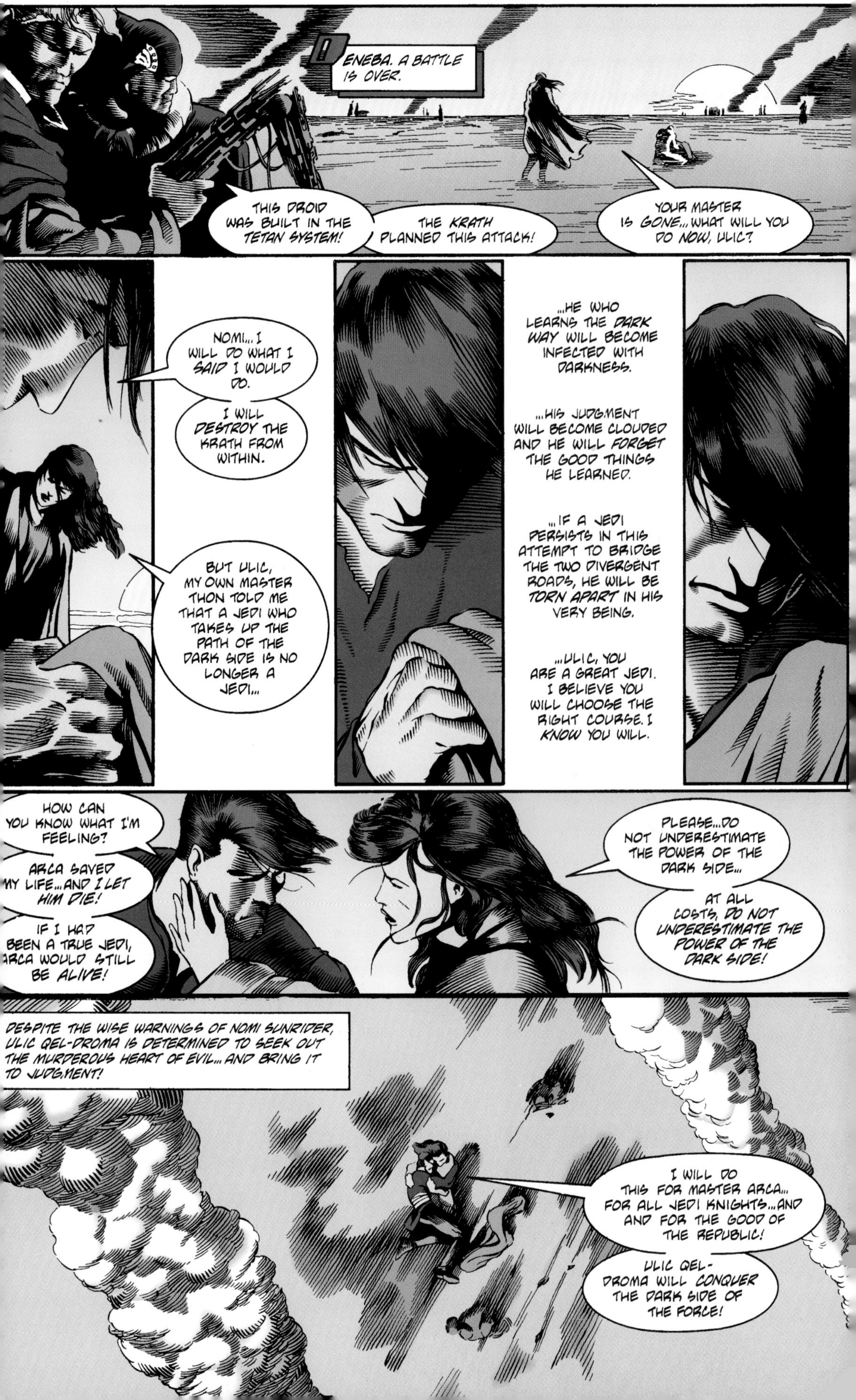
DENEBA. A BATTLE IS OVER.
THIS DROID WAS BUILT IN THE TETAN SYSTEM!
THE KRATH PLANNED THIS ATTACK!
YOUR MASTER IS GONE... WHAT WILL YOU DO NOW, ULIC?
NOMI... I WILL DO WHAT I SAID I WOULD DO.
I WILL DESTROY THE KRATH FROM WITHIN.
BUT ULIC, MY OWN MASTER THON TOLD ME THAT A JEDI WHO TAKES UP THE PATH OF THE DARK SIDE IS NO LONGER A JEDI...
...HE WHO LEARNS THE DARK WAY WILL BECOME INFECTED WITH DARKNESS.
...HIS JUDGMENT WILL BECOME CLOUDED AND HE WILL FORGET THE GOOD THINGS HE LEARNED.
...IF A JEDI PERSISTS IN THIS ATTEMPT TO BRIDGE THE TWO DIVERGENT ROADS, HE WILL BE TORN APART IN HIS VERY BEING.
...ULIC, YOU ARE A GREAT JEDI. I BELIEVE YOU WILL CHOOSE THE RIGHT COURSE. I KNOW YOU WILL.
HOW CAN YOU KNOW WHAT I'M FEELING?
ARCA SAVED MY LIFE... AND I LET HIM DIE!
IF I HAD BEEN A TRUE JEDI, ARCA WOULD STILL BE ALIVE!
PLEASE... DO NOT UNDERESTIMATE THE POWER OF THE DARK SIDE...
AT ALL COSTS, DO NOT UNDERESTIMATE THE POWER OF THE DARK SIDE!
DESPITE THE WISE WARNINGS OF NOMI SUNRIDER, ULIC QEL-DROMA IS DETERMINED TO SEEK OUT THE MURDEROUS HEART OF EVIL... AND BRING IT TO JUDGMENT!
I WILL DO THIS FOR MASTER ARCA... FOR ALL JEDI KNIGHTS... AND AND FOR THE GOOD OF THE REPUBLIC!
ULIC QEL-DROMA WILL CONQUER THE DARK SIDE OF THE FORCE!

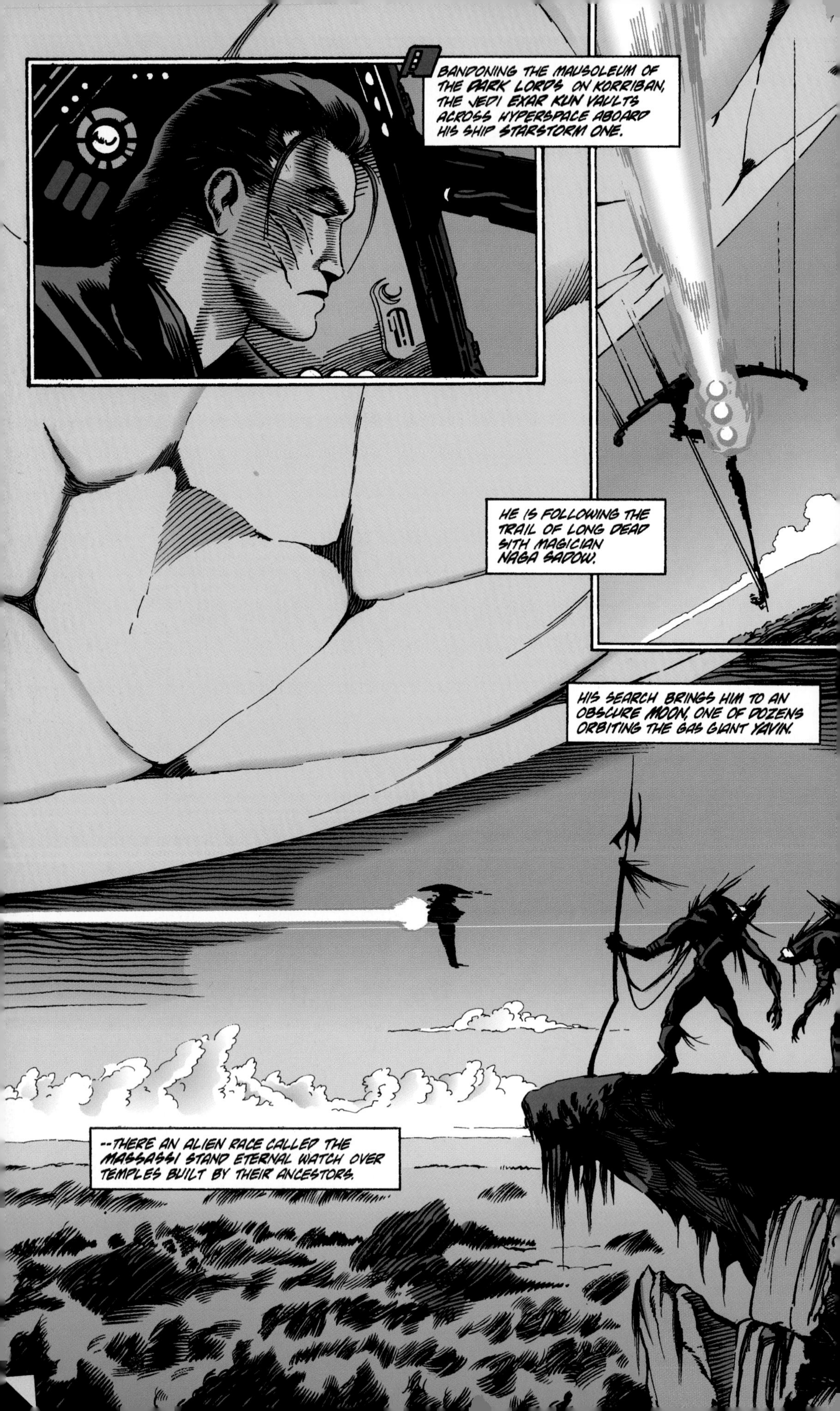
BANDONING THE MAUSOLEUM OF THE DARK LORDS ON KORRIBAN, THE JEDI EXAR KUN VAULTS ACROSS HYPERSPACE ABOARD HIS SHIP STARSTORM ONE.
HE IS FOLLOWING THE TRAIL OF LONG DEAD SITH MAGICIAN NAGA SADOW.
HIS SEARCH BRINGS HIM TO AN OBSCURE MOON, ONE OF DOZENS ORBITING THE GAS GIANT YAVIN.
--THERE AN ALIEN RACE CALLED THE MASSASSI STAND ETERNAL WATCH OVER TEMPLES BUILT BY THEIR ANCESTORS.

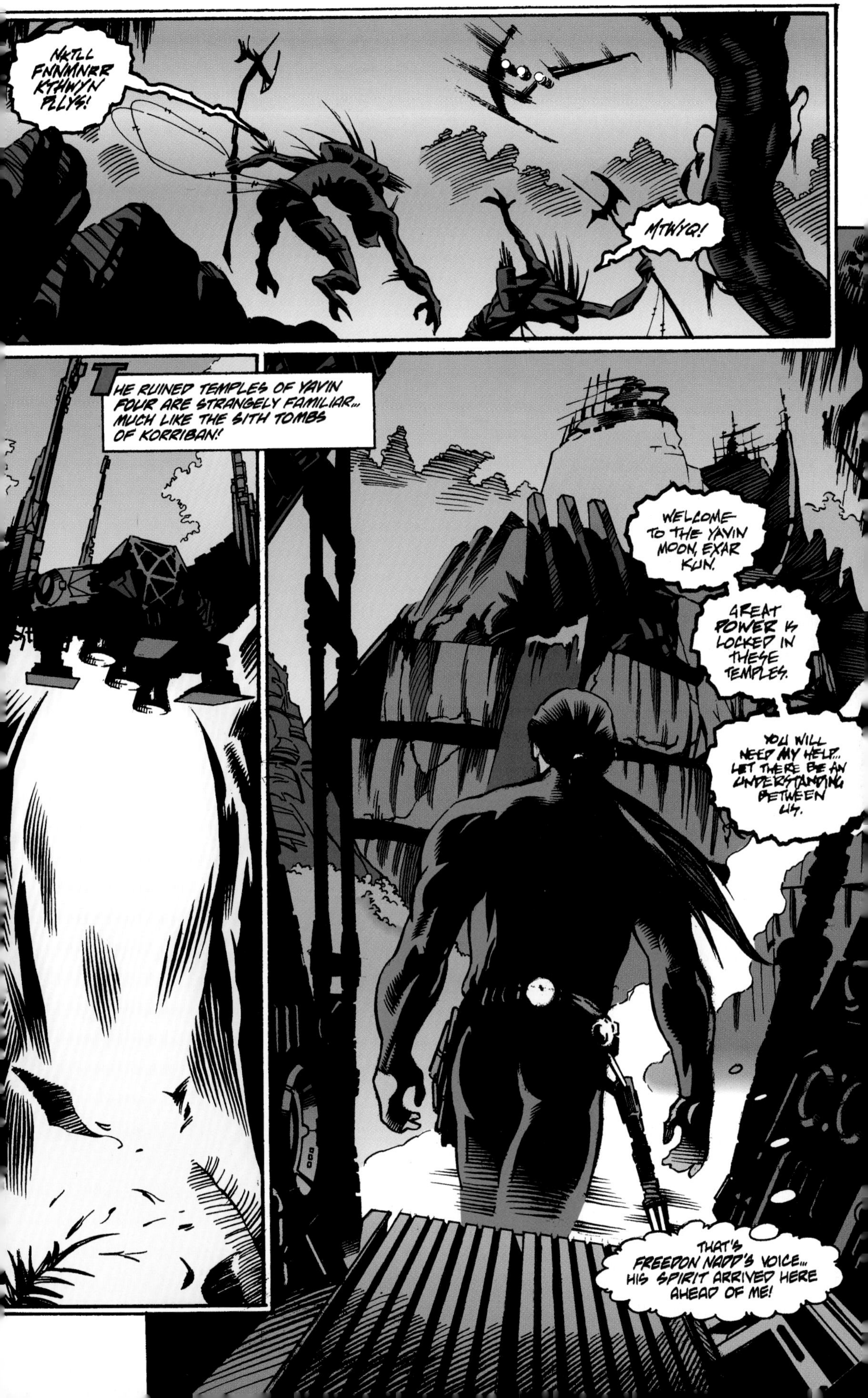
NKTLL FNNMNRR KTHWYN PLLYS!
MTWYQ!
THE RUINED TEMPLES OF YAVIN FOUR ARE STRANGELY FAMILIAR... MUCH LIKE THE SITH TOMBS OF KORRIBAN!
WELCOME TO THE YAVIN MOON, EXAR KUN.
GREAT POWER IS LOCKED IN THESE TEMPLES.
YOU WILL NEED MY HELP... LET THERE BE AN UNDERSTANDING BETWEEN US.
THAT'S FREEDON NADD'S VOICE... HIS SPIRIT ARRIVED HERE AHEAD OF ME!

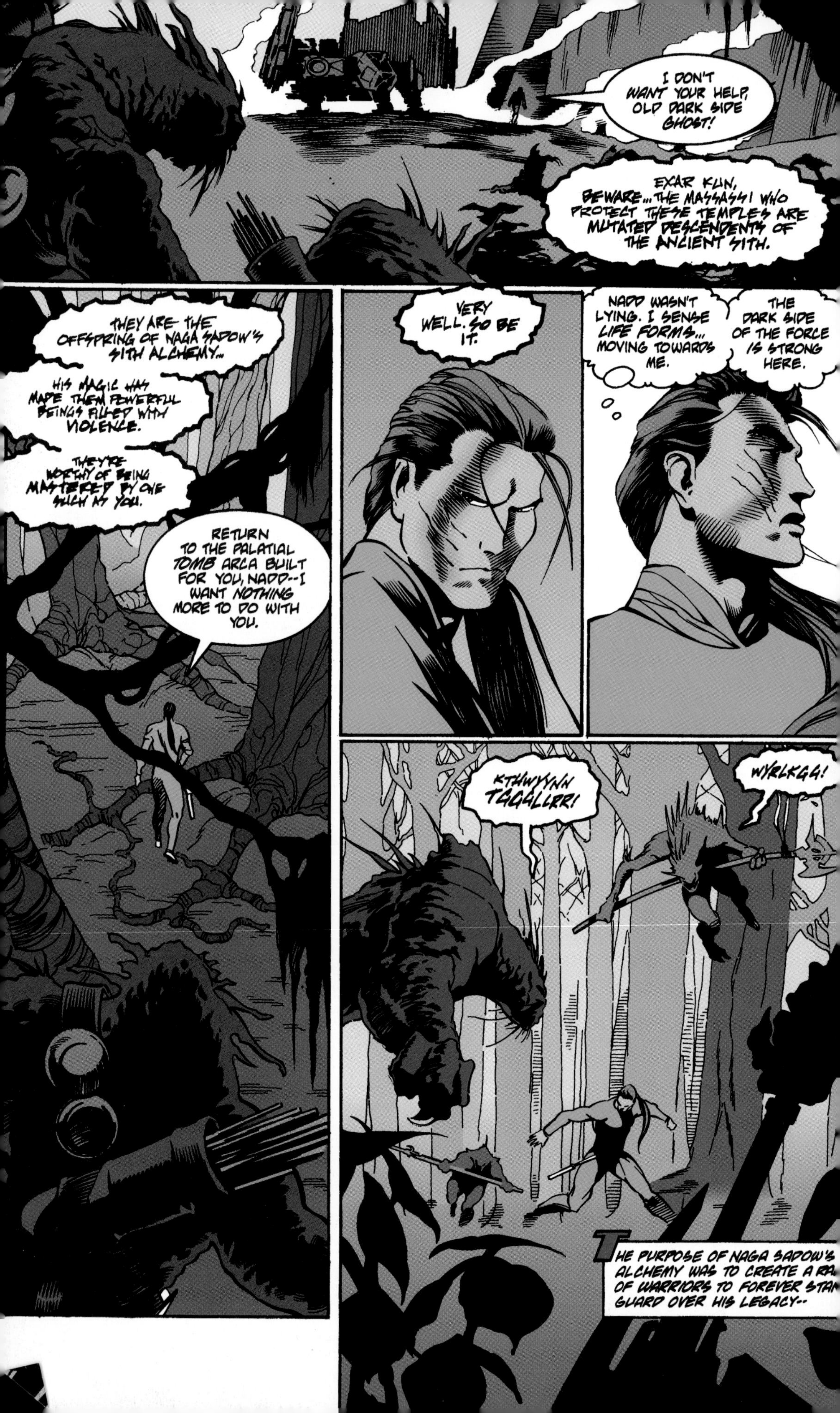
I DON'T WANT YOUR HELP, OLD DARK SIDE GHOST!
EXAR KUN, BEWARE... THE MASSASSI WHO PROTECT THESE TEMPLES ARE MUTATED DESCENDENTS OF THE ANCIENT SITH.
THEY ARE THE OFFSPRING OF NAGA SADOW'S SITH ALCHEMY...
HIS MAGIC HAS MADE THEM POWERFUL BEINGS FILLED WITH VIOLENCE.
THEY'RE WORTHY OF BEING MASTERED BY ONE SUCH AS YOU.
RETURN TO THE PALATIAL TOMB ARCA BUILT FOR YOU, NADD--I WANT NOTHING MORE TO DO WITH YOU.
VERY WELL. SO BE IT.
NADD WASN'T LYING. I SENSE LIFE FORMS... MOVING TOWARDS ME.
THE DARK SIDE OF THE FORCE IS STRONG HERE.
KTHWYYNN TGGGLLRR!
WYRLKGG!
THE PURPOSE OF NAGA SADOW'S ALCHEMY WAS TO CREATE A RA OF WARRIORS TO FOREVER STA GUARD OVER HIS LEGACY--

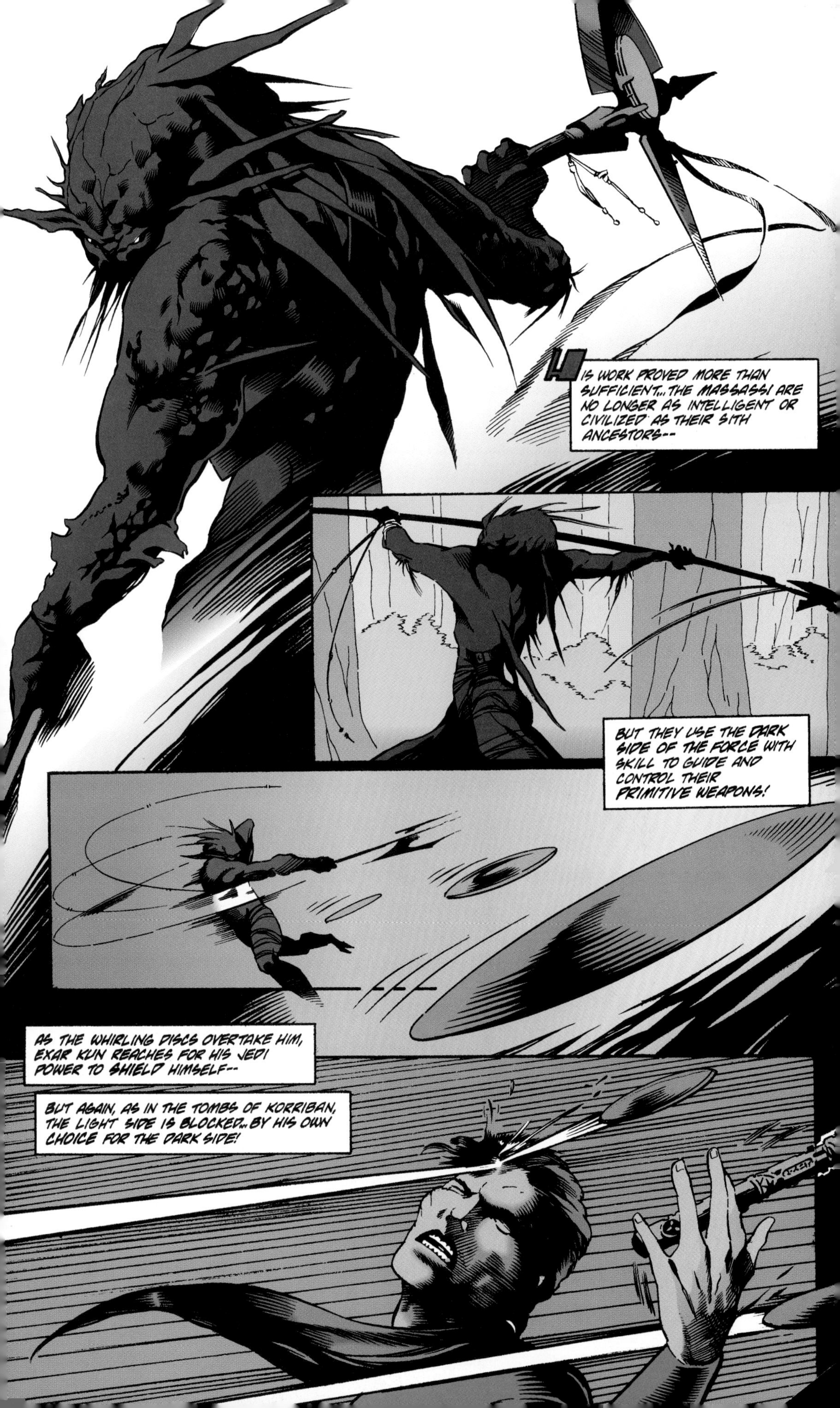
HIS WORK PROVED MORE THAN SUFFICIENT... THE MASSASSI ARE NO LONGER AS INTELLIGENT OR CIVILIZED AS THEIR SITH ANCESTORS--
BUT THEY USE THE DARK SIDE OF THE FORCE WITH SKILL TO GUIDE AND CONTROL THEIR PRIMITIVE WEAPONS!
AS THE WHIRLING DISCS OVERTAKE HIM, EXAR KUN REACHES FOR HIS JEDI POWER TO SHIELD HIMSELF--
BUT AGAIN, AS IN THE TOMBS OF KORRIBAN, THE LIGHT SIDE IS BLOCKED... BY HIS OWN CHOICE FOR THE DARK SIDE!

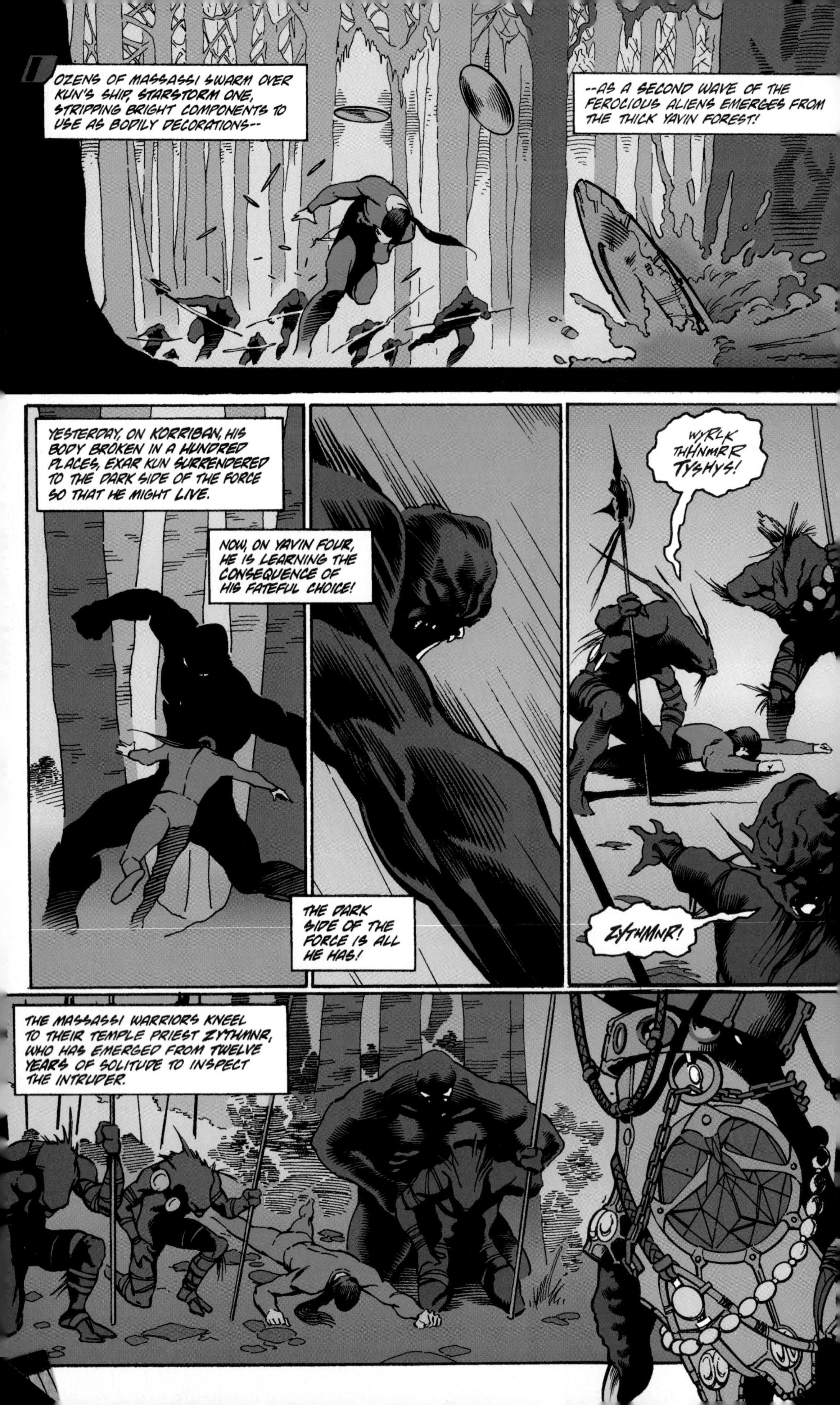
DOZENS OF MASSASSI SWARM OVER KUN'S SHIP, STARSTORM ONE, STRIPPING BRIGHT COMPONENTS TO USE AS BODILY DECORATIONS--
--AS A SECOND WAVE OF THE FEROCIOUS ALIENS EMERGES FROM THE THICK YAVIN FOREST!
YESTERDAY, ON KORRIBAN, HIS BODY BROKEN IN A HUNDRED PLACES, EXAR KUN SURRENDERED TO THE DARK SIDE OF THE FORCE SO THAT HE MIGHT LIVE.
NOW, ON YAVIN FOUR, HE IS LEARNING THE CONSEQUENCE OF HIS FATEFUL CHOICE!
THE DARK SIDE OF THE FORCE IS ALL HE HAS!
WYRLK THHNMRR TYSHYS!
ZYTHMNR!
THE MASSASSI WARRIORS KNEEL TO THEIR TEMPLE PRIEST ZYTHMNR, WHO HAS EMERGED FROM TWELVE YEARS OF SOLITUDE TO INSPECT THE INTRUDER.

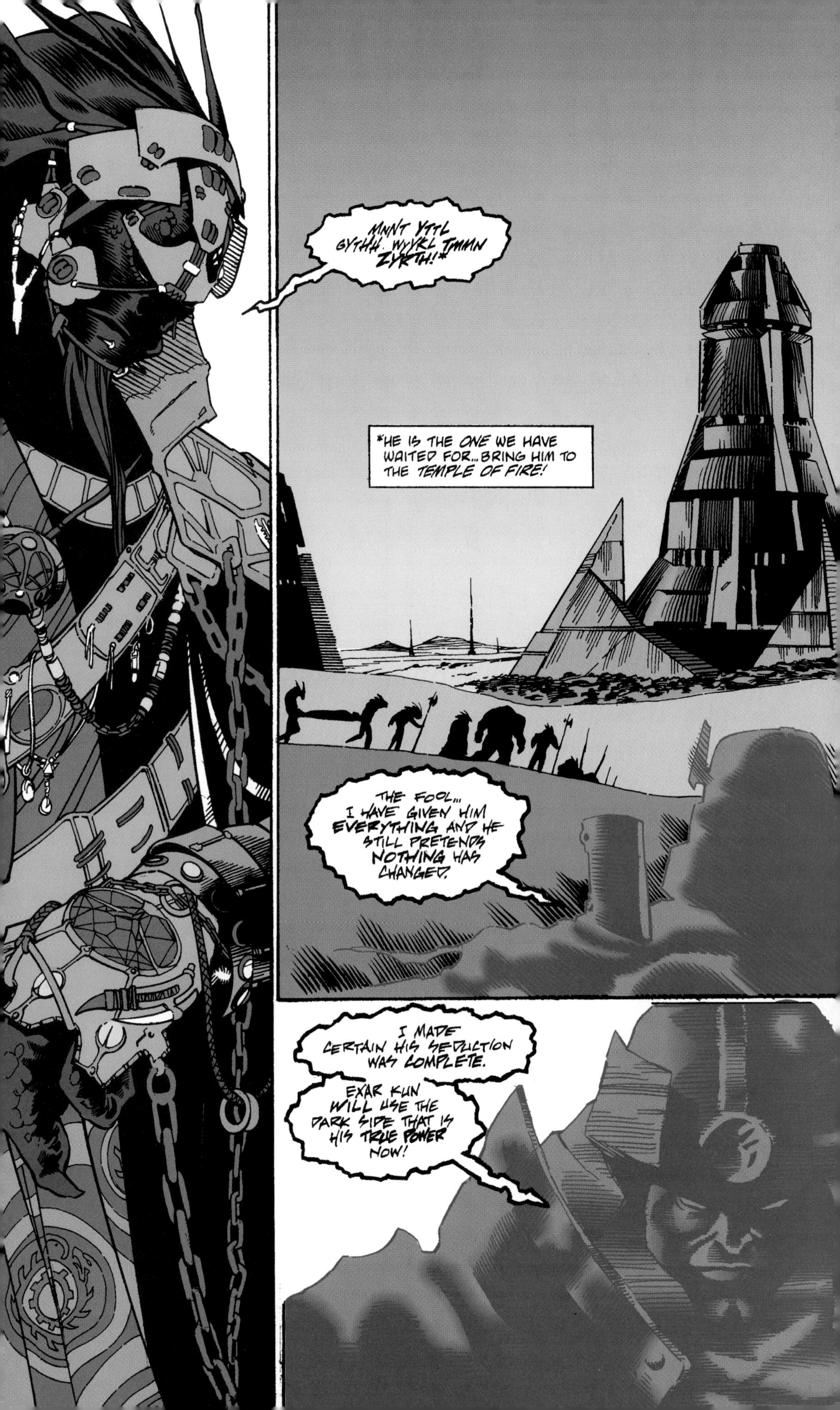
MNNT YTTL GYTHH. WYKL TMMN ZYRTH!*
*HE IS THE ONE WE HAVE WAITED FOR...BRING HIM TO THE TEMPLE OF FIRE!
THE FOOL... I HAVE GIVEN HIM EVERYTHING AND HE STILL PRETENDS NOTHING HAS CHANGED.
I MADE CERTAIN HIS SEDUCTION WAS COMPLETE.
EXAR KUN WILL USE THE DARK SIDE THAT IS HIS TRUE POWER NOW!

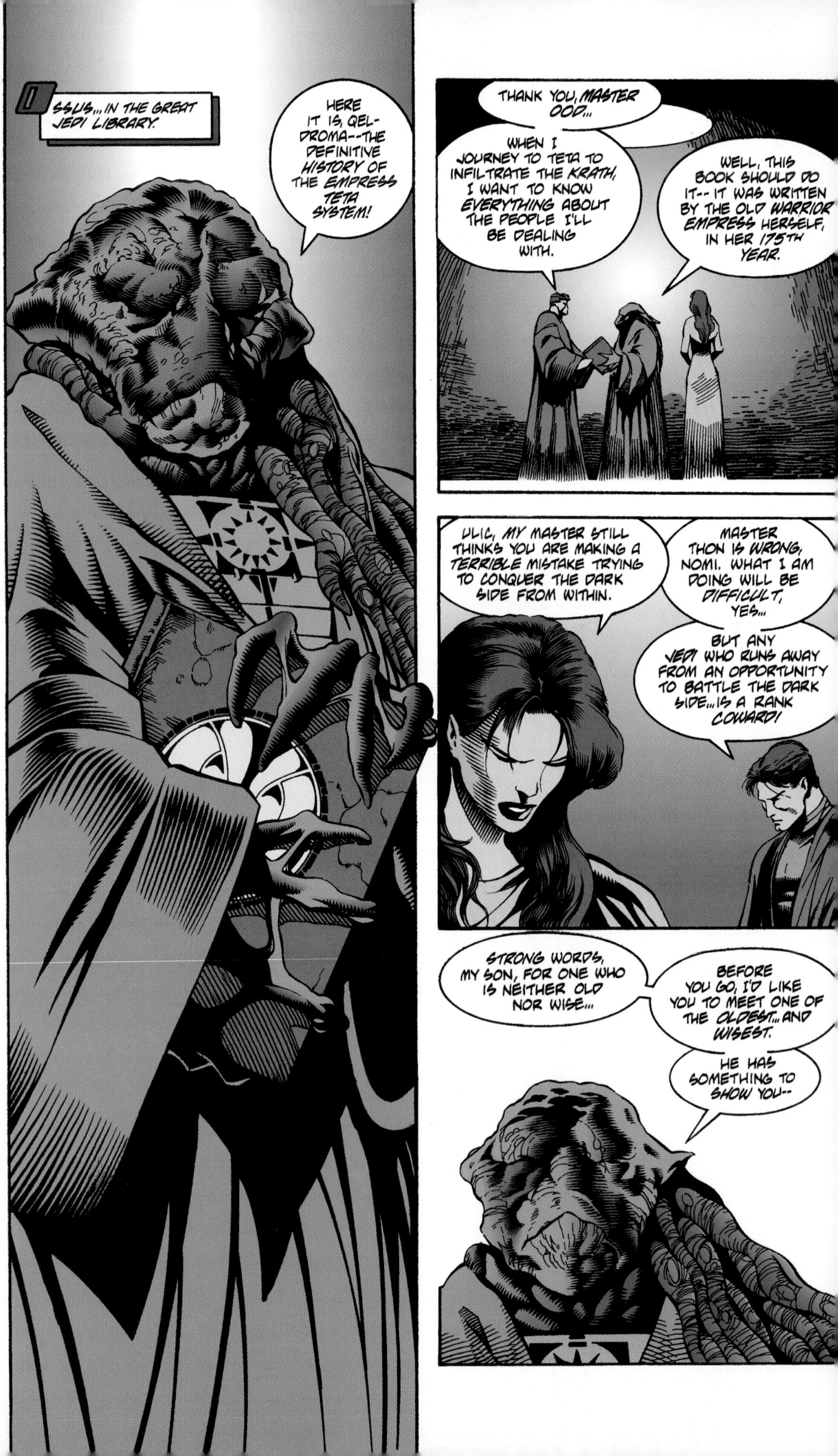
OSSUS... IN THE GREAT JEDI LIBRARY.
HERE IT IS, QEL-DROMA--THE DEFINITIVE HISTORY OF THE EMPRESS TETA SYSTEM!
THANK YOU, MASTER OOD...
WHEN I JOURNEY TO TETA TO INFILTRATE THE KRATH, I WANT TO KNOW EVERYTHING ABOUT THE PEOPLE I'LL BE DEALING WITH.
WELL, THIS BOOK SHOULD DO IT-- IT WAS WRITTEN BY THE OLD WARRIOR EMPRESS HERSELF, IN HER 175TH YEAR.
ULIC, MY MASTER STILL THINKS YOU ARE MAKING A TERRIBLE MISTAKE TRYING TO CONQUER THE DARK SIDE FROM WITHIN.
MASTER THON IS WRONG, NOMI. WHAT I AM DOING WILL BE DIFFICULT, YES...
BUT ANY JEDI WHO RUNS AWAY FROM AN OPPORTUNITY TO BATTLE THE DARK SIDE... IS A RANK COWARD!
STRONG WORDS, MY SON, FOR ONE WHO IS NEITHER OLD NOR WISE...
BEFORE YOU GO, I'D LIKE YOU TO MEET ONE OF THE OLDEST... AND WISEST.
HE HAS SOMETHING TO SHOW YOU--

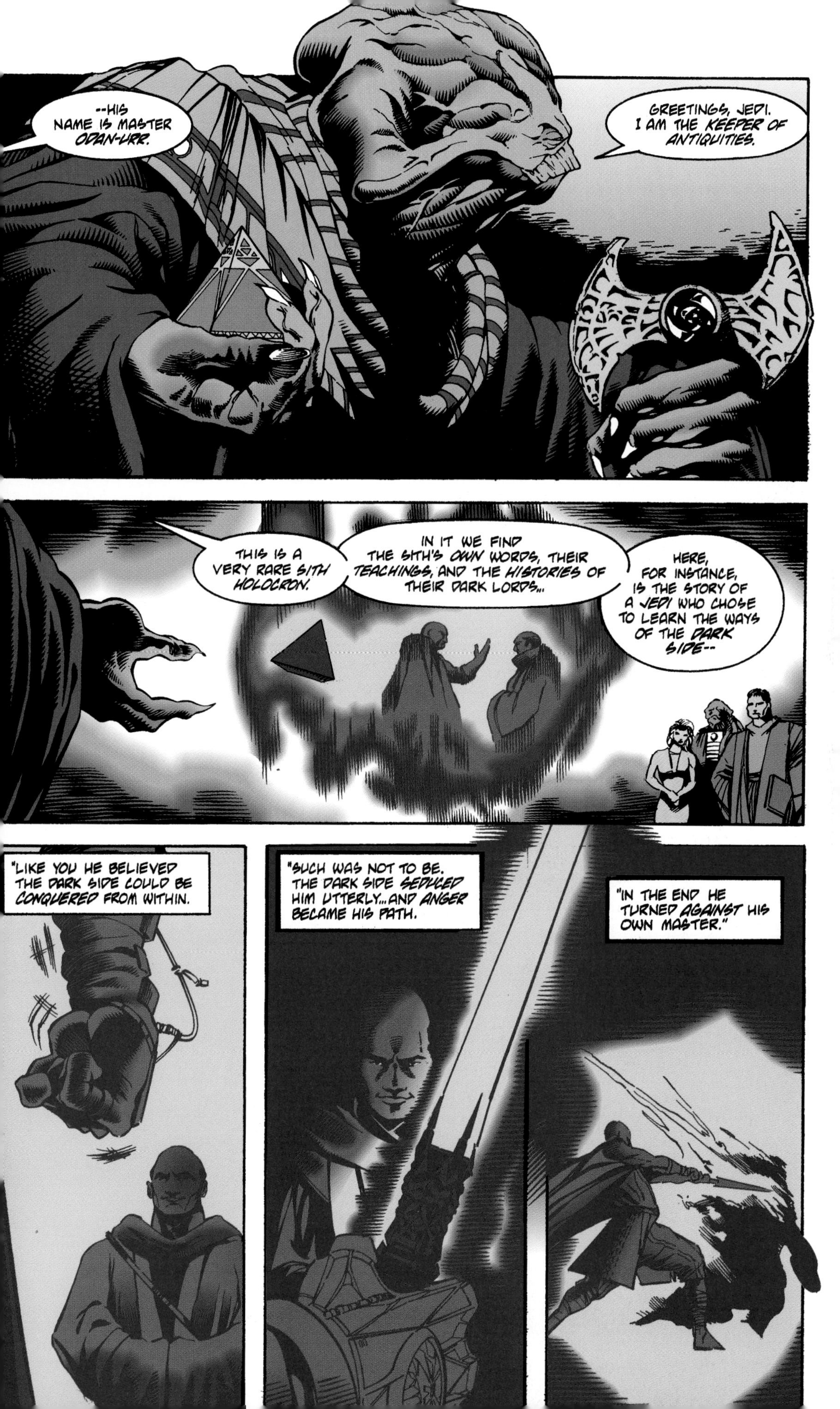
--HIS NAME IS MASTER *ODAN-URR.*
GREETINGS, JEDI. I AM THE *KEEPER OF ANTIQUITIES.*
THIS IS A VERY RARE SITH *HOLOCRON.*
IN IT WE FIND THE SITH'S *OWN* WORDS, THEIR *TEACHINGS*, AND THE *HISTORIES* OF THEIR DARK LORDS...
HERE, FOR INSTANCE, IS THE STORY OF A *JEDI* WHO CHOSE TO LEARN THE WAYS OF THE *DARK SIDE*--
"LIKE YOU HE BELIEVED THE DARK SIDE COULD BE *CONQUERED* FROM WITHIN.
"SUCH WAS NOT TO BE. THE DARK SIDE *SEDUCED* HIM UTTERLY...AND *ANGER* BECAME HIS PATH.
"IN THE END HE TURNED *AGAINST* HIS OWN MASTER."

ULIC IS STUNNED BY THE IMAGES OF A JEDI KNIGHT MURDERING HIS OWN TEACHER...
WHY DO YOU SHOW ME THIS--WHAT DOES IT HAVE TO DO WITH ME?
IS THIS HOW YOU DEMONSTRATE YOUR DISAPPROVAL OF MY CHOICE?
I NEED YOUR UNDERSTANDING, NOT YOUR DISAPPROVAL.
BECAUSE OF MY FAILURE, MY MASTER DIED AT THE HANDS OF THE EVIL KRATH.
ARCA WAS A VERY GREAT JEDI. IF SUCH BEGINNING MAGICIANS COULD KILL HIM, WHAT WILL THEY DO TO THE REST OF US--
WHAT WILL THEY DO TO YOU?
ULIC...MASTER ODAN-URR WANTS TO WARN YOU...ABOUT THE DARK SIDE OF THE FORCE.
NOMI, CAN'T YOU SEE... SOMEONE HAS TO PREVENT THIS EVIL FROM INFECTING THE GALAXY AS IT DID IN ANCIENT TIMES!
THESE MASTERS PREFER TO DO NOTHING!
YOU ARE A DETERMINED YOUNG MAN--
MAY THE FORCE BE WITH YOU.
THE JEDI MASTERS HAVE OFFERED THEIR WISDOM. THE REST IS UP TO YOU.
NOW GO.

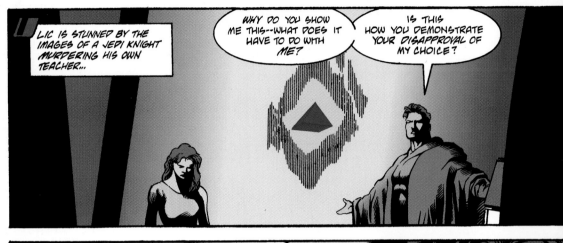

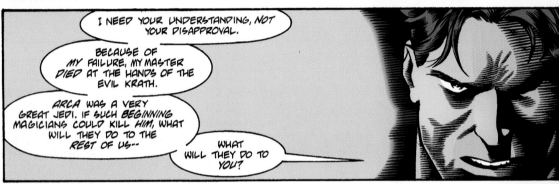

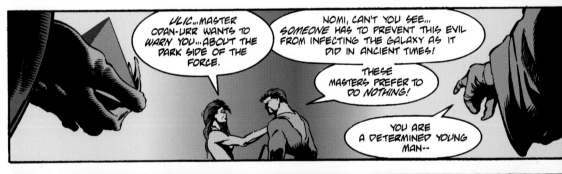

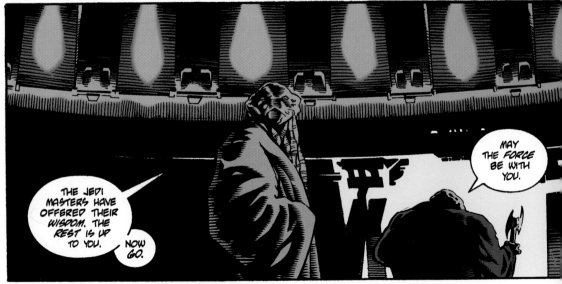

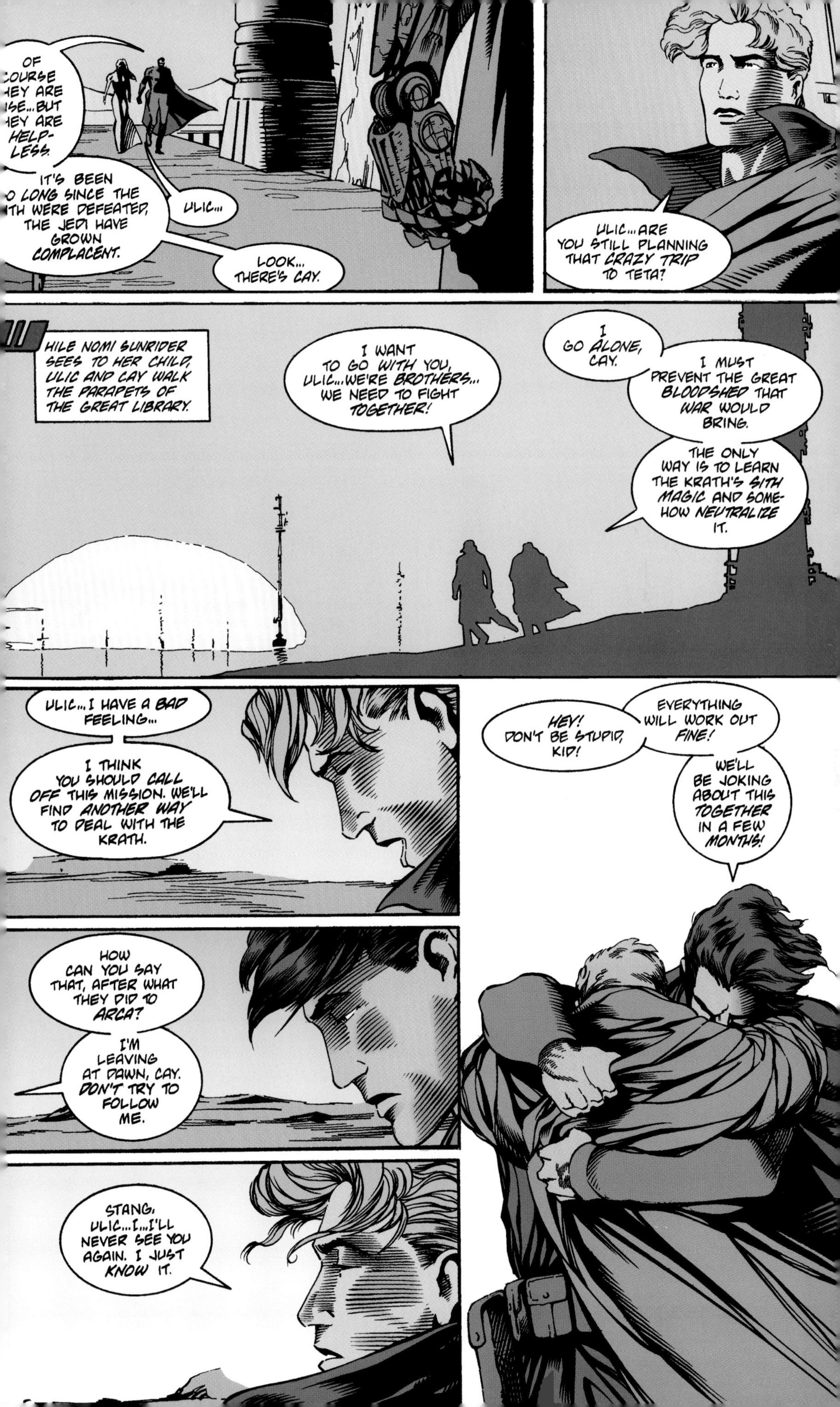
OF COURSE HEY ARE ISE...BUT HEY ARE HELP-LESS.
IT'S BEEN O LONG SINCE THE ITH WERE DEFEATED, THE JEDI HAVE GROWN COMPLACENT.
ULIC...
LOOK... THERE'S CAY.
ULIC...ARE YOU STILL PLANNING THAT CRAZY TRIP TO TETA?
HILE NOMI SUNRIDER SEES TO HER CHILD, ULIC AND CAY WALK THE PARAPETS OF THE GREAT LIBRARY.
I WANT TO GO WITH YOU, ULIC...WE'RE BROTHERS... WE NEED TO FIGHT TOGETHER!
I GO ALONE, CAY.
I MUST PREVENT THE GREAT BLOODSHED THAT WAR WOULD BRING.
THE ONLY WAY IS TO LEARN THE KRATH'S SITH MAGIC AND SOME-HOW NEUTRALIZE IT.
ULIC...I HAVE A BAD FEELING...
I THINK YOU SHOULD CALL OFF THIS MISSION. WE'LL FIND ANOTHER WAY TO DEAL WITH THE KRATH.
HOW CAN YOU SAY THAT, AFTER WHAT THEY DID TO ARCA?
I'M LEAVING AT DAWN, CAY. DON'T TRY TO FOLLOW ME.
STANG, ULIC...I...I'LL NEVER SEE YOU AGAIN. I JUST KNOW IT.
HEY! DON'T BE STUPID, KID!
EVERYTHING WILL WORK OUT FINE!
WE'LL BE JOKING ABOUT THIS TOGETHER IN A FEW MONTHS!

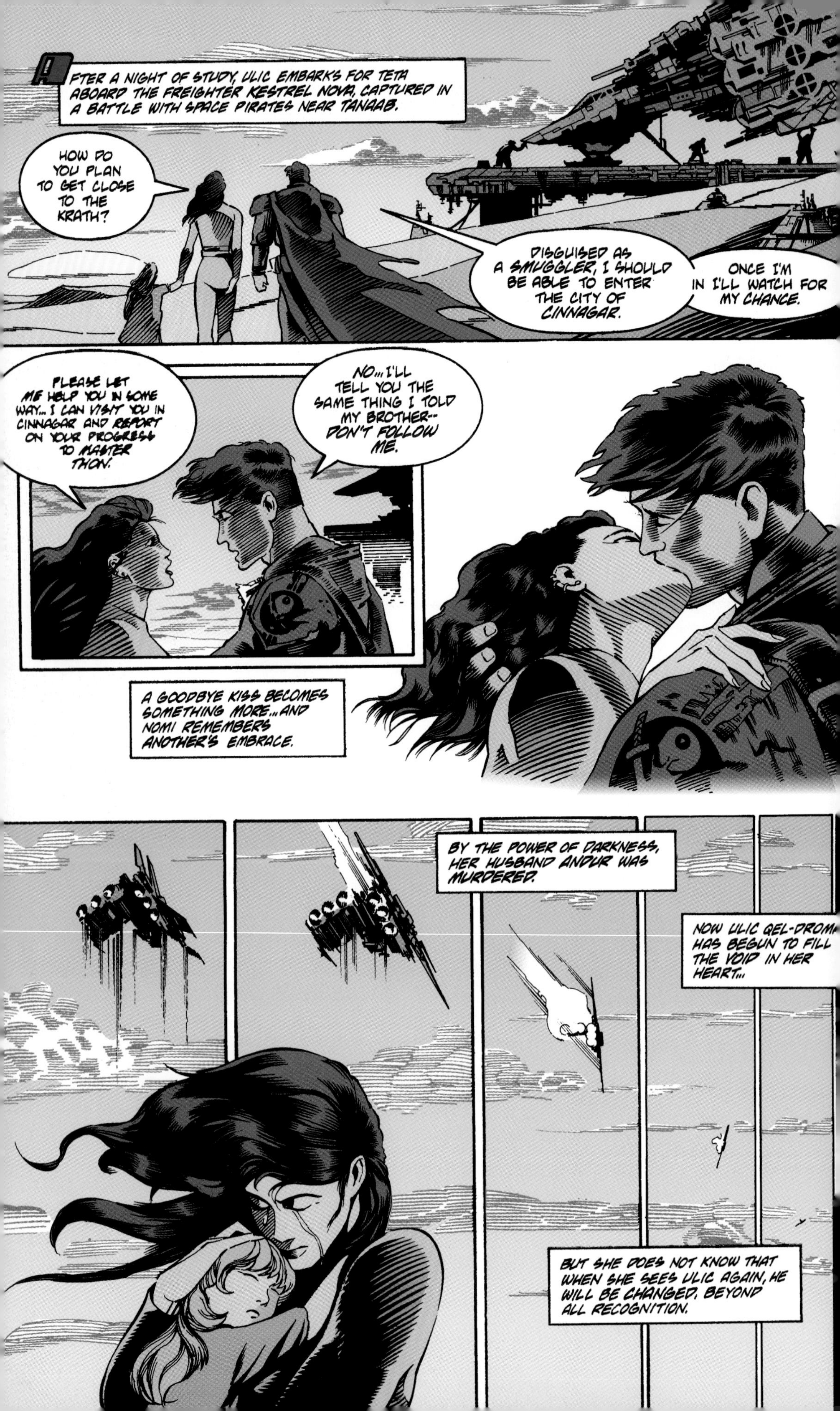
AFTER A NIGHT OF STUDY, ULIC EMBARKS FOR TETA ABOARD THE FREIGHTER KESTREL NOVA, CAPTURED IN A BATTLE WITH SPACE PIRATES NEAR TANAAB.
HOW DO YOU PLAN TO GET CLOSE TO THE KRATH?
DISGUISED AS A SMUGGLER, I SHOULD BE ABLE TO ENTER THE CITY OF CINNAGAR.
ONCE I'M IN I'LL WATCH FOR MY CHANCE.
PLEASE LET ME HELP YOU IN SOME WAY... I CAN VISIT YOU IN CINNAGAR AND REPORT ON YOUR PROGRESS TO MASTER THON.
NO... I'LL TELL YOU THE SAME THING I TOLD MY BROTHER-- DON'T FOLLOW ME.
A GOODBYE KISS BECOMES SOMETHING MORE... AND NOMI REMEMBERS ANOTHER'S EMBRACE.
BY THE POWER OF DARKNESS, HER HUSBAND ANDUR WAS MURDERED.
NOW ULIC QEL-DROMA HAS BEGUN TO FILL THE VOID IN HER HEART...
BUT SHE DOES NOT KNOW THAT WHEN SHE SEES ULIC AGAIN, HE WILL BE CHANGED, BEYOND ALL RECOGNITION.

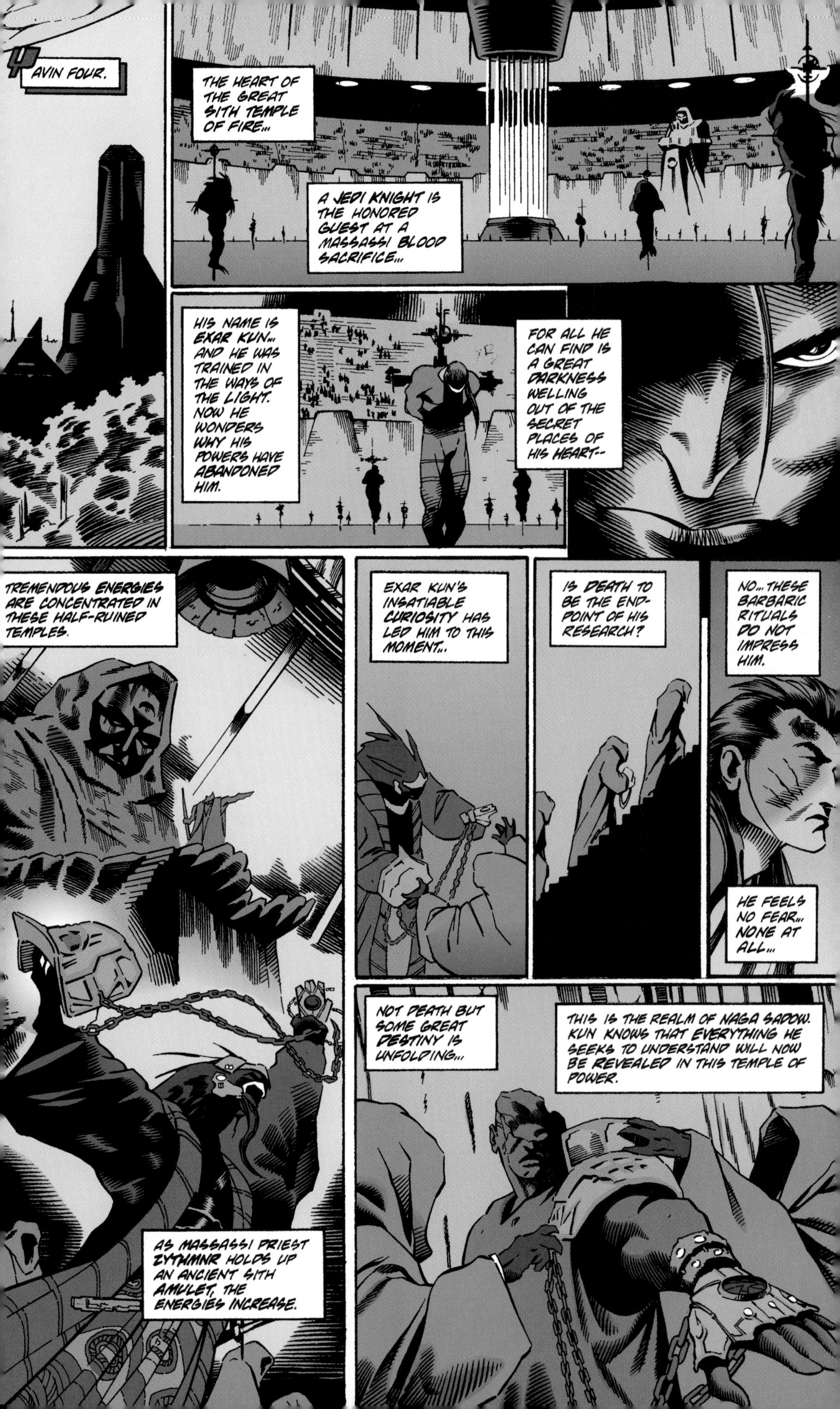
4
AVIN FOUR.
THE HEART OF THE GREAT SITH TEMPLE OF FIRE...
A JEDI KNIGHT IS THE HONORED GUEST AT A MASSASSI BLOOD SACRIFICE...
HIS NAME IS EXAR KUN... AND HE WAS TRAINED IN THE WAYS OF THE LIGHT. NOW HE WONDERS WHY HIS POWERS HAVE ABANDONED HIM.
FOR ALL HE CAN FIND IS A GREAT DARKNESS WELLING OUT OF THE SECRET PLACES OF HIS HEART--
TREMENDOUS ENERGIES ARE CONCENTRATED IN THESE HALF-RUINED TEMPLES.
AS MASSASSI PRIEST ZYTHMNR HOLDS UP AN ANCIENT SITH AMULET, THE ENERGIES INCREASE.
EXAR KUN'S INSATIABLE CURIOSITY HAS LED HIM TO THIS MOMENT...
IS DEATH TO BE THE END-POINT OF HIS RESEARCH?
NO... THESE BARBARIC RITUALS DO NOT IMPRESS HIM.
HE FEELS NO FEAR... NONE AT ALL...
NOT DEATH BUT SOME GREAT DESTINY IS UNFOLDING...
THIS IS THE REALM OF NAGA SADOW. KUN KNOWS THAT EVERYTHING HE SEEKS TO UNDERSTAND WILL NOW BE REVEALED IN THIS TEMPLE OF POWER.

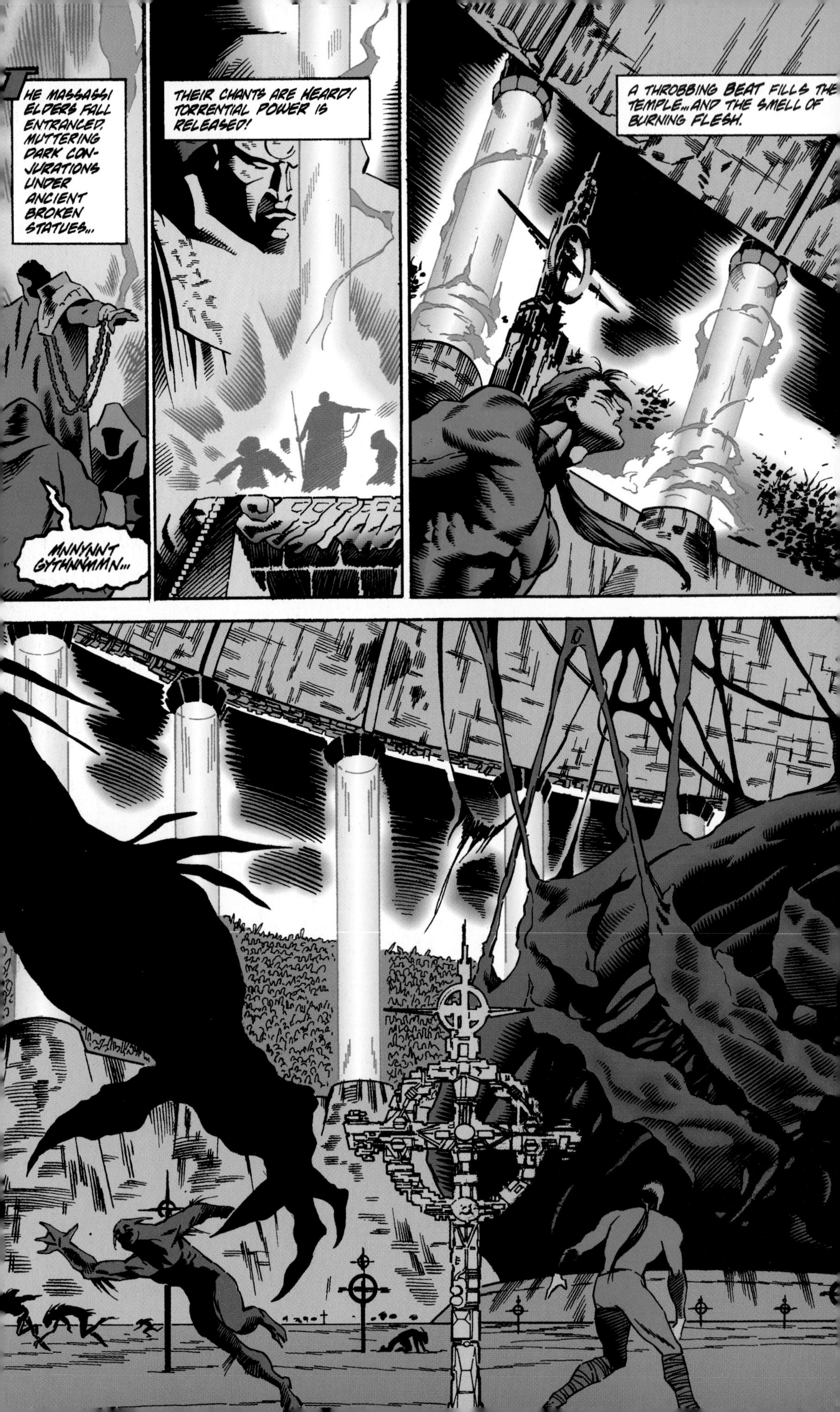
THE MASSASSI ELDERS FALL ENTRANCED, MUTTERING DARK CON-JURATIONS UNDER ANCIENT BROKEN STATUES...
MNNYNNT GYTHNNMMN...
THEIR CHANTS ARE HEARD! TORRENTIAL POWER IS RELEASED!
A THROBBING BEAT FILLS THE TEMPLE...AND THE SMELL OF BURNING FLESH.

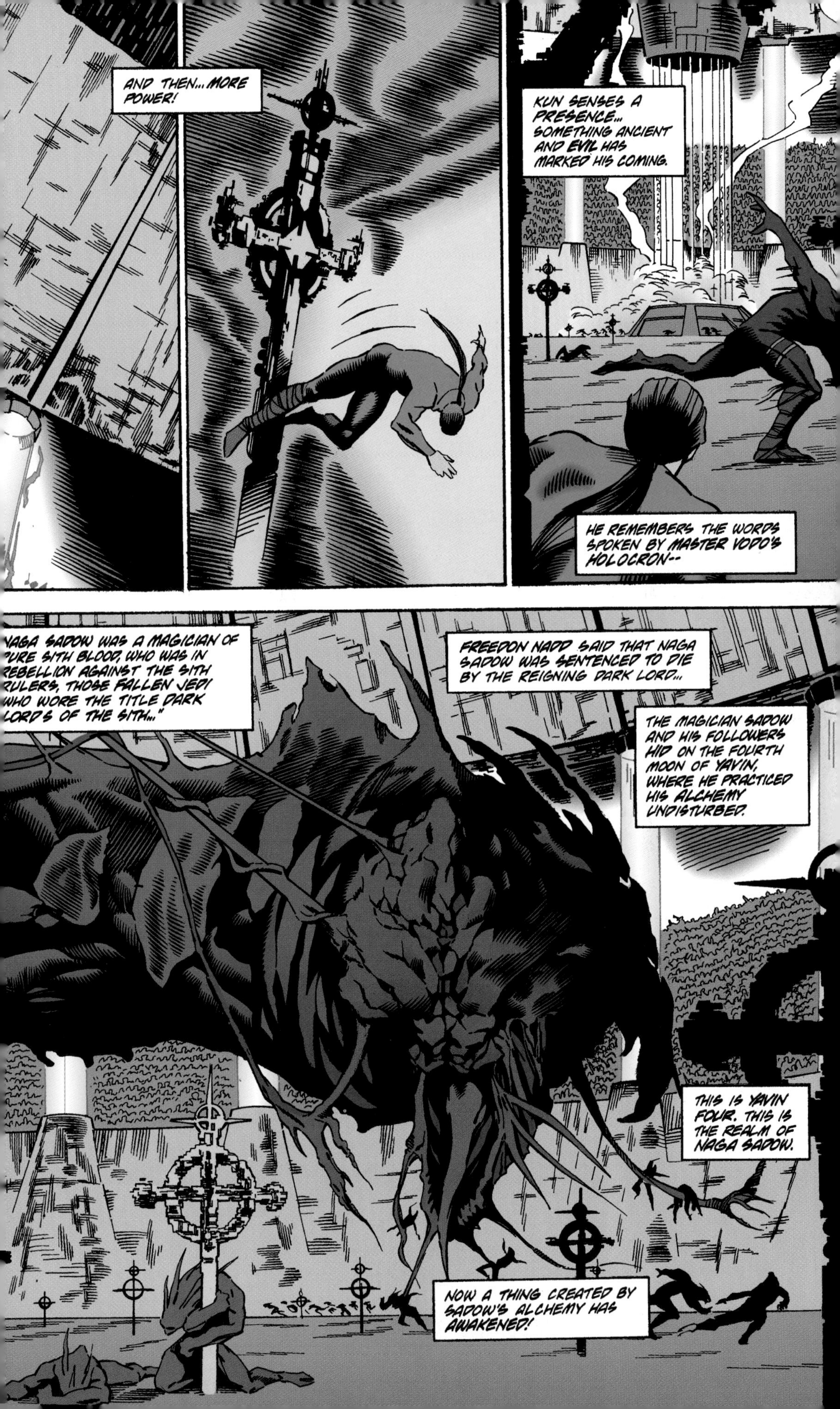
AND THEN... MORE POWER!
KUN SENSES A PRESENCE... SOMETHING ANCIENT AND EVIL HAS MARKED HIS COMING.
HE REMEMBERS THE WORDS SPOKEN BY MASTER VODO'S HOLOCRON--
NAGA SADOW WAS A MAGICIAN OF PURE SITH BLOOD, WHO WAS IN REBELLION AGAINST THE SITH RULERS, THOSE FALLEN JEDI WHO WORE THE TITLE DARK LORDS OF THE SITH..."
FREEDON NADD SAID THAT NAGA SADOW WAS SENTENCED TO DIE BY THE REIGNING DARK LORD...
THE MAGICIAN SADOW AND HIS FOLLOWERS HID ON THE FOURTH MOON OF YAVIN, WHERE HE PRACTICED HIS ALCHEMY UNDISTURBED.
THIS IS YAVIN FOUR. THIS IS THE REALM OF NAGA SADOW.
NOW A THING CREATED BY SADOW'S ALCHEMY HAS AWAKENED!

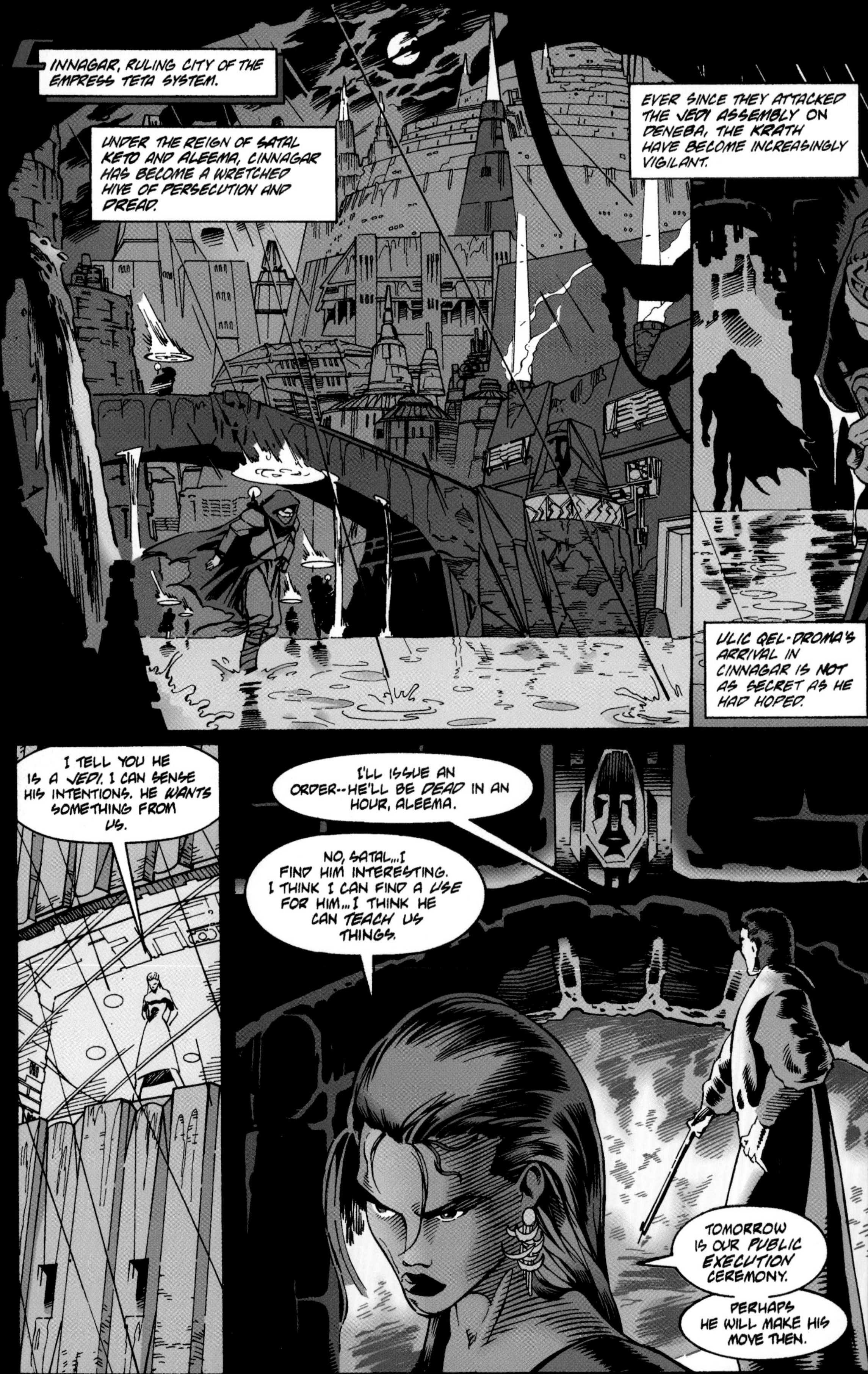
CINNAGAR, RULING CITY OF THE EMPRESS TETA SYSTEM.
UNDER THE REIGN OF SATAL KETO AND ALEEMA, CINNAGAR HAS BECOME A WRETCHED HIVE OF PERSECUTION AND DREAD.
EVER SINCE THEY ATTACKED THE JEDI ASSEMBLY ON DENEBA, THE KRATH HAVE BECOME INCREASINGLY VIGILANT.
ULIC QEL-DROMA'S ARRIVAL IN CINNAGAR IS NOT AS SECRET AS HE HAD HOPED.
I TELL YOU HE IS A JEDI. I CAN SENSE HIS INTENTIONS. HE WANTS SOMETHING FROM US.
I'LL ISSUE AN ORDER--HE'LL BE DEAD IN AN HOUR, ALEEMA.
NO, SATAL...I FIND HIM INTERESTING. I THINK I CAN FIND A USE FOR HIM...I THINK HE CAN TEACH US THINGS.
TOMORROW IS OUR PUBLIC EXECUTION CEREMONY.
PERHAPS HE WILL MAKE HIS MOVE THEN.

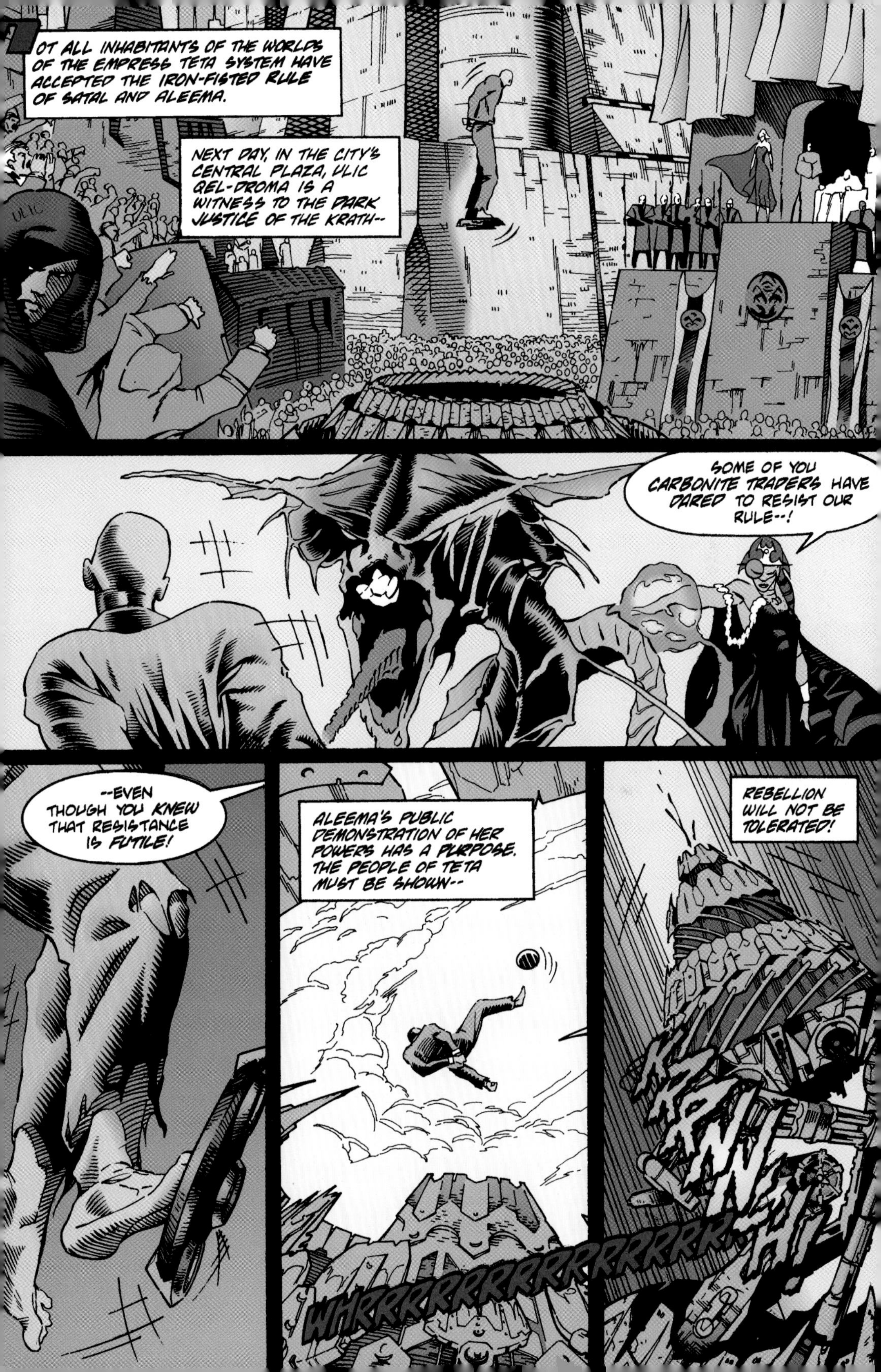
NOT ALL INHABITANTS OF THE WORLDS OF THE EMPRESS TETA SYSTEM HAVE ACCEPTED THE IRON-FISTED RULE OF SATAL AND ALEEMA.
NEXT DAY, IN THE CITY'S CENTRAL PLAZA, ULIC QEL-DROMA IS A WITNESS TO THE DARK JUSTICE OF THE KRATH--
ULIC
SOME OF YOU CARBONITE TRADERS HAVE DARED TO RESIST OUR RULE--!
--EVEN THOUGH YOU KNEW THAT RESISTANCE IS FUTILE!
ALEEMA'S PUBLIC DEMONSTRATION OF HER POWERS HAS A PURPOSE. THE PEOPLE OF TETA MUST BE SHOWN--
REBELLION WILL NOT BE TOLERATED!

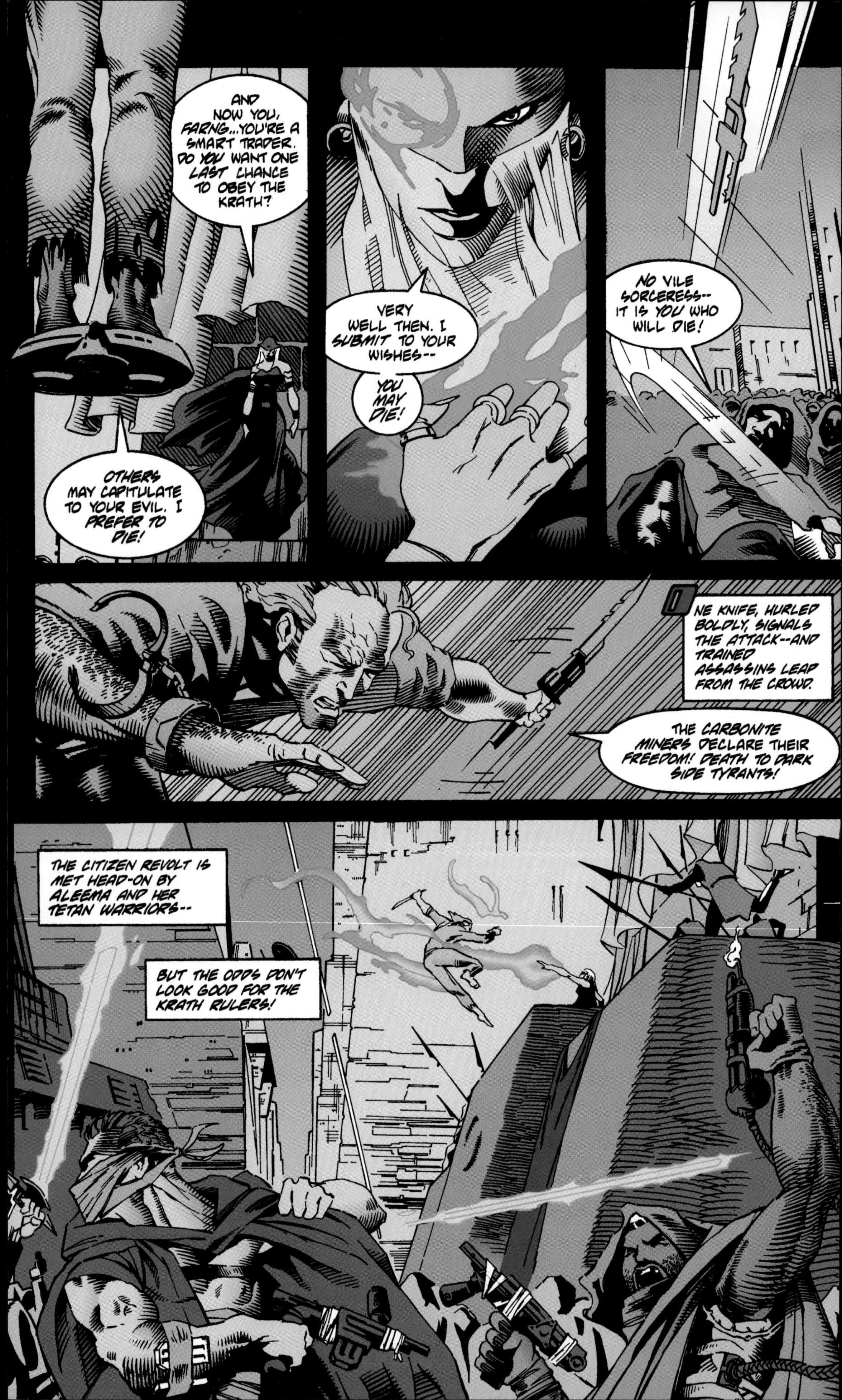
AND NOW YOU, FARNG...YOU'RE A SMART TRADER. DO YOU WANT ONE LAST CHANCE TO OBEY THE KRATH?
OTHERS MAY CAPITULATE TO YOUR EVIL. I PREFER TO DIE!
VERY WELL THEN. I SUBMIT TO YOUR WISHES--
YOU MAY DIE!
NO VILE SORCERESS-- IT IS YOU WHO WILL DIE!
ONE KNIFE, HURLED BOLDLY, SIGNALS THE ATTACK--AND TRAINED ASSASSINS LEAP FROM THE CROWD.
THE CARBONITE MINERS DECLARE THEIR FREEDOM! DEATH TO DARK SIDE TYRANTS!
THE CITIZEN REVOLT IS MET HEAD-ON BY ALEEMA AND HER TETAN WARRIORS--
BUT THE ODDS DON'T LOOK GOOD FOR THE KRATH RULERS!

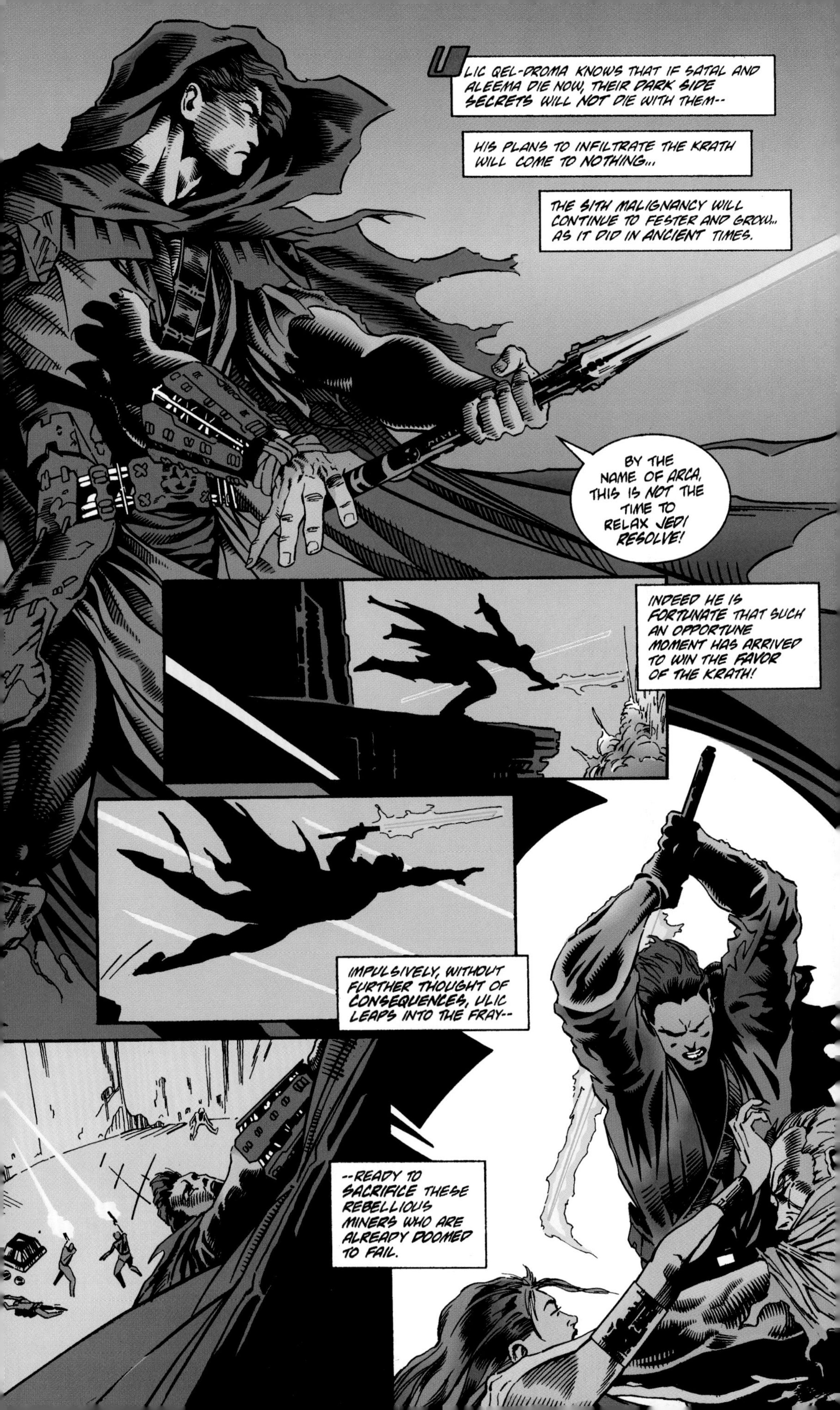
ULIC QEL-DROMA KNOWS THAT IF SATAL AND ALEEMA DIE NOW, THEIR DARK SIDE SECRETS WILL NOT DIE WITH THEM--
HIS PLANS TO INFILTRATE THE KRATH WILL COME TO NOTHING...
THE SITH MALIGNANCY WILL CONTINUE TO FESTER AND GROW... AS IT DID IN ANCIENT TIMES.
BY THE NAME OF ARCA, THIS IS NOT THE TIME TO RELAX JEDI RESOLVE!
INDEED HE IS FORTUNATE THAT SUCH AN OPPORTUNE MOMENT HAS ARRIVED TO WIN THE FAVOR OF THE KRATH!
IMPULSIVELY, WITHOUT FURTHER THOUGHT OF CONSEQUENCES, ULIC LEAPS INTO THE FRAY--
--READY TO SACRIFICE THESE REBELLIOUS MINERS WHO ARE ALREADY DOOMED TO FAIL.

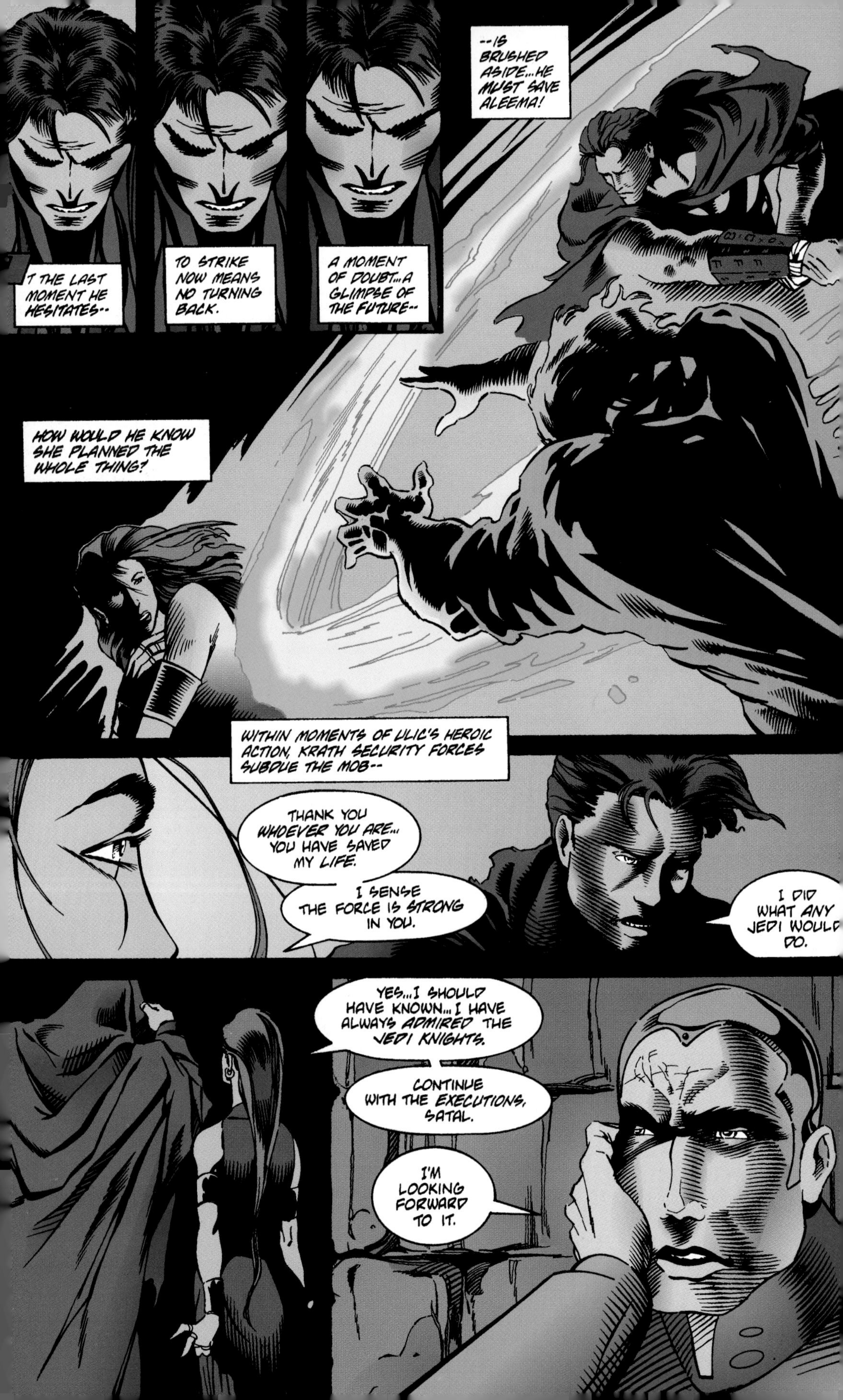

T THE LAST MOMENT HE HESITATES--
TO STRIKE NOW MEANS NO TURNING BACK.
A MOMENT OF DOUBT...A GLIMPSE OF THE FUTURE--
--IS BRUSHED ASIDE...HE MUST SAVE ALEEMA!
HOW WOULD HE KNOW SHE PLANNED THE WHOLE THING?
WITHIN MOMENTS OF ULIC'S HEROIC ACTION, KRATH SECURITY FORCES SUBDUE THE MOB--
THANK YOU WHOEVER YOU ARE... YOU HAVE SAVED MY LIFE.
I SENSE THE FORCE IS STRONG IN YOU.
I DID WHAT ANY JEDI WOULD DO.
YES...I SHOULD HAVE KNOWN...I HAVE ALWAYS ADMIRED THE JEDI KNIGHTS.
CONTINUE WITH THE EXECUTIONS, SATAL.
I'M LOOKING FORWARD TO IT.

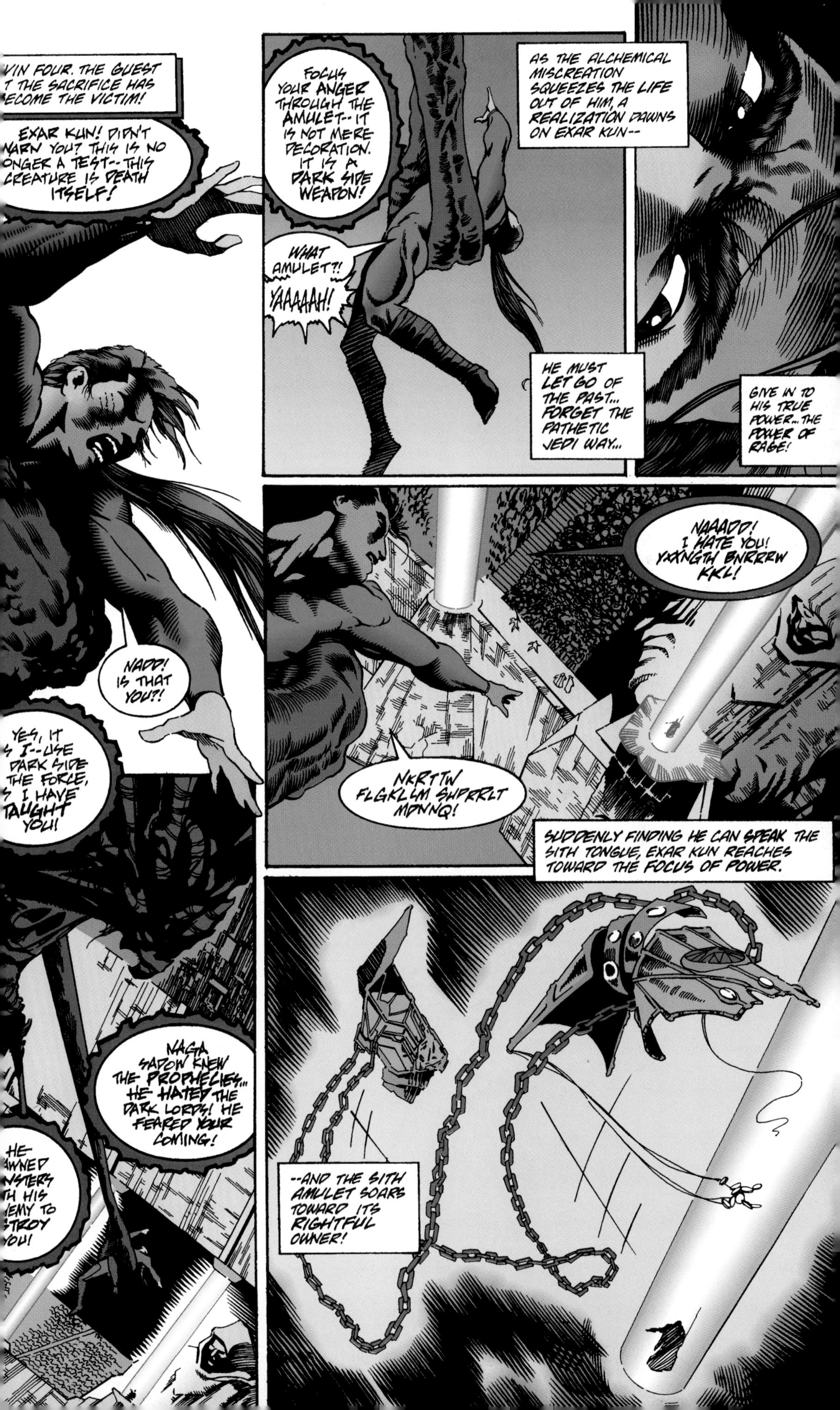

VIN FOUR. THE GUEST T THE SACRIFICE HAS ECOME THE VICTIM!
EXAR KUN! DIDN'T NARN YOU? THIS IS NO ONGER A TEST-- THIS CREATURE IS DEATH ITSELF!
FOCUS YOUR ANGER THROUGH THE AMULET-- IT IS NOT MERE DECORATION. IT IS A DARK SIDE WEAPON!
WHAT AMULET?!
YAAAAAH!
AS THE ALCHEMICAL MISCREATION SQUEEZES THE LIFE OUT OF HIM, A REALIZATION DAWNS ON EXAR KUN--
HE MUST LET GO OF THE PAST... FORGET THE PATHETIC JEDI WAY...
GIVE IN TO HIS TRUE POWER... THE POWER OF RAGE!
NADD! IS THAT YOU?!
YES, IT S I--USE DARK SIDE THE FORCE, S I HAVE TAUGHT YOU!
NAAADD! I HATE YOU! YXXNGTH BNRRRW KKL!
NKRTTW FLGKLLM SHPRRLT MDNNQ!
SUDDENLY FINDING HE CAN SPEAK THE SITH TONGUE, EXAR KUN REACHES TOWARD THE FOCUS OF POWER.
NAGA SADOW KNEW THE PROPHECIES... HE HATED THE DARK LORDS! HE FEARED YOUR COMING!
HE- AWNED NSTERS TH HIS EMY TO STROY YOU!
--AND THE SITH AMULET SOARS TOWARD ITS RIGHTFUL OWNER!

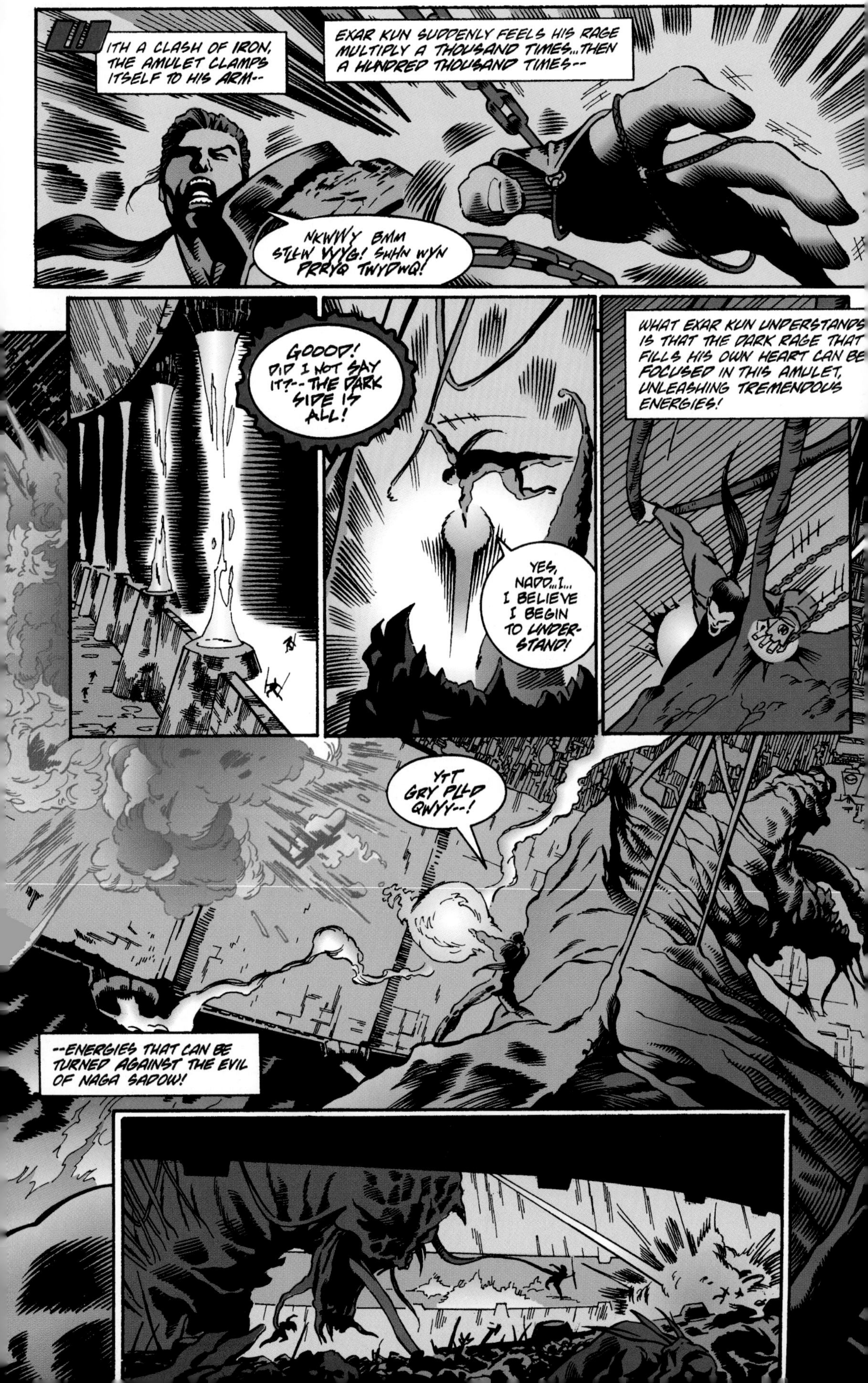

ITH A CLASH OF IRON, THE AMULET CLAMPS ITSELF TO HIS ARM--
EXAR KUN SUDDENLY FEELS HIS RAGE MULTIPLY A THOUSAND TIMES...THEN A HUNDRED THOUSAND TIMES--
NKWWY BMM STLLW VYYG! SHHN WYN PRRYQ TWYDWQ!
GOOOD! DID I NOT SAY IT?--THE DARK SIDE IS ALL!
YES, NADD...I... I BELIEVE I BEGIN TO UNDERSTAND!
WHAT EXAR KUN UNDERSTANDS IS THAT THE DARK RAGE THAT FILLS HIS OWN HEART CAN BE FOCUSED IN THIS AMULET, UNLEASHING TREMENDOUS ENERGIES!
YTT GRY PLLD QWYY--!
--ENERGIES THAT CAN BE TURNED AGAINST THE EVIL OF NAGA SADOW!

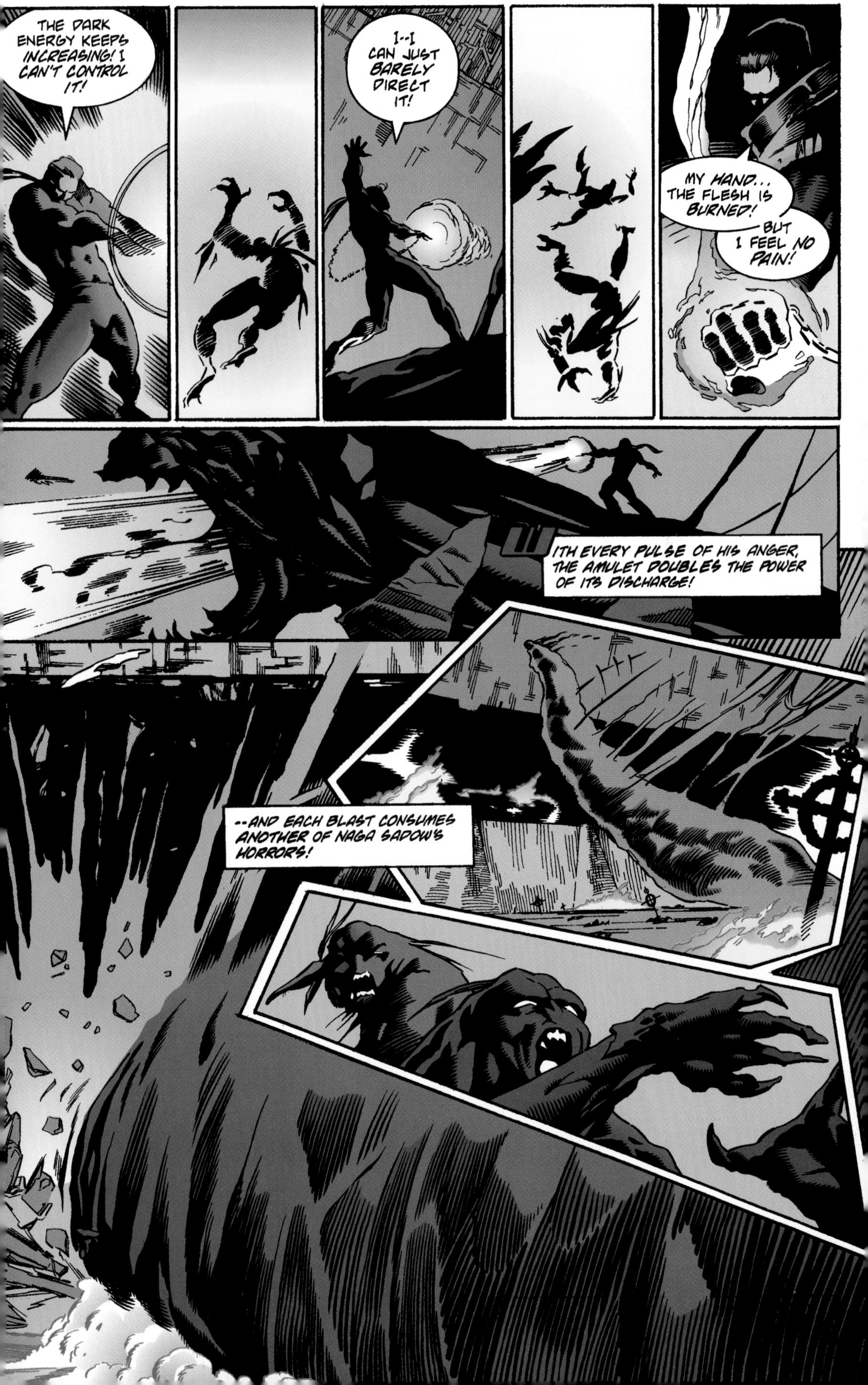
THE DARK ENERGY KEEPS INCREASING! I CAN'T CONTROL IT!
I--I CAN JUST BARELY DIRECT IT!
MY HAND... THE FLESH IS BURNED!
BUT I FEEL NO PAIN!
ITH EVERY PULSE OF HIS ANGER, THE AMULET DOUBLES THE POWER OF ITS DISCHARGE!
--AND EACH BLAST CONSUMES ANOTHER OF NAGA SADOW'S HORRORS!

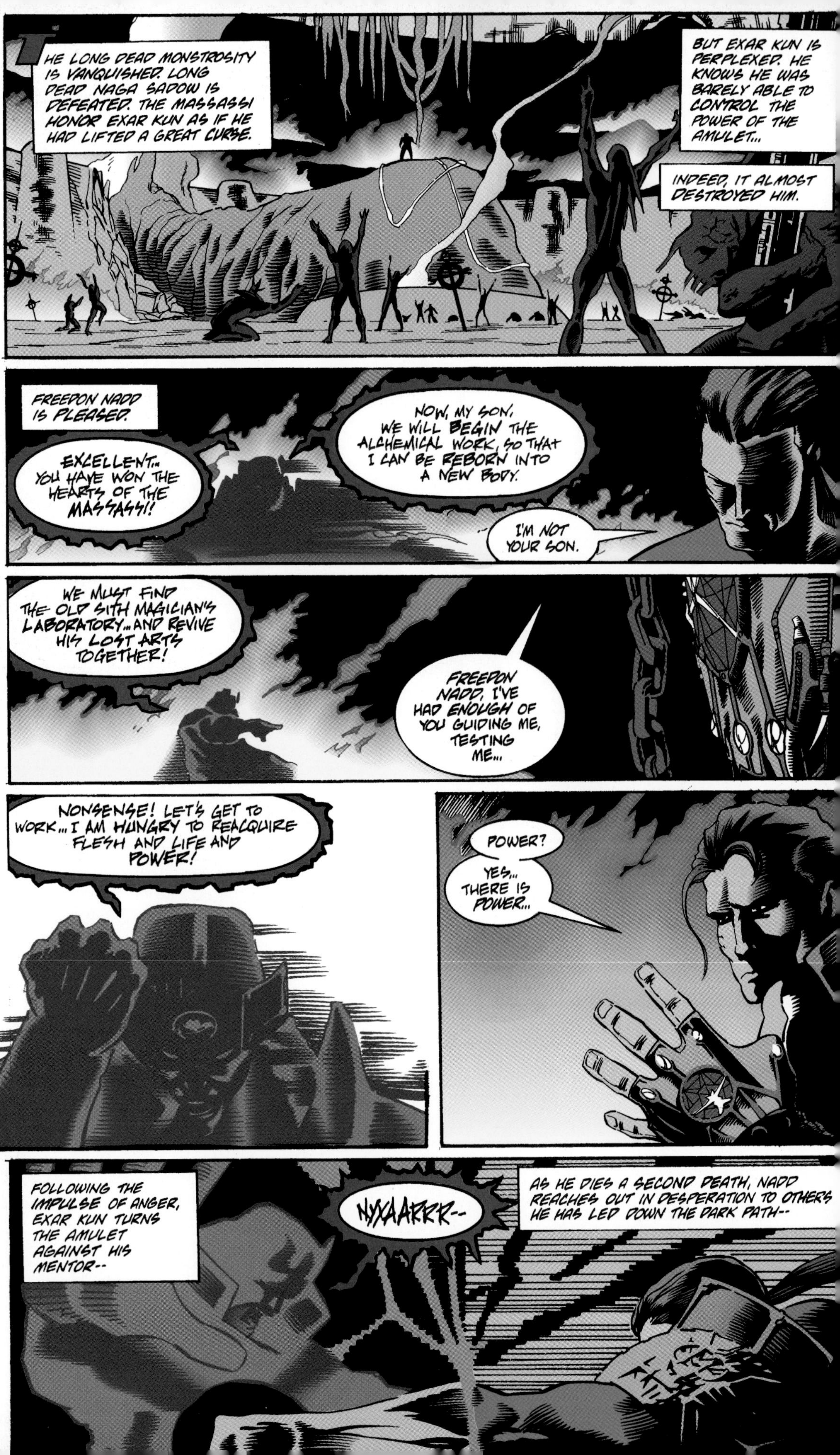
THE LONG DEAD MONSTROSITY IS VANQUISHED. LONG DEAD NAGA SADOW IS DEFEATED. THE MASSASSI HONOR EXAR KUN AS IF HE HAD LIFTED A GREAT CURSE.
BUT EXAR KUN IS PERPLEXED. HE KNOWS HE WAS BARELY ABLE TO CONTROL THE POWER OF THE AMULET...
INDEED, IT ALMOST DESTROYED HIM.
FREEDON NADD IS PLEASED.
EXCELLENT... YOU HAVE WON THE HEARTS OF THE MASSASSI!
NOW, MY SON, WE WILL BEGIN THE ALCHEMICAL WORK, SO THAT I CAN BE REBORN INTO A NEW BODY.
I'M NOT YOUR SON.
WE MUST FIND THE OLD SITH MAGICIAN'S LABORATORY... AND REVIVE HIS LOST ARTS TOGETHER!
FREEDON NADD, I'VE HAD ENOUGH OF YOU GUIDING ME, TESTING ME...
NONSENSE! LET'S GET TO WORK... I AM HUNGRY TO REACQUIRE FLESH AND LIFE AND POWER!
POWER?
YES... THERE IS POWER...
FOLLOWING THE IMPULSE OF ANGER, EXAR KUN TURNS THE AMULET AGAINST HIS MENTOR--
NYXAARRR--
AS HE DIES A SECOND DEATH, NADD REACHES OUT IN DESPERATION TO OTHERS HE HAS LED DOWN THE DARK PATH--

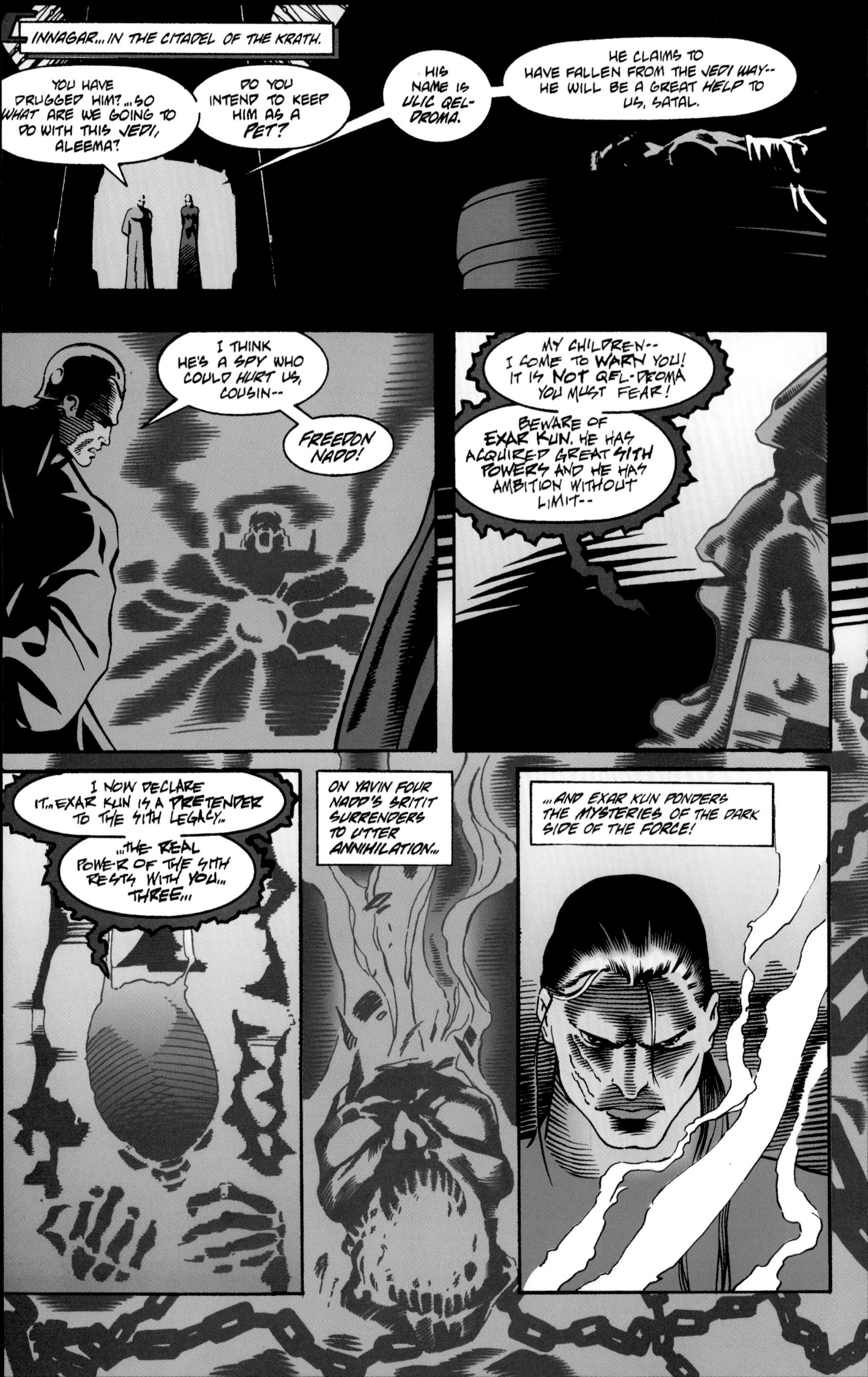

INNAGAR...IN THE CITADEL OF THE KRATH.
YOU HAVE DRUGGED HIM?...SO WHAT ARE WE GOING TO DO WITH THIS JEDI, ALEEMA?
DO YOU INTEND TO KEEP HIM AS A PET?
HIS NAME IS ULIC QEL-DROMA.
HE CLAIMS TO HAVE FALLEN FROM THE JEDI WAY-- HE WILL BE A GREAT HELP TO US, SATAL.
I THINK HE'S A SPY WHO COULD HURT US, COUSIN--
FREEDON NADD!
MY CHILDREN-- I COME TO WARN YOU! IT IS NOT QEL-DROMA YOU MUST FEAR!
BEWARE OF EXAR KUN. HE HAS ACQUIRED GREAT SITH POWERS AND HE HAS AMBITION WITHOUT LIMIT--
I NOW DECLARE IT...EXAR KUN IS A PRETENDER TO THE SITH LEGACY...
...THE REAL POWER OF THE SITH RESTS WITH YOU... THREE...
ON YAVIN FOUR NADD'S SPIRIT SURRENDERS TO UTTER ANNIHILATION...
...AND EXAR KUN PONDERS THE MYSTERIES OF THE DARK SIDE OF THE FORCE!

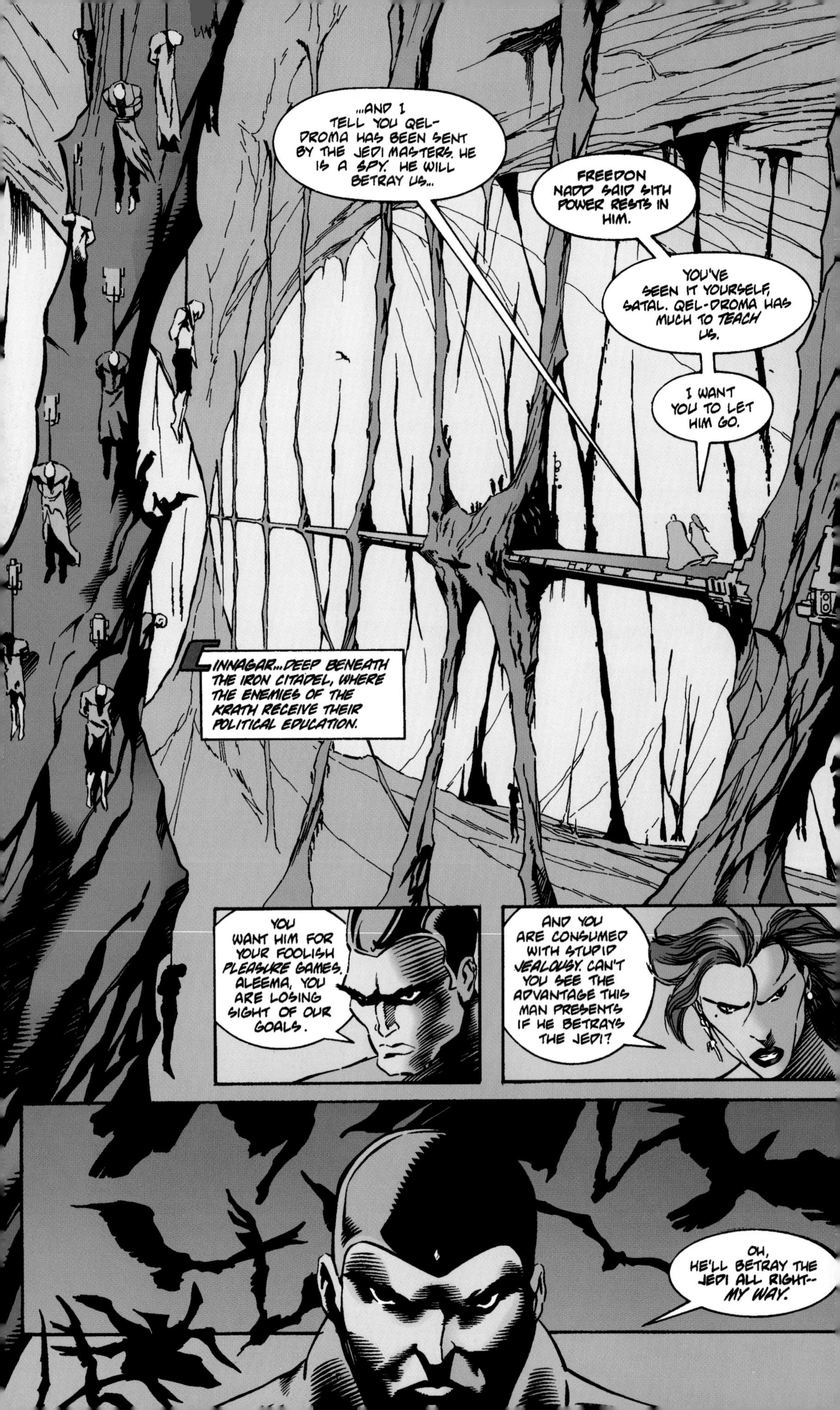
INNAGAR...DEEP BENEATH THE IRON CITADEL, WHERE THE ENEMIES OF THE KRATH RECEIVE THEIR POLITICAL EDUCATION.
...AND I TELL YOU QEL-DROMA HAS BEEN SENT BY THE JEDI MASTERS. HE IS A SPY. HE WILL BETRAY US...
FREEDON NADD SAID SITH POWER RESTS IN HIM.
YOU'VE SEEN IT YOURSELF, SATAL. QEL-DROMA HAS MUCH TO TEACH US.
I WANT YOU TO LET HIM GO.
YOU WANT HIM FOR YOUR FOOLISH PLEASURE GAMES, ALEEMA. YOU ARE LOSING SIGHT OF OUR GOALS.
AND YOU ARE CONSUMED WITH STUPID JEALOUSY. CAN'T YOU SEE THE ADVANTAGE THIS MAN PRESENTS IF HE BETRAYS THE JEDI?
OH, HE'LL BETRAY THE JEDI ALL RIGHT-- MY WAY.

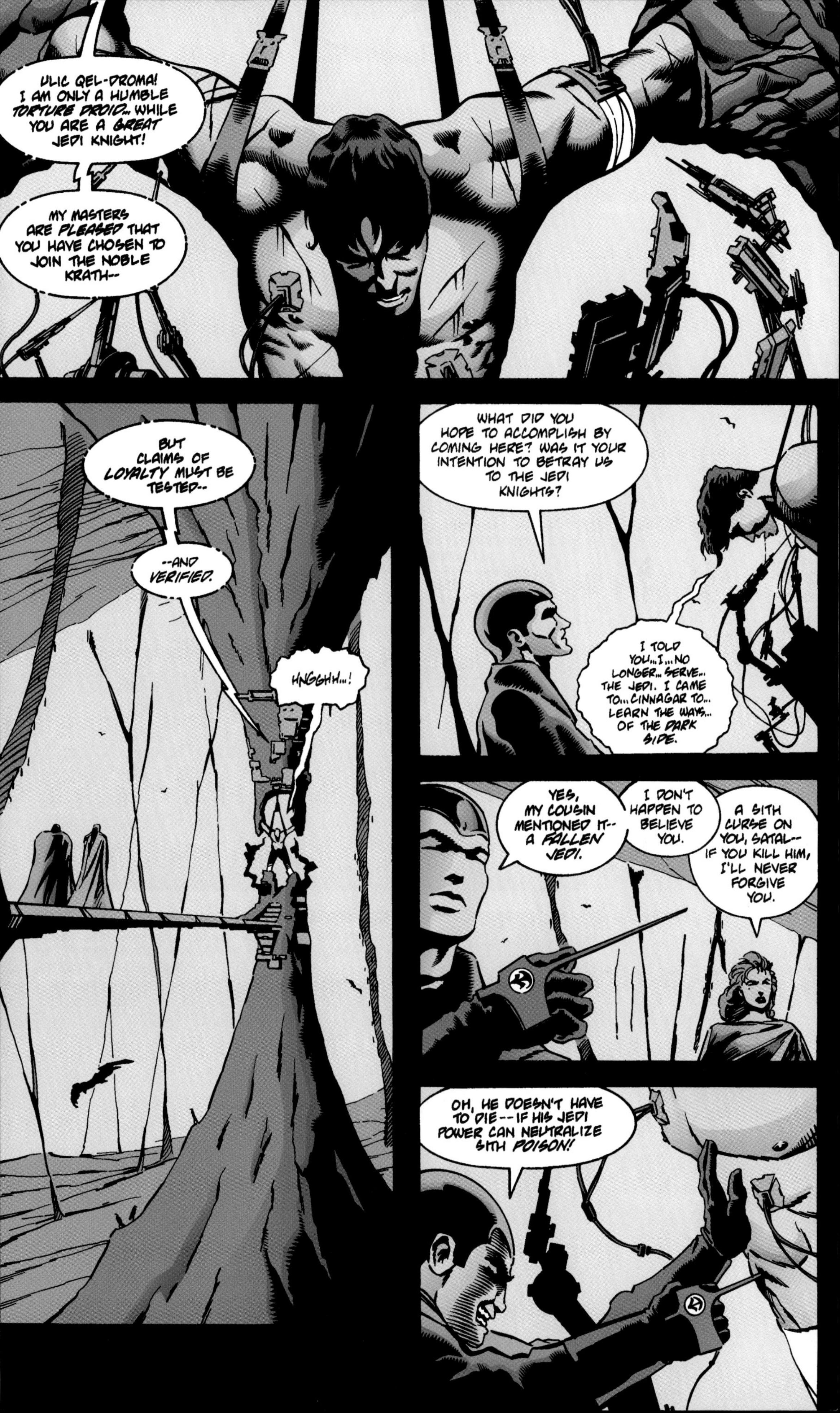
ULIC QEL-DROMA! I AM ONLY A HUMBLE TORTURE DROID... WHILE YOU ARE A GREAT JEDI KNIGHT!
MY MASTERS ARE PLEASED THAT YOU HAVE CHOSEN TO JOIN THE NOBLE KRATH--
BUT CLAIMS OF LOYALTY MUST BE TESTED--
--AND VERIFIED.
HNGGHH...!
WHAT DID YOU HOPE TO ACCOMPLISH BY COMING HERE? WAS IT YOUR INTENTION TO BETRAY US TO THE JEDI KNIGHTS?
I TOLD YOU...I...NO LONGER... SERVE... THE JEDI. I CAME TO...CINNAGAR TO... LEARN THE WAYS... OF THE DARK SIDE.
YES, MY COUSIN MENTIONED IT-- A FALLEN JEDI.
I DON'T HAPPEN TO BELIEVE YOU.
A SITH CURSE ON YOU, SATAL-- IF YOU KILL HIM, I'LL NEVER FORGIVE YOU.
OH, HE DOESN'T HAVE TO DIE--IF HIS JEDI POWER CAN NEUTRALIZE SITH POISON!

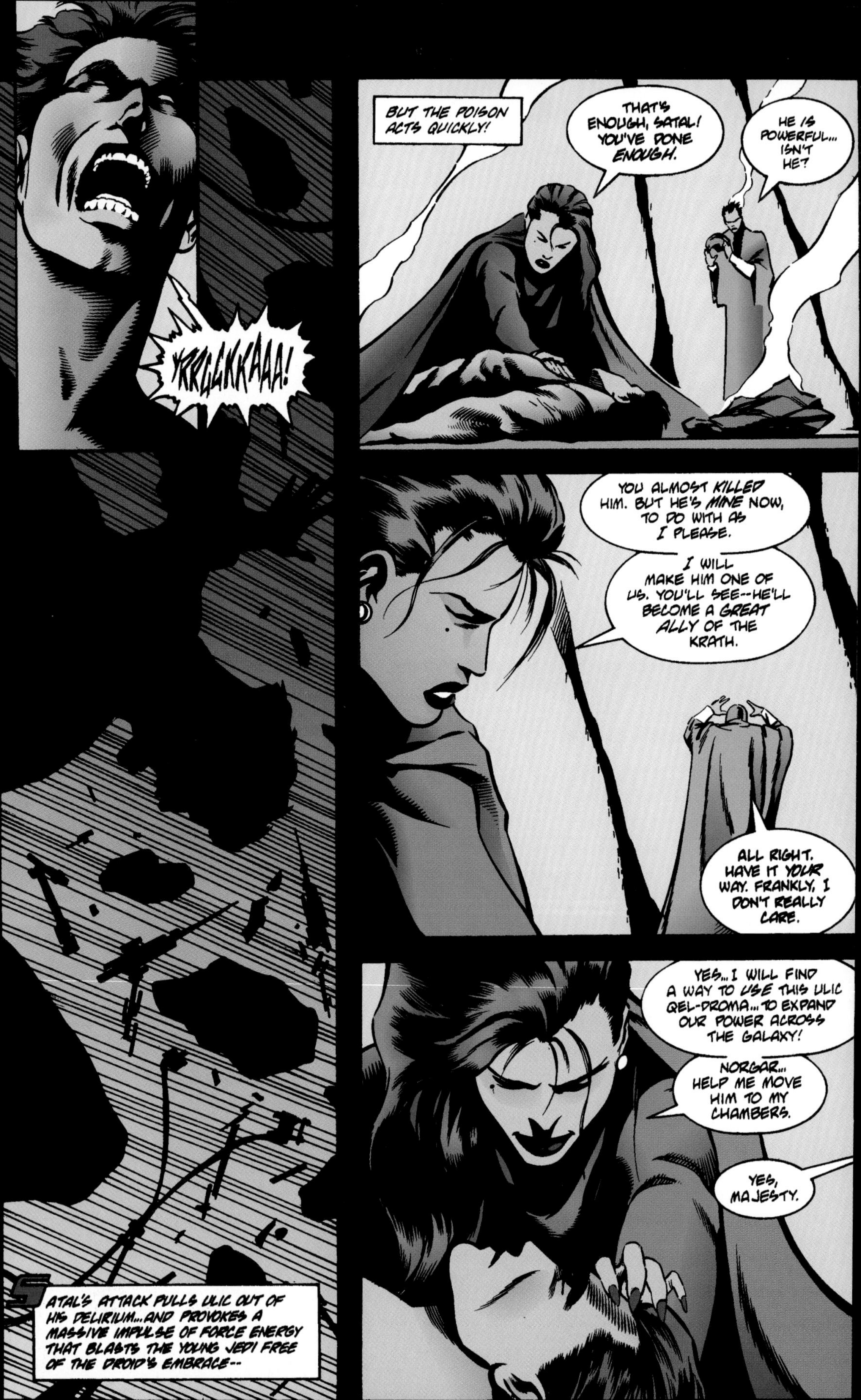
YRRGGKKAAA!
BUT THE POISON ACTS QUICKLY!
THAT'S ENOUGH, SATAL! YOU'VE DONE ENOUGH.
HE IS POWERFUL... ISN'T HE?
YOU ALMOST KILLED HIM. BUT HE'S MINE NOW, TO DO WITH AS I PLEASE.
I WILL MAKE HIM ONE OF US. YOU'LL SEE--HE'LL BECOME A GREAT ALLY OF THE KRATH.
ALL RIGHT. HAVE IT YOUR WAY. FRANKLY, I DON'T REALLY CARE.
YES... I WILL FIND A WAY TO USE THIS ULIC QEL-DROMA... TO EXPAND OUR POWER ACROSS THE GALAXY!
NORGAR... HELP ME MOVE HIM TO MY CHAMBERS.
YES, MAJESTY.
ATAL'S ATTACK PULLS ULIC OUT OF HIS DELIRIUM... AND PROVOKES A MASSIVE IMPULSE OF FORCE ENERGY THAT BLASTS THE YOUNG JEDI FREE OF THE DROID'S EMBRACE--

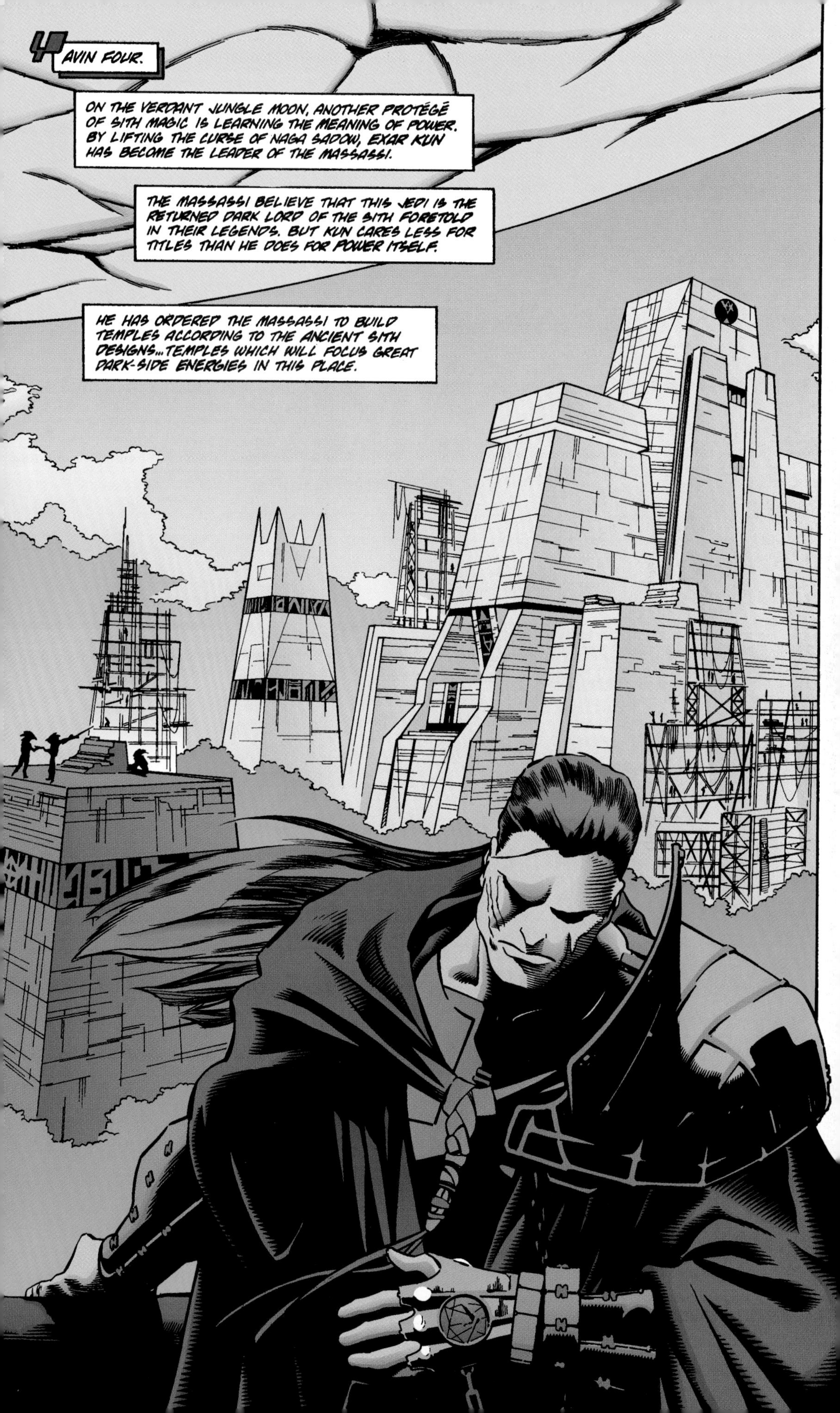
YAVIN FOUR.
ON THE VERDANT JUNGLE MOON, ANOTHER PROTÉGÉ OF SITH MAGIC IS LEARNING THE MEANING OF POWER. BY LIFTING THE CURSE OF NAGA SADOW, EXAR KUN HAS BECOME THE LEADER OF THE MASSASSI.
THE MASSASSI BELIEVE THAT THIS JEDI IS THE RETURNED DARK LORD OF THE SITH FORETOLD IN THEIR LEGENDS. BUT KUN CARES LESS FOR TITLES THAN HE DOES FOR POWER ITSELF.
HE HAS ORDERED THE MASSASSI TO BUILD TEMPLES ACCORDING TO THE ANCIENT SITH DESIGNS...TEMPLES WHICH WILL FOCUS GREAT DARK-SIDE ENERGIES IN THIS PLACE.

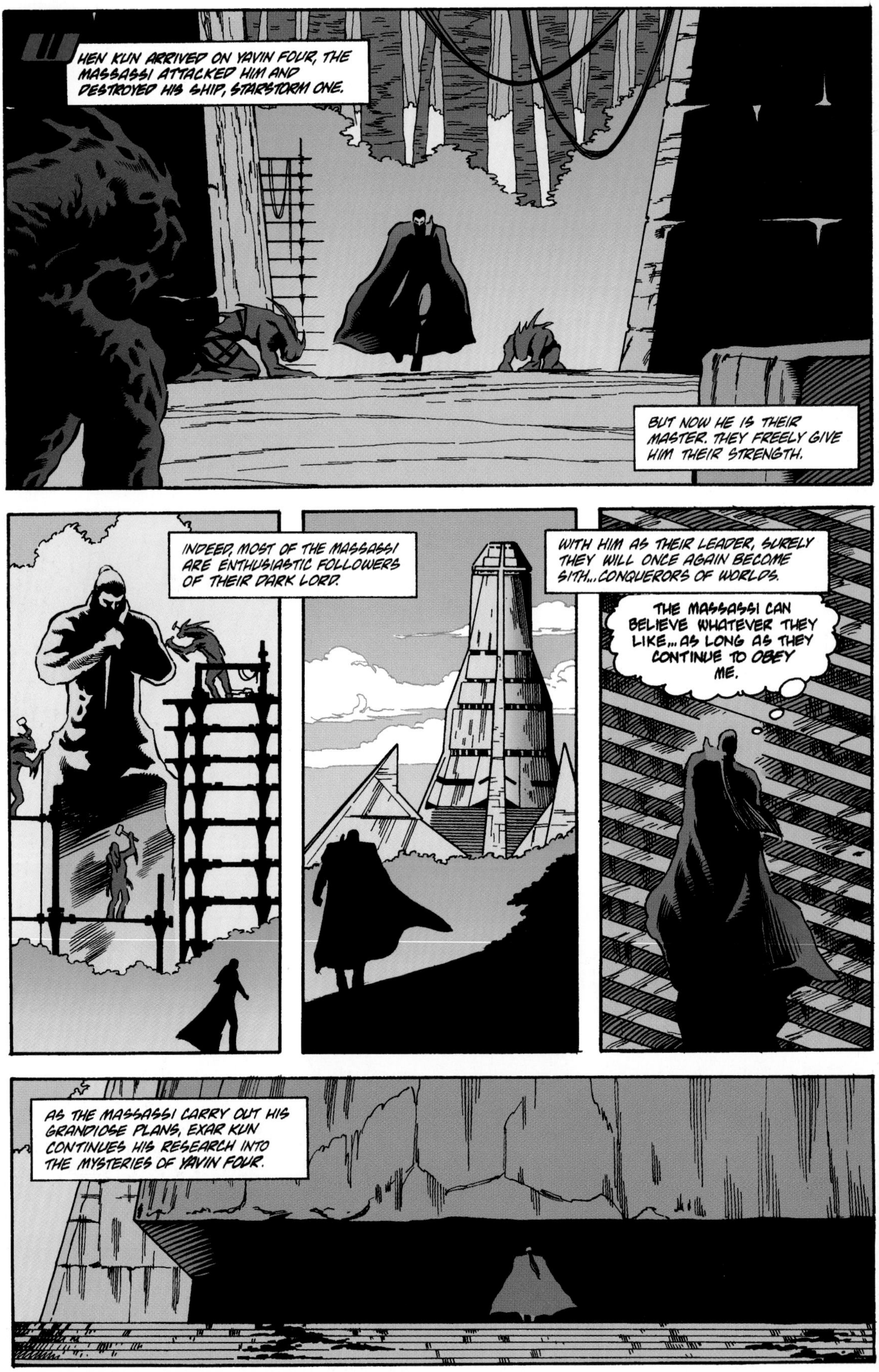
WHEN KUN ARRIVED ON YAVIN FOUR, THE MASSASSI ATTACKED HIM AND DESTROYED HIS SHIP, STARSTORM ONE.
BUT NOW HE IS THEIR MASTER. THEY FREELY GIVE HIM THEIR STRENGTH.
INDEED, MOST OF THE MASSASSI ARE ENTHUSIASTIC FOLLOWERS OF THEIR DARK LORD.
WITH HIM AS THEIR LEADER, SURELY THEY WILL ONCE AGAIN BECOME SITH...CONQUERORS OF WORLDS.
THE MASSASSI CAN BELIEVE WHATEVER THEY LIKE...AS LONG AS THEY CONTINUE TO OBEY ME.
AS THE MASSASSI CARRY OUT HIS GRANDIOSE PLANS, EXAR KUN CONTINUES HIS RESEARCH INTO THE MYSTERIES OF YAVIN FOUR.

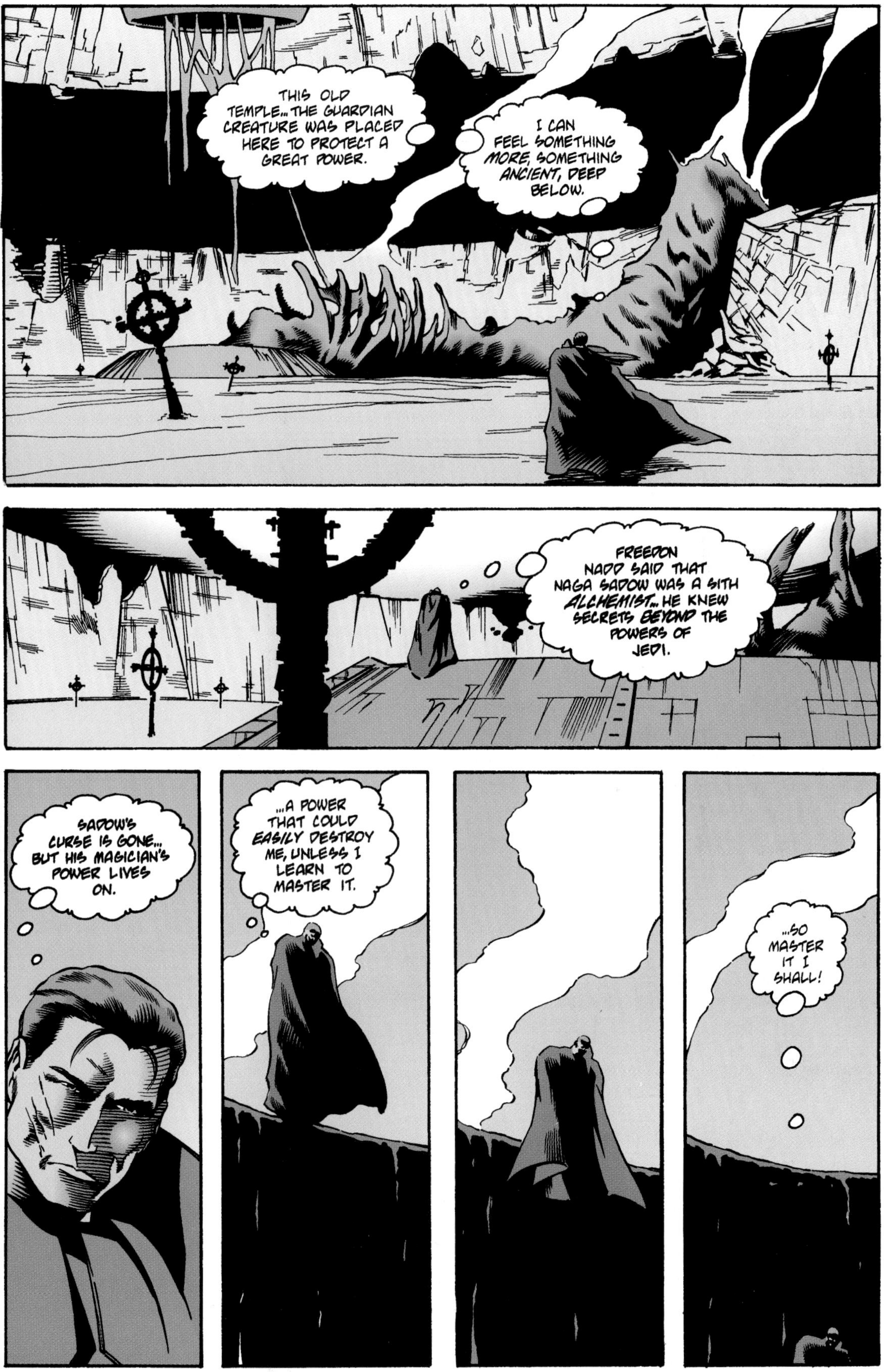
THIS OLD TEMPLE... THE GUARDIAN CREATURE WAS PLACED HERE TO PROTECT A GREAT POWER.
I CAN FEEL SOMETHING MORE, SOMETHING ANCIENT, DEEP BELOW.
FREEDON NADD SAID THAT NAGA SADOW WAS A SITH ALCHEMIST... HE KNEW SECRETS BEYOND THE POWERS OF JEDI.
SADOW'S CURSE IS GONE... BUT HIS MAGICIAN'S POWER LIVES ON.
...A POWER THAT COULD EASILY DESTROY ME, UNLESS I LEARN TO MASTER IT.
...SO MASTER IT I SHALL!

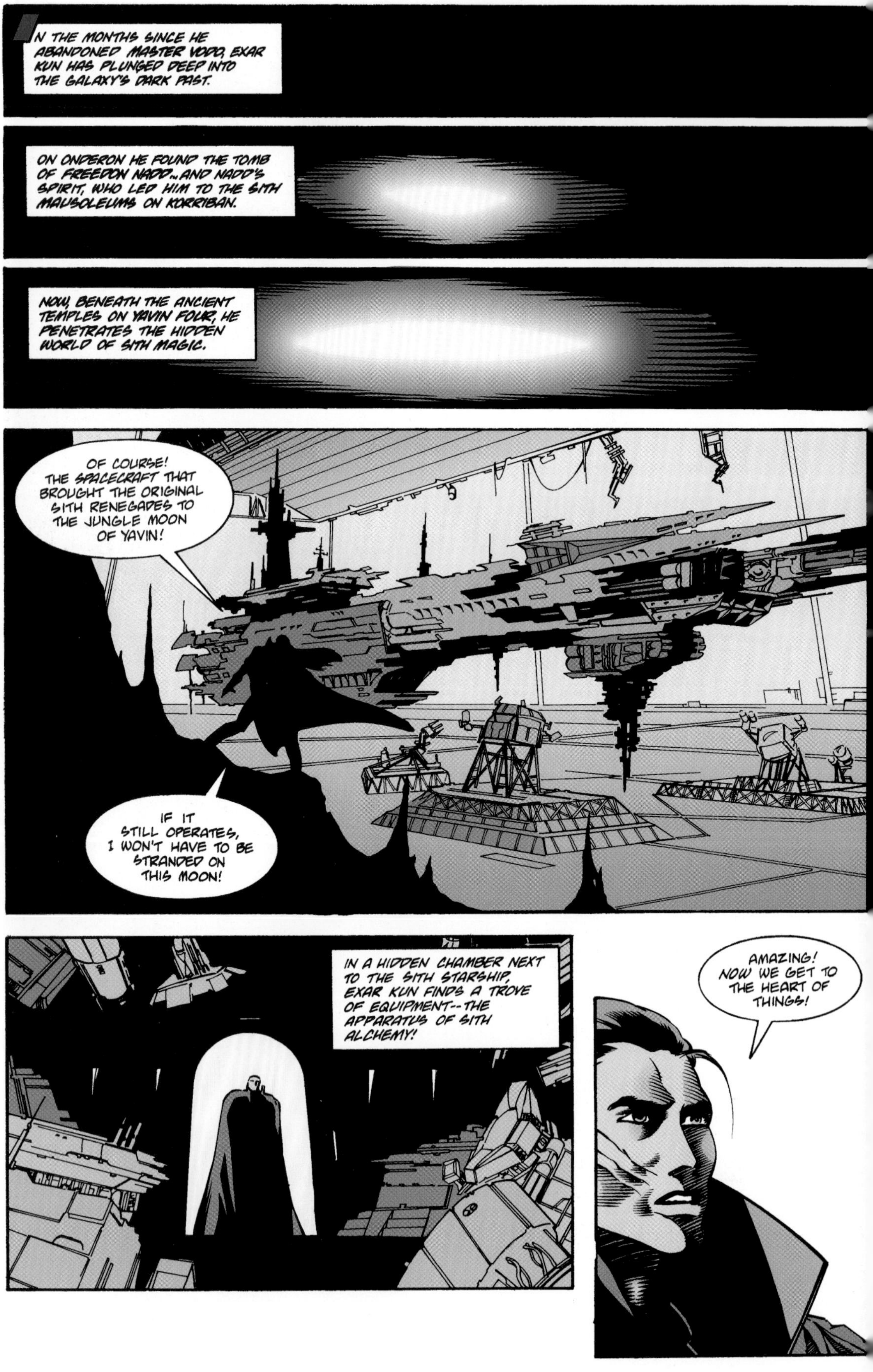
IN THE MONTHS SINCE HE ABANDONED MASTER VODO, EXAR KUN HAS PLUNGED DEEP INTO THE GALAXY'S DARK PAST.
ON ONDERON HE FOUND THE TOMB OF FREEDON NADD...AND NADD'S SPIRIT, WHO LED HIM TO THE SITH MAUSOLEUMS ON KORRIBAN.
NOW, BENEATH THE ANCIENT TEMPLES ON YAVIN FOUR, HE PENETRATES THE HIDDEN WORLD OF SITH MAGIC.
OF COURSE! THE SPACECRAFT THAT BROUGHT THE ORIGINAL SITH RENEGADES TO THE JUNGLE MOON OF YAVIN!
IF IT STILL OPERATES, I WON'T HAVE TO BE STRANDED ON THIS MOON!
IN A HIDDEN CHAMBER NEXT TO THE SITH STARSHIP, EXAR KUN FINDS A TROVE OF EQUIPMENT--THE APPARATUS OF SITH ALCHEMY!
AMAZING! NOW WE GET TO THE HEART OF THINGS!

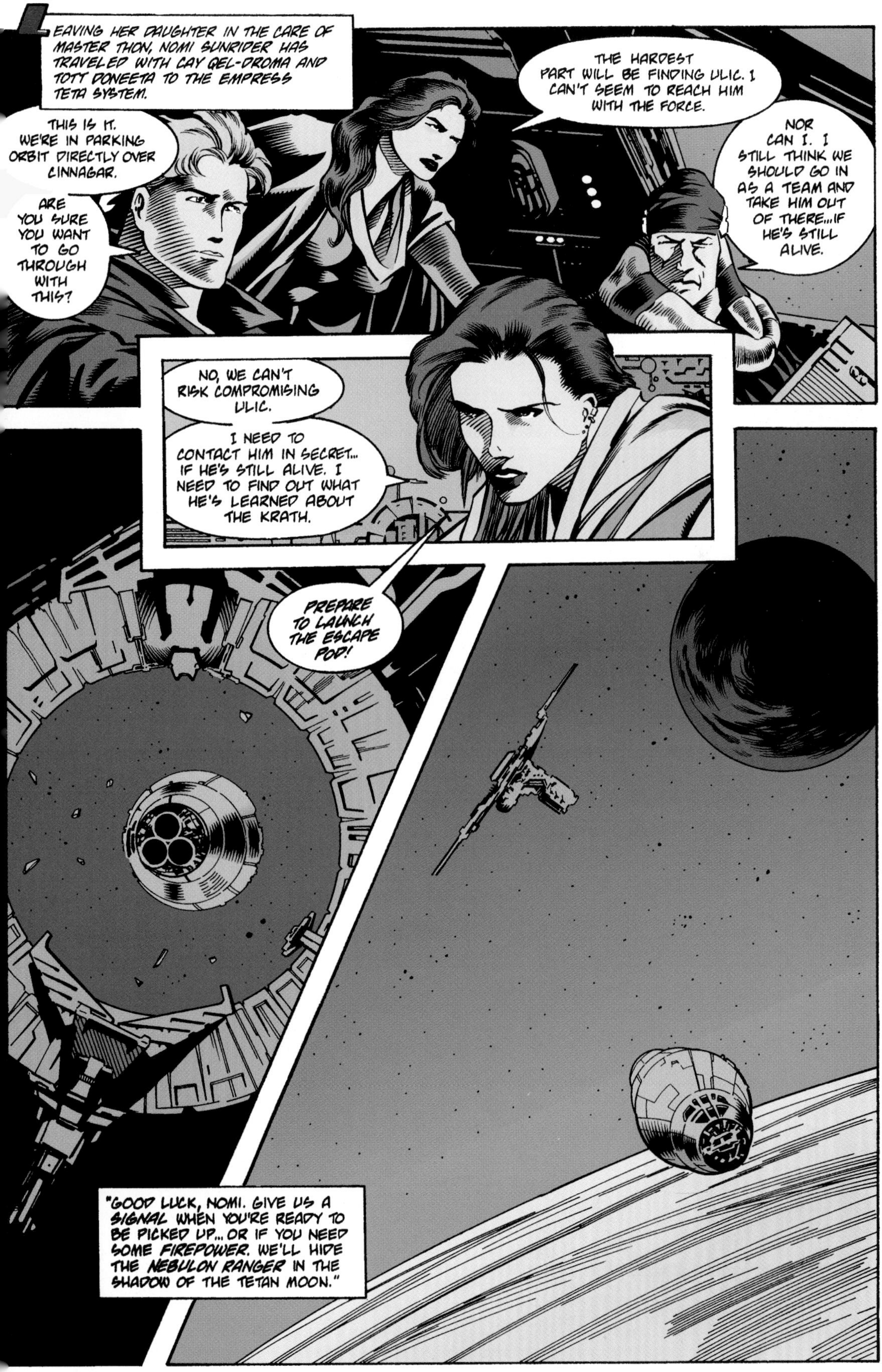
LEAVING HER DAUGHTER IN THE CARE OF MASTER THON, NOMI SUNRIDER HAS TRAVELED WITH CAY QEL-DROMA AND TOTT DONEETA TO THE EMPRESS TETA SYSTEM.
THIS IS IT. WE'RE IN PARKING ORBIT DIRECTLY OVER CINNAGAR.
ARE YOU SURE YOU WANT TO GO THROUGH WITH THIS?
THE HARDEST PART WILL BE FINDING ULIC. I CAN'T SEEM TO REACH HIM WITH THE FORCE.
NOR CAN I. I STILL THINK WE SHOULD GO IN AS A TEAM AND TAKE HIM OUT OF THERE...IF HE'S STILL ALIVE.
NO, WE CAN'T RISK COMPROMISING ULIC.
I NEED TO CONTACT HIM IN SECRET... IF HE'S STILL ALIVE. I NEED TO FIND OUT WHAT HE'S LEARNED ABOUT THE KRATH.
PREPARE TO LAUNCH THE ESCAPE POD!
"GOOD LUCK, NOMI. GIVE US A SIGNAL WHEN YOU'RE READY TO BE PICKED UP... OR IF YOU NEED SOME FIREPOWER. WE'LL HIDE THE NEBULON RANGER IN THE SHADOW OF THE TETAN MOON."

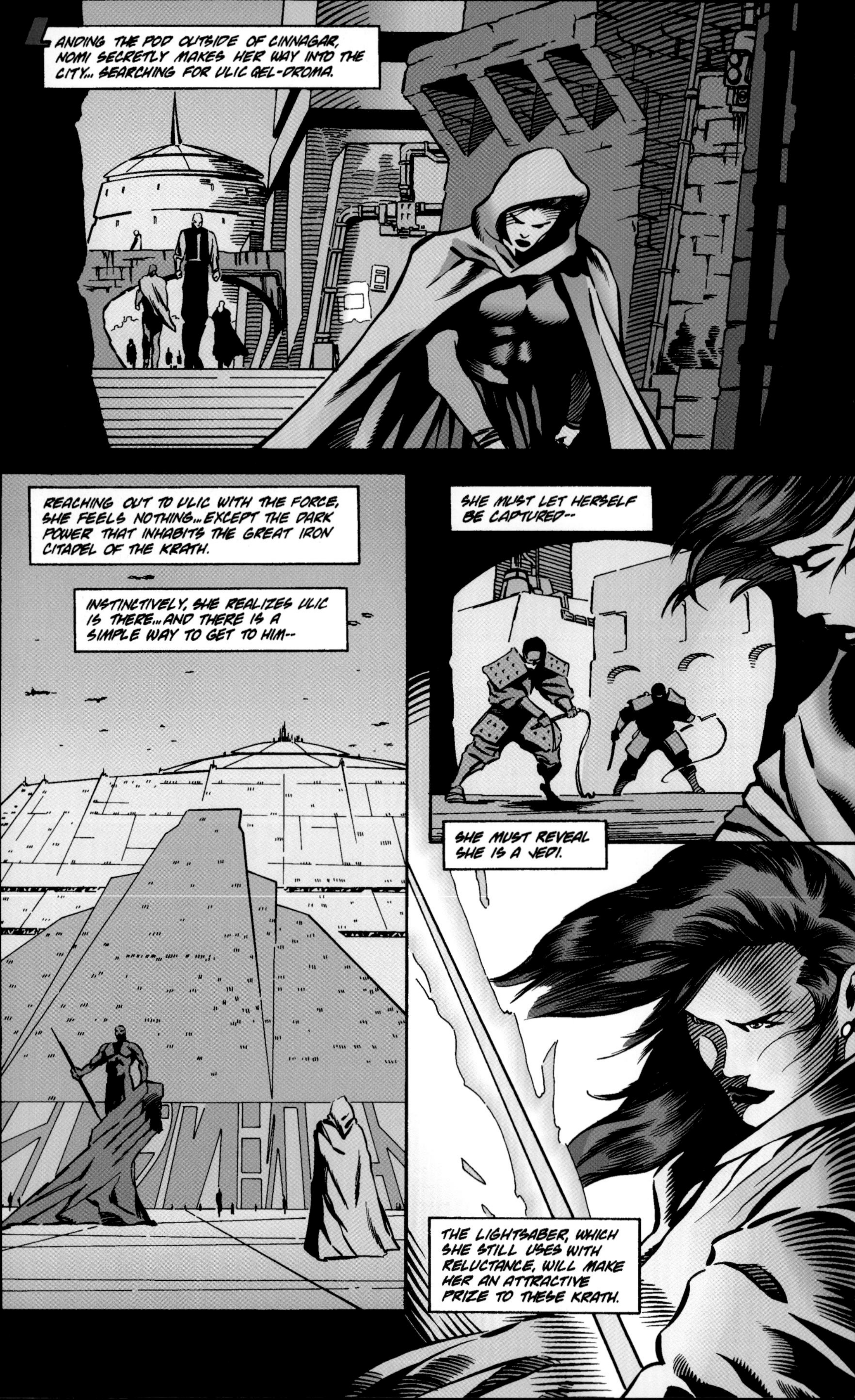
LANDING THE POD OUTSIDE OF CINNAGAR, NOMI SECRETLY MAKES HER WAY INTO THE CITY... SEARCHING FOR ULIC QEL-DROMA.
REACHING OUT TO ULIC WITH THE FORCE, SHE FEELS NOTHING...EXCEPT THE DARK POWER THAT INHABITS THE GREAT IRON CITADEL OF THE KRATH.
INSTINCTIVELY, SHE REALIZES ULIC IS THERE...AND THERE IS A SIMPLE WAY TO GET TO HIM--
SHE MUST LET HERSELF BE CAPTURED--
SHE MUST REVEAL SHE IS A JEDI.
THE LIGHTSABER, WHICH SHE STILL USES WITH RELUCTANCE, WILL MAKE HER AN ATTRACTIVE PRIZE TO THESE KRATH.

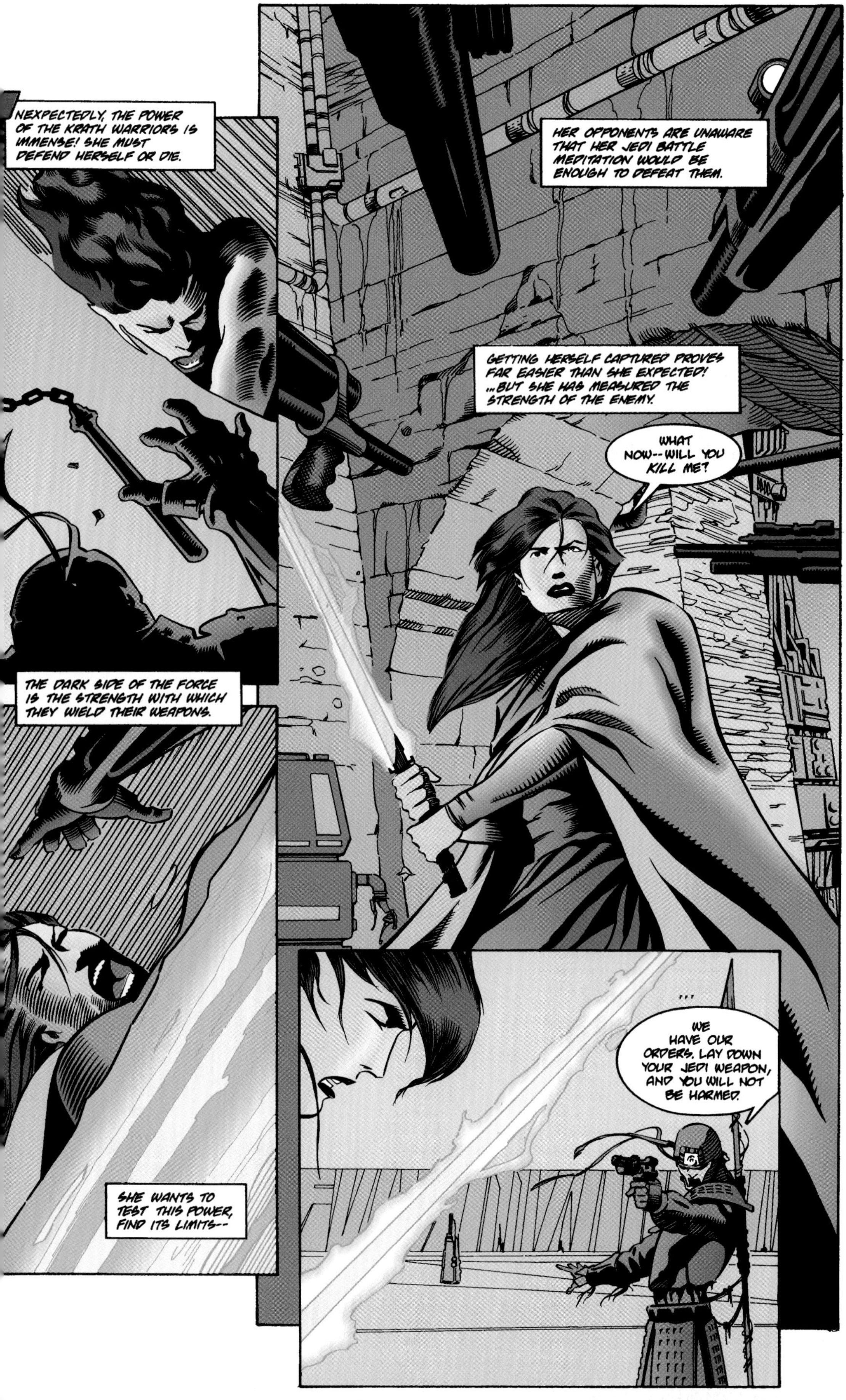
NEXPECTEDLY, THE POWER OF THE KRATH WARRIORS IS IMMENSE! SHE MUST DEFEND HERSELF OR DIE.
THE DARK SIDE OF THE FORCE IS THE STRENGTH WITH WHICH THEY WIELD THEIR WEAPONS.
SHE WANTS TO TEST THIS POWER, FIND ITS LIMITS--
HER OPPONENTS ARE UNAWARE THAT HER JEDI BATTLE MEDITATION WOULD BE ENOUGH TO DEFEAT THEM.
GETTING HERSELF CAPTURED PROVES FAR EASIER THAN SHE EXPECTED! ...BUT SHE HAS MEASURED THE STRENGTH OF THE ENEMY.
WHAT NOW--WILL YOU KILL ME?
...
WE HAVE OUR ORDERS. LAY DOWN YOUR JEDI WEAPON, AND YOU WILL NOT BE HARMED.

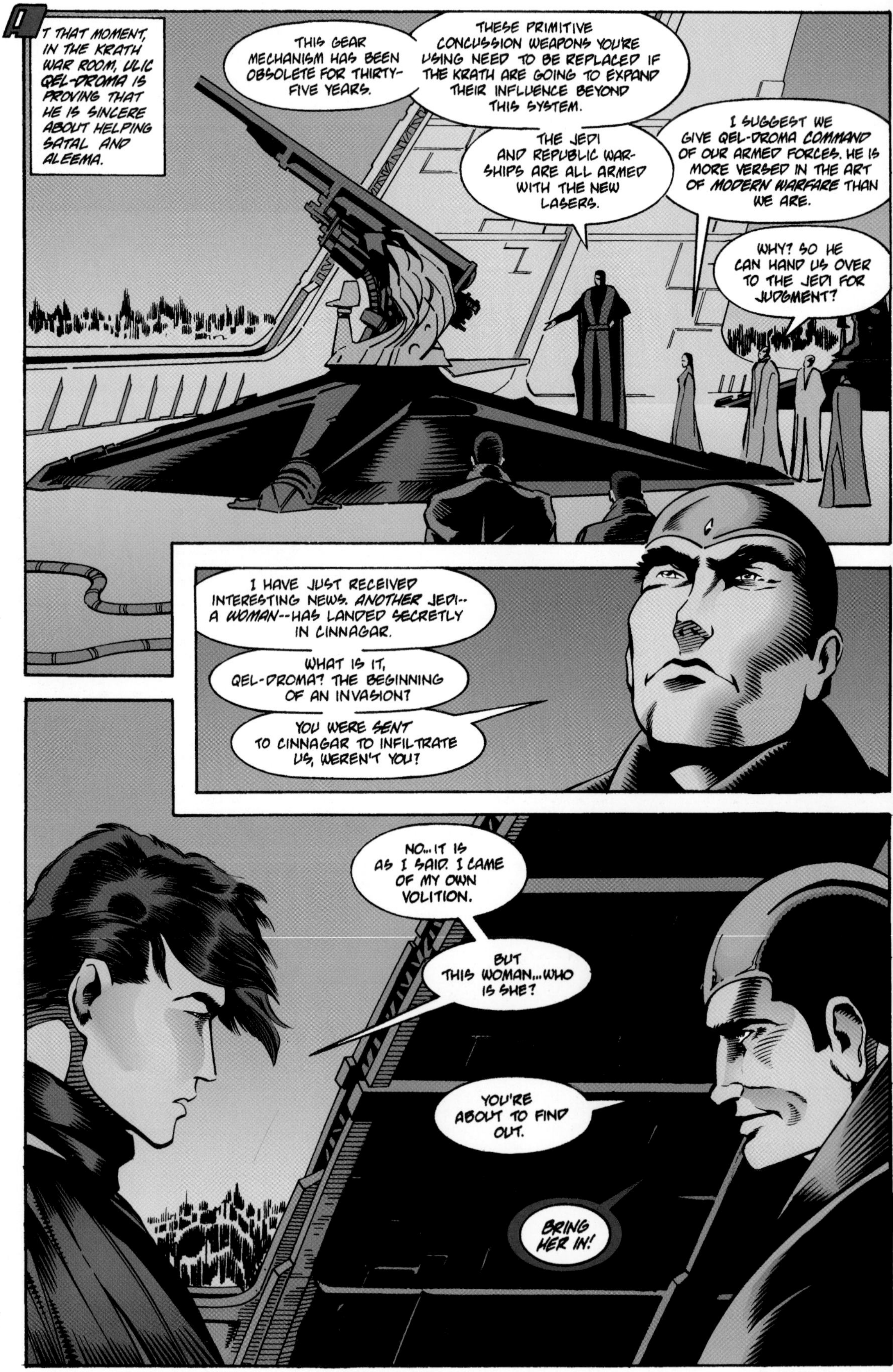
AT THAT MOMENT, IN THE KRATH WAR ROOM, ULIC QEL-DROMA IS PROVING THAT HE IS SINCERE ABOUT HELPING SATAL AND ALEEMA.
THIS GEAR MECHANISM HAS BEEN OBSOLETE FOR THIRTY-FIVE YEARS.
THESE PRIMITIVE CONCUSSION WEAPONS YOU'RE USING NEED TO BE REPLACED IF THE KRATH ARE GOING TO EXPAND THEIR INFLUENCE BEYOND THIS SYSTEM.
THE JEDI AND REPUBLIC WAR-SHIPS ARE ALL ARMED WITH THE NEW LASERS.
I SUGGEST WE GIVE QEL-DROMA COMMAND OF OUR ARMED FORCES. HE IS MORE VERSED IN THE ART OF MODERN WARFARE THAN WE ARE.
WHY? SO HE CAN HAND US OVER TO THE JEDI FOR JUDGMENT?
I HAVE JUST RECEIVED INTERESTING NEWS. ANOTHER JEDI--A WOMAN--HAS LANDED SECRETLY IN CINNAGAR.
WHAT IS IT, QEL-DROMA? THE BEGINNING OF AN INVASION?
YOU WERE SENT TO CINNAGAR TO INFILTRATE US, WEREN'T YOU?
NO... IT IS AS I SAID. I CAME OF MY OWN VOLITION.
BUT THIS WOMAN... WHO IS SHE?
YOU'RE ABOUT TO FIND OUT.
BRING HER IN!

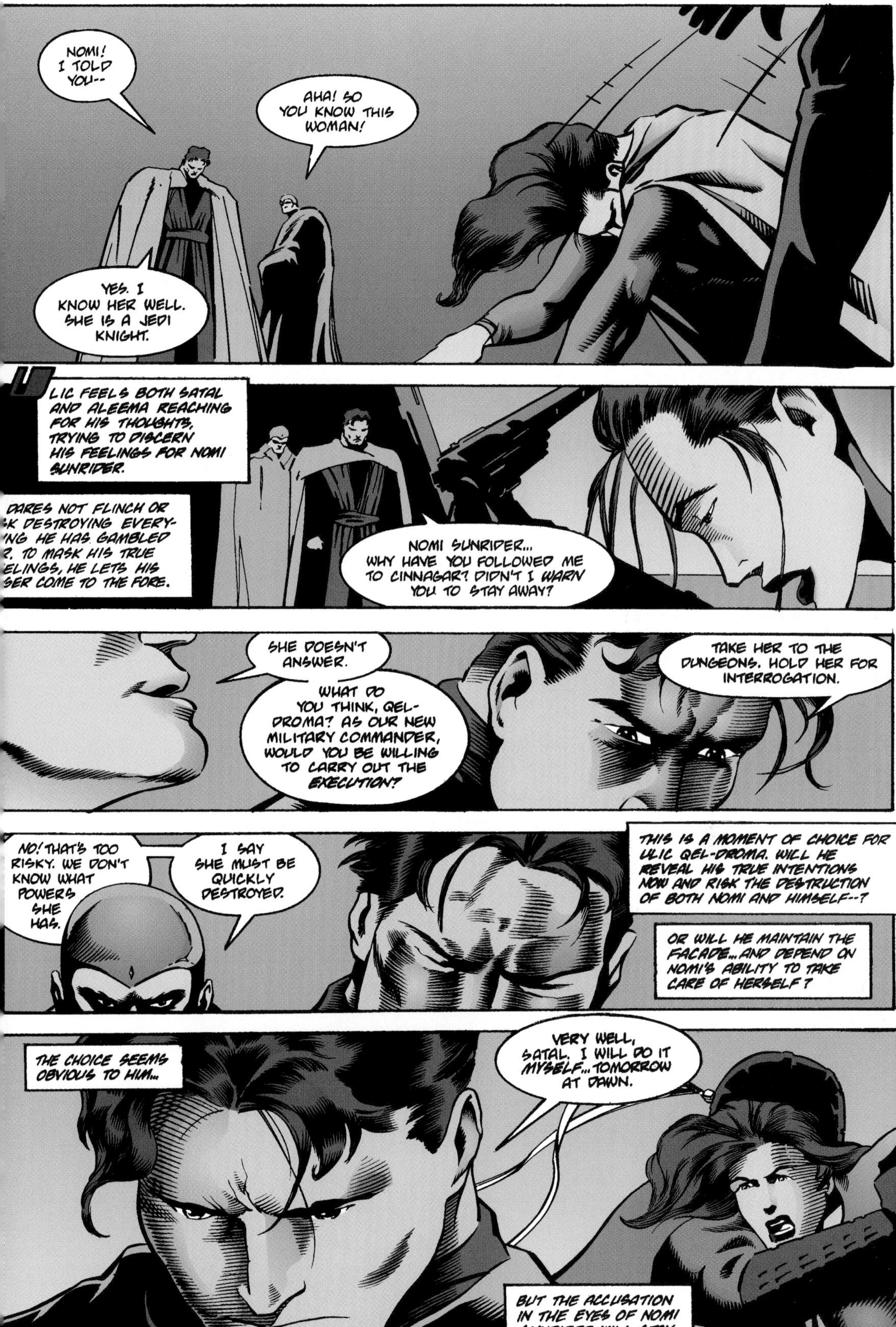
NOMI! I TOLD YOU--
AHA! SO YOU KNOW THIS WOMAN!
YES. I KNOW HER WELL. SHE IS A JEDI KNIGHT.
ULIC FEELS BOTH SATAL AND ALEEMA REACHING FOR HIS THOUGHTS, TRYING TO DISCERN HIS FEELINGS FOR NOMI SUNRIDER.
DARES NOT FLINCH OR K DESTROYING EVERY- NG HE HAS GAMBLED R. TO MASK HIS TRUE ELINGS, HE LETS HIS SER COME TO THE FORE.
NOMI SUNRIDER... WHY HAVE YOU FOLLOWED ME TO CINNAGAR? DIDN'T I WARN YOU TO STAY AWAY?
SHE DOESN'T ANSWER.
WHAT DO YOU THINK, QEL-DROMA? AS OUR NEW MILITARY COMMANDER, WOULD YOU BE WILLING TO CARRY OUT THE EXECUTION?
TAKE HER TO THE DUNGEONS. HOLD HER FOR INTERROGATION.
NO! THAT'S TOO RISKY. WE DON'T KNOW WHAT POWERS SHE HAS.
I SAY SHE MUST BE QUICKLY DESTROYED.
THIS IS A MOMENT OF CHOICE FOR ULIC QEL-DROMA. WILL HE REVEAL HIS TRUE INTENTIONS NOW AND RISK THE DESTRUCTION OF BOTH NOMI AND HIMSELF--?
OR WILL HE MAINTAIN THE FACADE...AND DEPEND ON NOMI'S ABILITY TO TAKE CARE OF HERSELF?
THE CHOICE SEEMS OBVIOUS TO HIM...
VERY WELL, SATAL. I WILL DO IT MYSELF...TOMORROW AT DAWN.
BUT THE ACCUSATION IN THE EYES OF NOMI SUNRIDER WILL STAY WITH HIM FOR THE REST OF HIS LIFE.

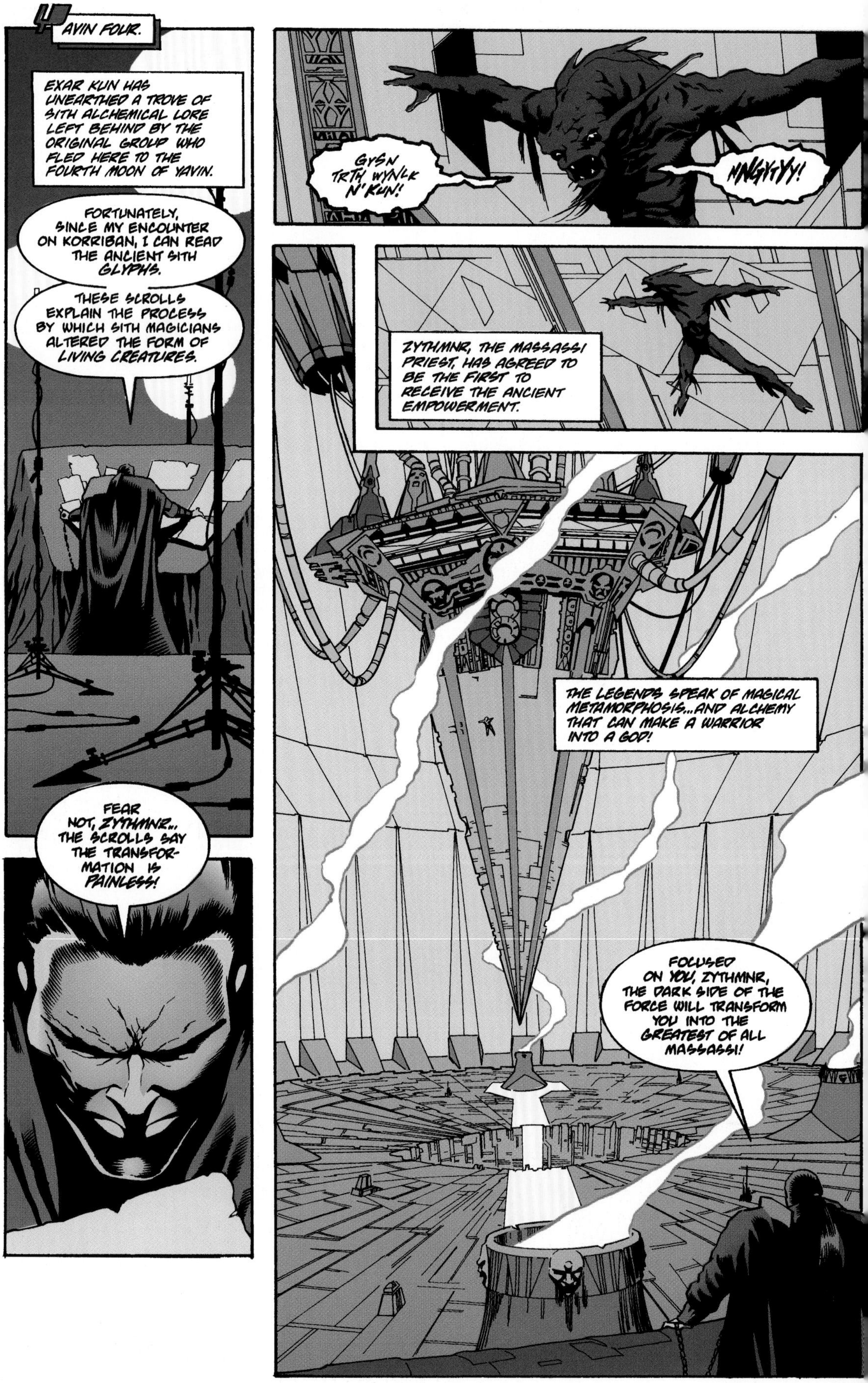
YAVIN FOUR.
EXAR KUN HAS UNEARTHED A TROVE OF SITH ALCHEMICAL LORE LEFT BEHIND BY THE ORIGINAL GROUP WHO FLED HERE TO THE FOURTH MOON OF YAVIN.
FORTUNATELY, SINCE MY ENCOUNTER ON KORRIBAN, I CAN READ THE ANCIENT SITH GLYPHS.
THESE SCROLLS EXPLAIN THE PROCESS BY WHICH SITH MAGICIANS ALTERED THE FORM OF LIVING CREATURES.
GYSN TRTH WYNLK N'KUN!
NNGYYYY!
FEAR NOT, ZYTHMNR.. THE SCROLLS SAY THE TRANSFORMATION IS PAINLESS!
ZYTHMNR, THE MASSASSI PRIEST, HAS AGREED TO BE THE FIRST TO RECEIVE THE ANCIENT EMPOWERMENT.
THE LEGENDS SPEAK OF MAGICAL METAMORPHOSIS...AND ALCHEMY THAT CAN MAKE A WARRIOR INTO A GOD!
FOCUSED ON YOU, ZYTHMNR, THE DARK SIDE OF THE FORCE WILL TRANSFORM YOU INTO THE GREATEST OF ALL MASSASSI!

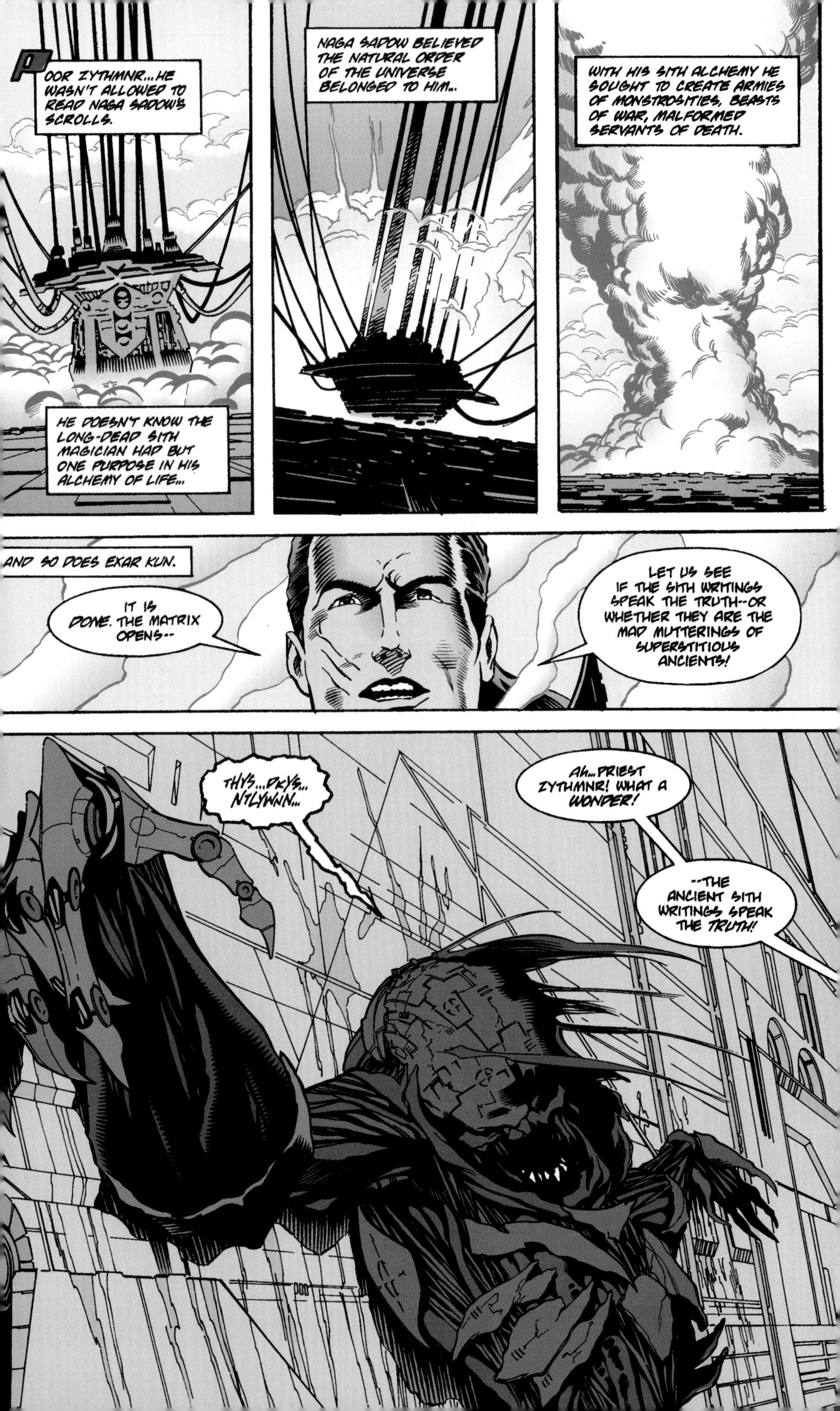
POOR ZYTHMNR... HE WASN'T ALLOWED TO READ NAGA SADOW'S SCROLLS.
HE DOESN'T KNOW THE LONG-DEAD SITH MAGICIAN HAD BUT ONE PURPOSE IN HIS ALCHEMY OF LIFE...
NAGA SADOW BELIEVED THE NATURAL ORDER OF THE UNIVERSE BELONGED TO HIM...
WITH HIS SITH ALCHEMY HE SOUGHT TO CREATE ARMIES OF MONSTROSITIES, BEASTS OF WAR, MALFORMED SERVANTS OF DEATH.
AND SO DOES EXAR KUN.
IT IS DONE. THE MATRIX OPENS--
LET US SEE IF THE SITH WRITINGS SPEAK THE TRUTH--OR WHETHER THEY ARE THE MAD MUTTERINGS OF SUPERSTITIOUS ANCIENTS!
THYS...DKYS... NTLYWNN...
AH...PRIEST ZYTHMNR! WHAT A WONDER!
--THE ANCIENT SITH WRITINGS SPEAK THE TRUTH!

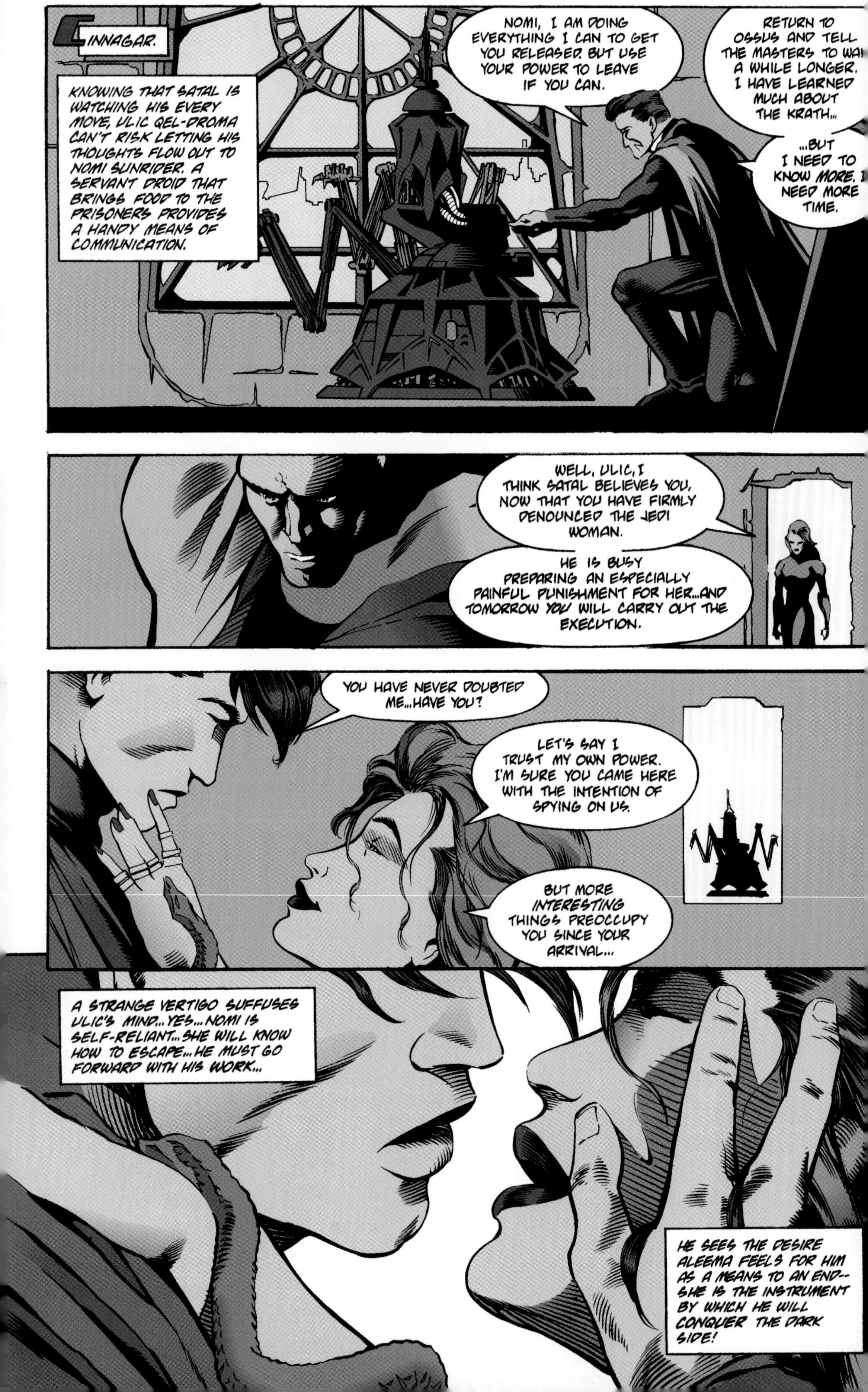
CINNAGAR.
KNOWING THAT SATAL IS WATCHING HIS EVERY MOVE, ULIC QEL-DROMA CAN'T RISK LETTING HIS THOUGHTS FLOW OUT TO NOMI SUNRIDER. A SERVANT DROID THAT BRINGS FOOD TO THE PRISONERS PROVIDES A HANDY MEANS OF COMMUNICATION.
NOMI, I AM DOING EVERYTHING I CAN TO GET YOU RELEASED. BUT USE YOUR POWER TO LEAVE IF YOU CAN.
RETURN TO OSSUS AND TELL THE MASTERS TO WA A WHILE LONGER. I HAVE LEARNED MUCH ABOUT THE KRATH...
...BUT I NEED TO KNOW MORE. I NEED MORE TIME.
WELL, ULIC, I THINK SATAL BELIEVES YOU, NOW THAT YOU HAVE FIRMLY DENOUNCED THE JEDI WOMAN.
HE IS BUSY PREPARING AN ESPECIALLY PAINFUL PUNISHMENT FOR HER...AND TOMORROW YOU WILL CARRY OUT THE EXECUTION.
YOU HAVE NEVER DOUBTED ME...HAVE YOU?
LET'S SAY I TRUST MY OWN POWER. I'M SURE YOU CAME HERE WITH THE INTENTION OF SPYING ON US.
BUT MORE INTERESTING THINGS PREOCCUPY YOU SINCE YOUR ARRIVAL...
A STRANGE VERTIGO SUFFUSES ULIC'S MIND...YES...NOMI IS SELF-RELIANT...SHE WILL KNOW HOW TO ESCAPE...HE MUST GO FORWARD WITH HIS WORK...
HE SEES THE DESIRE ALEEMA FEELS FOR HIM AS A MEANS TO AN END--SHE IS THE INSTRUMENT BY WHICH HE WILL CONQUER THE DARK SIDE!

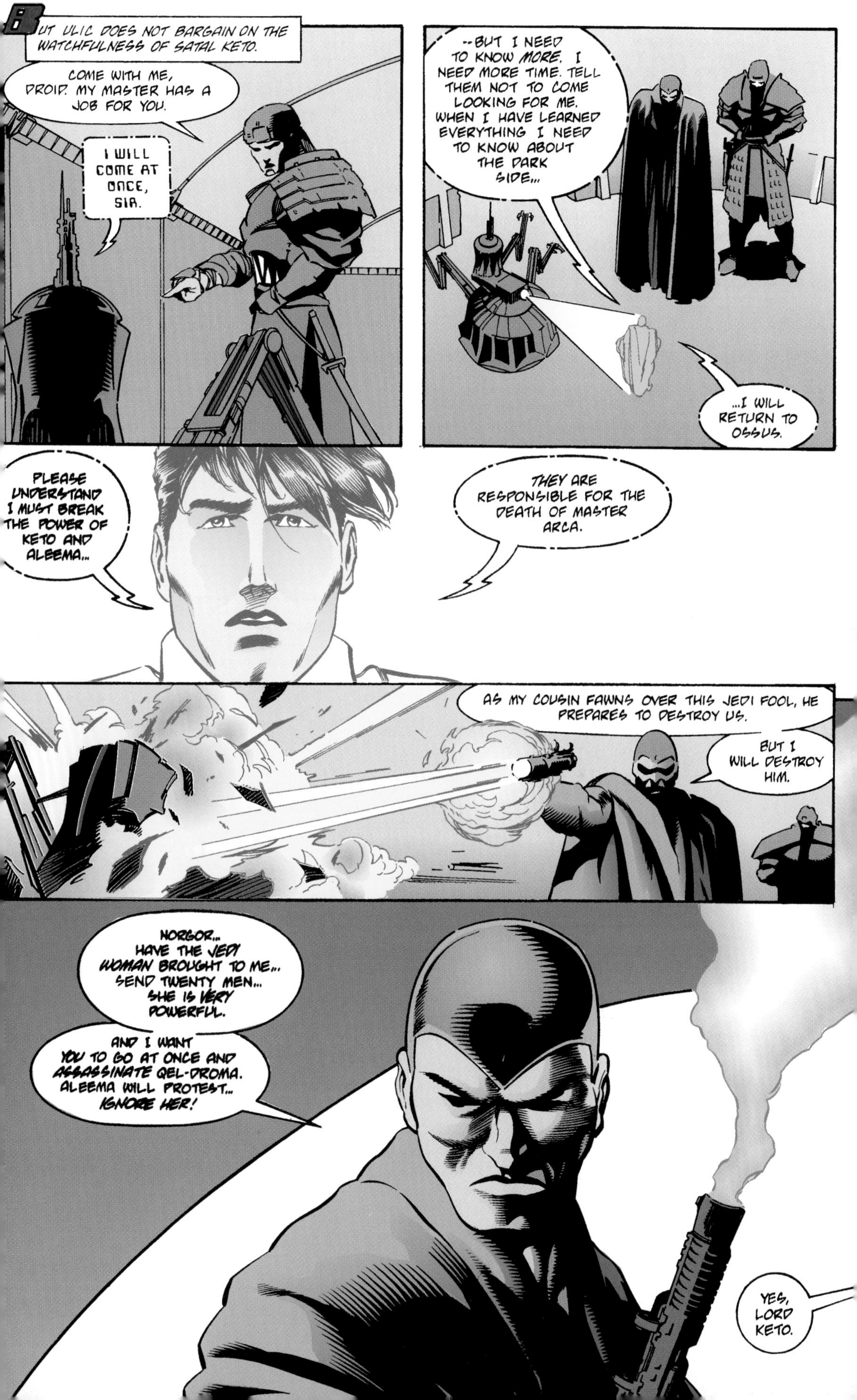
BUT ULIC DOES NOT BARGAIN ON THE WATCHFULNESS OF SATAL KETO.
COME WITH ME, DROID. MY MASTER HAS A JOB FOR YOU.
I WILL COME AT ONCE, SIR.
--BUT I NEED TO KNOW MORE. I NEED MORE TIME. TELL THEM NOT TO COME LOOKING FOR ME. WHEN I HAVE LEARNED EVERYTHING I NEED TO KNOW ABOUT THE DARK SIDE...
...I WILL RETURN TO OSSUS.
PLEASE UNDERSTAND I MUST BREAK THE POWER OF KETO AND ALEEMA...
THEY ARE RESPONSIBLE FOR THE DEATH OF MASTER ARCA.
AS MY COUSIN FAWNS OVER THIS JEDI FOOL, HE PREPARES TO DESTROY US.
BUT I WILL DESTROY HIM.
NORGOR... HAVE THE JEDI WOMAN BROUGHT TO ME... SEND TWENTY MEN... SHE IS VERY POWERFUL.
AND I WANT YOU TO GO AT ONCE AND ASSASSINATE QEL-DROMA. ALEEMA WILL PROTEST... IGNORE HER!
YES, LORD KETO.

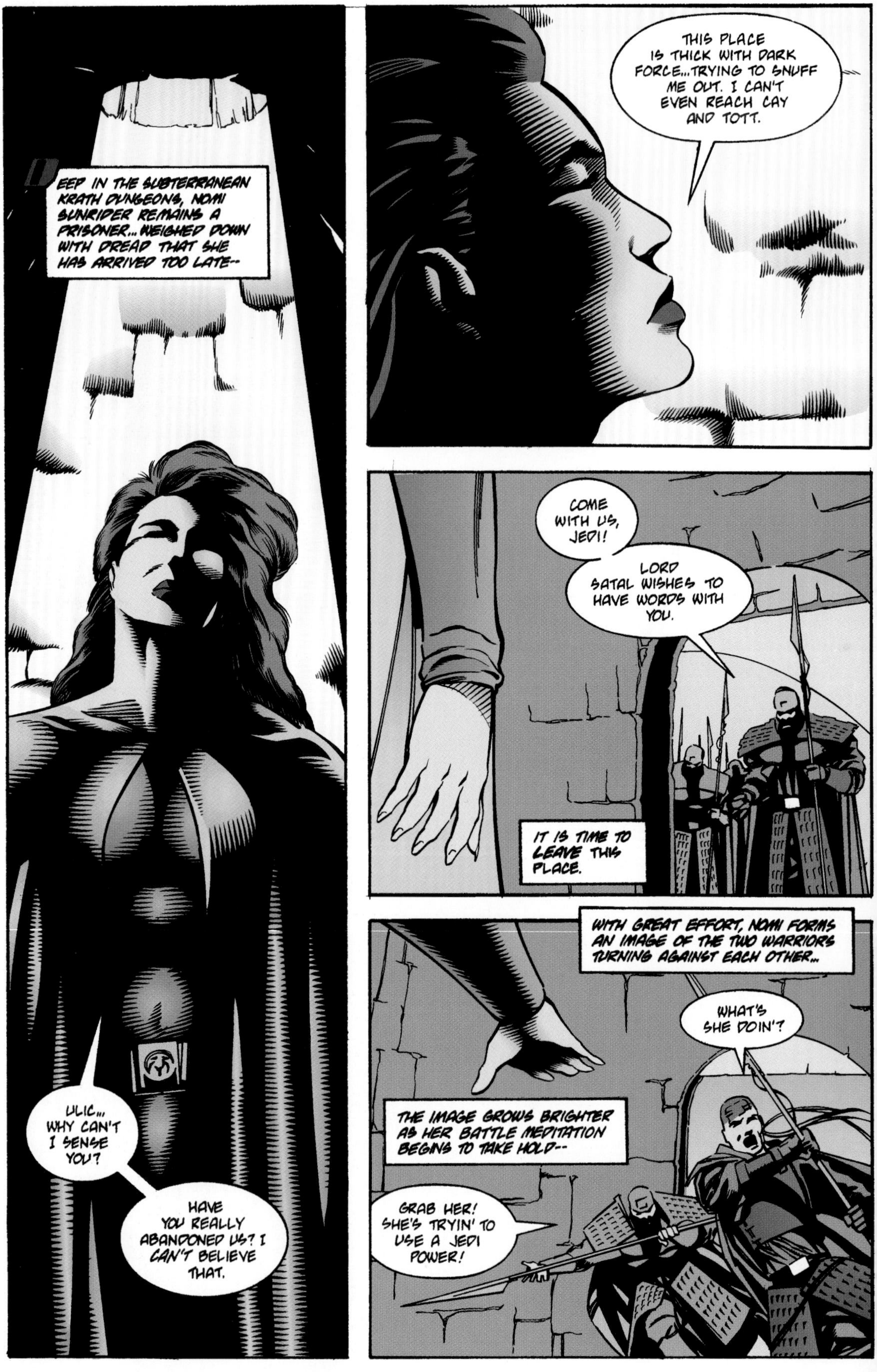
EEP IN THE SUBTERRANEAN KRATH DUNGEONS, NOMI SUNRIDER REMAINS A PRISONER... WEIGHED DOWN WITH DREAD THAT SHE HAS ARRIVED TOO LATE--
ULIC... WHY CAN'T I SENSE YOU?
HAVE YOU REALLY ABANDONED US? I CAN'T BELIEVE THAT.
THIS PLACE IS THICK WITH DARK FORCE...TRYING TO SNUFF ME OUT. I CAN'T EVEN REACH CAY AND TOTT.
COME WITH US, JEDI!
LORD SATAL WISHES TO HAVE WORDS WITH YOU.
IT IS TIME TO LEAVE THIS PLACE.
WITH GREAT EFFORT, NOMI FORMS AN IMAGE OF THE TWO WARRIORS TURNING AGAINST EACH OTHER...
WHAT'S SHE DOIN'?
THE IMAGE GROWS BRIGHTER AS HER BATTLE MEDITATION BEGINS TO TAKE HOLD--
GRAB HER! SHE'S TRYIN' TO USE A JEDI POWER!

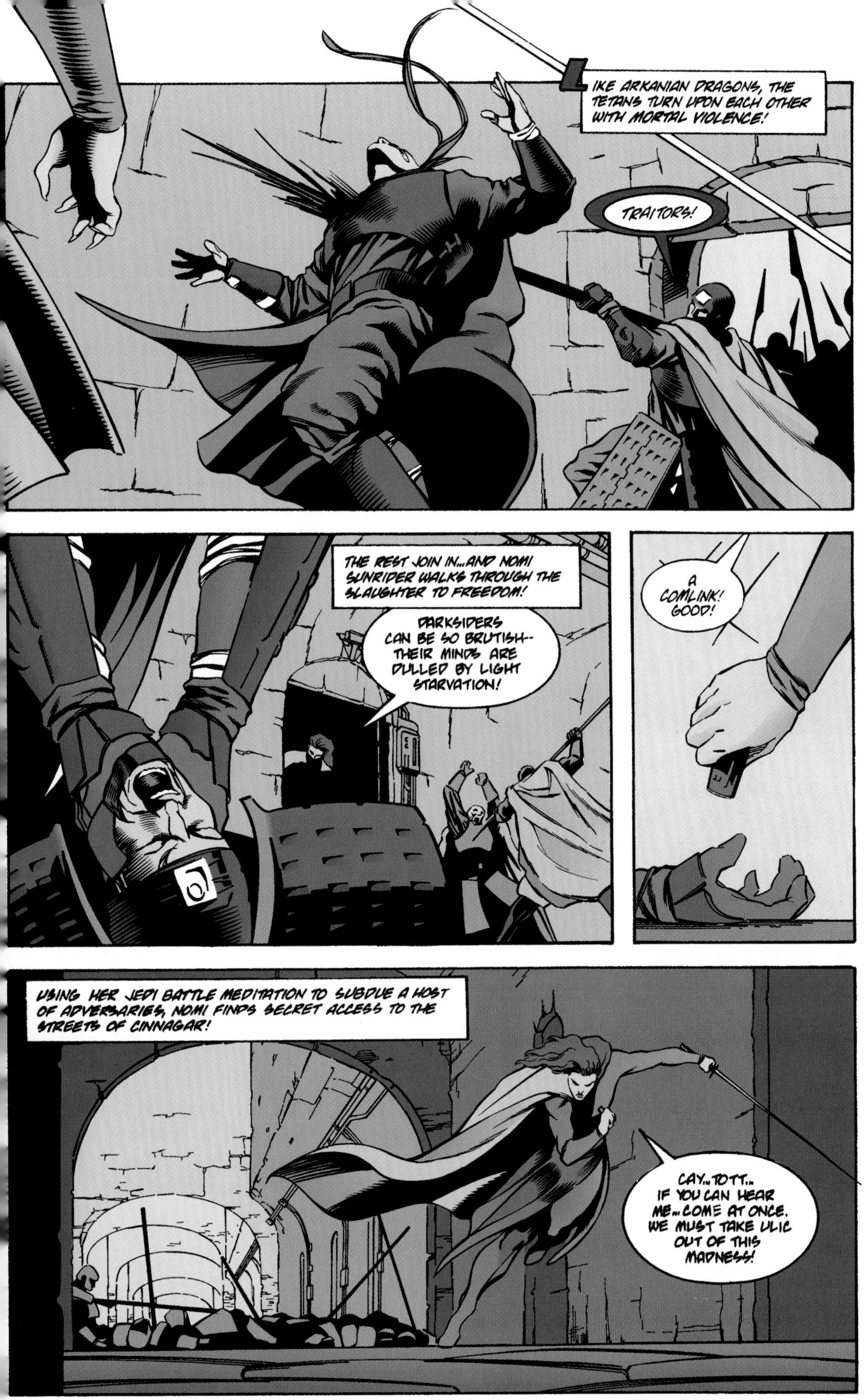
LIKE ARKANIAN DRAGONS, THE TETANS TURN UPON EACH OTHER WITH MORTAL VIOLENCE!
TRAITORS!
THE REST JOIN IN...AND NOMI SUNRIDER WALKS THROUGH THE SLAUGHTER TO FREEDOM!
DARKSIDERS CAN BE SO BRUTISH-- THEIR MINDS ARE DULLED BY LIGHT STARVATION!
A COMLINK! GOOD!
USING HER JEDI BATTLE MEDITATION TO SUBDUE A HOST OF ADVERSARIES, NOMI FINDS SECRET ACCESS TO THE STREETS OF CINNAGAR!
CAY...TOTT... IF YOU CAN HEAR ME...COME AT ONCE. WE MUST TAKE ULIC OUT OF THIS MADNESS!

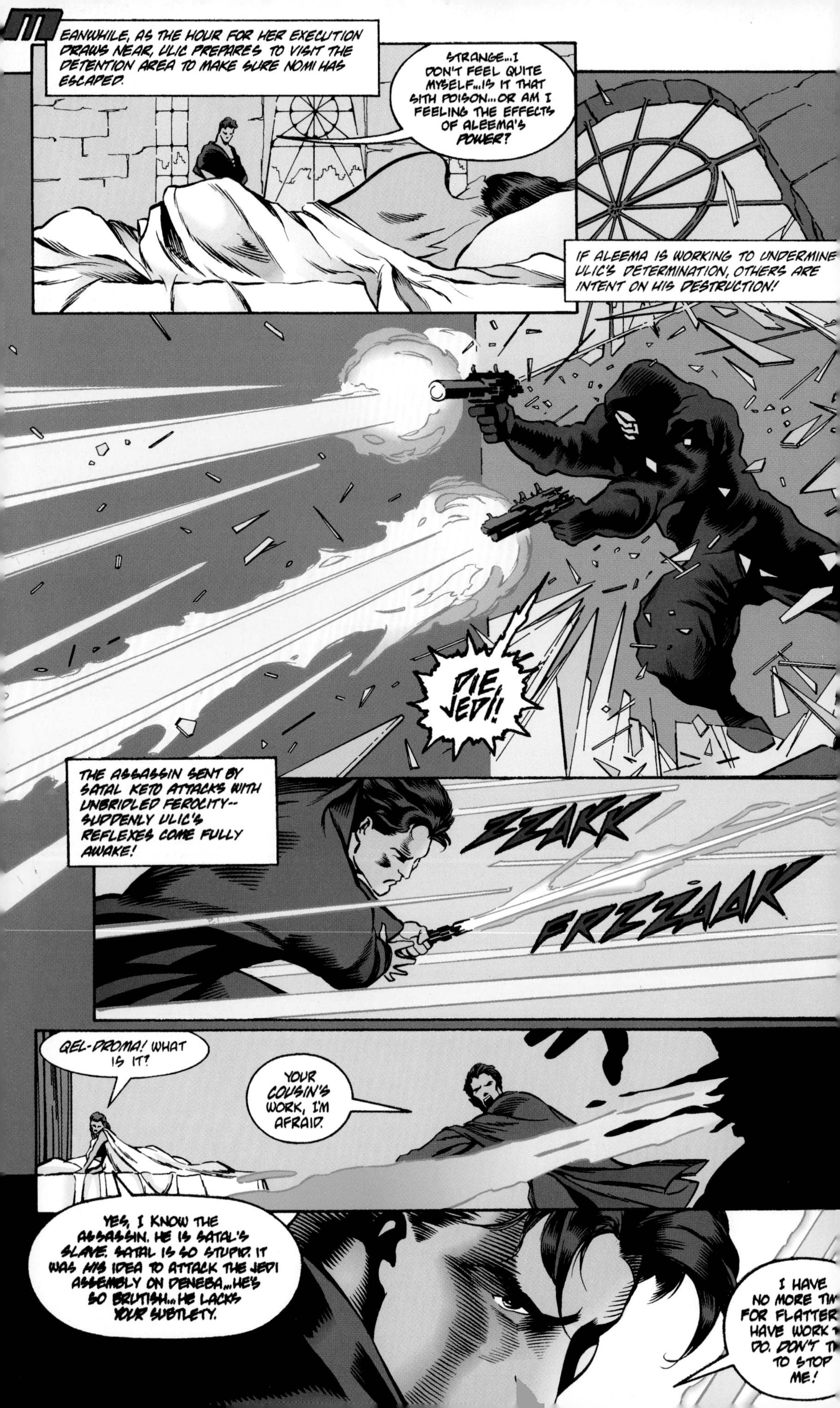
MEANWHILE, AS THE HOUR FOR HER EXECUTION DRAWS NEAR, ULIC PREPARES TO VISIT THE DETENTION AREA TO MAKE SURE NOMI HAS ESCAPED.
STRANGE...I DON'T FEEL QUITE MYSELF...IS IT THAT SITH POISON...OR AM I FEELING THE EFFECTS OF ALEEMA'S POWER?
IF ALEEMA IS WORKING TO UNDERMINE ULIC'S DETERMINATION, OTHERS ARE INTENT ON HIS DESTRUCTION!
DIE, JEDI!!
THE ASSASSIN SENT BY SATAL KETO ATTACKS WITH UNBRIDLED FEROCITY-- SUDDENLY ULIC'S REFLEXES COME FULLY AWAKE!
ZZAKK
FRZZAAK
QEL-DROMA! WHAT IS IT?
YOUR COUSIN'S WORK, I'M AFRAID.
YES, I KNOW THE ASSASSIN. HE IS SATAL'S SLAVE. SATAL IS SO STUPID. IT WAS HIS IDEA TO ATTACK THE JEDI ASSEMBLY ON DENEBA...HE'S SO BRUTISH...HE LACKS YOUR SUBTLETY.

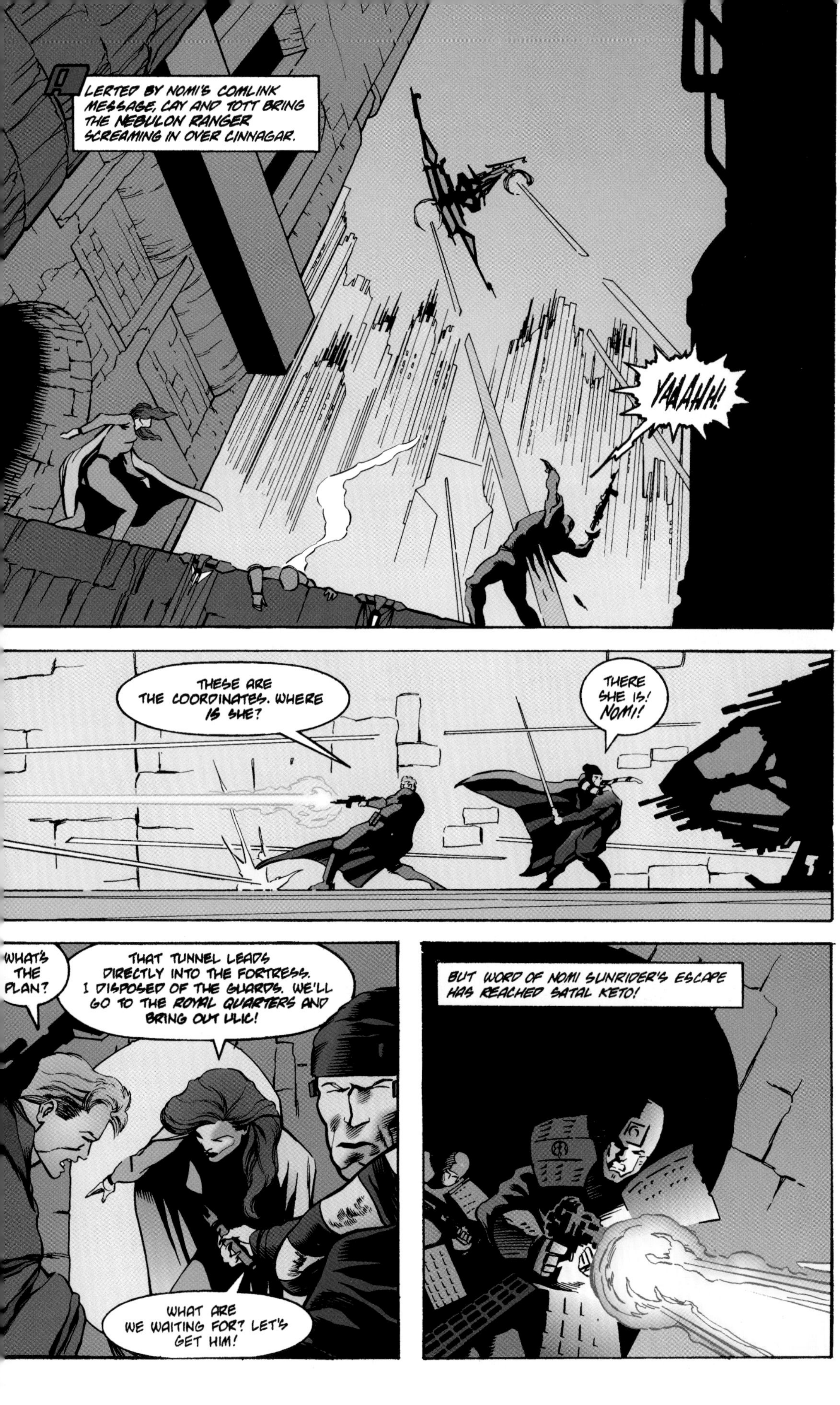
ALERTED BY NOMI'S COMLINK MESSAGE, CAY AND TOTT BRING THE NEBULON RANGER SCREAMING IN OVER CINNAGAR.
YAAAHH!
THESE ARE THE COORDINATES. WHERE IS SHE?
THERE SHE IS! NOMI!
WHAT'S THE PLAN?
THAT TUNNEL LEADS DIRECTLY INTO THE FORTRESS. I DISPOSED OF THE GUARDS. WE'LL GO TO THE ROYAL QUARTERS AND BRING OUT ULIC!
WHAT ARE WE WAITING FOR? LET'S GET HIM!
BUT WORD OF NOMI SUNRIDER'S ESCAPE HAS REACHED SATAL KETO!

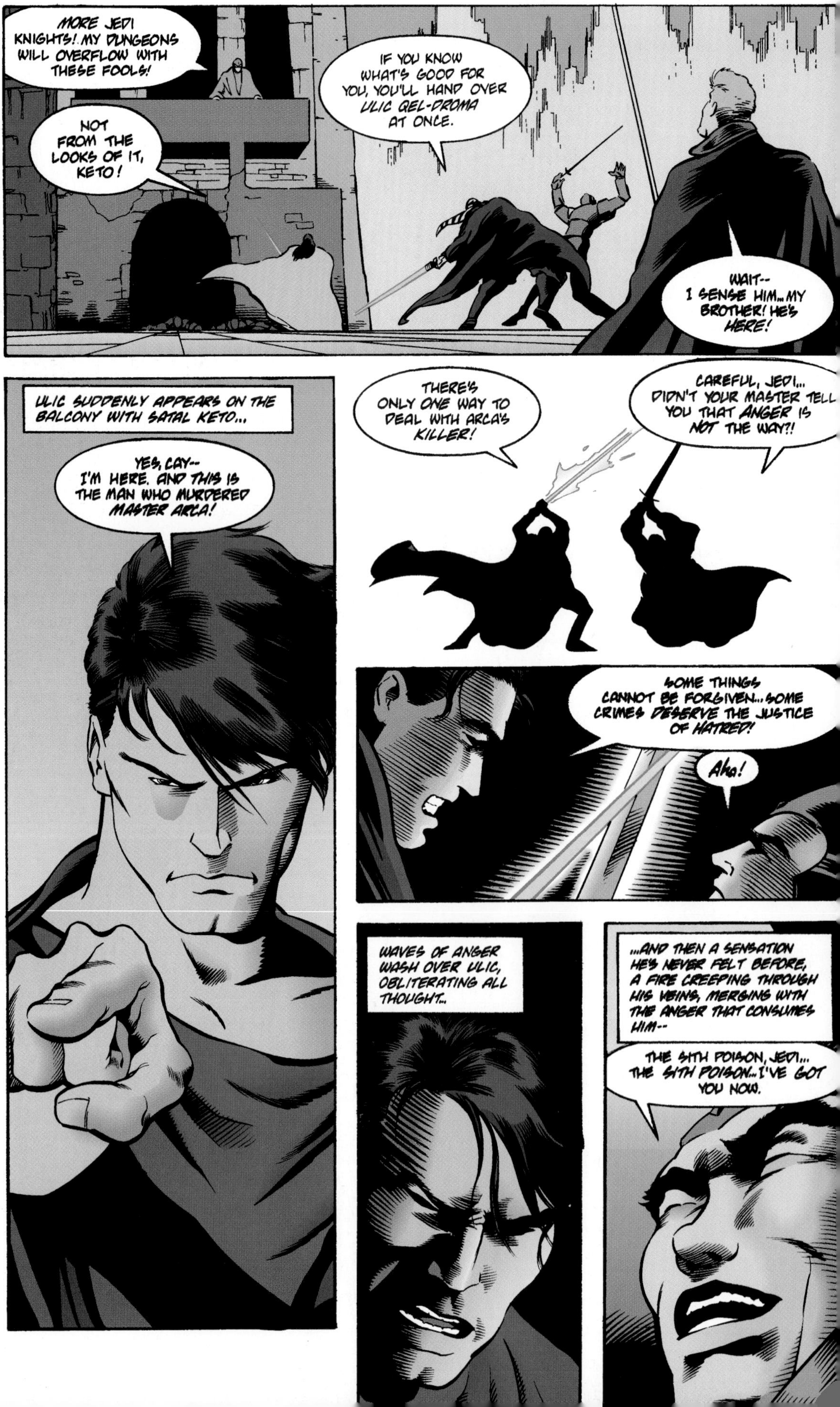
MORE JEDI KNIGHTS! MY DUNGEONS WILL OVERFLOW WITH THESE FOOLS!
NOT FROM THE LOOKS OF IT, KETO!
IF YOU KNOW WHAT'S GOOD FOR YOU, YOU'LL HAND OVER ULIC QEL-DROMA AT ONCE.
WAIT-- I SENSE HIM... MY BROTHER! HE'S HERE!
ULIC SUDDENLY APPEARS ON THE BALCONY WITH SATAL KETO...
YES, CAY-- I'M HERE. AND THIS IS THE MAN WHO MURDERED MASTER ARCA!
THERE'S ONLY ONE WAY TO DEAL WITH ARCA'S KILLER!
CAREFUL, JEDI... DIDN'T YOUR MASTER TELL YOU THAT ANGER IS NOT THE WAY?!
SOME THINGS CANNOT BE FORGIVEN... SOME CRIMES DESERVE THE JUSTICE OF HATRED!
Aha!
WAVES OF ANGER WASH OVER ULIC, OBLITERATING ALL THOUGHT...
...AND THEN A SENSATION HE'S NEVER FELT BEFORE, A FIRE CREEPING THROUGH HIS VEINS, MERGING WITH THE ANGER THAT CONSUMES HIM--
THE SITH POISON, JEDI... THE SITH POISON... I'VE GOT YOU NOW.

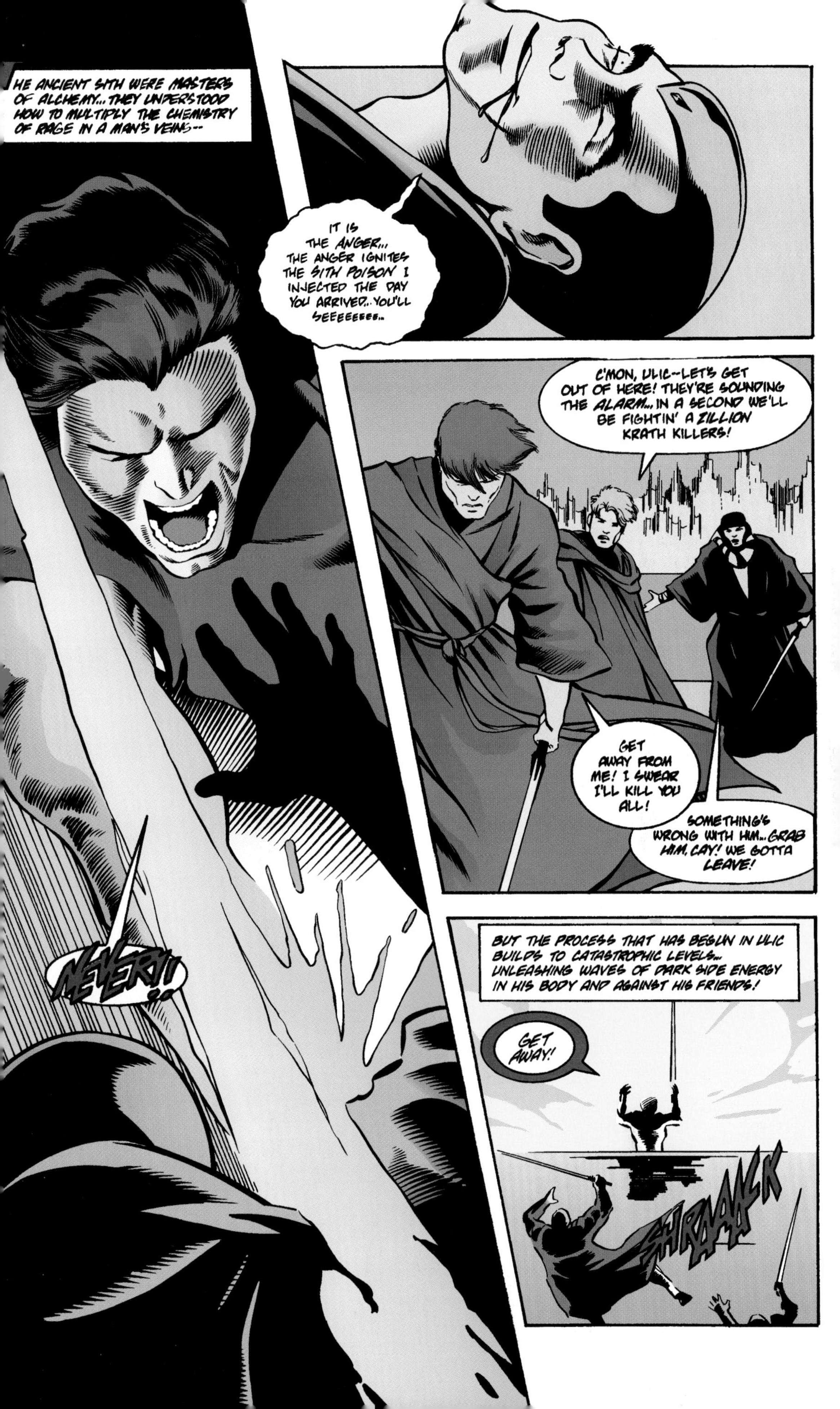
HE ANCIENT SITH WERE MASTERS OF ALCHEMY... THEY UNDERSTOOD HOW TO MULTIPLY THE CHEMISTRY OF RAGE IN A MAN'S VEINS--
IT IS THE ANGER... THE ANGER IGNITES THE SITH POISON I INJECTED THE DAY YOU ARRIVED... YOU'LL SEEEEEEEE...
NEVER!!
C'MON, ULIC--LET'S GET OUT OF HERE! THEY'RE SOUNDING THE ALARM... IN A SECOND WE'LL BE FIGHTIN' A ZILLION KRATH KILLERS!
GET AWAY FROM ME! I SWEAR I'LL KILL YOU ALL!
SOMETHING'S WRONG WITH HIM... GRAB HIM, CAY! WE GOTTA LEAVE!
BUT THE PROCESS THAT HAS BEGUN IN ULIC BUILDS TO CATASTROPHIC LEVELS... UNLEASHING WAVES OF DARK SIDE ENERGY IN HIS BODY AND AGAINST HIS FRIENDS!
GET AWAY!
SHRAAAK

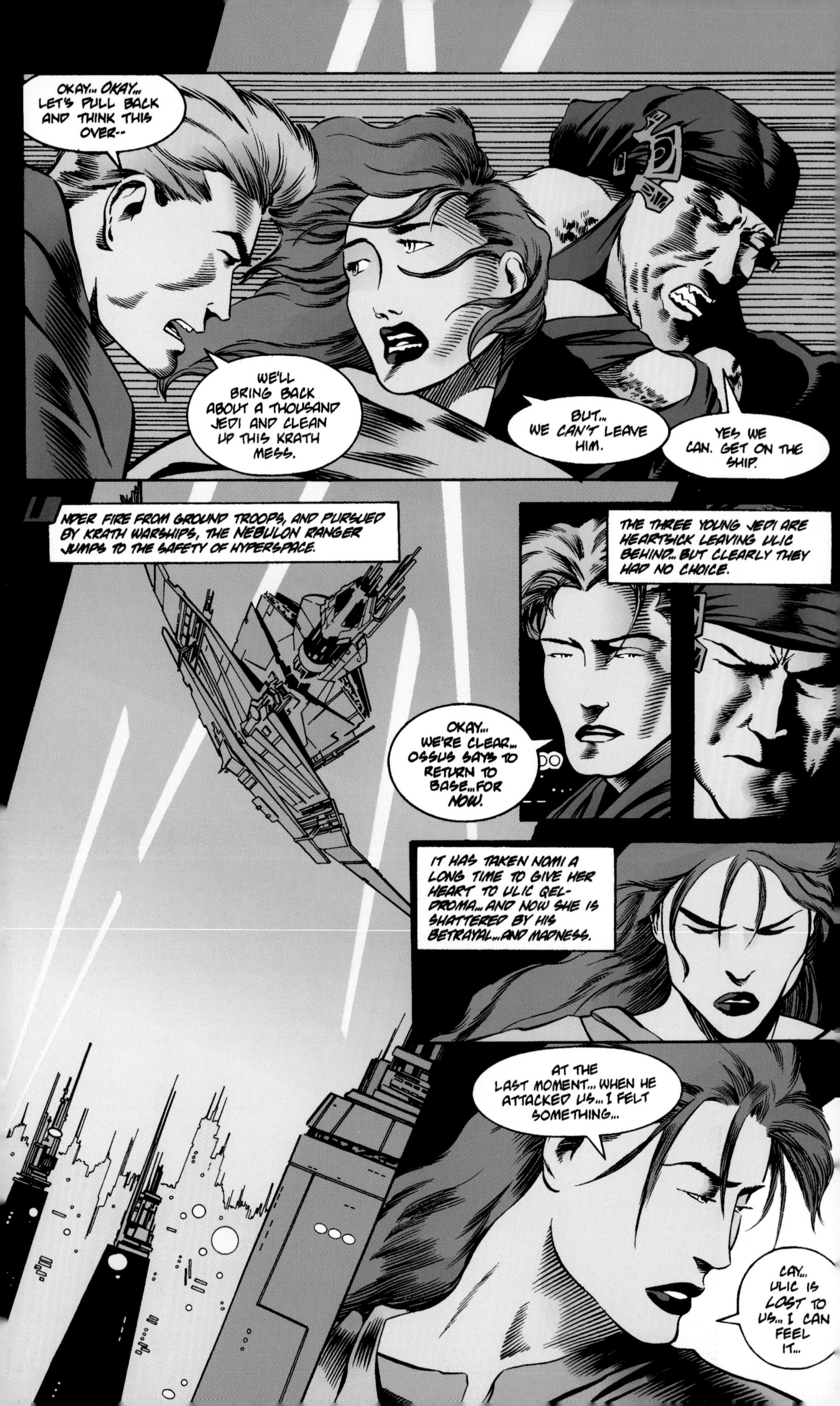
OKAY... OKAY... LET'S PULL BACK AND THINK THIS OVER--
WE'LL BRING BACK ABOUT A THOUSAND JEDI AND CLEAN UP THIS KRATH MESS.
BUT... WE CAN'T LEAVE HIM.
YES WE CAN. GET ON THE SHIP.
UNDER FIRE FROM GROUND TROOPS, AND PURSUED BY KRATH WARSHIPS, THE NEBULON RANGER JUMPS TO THE SAFETY OF HYPERSPACE.
THE THREE YOUNG JEDI ARE HEARTSICK LEAVING ULIC BEHIND... BUT CLEARLY THEY HAD NO CHOICE.
OKAY... WE'RE CLEAR... OSSUS SAYS TO RETURN TO BASE...FOR NOW.
IT HAS TAKEN NOMI A LONG TIME TO GIVE HER HEART TO ULIC QEL-DROMA... AND NOW SHE IS SHATTERED BY HIS BETRAYAL...AND MADNESS.
AT THE LAST MOMENT... WHEN HE ATTACKED US... I FELT SOMETHING...
CAY... ULIC IS LOST TO US... I CAN FEEL IT...

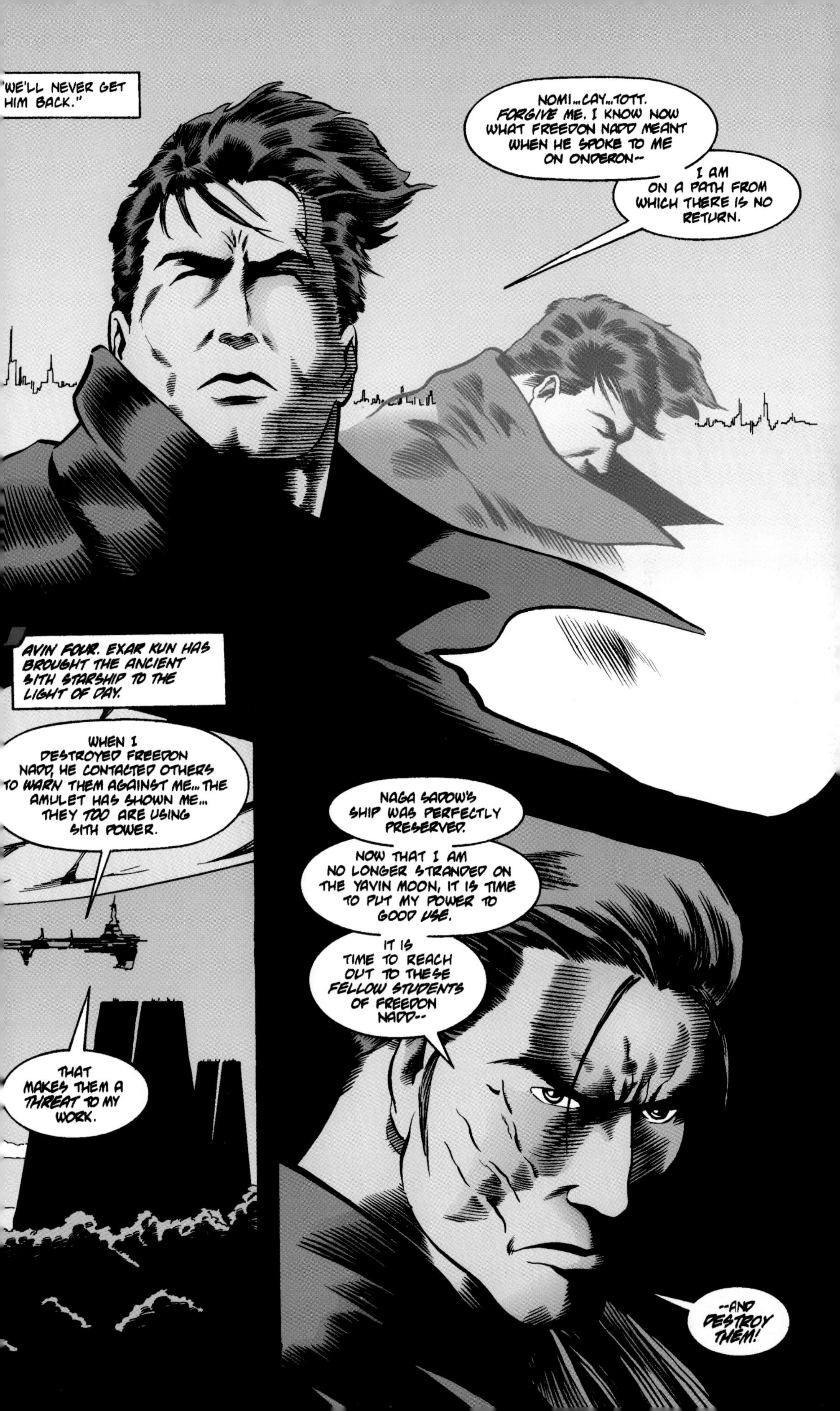
"WE'LL NEVER GET HIM BACK."
NOMI...CAY...TOTT. FORGIVE ME. I KNOW NOW WHAT FREEDON NADD MEANT WHEN HE SPOKE TO ME ON ONDERON--
I AM ON A PATH FROM WHICH THERE IS NO RETURN.
AVIN FOUR. EXAR KUN HAS BROUGHT THE ANCIENT SITH STARSHIP TO THE LIGHT OF DAY.
WHEN I DESTROYED FREEDON NADD, HE CONTACTED OTHERS TO WARN THEM AGAINST ME... THE AMULET HAS SHOWN ME... THEY TOO ARE USING SITH POWER.
THAT MAKES THEM A THREAT TO MY WORK.
NAGA SADOW'S SHIP WAS PERFECTLY PRESERVED.
NOW THAT I AM NO LONGER STRANDED ON THE YAVIN MOON, IT IS TIME TO PUT MY POWER TO GOOD USE.
IT IS TIME TO REACH OUT TO THESE FELLOW STUDENTS OF FREEDON NADD--
--AND DESTROY THEM!

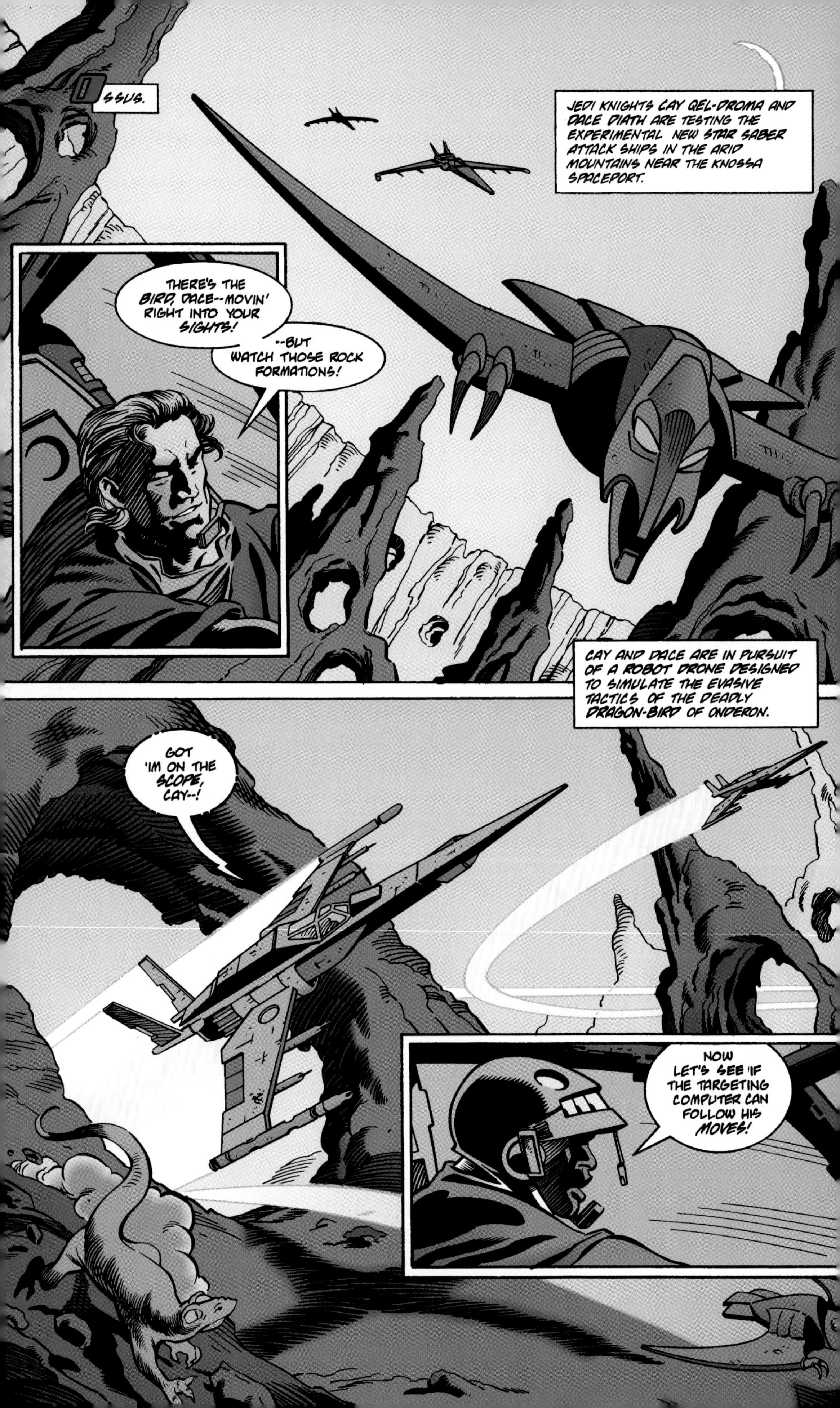
OSSUS.
JEDI KNIGHTS CAY QEL-DROMA AND DACE DIATH ARE TESTING THE EXPERIMENTAL NEW STAR SABER ATTACK SHIPS IN THE ARID MOUNTAINS NEAR THE KNOSSA SPACEPORT.
THERE'S THE BIRD, DACE--MOVIN' RIGHT INTO YOUR SIGHTS!
--BUT WATCH THOSE ROCK FORMATIONS!
CAY AND DACE ARE IN PURSUIT OF A ROBOT DRONE DESIGNED TO SIMULATE THE EVASIVE TACTICS OF THE DEADLY DRAGON-BIRD OF ONDERON.
GOT 'IM ON THE SCOPE, CAY--!
NOW LET'S SEE IF THE TARGETING COMPUTER CAN FOLLOW HIS MOVES!

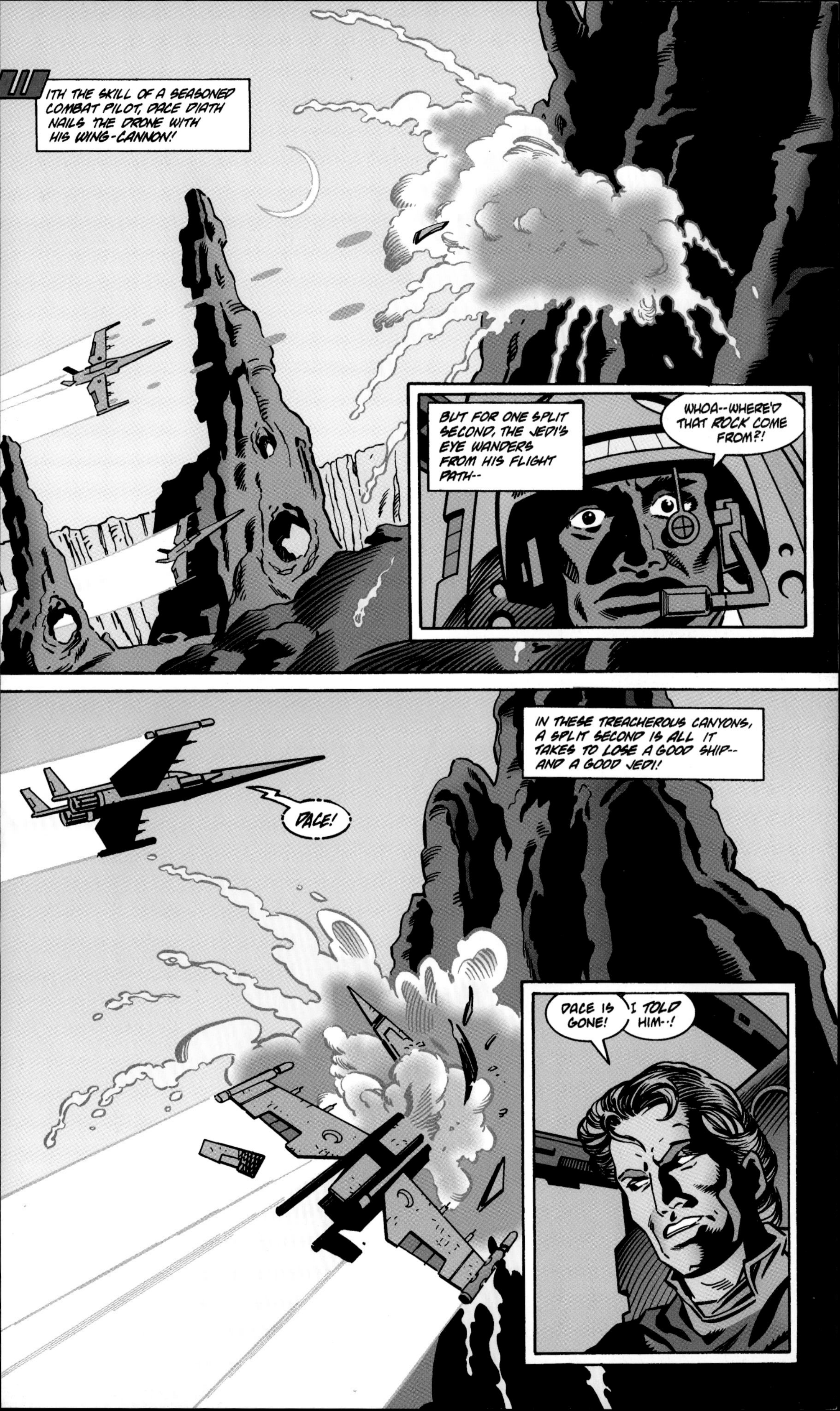
WITH THE SKILL OF A SEASONED COMBAT PILOT, DACE DIATH NAILS THE DRONE WITH HIS WING-CANNON!
BUT FOR ONE SPLIT SECOND, THE JEDI'S EYE WANDERS FROM HIS FLIGHT PATH--
WHOA--WHERE'D THAT ROCK COME FROM?!
IN THESE TREACHEROUS CANYONS, A SPLIT SECOND IS ALL IT TAKES TO LOSE A GOOD SHIP-- AND A GOOD JEDI!
DACE!
DACE IS GONE!
I TOLD HIM--!

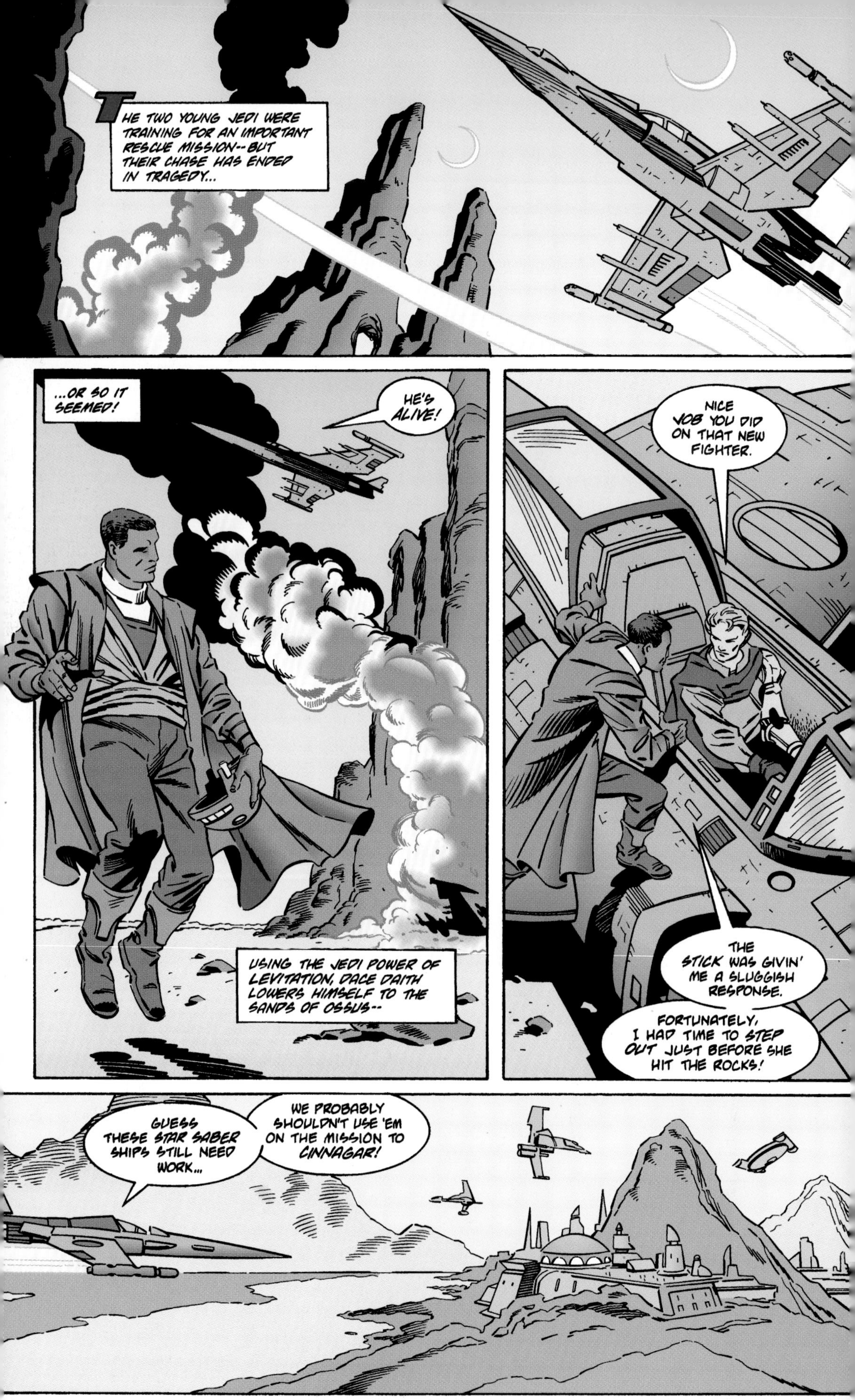
THE TWO YOUNG JEDI WERE TRAINING FOR AN IMPORTANT RESCUE MISSION--BUT THEIR CHASE HAS ENDED IN TRAGEDY...
...OR SO IT SEEMED!
HE'S ALIVE!
USING THE JEDI POWER OF LEVITATION, DACE DAITH LOWERS HIMSELF TO THE SANDS OF OSSUS--
NICE JOB YOU DID ON THAT NEW FIGHTER.
THE STICK WAS GIVIN' ME A SLUGGISH RESPONSE.
FORTUNATELY, I HAD TIME TO STEP OUT JUST BEFORE SHE HIT THE ROCKS!
GUESS THESE STAR SABER SHIPS STILL NEED WORK...
WE PROBABLY SHOULDN'T USE 'EM ON THE MISSION TO CINNAGAR!

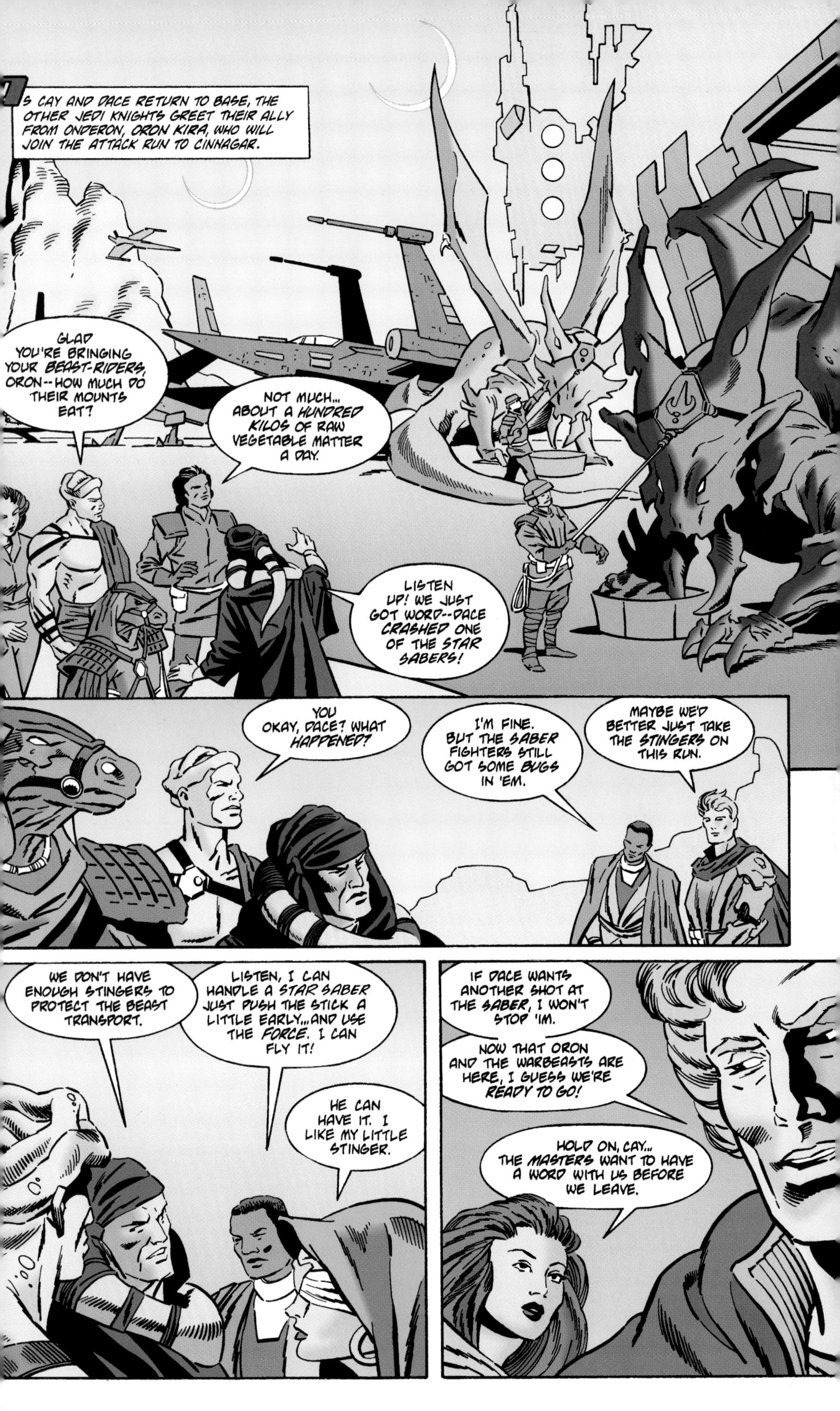
AS CAY AND DACE RETURN TO BASE, THE OTHER JEDI KNIGHTS GREET THEIR ALLY FROM ONDERON, ORON KIRA, WHO WILL JOIN THE ATTACK RUN TO CINNAGAR.
GLAD YOU'RE BRINGING YOUR BEAST-RIDERS, ORON--HOW MUCH DO THEIR MOUNTS EAT?
NOT MUCH... ABOUT A HUNDRED KILOS OF RAW VEGETABLE MATTER A DAY.
LISTEN UP! WE JUST GOT WORD--DACE CRASHED ONE OF THE STAR SABERS!
YOU OKAY, DACE? WHAT HAPPENED?
I'M FINE. BUT THE SABER FIGHTERS STILL GOT SOME BUGS IN 'EM.
MAYBE WE'D BETTER JUST TAKE THE STINGERS ON THIS RUN.
WE DON'T HAVE ENOUGH STINGERS TO PROTECT THE BEAST TRANSPORT.
LISTEN, I CAN HANDLE A STAR SABER JUST PUSH THE STICK A LITTLE EARLY...AND USE THE FORCE. I CAN FLY IT!
HE CAN HAVE IT. I LIKE MY LITTLE STINGER.
IF DACE WANTS ANOTHER SHOT AT THE SABER, I WON'T STOP 'IM.
NOW THAT ORON AND THE WARBEASTS ARE HERE, I GUESS WE'RE READY TO GO!
HOLD ON, CAY... THE MASTERS WANT TO HAVE A WORD WITH US BEFORE WE LEAVE.

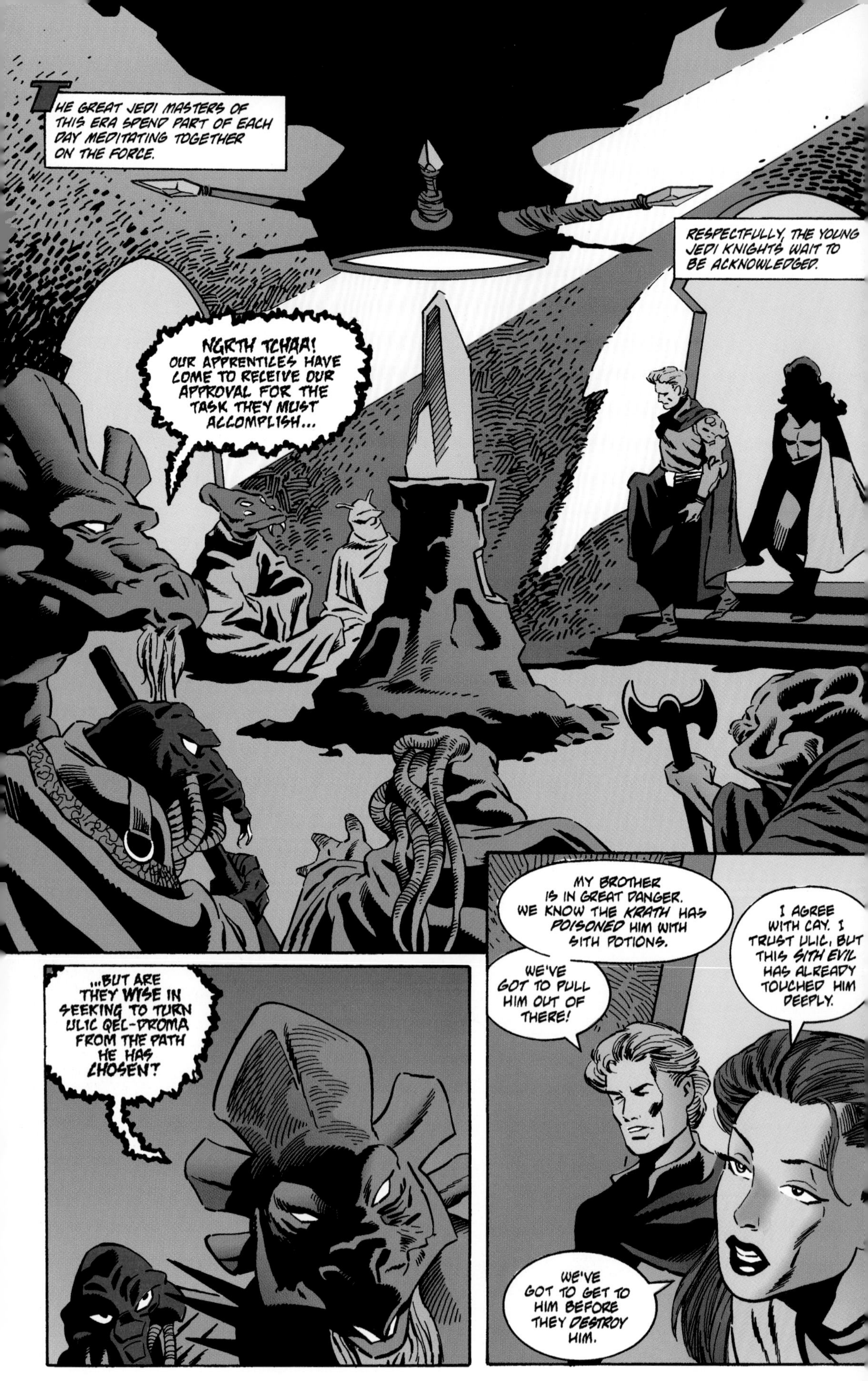
THE GREAT JEDI MASTERS OF THIS ERA SPEND PART OF EACH DAY MEDITATING TOGETHER ON THE FORCE.
RESPECTFULLY, THE YOUNG JEDI KNIGHTS WAIT TO BE ACKNOWLEDGED.
NGRTH TCHAA! OUR APPRENTICES HAVE COME TO RECEIVE OUR APPROVAL FOR THE TASK THEY MUST ACCOMPLISH...
...BUT ARE THEY WISE IN SEEKING TO TURN ULIC QEL-DROMA FROM THE PATH HE HAS CHOSEN?
MY BROTHER IS IN GREAT DANGER. WE KNOW THE KRATH HAS POISONED HIM WITH SITH POTIONS.
WE'VE GOT TO PULL HIM OUT OF THERE!
I AGREE WITH CAY. I TRUST ULIC, BUT THIS SITH EVIL HAS ALREADY TOUCHED HIM DEEPLY.
WE'VE GOT TO GET TO HIM BEFORE THEY DESTROY HIM.

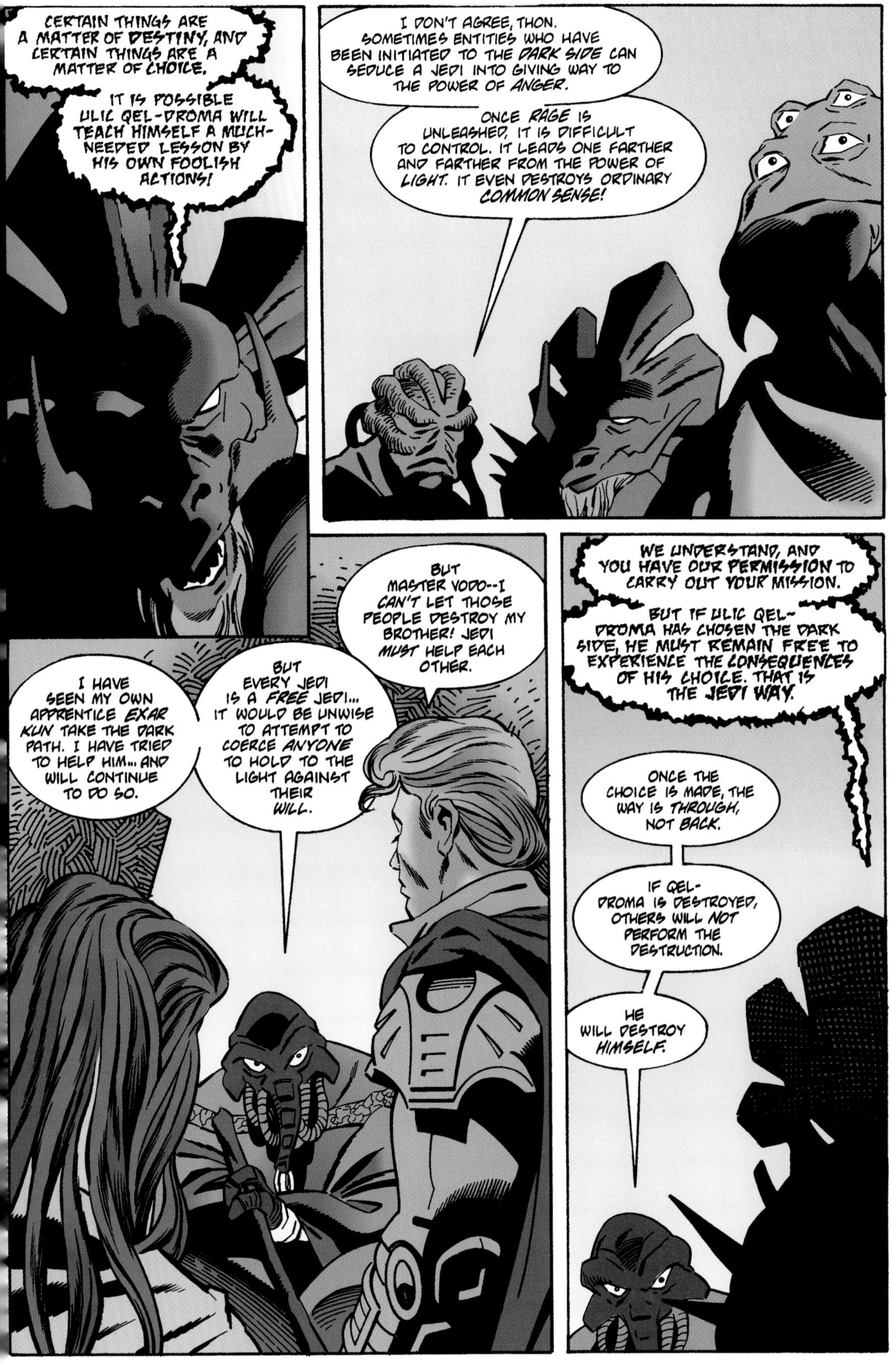
CERTAIN THINGS ARE A MATTER OF DESTINY, AND CERTAIN THINGS ARE A MATTER OF CHOICE.
IT IS POSSIBLE ULIC QEL-DROMA WILL TEACH HIMSELF A MUCH-NEEDED LESSON BY HIS OWN FOOLISH ACTIONS!
I DON'T AGREE, THON. SOMETIMES ENTITIES WHO HAVE BEEN INITIATED TO THE DARK SIDE CAN SEDUCE A JEDI INTO GIVING WAY TO THE POWER OF ANGER.
ONCE RAGE IS UNLEASHED, IT IS DIFFICULT TO CONTROL. IT LEADS ONE FARTHER AND FARTHER FROM THE POWER OF LIGHT. IT EVEN DESTROYS ORDINARY COMMON SENSE!
BUT MASTER VODO--I CAN'T LET THOSE PEOPLE DESTROY MY BROTHER! JEDI MUST HELP EACH OTHER.
I HAVE SEEN MY OWN APPRENTICE EXAR KUN TAKE THE DARK PATH. I HAVE TRIED TO HELP HIM... AND WILL CONTINUE TO DO SO.
BUT EVERY JEDI IS A FREE JEDI... IT WOULD BE UNWISE TO ATTEMPT TO COERCE ANYONE TO HOLD TO THE LIGHT AGAINST THEIR WILL.
WE UNDERSTAND, AND YOU HAVE OUR PERMISSION TO CARRY OUT YOUR MISSION.
BUT IF ULIC QEL-DROMA HAS CHOSEN THE DARK SIDE, HE MUST REMAIN FREE TO EXPERIENCE THE CONSEQUENCES OF HIS CHOICE. THAT IS THE JEDI WAY.
ONCE THE CHOICE IS MADE, THE WAY IS THROUGH, NOT BACK.
IF QEL-DROMA IS DESTROYED, OTHERS WILL NOT PERFORM THE DESTRUCTION.
HE WILL DESTROY HIMSELF.

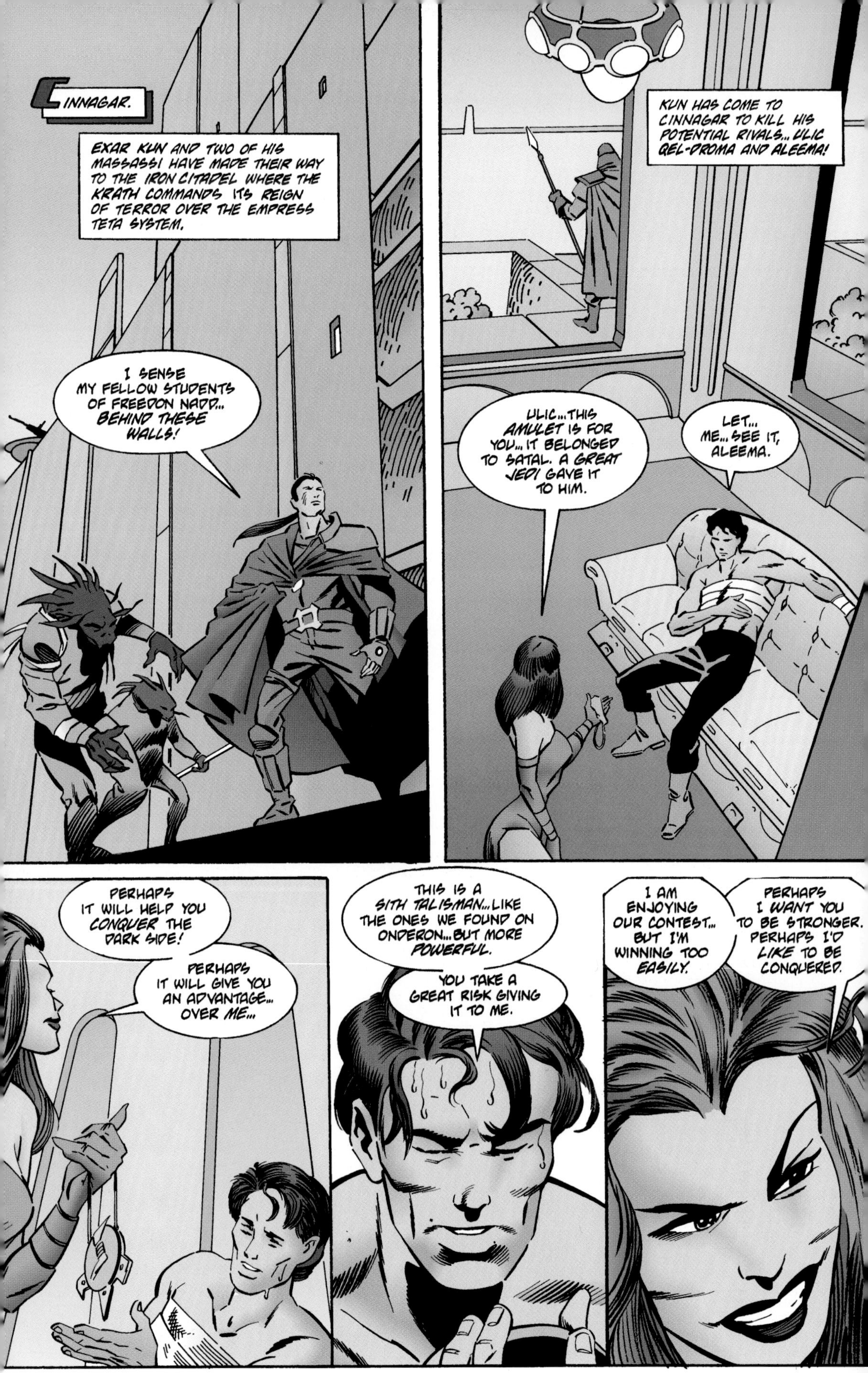
CINNAGAR.
EXAR KUN AND TWO OF HIS MASSASSI HAVE MADE THEIR WAY TO THE IRON CITADEL WHERE THE KRATH COMMANDS ITS REIGN OF TERROR OVER THE EMPRESS TETA SYSTEM.
I SENSE MY FELLOW STUDENTS OF FREEDON NADD... BEHIND THESE WALLS!
KUN HAS COME TO CINNAGAR TO KILL HIS POTENTIAL RIVALS... ULIC QEL-DROMA AND ALEEMA!
ULIC... THIS AMULET IS FOR YOU... IT BELONGED TO SATAL. A GREAT JEDI GAVE IT TO HIM.
LET... ME... SEE IT, ALEEMA.
PERHAPS IT WILL HELP YOU CONQUER THE DARK SIDE!
PERHAPS IT WILL GIVE YOU AN ADVANTAGE... OVER ME...
THIS IS A SITH TALISMAN... LIKE THE ONES WE FOUND ON ONDERON... BUT MORE POWERFUL.
YOU TAKE A GREAT RISK GIVING IT TO ME.
I AM ENJOYING OUR CONTEST... BUT I'M WINNING TOO EASILY.
PERHAPS I WANT YOU TO BE STRONGER. PERHAPS I'D LIKE TO BE CONQUERED.

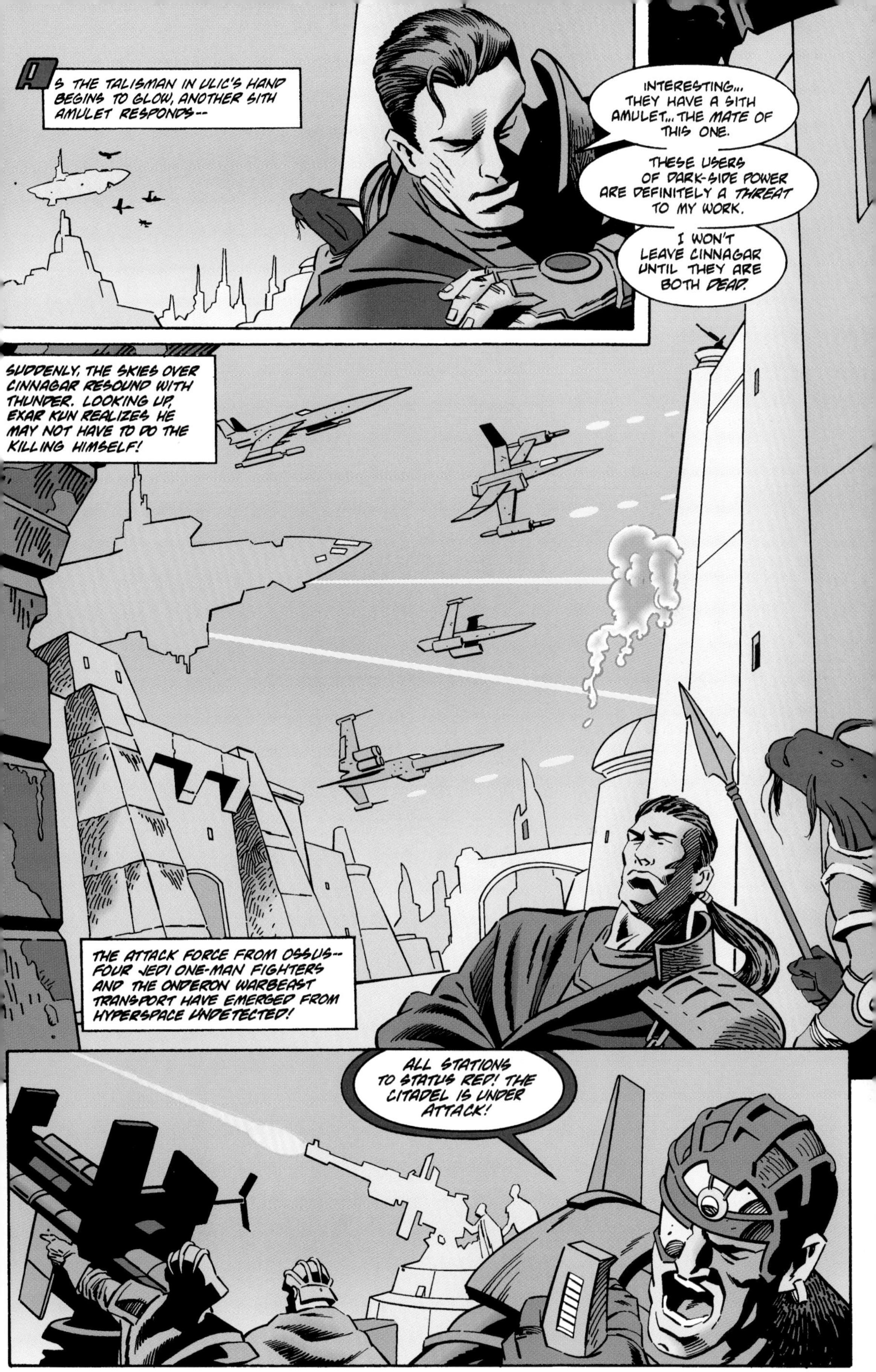
AS THE TALISMAN IN ULIC'S HAND BEGINS TO GLOW, ANOTHER SITH AMULET RESPONDS--
INTERESTING... THEY HAVE A SITH AMULET... THE MATE OF THIS ONE.
THESE USERS OF DARK-SIDE POWER ARE DEFINITELY A THREAT TO MY WORK.
I WON'T LEAVE CINNAGAR UNTIL THEY ARE BOTH DEAD.
SUDDENLY, THE SKIES OVER CINNAGAR RESOUND WITH THUNDER. LOOKING UP, EXAR KUN REALIZES HE MAY NOT HAVE TO DO THE KILLING HIMSELF!
THE ATTACK FORCE FROM OSSUS-- FOUR JEDI ONE-MAN FIGHTERS AND THE ONDERON WARBEAST TRANSPORT HAVE EMERGED FROM HYPERSPACE UNDETECTED!
ALL STATIONS TO STATUS RED! THE CITADEL IS UNDER ATTACK!

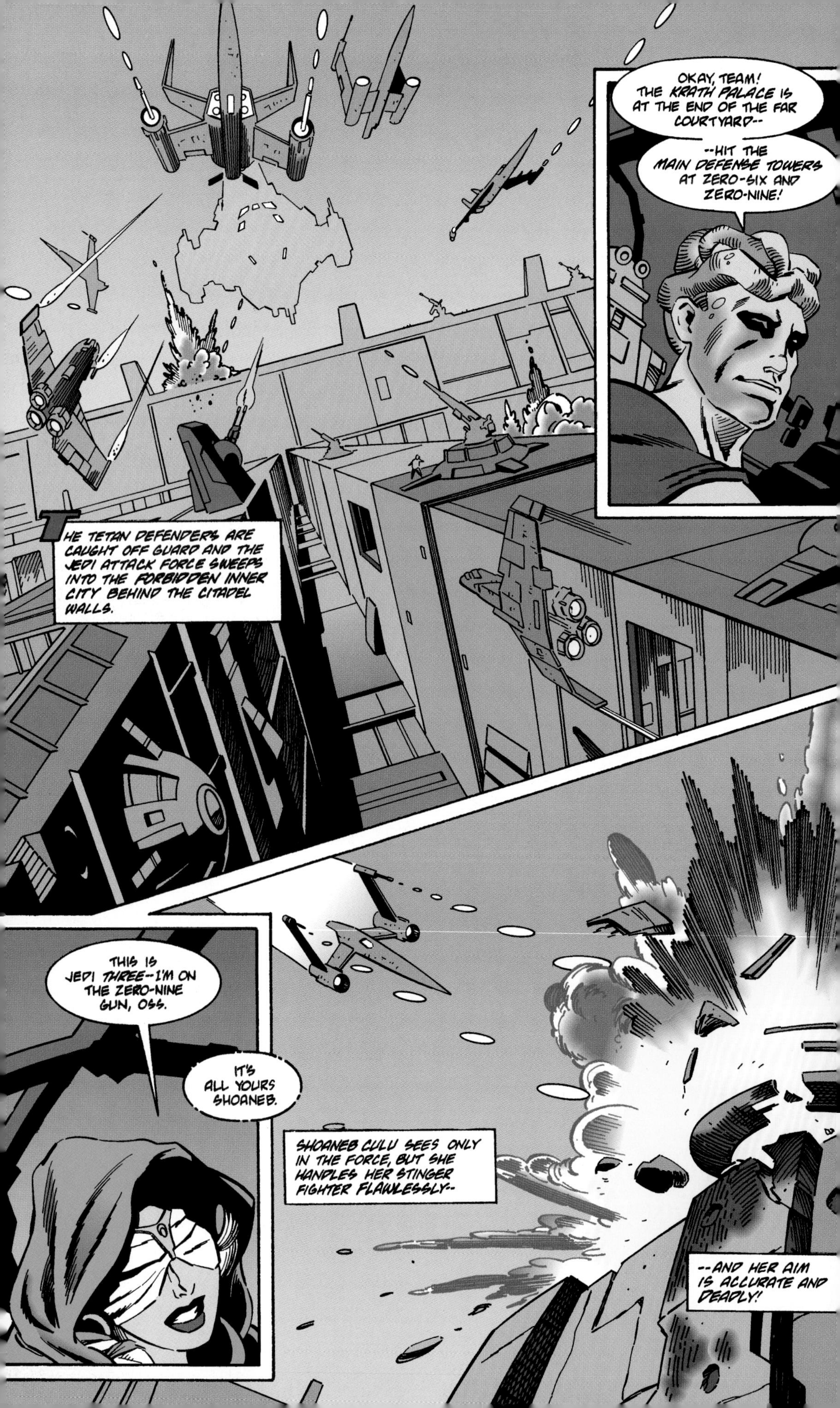
OKAY, TEAM! THE KRATH PALACE IS AT THE END OF THE FAR COURTYARD--
--HIT THE MAIN DEFENSE TOWERS AT ZERO-SIX AND ZERO-NINE!
THE TETAN DEFENDERS ARE CAUGHT OFF GUARD AND THE JEDI ATTACK FORCE SWEEPS INTO THE FORBIDDEN INNER CITY BEHIND THE CITADEL WALLS.
THIS IS JEDI THREE--I'M ON THE ZERO-NINE GUN, OSS.
IT'S ALL YOURS SHOANEB.
SHOANEB CULU SEES ONLY IN THE FORCE, BUT SHE HANDLES HER STINGER FIGHTER FLAWLESSLY--
--AND HER AIM IS ACCURATE AND DEADLY!

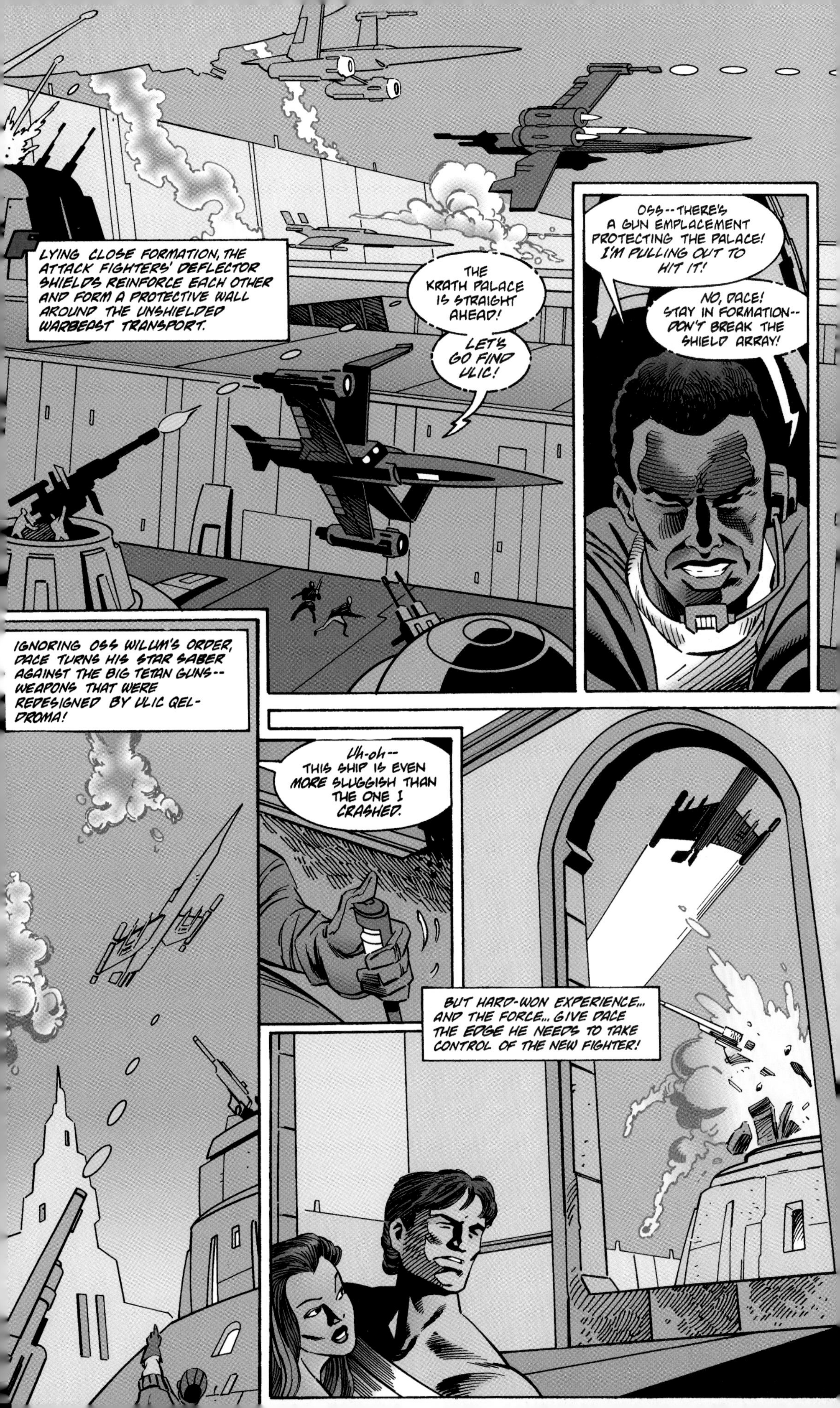
LYING CLOSE FORMATION, THE ATTACK FIGHTERS' DEFLECTOR SHIELDS REINFORCE EACH OTHER AND FORM A PROTECTIVE WALL AROUND THE UNSHIELDED WARBEAST TRANSPORT.
THE KRATH PALACE IS STRAIGHT AHEAD!
LET'S GO FIND ULIC!
OSS--THERE'S A GUN EMPLACEMENT PROTECTING THE PALACE! I'M PULLING OUT TO HIT IT!
NO, DACE! STAY IN FORMATION--DON'T BREAK THE SHIELD ARRAY!
IGNORING OSS WILUM'S ORDER, DACE TURNS HIS STAR SABER AGAINST THE BIG TETAN GUNS--WEAPONS THAT WERE REDESIGNED BY ULIC QEL-DROMA!
Uh-oh--THIS SHIP IS EVEN MORE SLUGGISH THAN THE ONE I CRASHED.
BUT HARD-WON EXPERIENCE... AND THE FORCE... GIVE DACE THE EDGE HE NEEDS TO TAKE CONTROL OF THE NEW FIGHTER!

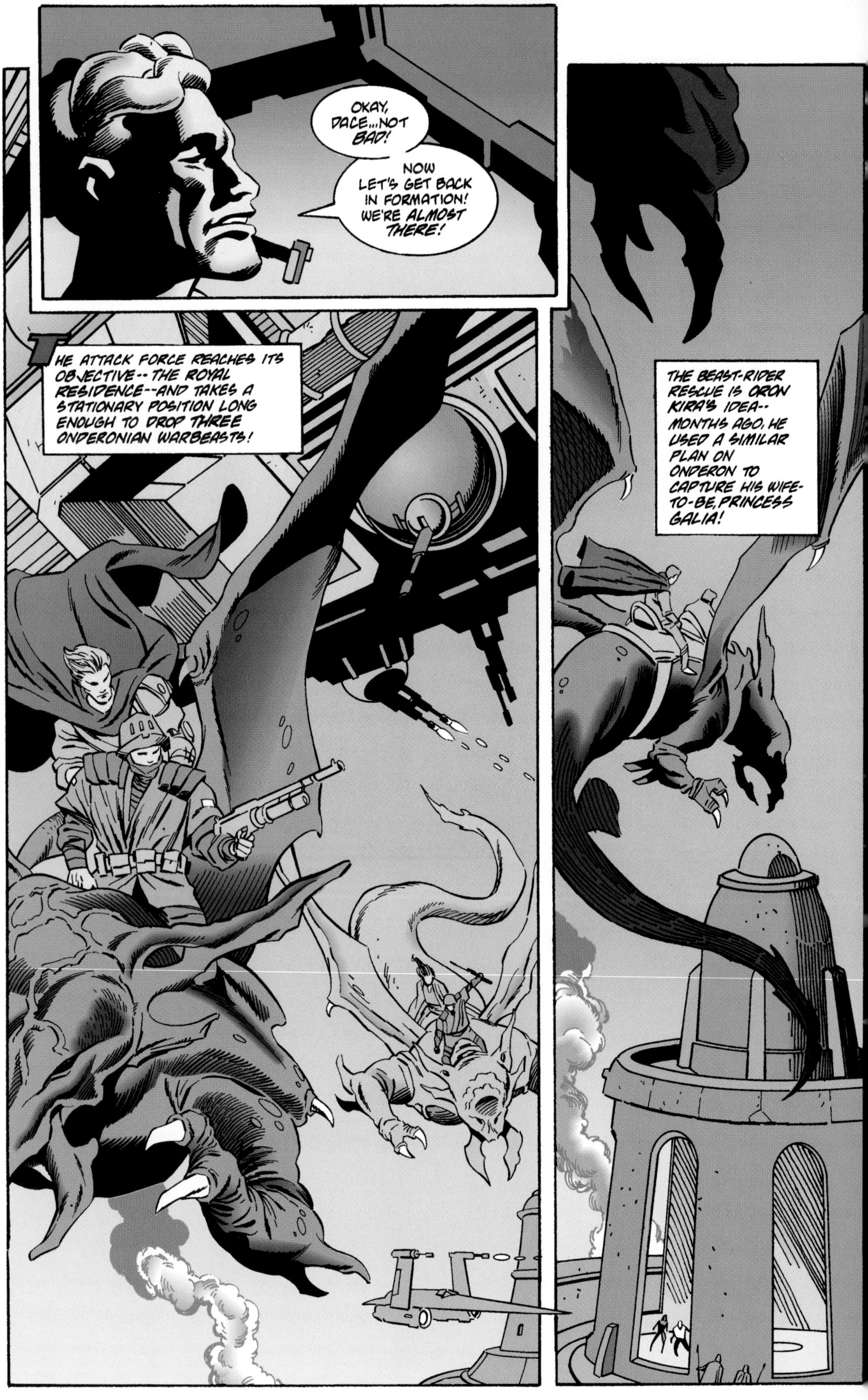
OKAY, DACE...NOT BAD!
NOW LET'S GET BACK IN FORMATION! WE'RE ALMOST THERE!
THE ATTACK FORCE REACHES ITS OBJECTIVE--THE ROYAL RESIDENCE--AND TAKES A STATIONARY POSITION LONG ENOUGH TO DROP THREE ONDERONIAN WARBEASTS!
THE BEAST-RIDER RESCUE IS ORON KIRA'S IDEA--MONTHS AGO, HE USED A SIMILAR PLAN ON ONDERON TO CAPTURE HIS WIFE-TO-BE, PRINCESS GALIA!

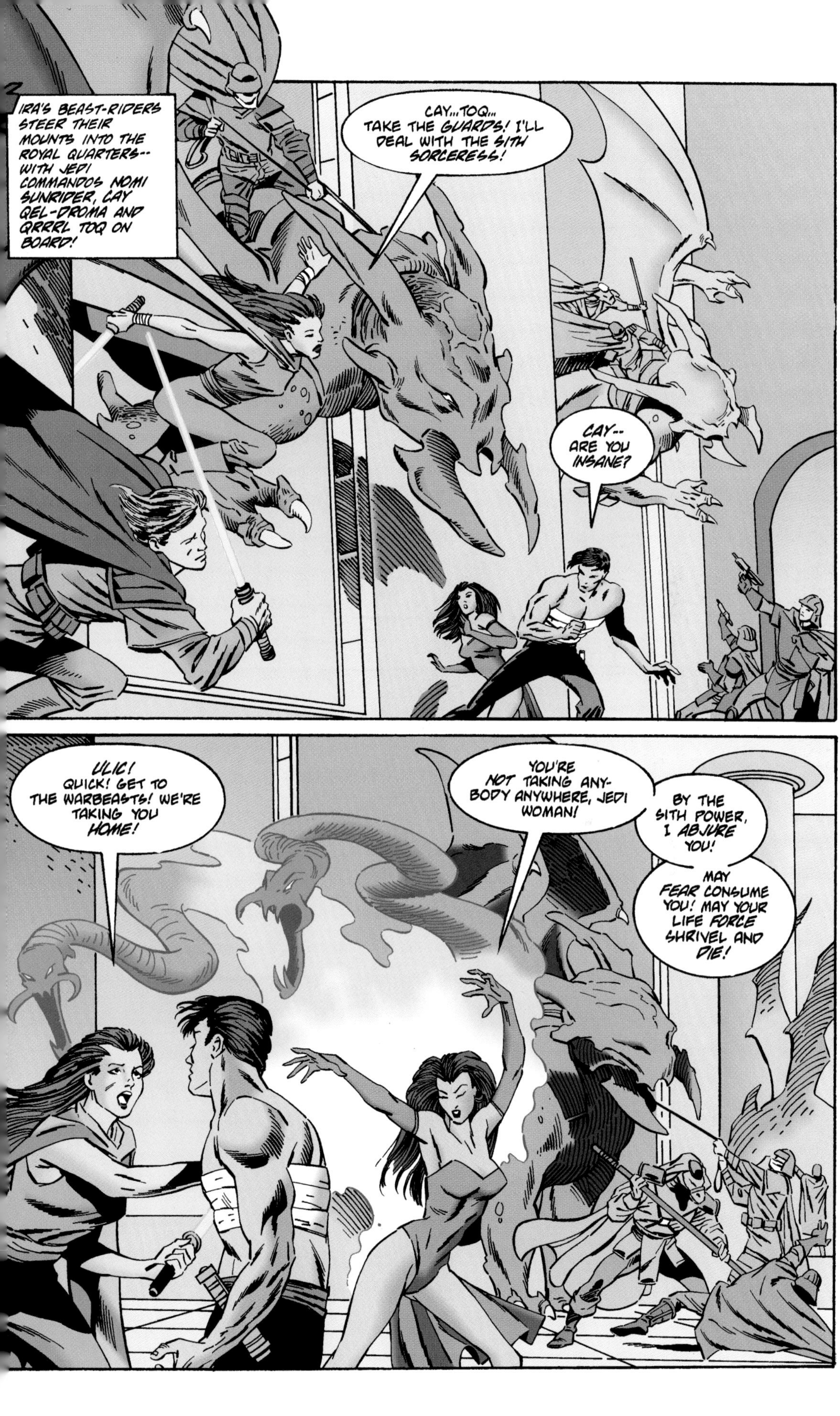
IRA'S BEAST-RIDERS STEER THEIR MOUNTS INTO THE ROYAL QUARTERS-- WITH JEDI COMMANDOS NOMI SUNRIDER, CAY QEL-DROMA AND QRRRL TOQ ON BOARD!
CAY... TOQ... TAKE THE GUARDS! I'LL DEAL WITH THE SITH SORCERESS!
CAY-- ARE YOU INSANE?
ULIC! QUICK! GET TO THE WARBEASTS! WE'RE TAKING YOU HOME!
YOU'RE NOT TAKING ANYBODY ANYWHERE, JEDI WOMAN!
BY THE SITH POWER, I ABJURE YOU!
MAY FEAR CONSUME YOU! MAY YOUR LIFE FORCE SHRIVEL AND DIE!

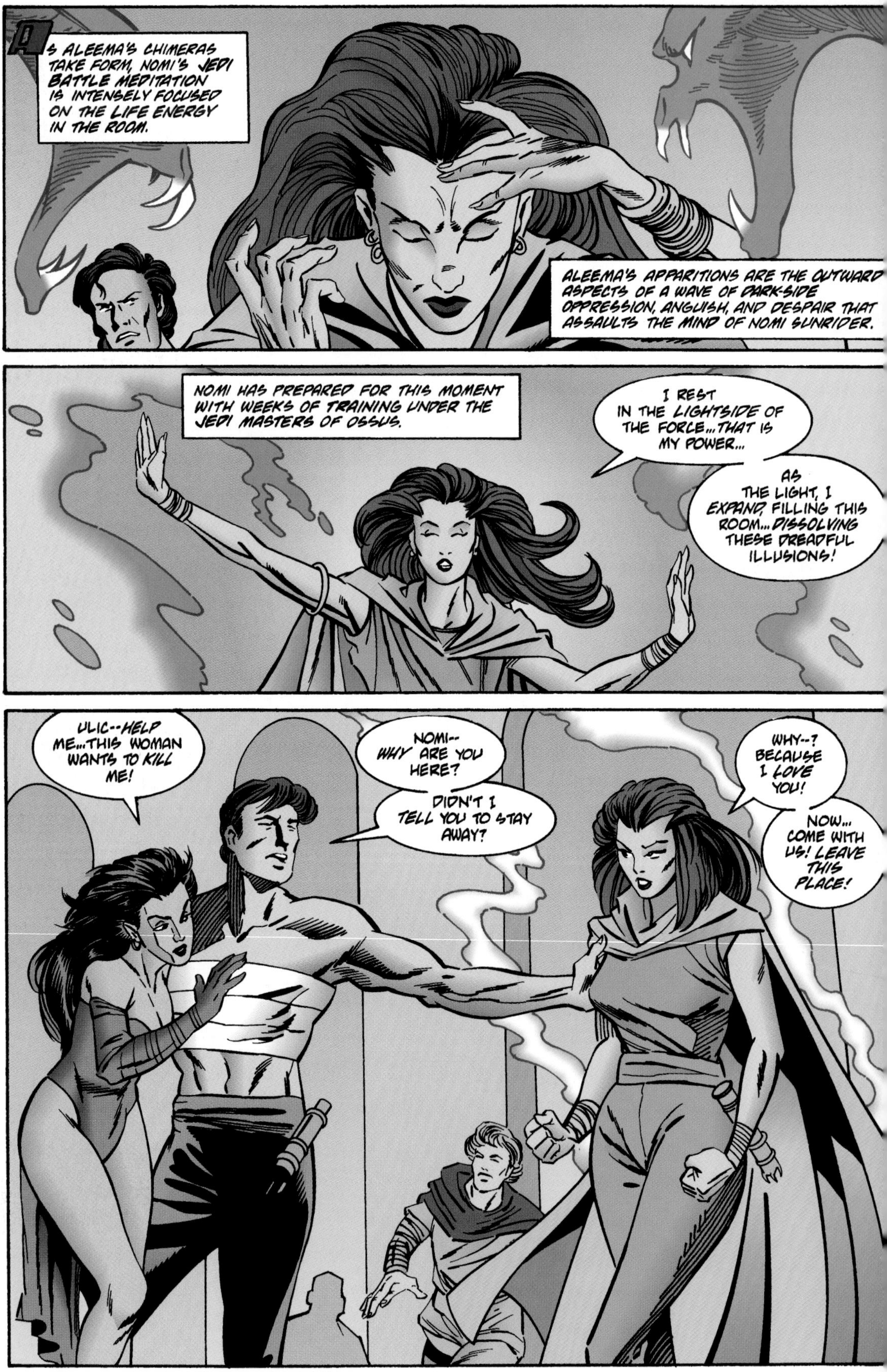
As Aleema's chimeras take form, Nomi's Jedi battle meditation is intensely focused on the life energy in the room.
Aleema's apparitions are the outward aspects of a wave of dark-side oppression, anguish, and despair that assaults the mind of Nomi Sunrider.
Nomi has prepared for this moment with weeks of training under the Jedi Masters of Ossus.
I rest in the lightside of the Force...that is my power...
As the light, I expand, filling this room...dissolving these dreadful illusions!
Ulic--help me...this woman wants to kill me!
Nomi-- why are you here?
Didn't I tell you to stay away?
Why--? Because I love you!
Now... come with us! Leave this place!

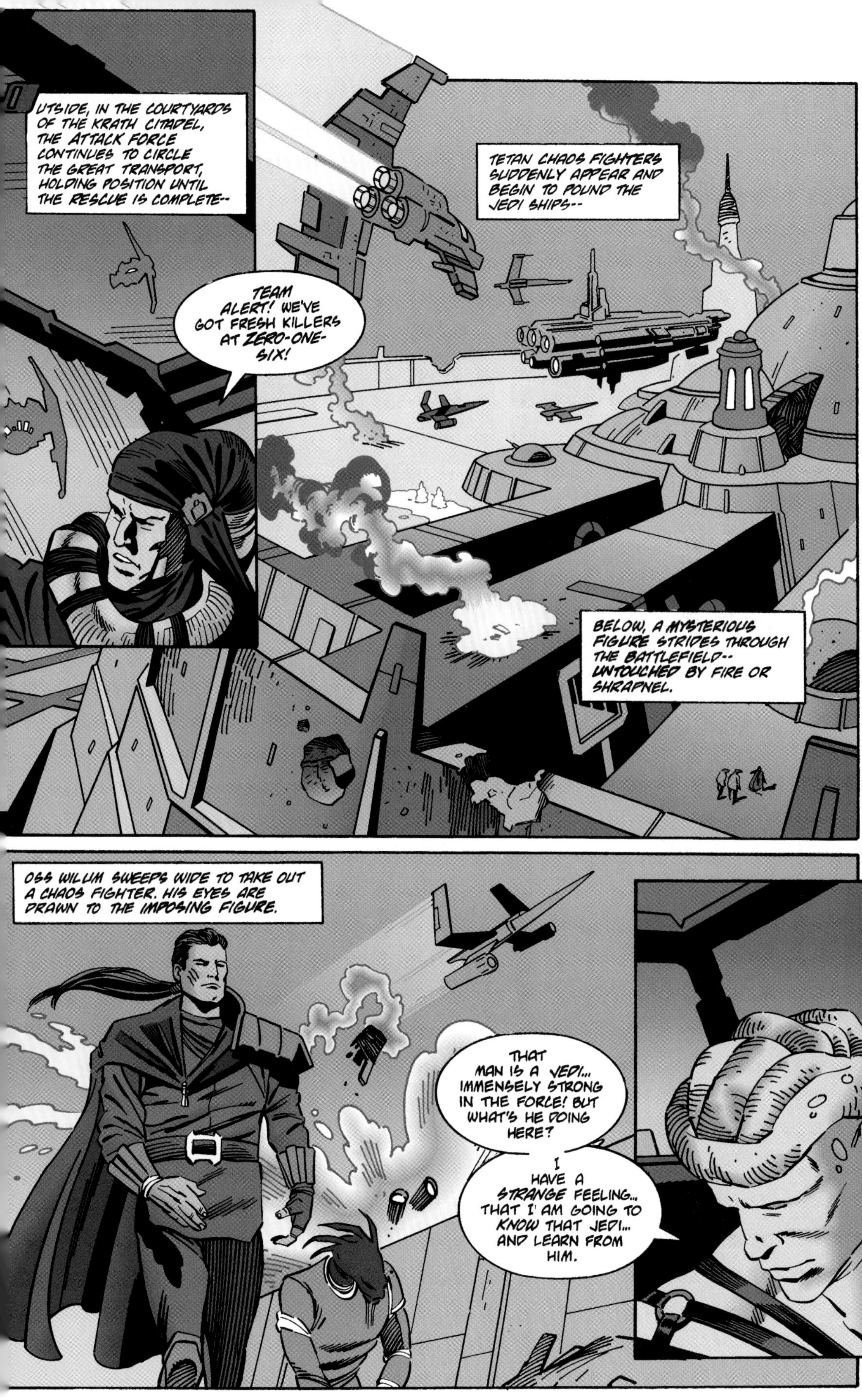
UTSIDE, IN THE COURTYARDS OF THE KRATH CITADEL, THE ATTACK FORCE CONTINUES TO CIRCLE THE GREAT TRANSPORT, HOLDING POSITION UNTIL THE RESCUE IS COMPLETE--
TEAM ALERT! WE'VE GOT FRESH KILLERS AT ZERO-ONE-SIX!
TETAN CHAOS FIGHTERS SUDDENLY APPEAR AND BEGIN TO POUND THE JEDI SHIPS--
BELOW, A MYSTERIOUS FIGURE STRIDES THROUGH THE BATTLEFIELD-- UNTOUCHED BY FIRE OR SHRAPNEL.
OSS WILUM SWEEPS WIDE TO TAKE OUT A CHAOS FIGHTER. HIS EYES ARE DRAWN TO THE IMPOSING FIGURE.
THAT MAN IS A JEDI... IMMENSELY STRONG IN THE FORCE! BUT WHAT'S HE DOING HERE?
I HAVE A STRANGE FEELING... THAT I AM GOING TO KNOW THAT JEDI... AND LEARN FROM HIM.

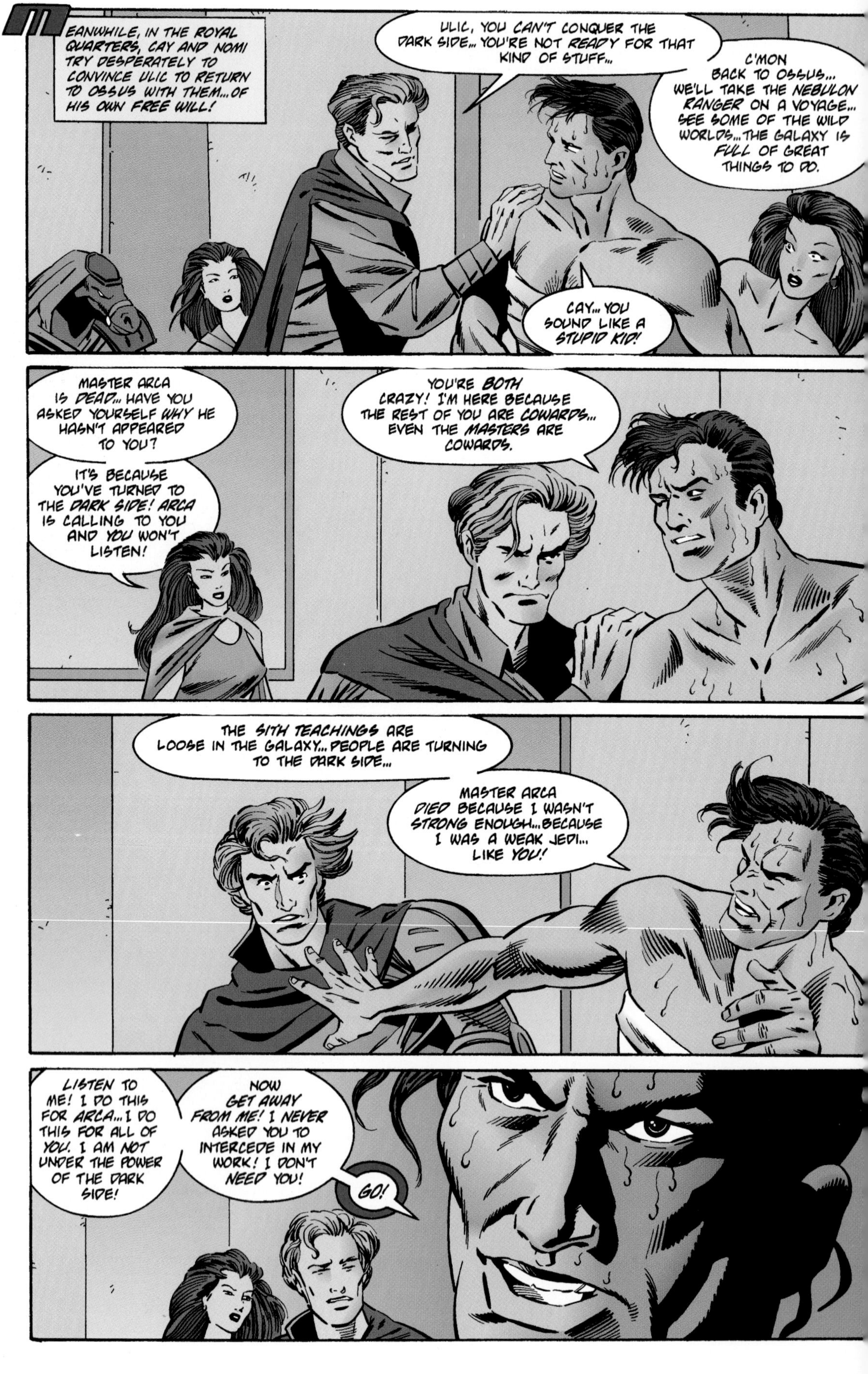
MEANWHILE, IN THE ROYAL QUARTERS, CAY AND NOMI TRY DESPERATELY TO CONVINCE ULIC TO RETURN TO OSSUS WITH THEM... OF HIS OWN FREE WILL!
ULIC, YOU CAN'T CONQUER THE DARK SIDE... YOU'RE NOT READY FOR THAT KIND OF STUFF...
C'MON BACK TO OSSUS... WE'LL TAKE THE NEBULON RANGER ON A VOYAGE... SEE SOME OF THE WILD WORLDS... THE GALAXY IS FULL OF GREAT THINGS TO DO.
CAY... YOU SOUND LIKE A STUPID KID!
MASTER ARCA IS DEAD... HAVE YOU ASKED YOURSELF WHY HE HASN'T APPEARED TO YOU?
IT'S BECAUSE YOU'VE TURNED TO THE DARK SIDE! ARCA IS CALLING TO YOU AND YOU WON'T LISTEN!
YOU'RE BOTH CRAZY! I'M HERE BECAUSE THE REST OF YOU ARE COWARDS... EVEN THE MASTERS ARE COWARDS.
THE SITH TEACHINGS ARE LOOSE IN THE GALAXY... PEOPLE ARE TURNING TO THE DARK SIDE...
MASTER ARCA DIED BECAUSE I WASN'T STRONG ENOUGH... BECAUSE I WAS A WEAK JEDI... LIKE YOU!
LISTEN TO ME! I DO THIS FOR ARCA... I DO THIS FOR ALL OF YOU. I AM NOT UNDER THE POWER OF THE DARK SIDE!
NOW GET AWAY FROM ME! I NEVER ASKED YOU TO INTERCEDE IN MY WORK! I DON'T NEED YOU!
GO!

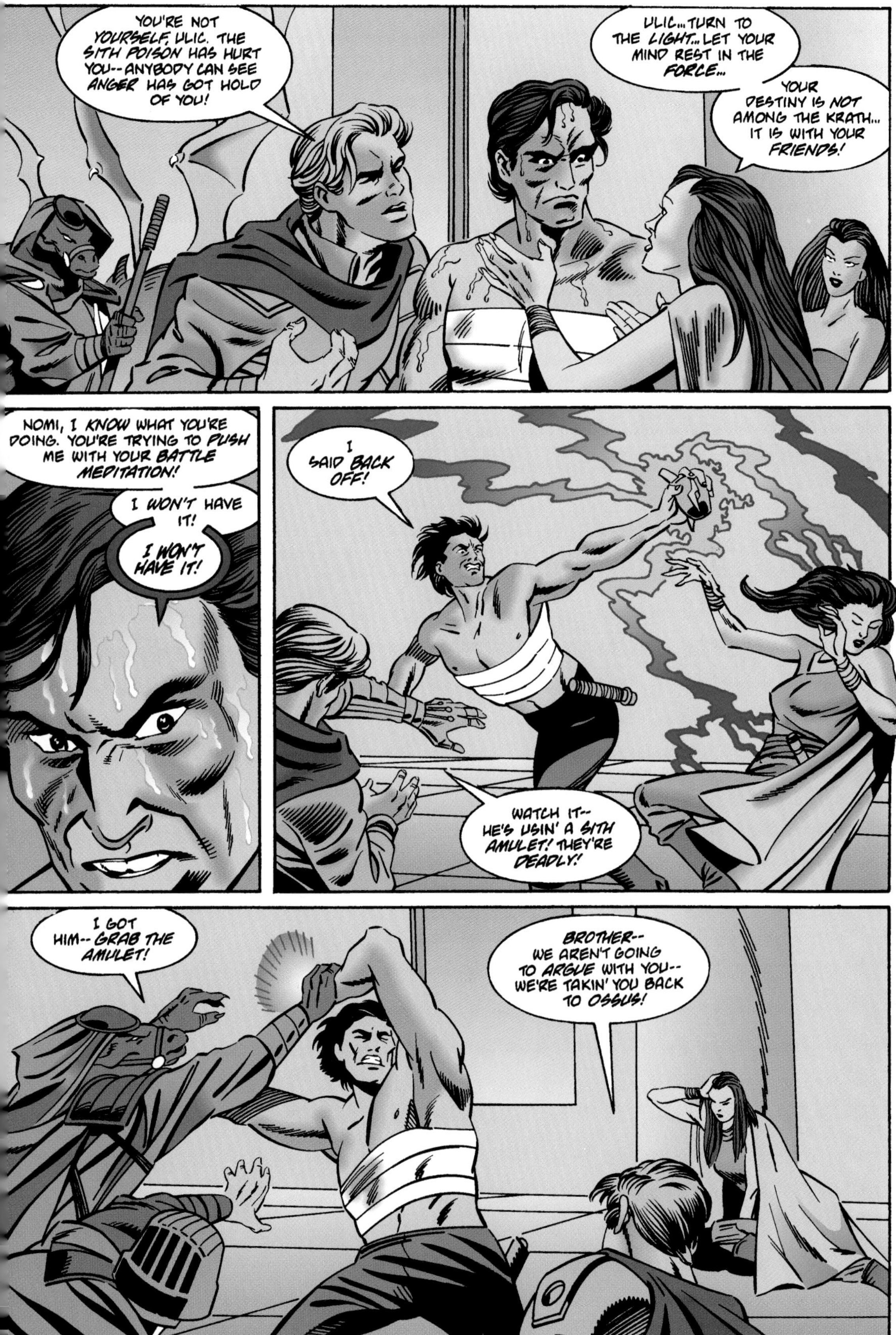

YOU'RE NOT YOURSELF, ULIC. THE SITH POISON HAS HURT YOU--ANYBODY CAN SEE ANGER HAS GOT HOLD OF YOU!
ULIC...TURN TO THE LIGHT...LET YOUR MIND REST IN THE FORCE...
YOUR DESTINY IS NOT AMONG THE KRATH... IT IS WITH YOUR FRIENDS!
NOMI, I KNOW WHAT YOU'RE DOING. YOU'RE TRYING TO PUSH ME WITH YOUR BATTLE MEDITATION!
I WON'T HAVE IT!
I WON'T HAVE IT!
I SAID BACK OFF!
WATCH IT-- HE'S USIN' A SITH AMULET! THEY'RE DEADLY!
I GOT HIM--GRAB THE AMULET!
BROTHER-- WE AREN'T GOING TO ARGUE WITH YOU-- WE'RE TAKIN' YOU BACK TO OSSUS!

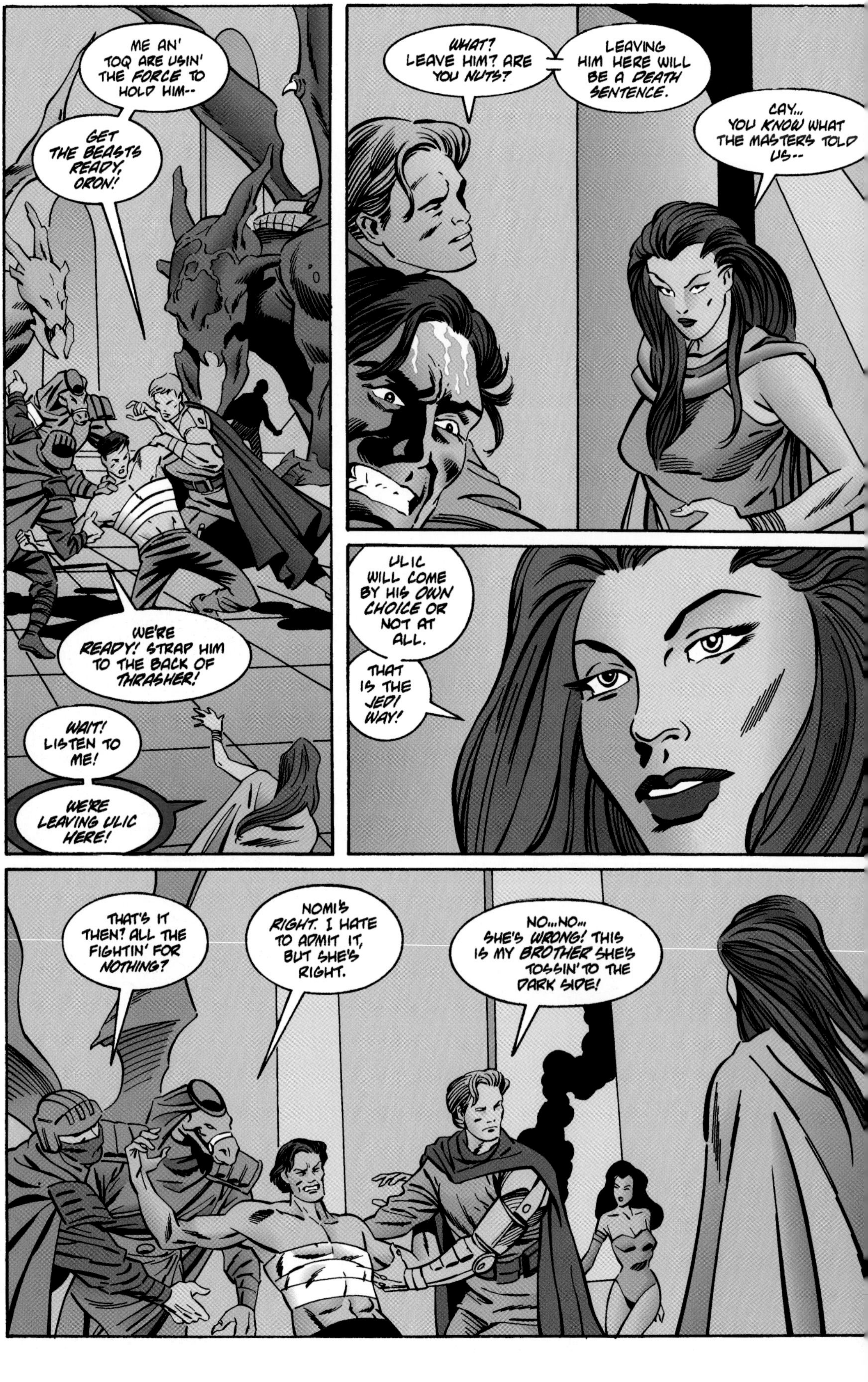
ME AN' TOQ ARE USIN' THE FORCE TO HOLD HIM--
GET THE BEASTS READY, ORON!
WE'RE READY! STRAP HIM TO THE BACK OF THRASHER!
WAIT! LISTEN TO ME!
WE'RE LEAVING ULIC HERE!
WHAT? LEAVE HIM? ARE YOU NUTS?
LEAVING HIM HERE WILL BE A DEATH SENTENCE.
CAY... YOU KNOW WHAT THE MASTERS TOLD US--
ULIC WILL COME BY HIS OWN CHOICE OR NOT AT ALL.
THAT IS THE JEDI WAY!
THAT'S IT THEN? ALL THE FIGHTIN' FOR NOTHING?
NOMI'S RIGHT. I HATE TO ADMIT IT, BUT SHE'S RIGHT.
NO...NO... SHE'S WRONG! THIS IS MY BROTHER SHE'S TOSSIN' TO THE DARK SIDE!

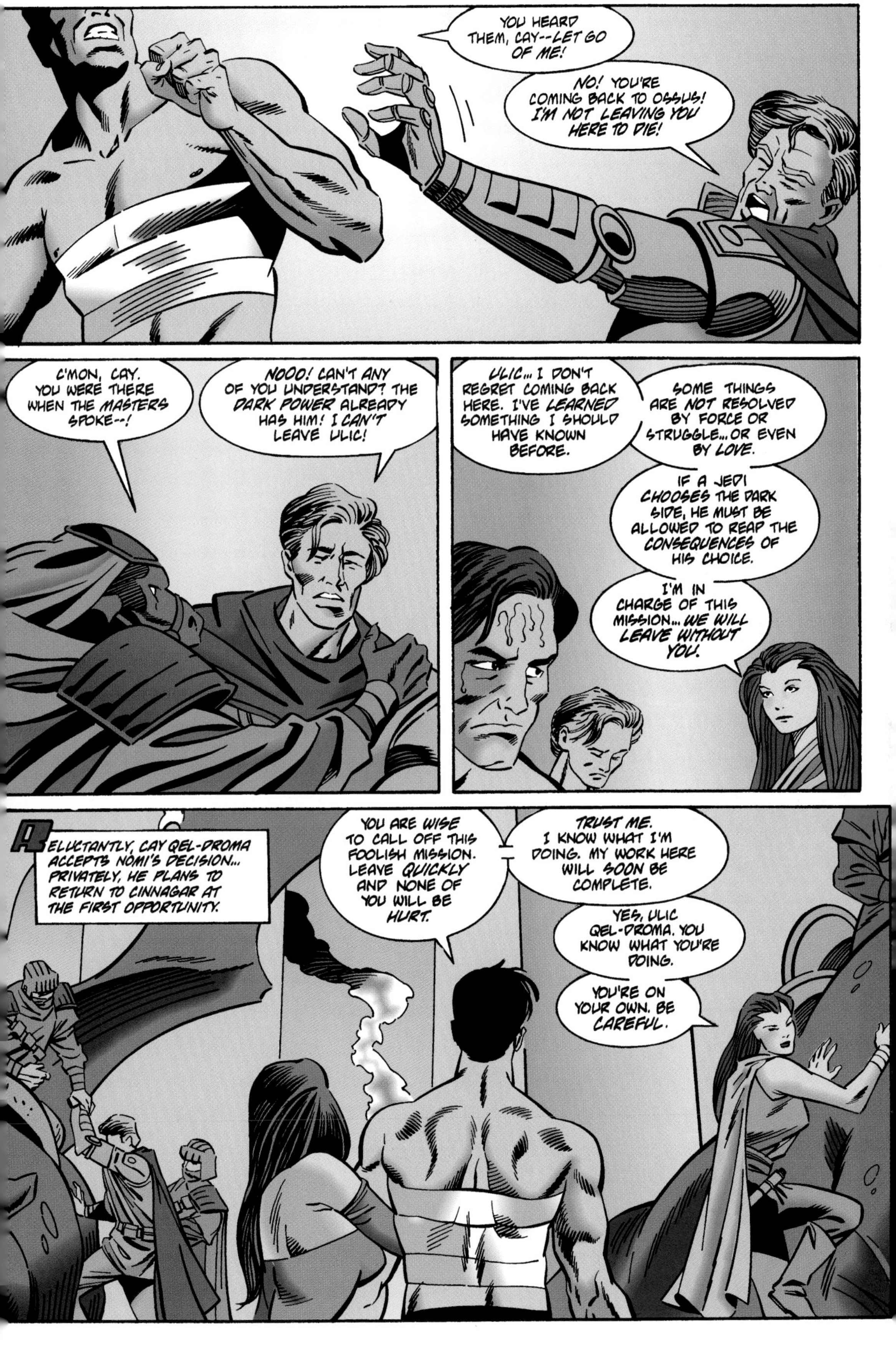
YOU HEARD THEM, CAY--LET GO OF ME!
NO! YOU'RE COMING BACK TO OSSUS! I'M NOT LEAVING YOU HERE TO DIE!
C'MON, CAY. YOU WERE THERE WHEN THE MASTERS SPOKE--!
NOOO! CAN'T ANY OF YOU UNDERSTAND? THE DARK POWER ALREADY HAS HIM! I CAN'T LEAVE ULIC!
ULIC... I DON'T REGRET COMING BACK HERE. I'VE LEARNED SOMETHING I SHOULD HAVE KNOWN BEFORE.
SOME THINGS ARE NOT RESOLVED BY FORCE OR STRUGGLE... OR EVEN BY LOVE.
IF A JEDI CHOOSES THE DARK SIDE, HE MUST BE ALLOWED TO REAP THE CONSEQUENCES OF HIS CHOICE.
I'M IN CHARGE OF THIS MISSION... WE WILL LEAVE WITHOUT YOU.
RELUCTANTLY, CAY QEL-DROMA ACCEPTS NOMI'S DECISION... PRIVATELY, HE PLANS TO RETURN TO CINNAGAR AT THE FIRST OPPORTUNITY.
YOU ARE WISE TO CALL OFF THIS FOOLISH MISSION. LEAVE QUICKLY AND NONE OF YOU WILL BE HURT.
TRUST ME. I KNOW WHAT I'M DOING. MY WORK HERE WILL SOON BE COMPLETE.
YES, ULIC QEL-DROMA. YOU KNOW WHAT YOU'RE DOING.
YOU'RE ON YOUR OWN. BE CAREFUL.

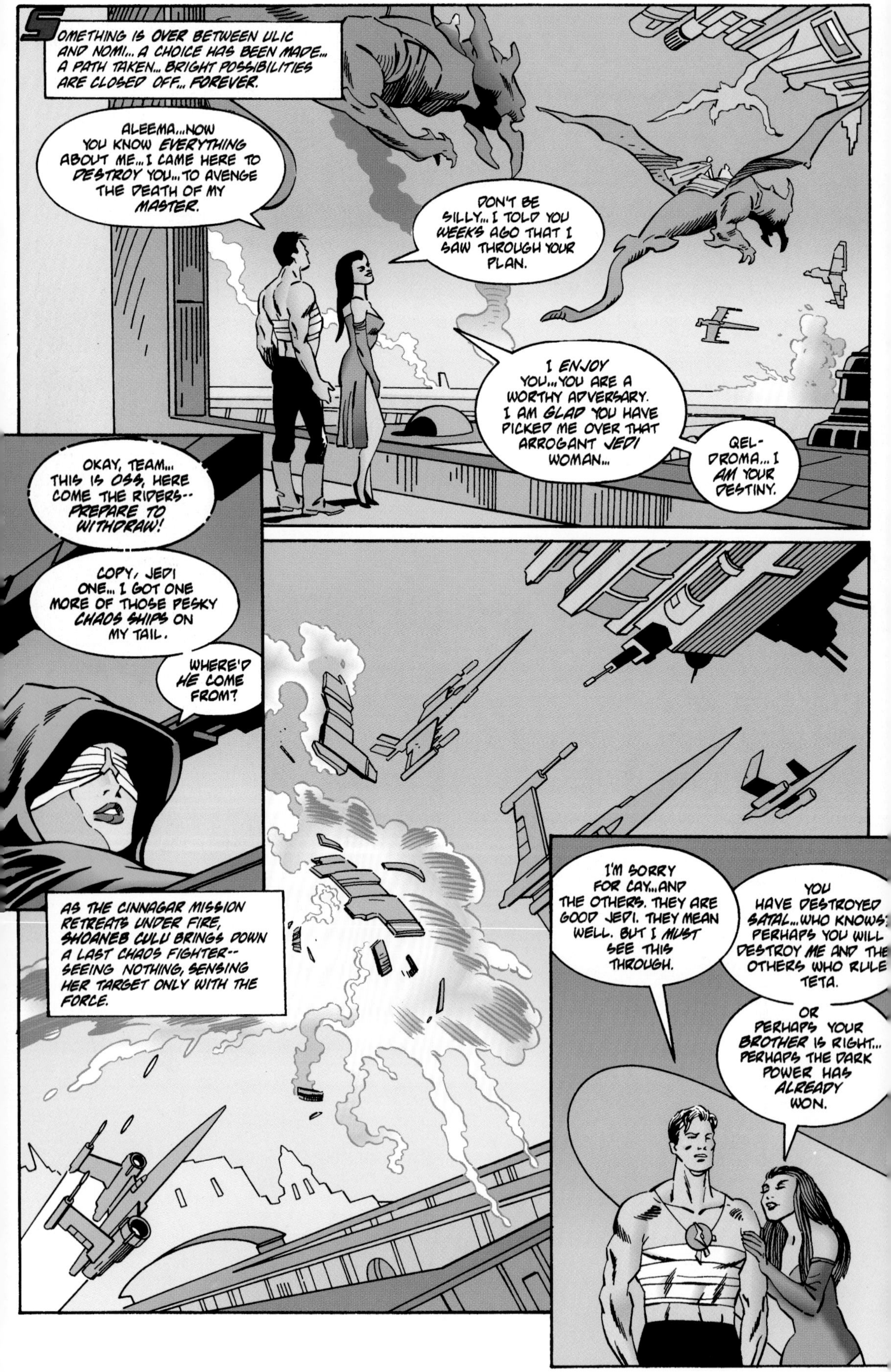

SOMETHING IS OVER BETWEEN ULIC AND NOMI... A CHOICE HAS BEEN MADE... A PATH TAKEN... BRIGHT POSSIBILITIES ARE CLOSED OFF... FOREVER.
ALEEMA...NOW YOU KNOW EVERYTHING ABOUT ME...I CAME HERE TO DESTROY YOU...TO AVENGE THE DEATH OF MY MASTER.
DON'T BE SILLY...I TOLD YOU WEEKS AGO THAT I SAW THROUGH YOUR PLAN.
I ENJOY YOU...YOU ARE A WORTHY ADVERSARY. I AM GLAD YOU HAVE PICKED ME OVER THAT ARROGANT JEDI WOMAN...
QEL-DROMA... I AM YOUR DESTINY.
OKAY, TEAM... THIS IS OSS, HERE COME THE RIDERS-- PREPARE TO WITHDRAW!
COPY, JEDI ONE... I GOT ONE MORE OF THOSE PESKY CHAOS SHIPS ON MY TAIL.
WHERE'D HE COME FROM?
AS THE CINNAGAR MISSION RETREATS UNDER FIRE, SHOANEB CULU BRINGS DOWN A LAST CHAOS FIGHTER-- SEEING NOTHING, SENSING HER TARGET ONLY WITH THE FORCE.
I'M SORRY FOR CAY...AND THE OTHERS. THEY ARE GOOD JEDI. THEY MEAN WELL. BUT I MUST SEE THIS THROUGH.
YOU HAVE DESTROYED SATAL...WHO KNOWS: PERHAPS YOU WILL DESTROY ME AND THE OTHERS WHO RULE TETA.
OR PERHAPS YOUR BROTHER IS RIGHT... PERHAPS THE DARK POWER HAS ALREADY WON.

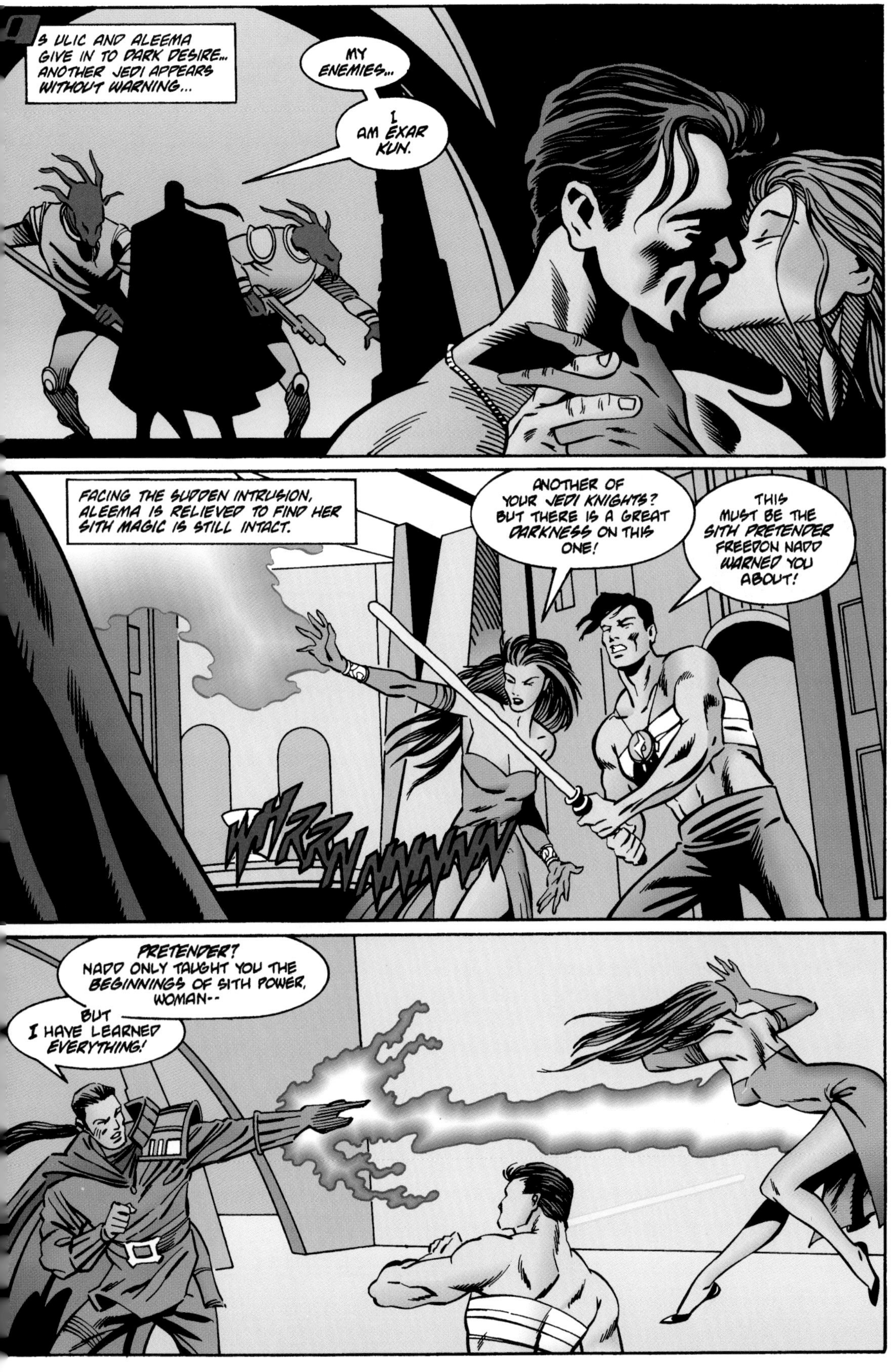
S ULIC AND ALEEMA GIVE IN TO DARK DESIRE... ANOTHER JEDI APPEARS WITHOUT WARNING...
MY ENEMIES...
I AM EXAR KUN.
FACING THE SUDDEN INTRUSION, ALEEMA IS RELIEVED TO FIND HER SITH MAGIC IS STILL INTACT.
ANOTHER OF YOUR JEDI KNIGHTS? BUT THERE IS A GREAT DARKNESS ON THIS ONE!
THIS MUST BE THE SITH PRETENDER FREEDON NADD WARNED YOU ABOUT!
PRETENDER? NADD ONLY TAUGHT YOU THE BEGINNINGS OF SITH POWER, WOMAN--
BUT I HAVE LEARNED EVERYTHING!

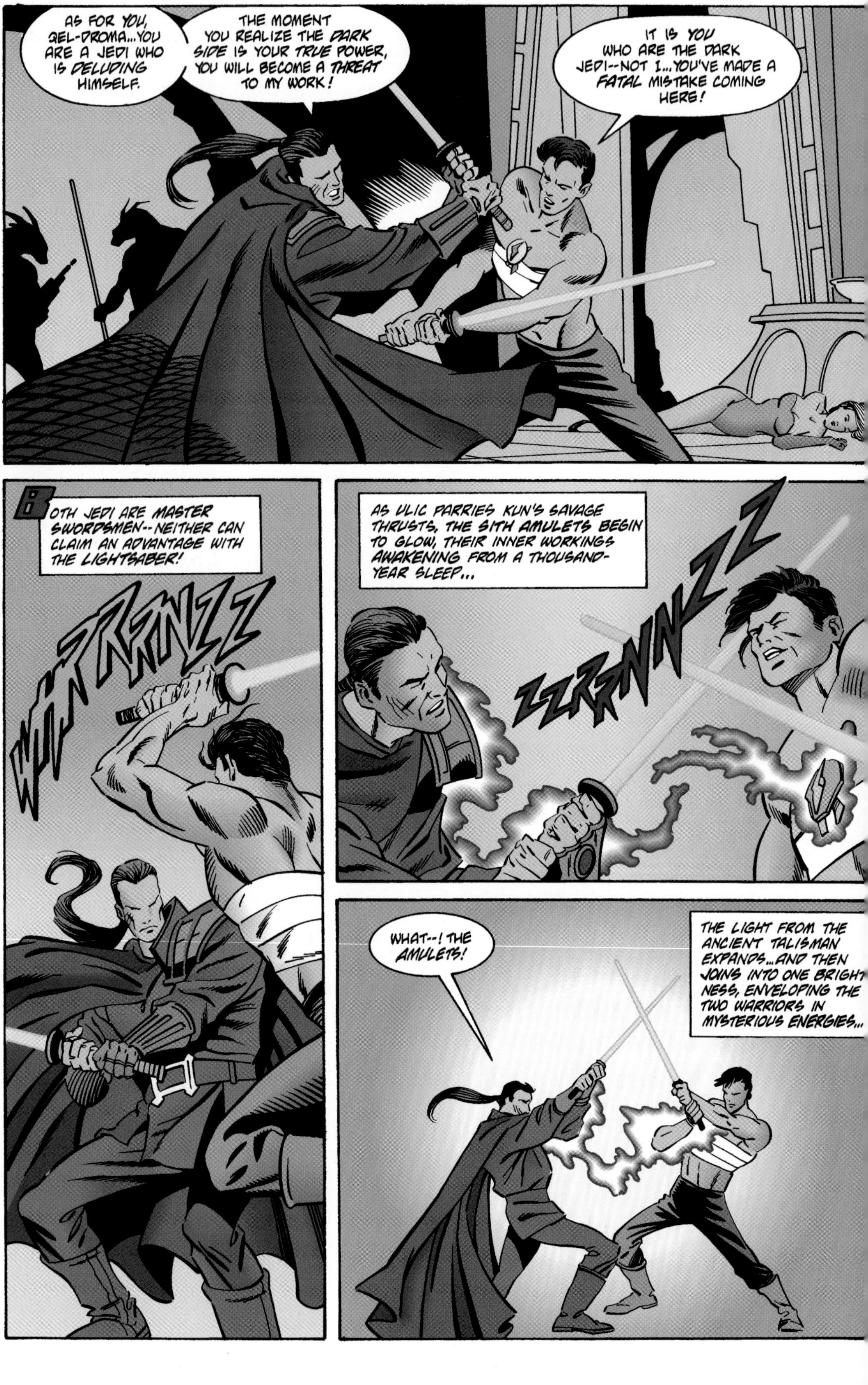
AS FOR YOU, QEL-DROMA...YOU ARE A JEDI WHO IS DELUDING HIMSELF.
THE MOMENT YOU REALIZE THE DARK SIDE IS YOUR TRUE POWER, YOU WILL BECOME A THREAT TO MY WORK!
IT IS YOU WHO ARE THE DARK JEDI--NOT I...YOU'VE MADE A FATAL MISTAKE COMING HERE!
BOTH JEDI ARE MASTER SWORDSMEN--NEITHER CAN CLAIM AN ADVANTAGE WITH THE LIGHTSABER!
WHHRRNZZ
AS ULIC PARRIES KUN'S SAVAGE THRUSTS, THE SITH AMULETS BEGIN TO GLOW, THEIR INNER WORKINGS AWAKENING FROM A THOUSAND-YEAR SLEEP...
ZZRRNNNZZ
WHAT--! THE AMULETS!
THE LIGHT FROM THE ANCIENT TALISMAN EXPANDS...AND THEN JOINS INTO ONE BRIGHTNESS, ENVELOPING THE TWO WARRIORS IN MYSTERIOUS ENERGIES...

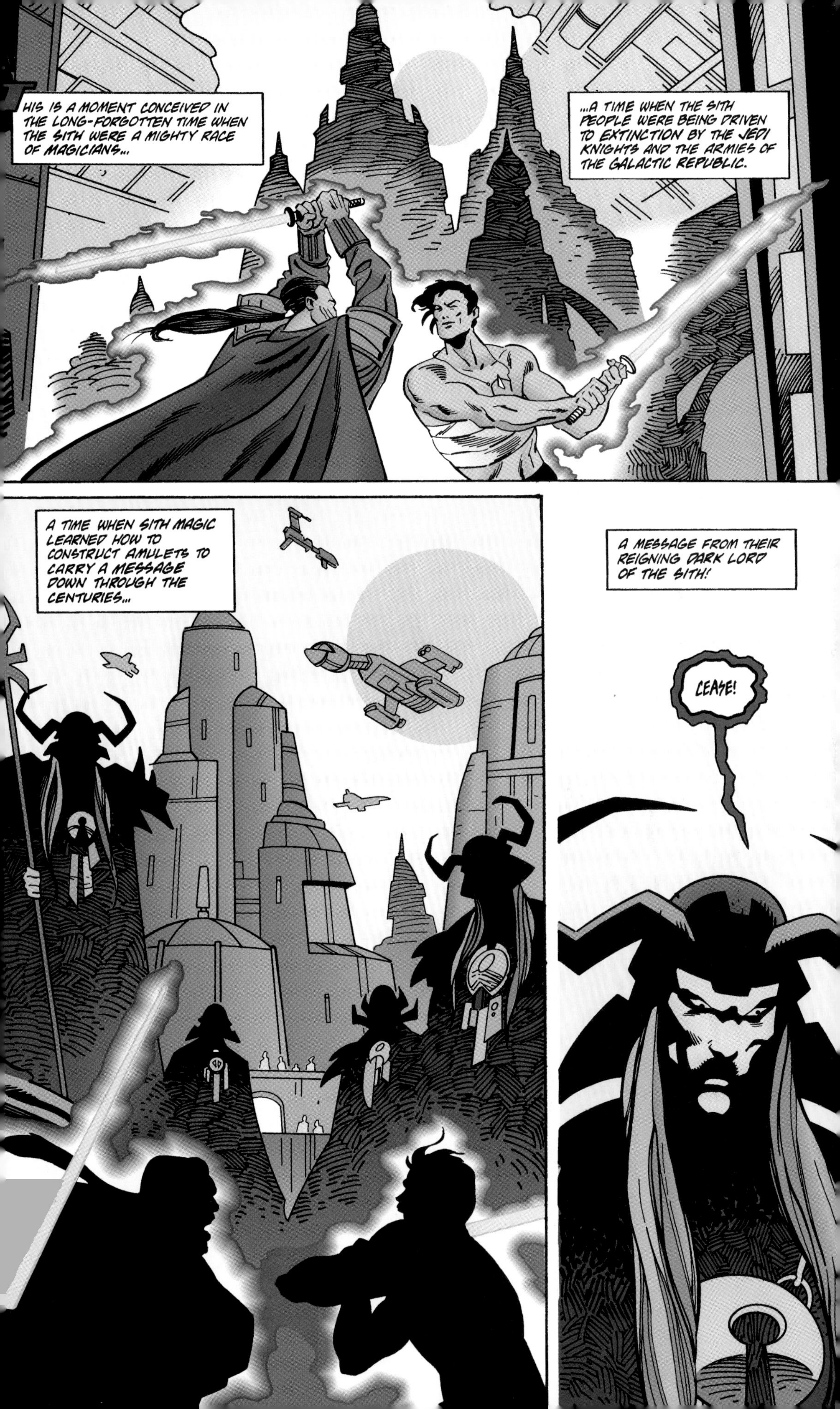
HIS IS A MOMENT CONCEIVED IN THE LONG-FORGOTTEN TIME WHEN THE SITH WERE A MIGHTY RACE OF MAGICIANS...
...A TIME WHEN THE SITH PEOPLE WERE BEING DRIVEN TO EXTINCTION BY THE JEDI KNIGHTS AND THE ARMIES OF THE GALACTIC REPUBLIC.
A TIME WHEN SITH MAGIC LEARNED HOW TO CONSTRUCT AMULETS TO CARRY A MESSAGE DOWN THROUGH THE CENTURIES...
A MESSAGE FROM THEIR REIGNING DARK LORD OF THE SITH!
CEASE!

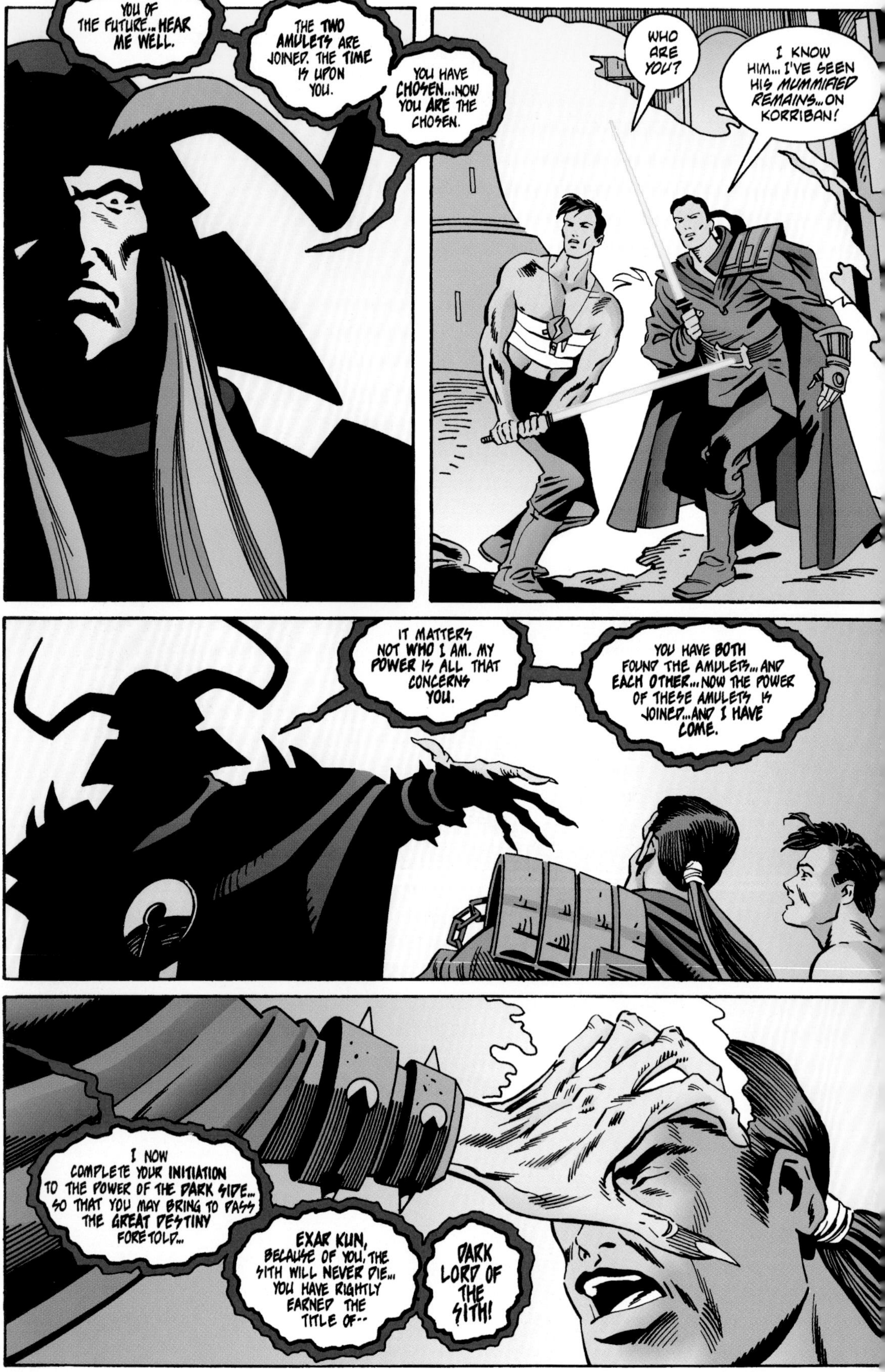
YOU OF THE FUTURE... HEAR ME WELL.
THE TWO AMULETS ARE JOINED. THE TIME IS UPON YOU.
YOU HAVE CHOSEN...NOW YOU ARE THE CHOSEN.
WHO ARE YOU?
I KNOW HIM... I'VE SEEN HIS MUMMIFIED REMAINS...ON KORRIBAN!
IT MATTERS NOT WHO I AM. MY POWER IS ALL THAT CONCERNS YOU.
YOU HAVE BOTH FOUND THE AMULETS...AND EACH OTHER...NOW THE POWER OF THESE AMULETS IS JOINED...AND I HAVE COME.
I NOW COMPLETE YOUR INITIATION TO THE POWER OF THE DARK SIDE... SO THAT YOU MAY BRING TO PASS THE GREAT DESTINY FORETOLD...
EXAR KUN, BECAUSE OF YOU, THE SITH WILL NEVER DIE... YOU HAVE RIGHTLY EARNED THE TITLE OF--
DARK LORD OF THE SITH!

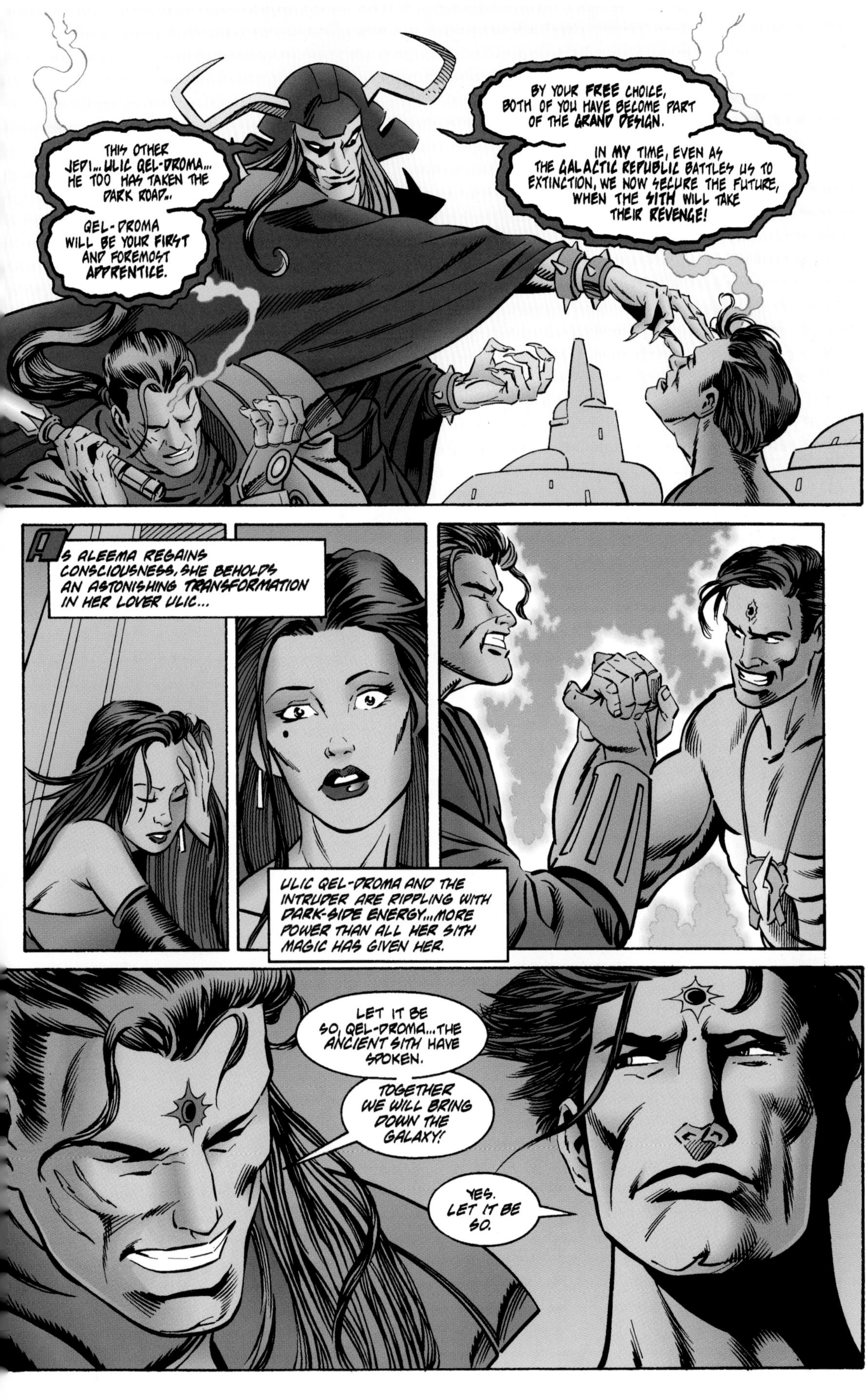
THIS OTHER JEDI... ULIC QEL-DROMA... HE TOO HAS TAKEN THE DARK ROAD...
QEL-DROMA WILL BE YOUR FIRST AND FOREMOST APPRENTICE.
BY YOUR FREE CHOICE, BOTH OF YOU HAVE BECOME PART OF THE GRAND DESIGN.
IN MY TIME, EVEN AS THE GALACTIC REPUBLIC BATTLES US TO EXTINCTION, WE NOW SECURE THE FUTURE, WHEN THE SITH WILL TAKE THEIR REVENGE!
AS ALEEMA REGAINS CONSCIOUSNESS, SHE BEHOLDS AN ASTONISHING TRANSFORMATION IN HER LOVER ULIC...
ULIC QEL-DROMA AND THE INTRUDER ARE RIPPLING WITH DARK-SIDE ENERGY...MORE POWER THAN ALL HER SITH MAGIC HAS GIVEN HER.
LET IT BE SO, QEL-DROMA...THE ANCIENT SITH HAVE SPOKEN.
TOGETHER WE WILL BRING DOWN THE GALAXY!
YES. LET IT BE SO.

The Artist Behind the Covers

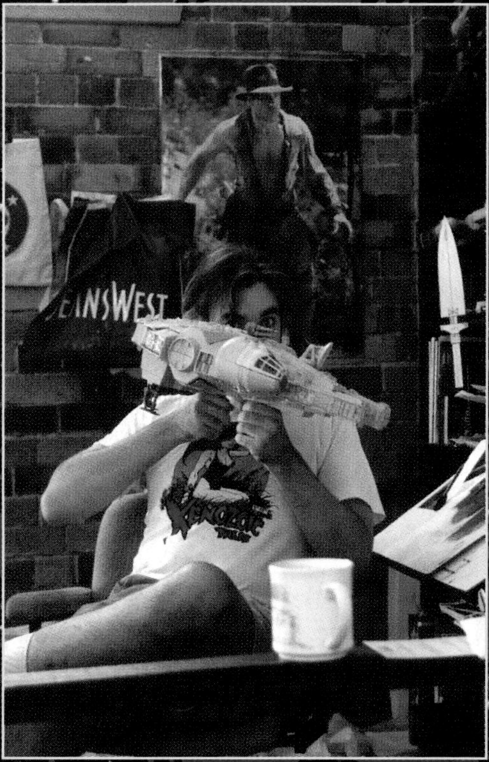

Hugh Fleming

*H*ugh Fleming, one of the best artists in the business, has been making a splash in recent years illustrating various *Star Wars* and *Indiana Jones* comic-book covers for Dark Horse Comics. His semi-photo-realistic painting style combines the character likenesses that *Star Wars* and Indy fans have come to expect, with a striking sense of light, texture, and wonder. In a very short time, Fleming has built up quite a fan following with his cover work on *Indiana Jones: Thunder in the Orient* and *Star Wars: Tales of the Jedi - Dark Lords of the Sith,* the latter of which is featured on the following pages.

A love of comics that began as a child is what eventually led Fleming to pursue work in the comics field. Primarily self-taught, he'd worked as a commercial artist for a few years but didn't like it much. Fleming finds that work becomes a real chore for him if he's not interested in what he's doing. In 1988, a friend and fellow movie buff helped rekindle Hugh's interest in comics. Says Hugh, "I saw some of the new stuff that the [comics] industry was serving up and it renewed my interest."

Drew Struzan, who worked on, among other things, *Indiana Jones* and *Star Wars* movie posters, was a major influence on Hugh's style. Struzan uses gesso — a type of modeling paste — as a thick undercoat, to produce a textured and stylistically bold image, with noticeable loops, whirls, and patterns. This style — as well as the familiar, montage, movie-poster style composition — is something that Hugh very consciously tries to achieve. He likes the effects montage can accomplish and admits that it's easier: "You can slap different things onto a page . . . [and they] don't have to relate directly to each other in terms of lighting and perspective."

Hugh's also a fan of Steve Rude's and Bill Sienkiewicz's painting styles. Talking about the infusion of stylistic influences, Hugh explains that, for him, there are different levels of influence. He points out that if he likes something about someone else's style, "it's going to trickle through," even if it's not obvious to the casual observer. You wouldn't necessarily see anything of Sienkiewicz's style in Hugh's painting, but, he says, "I'd like to think there's a little bit of Steve Rude in there and a fair proportion of Struzan." Hugh also considers among his influences and inspirations Dave Stevens, J.W. Waterhouse, and Alphonse Mucha.

Hugh Fleming lives and works in Brisbane, Australia. He is insanely happy and if he had his life to live over, he would do it all the same way again.

Except next time, he'd skip seeing any of the Batman movies.

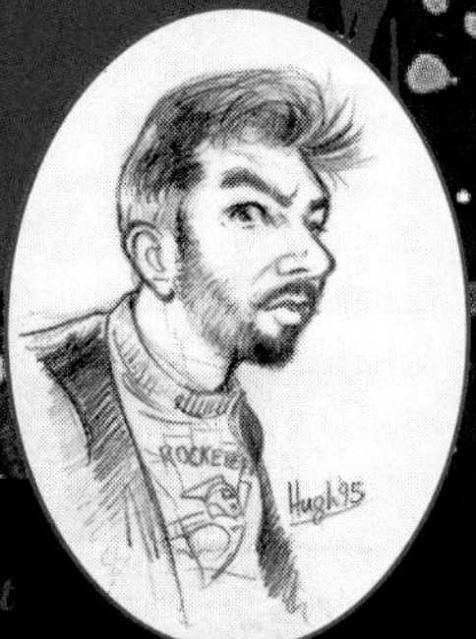
Hugh'95

Self-portrait

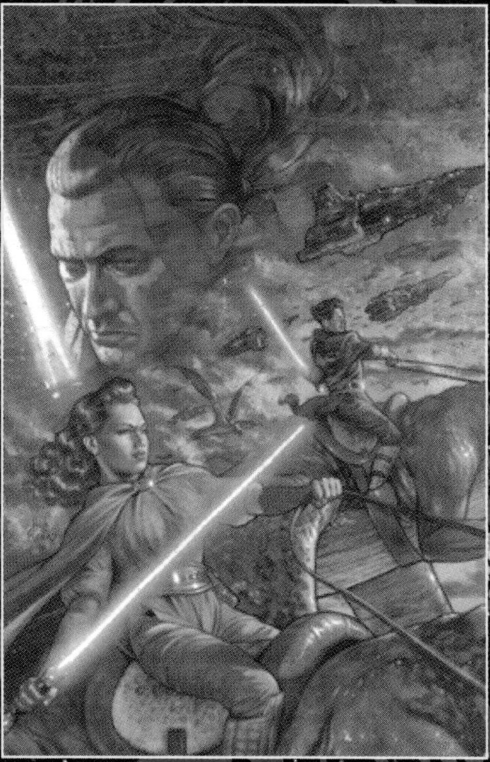

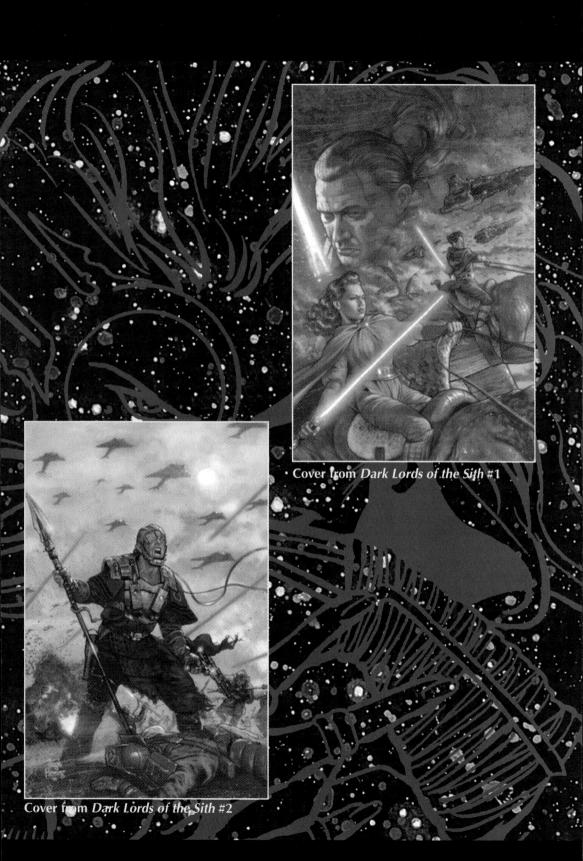

Cover from *Dark Lords of the Sith* #1

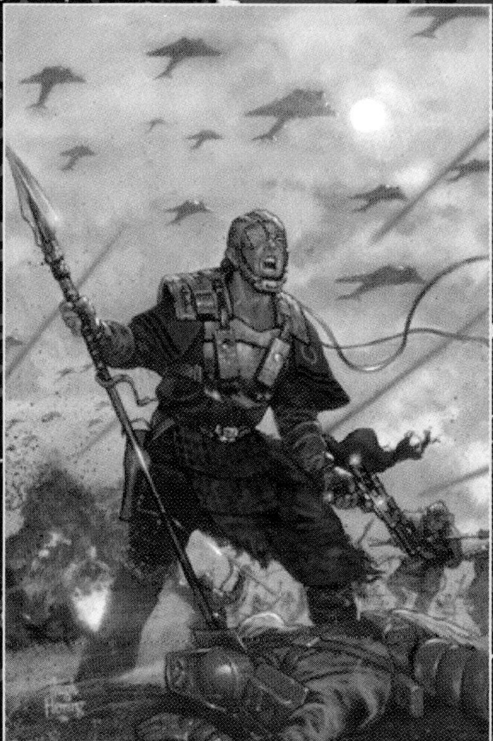

Cover from *Dark Lords of the Sith* #2

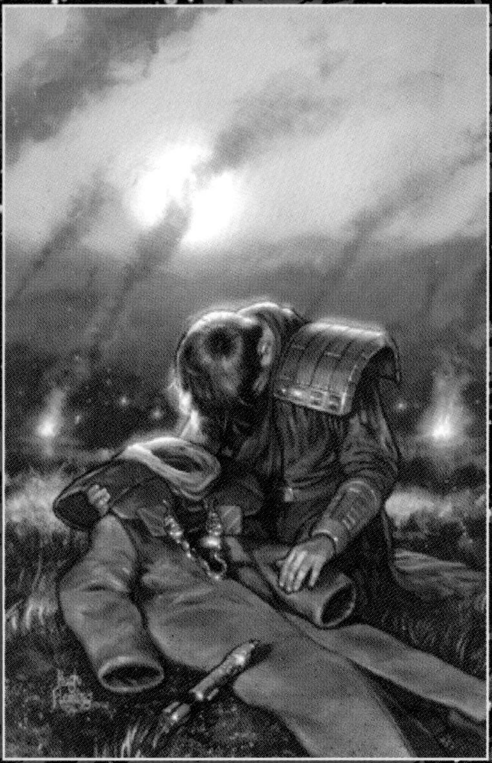

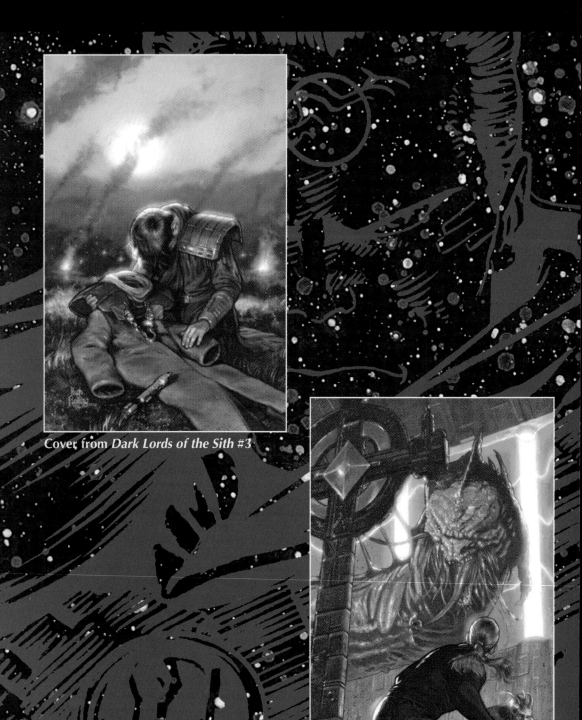

Cover from *Dark Lords of the Sith* #3

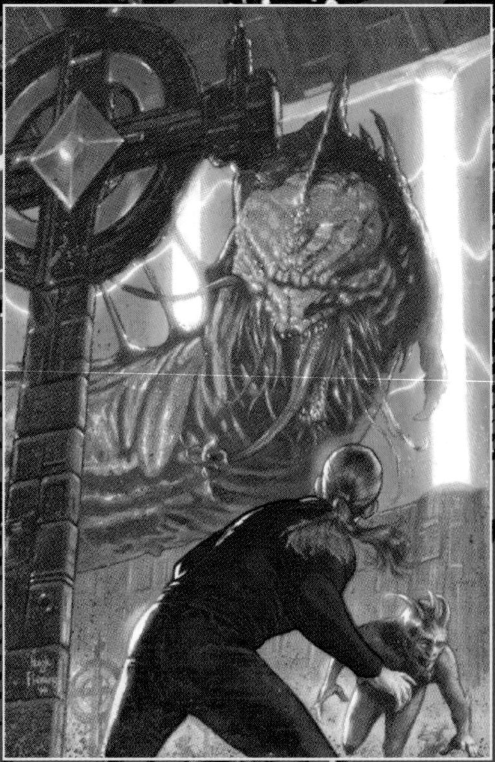

Cover from *Dark Lords of the Sith* #4

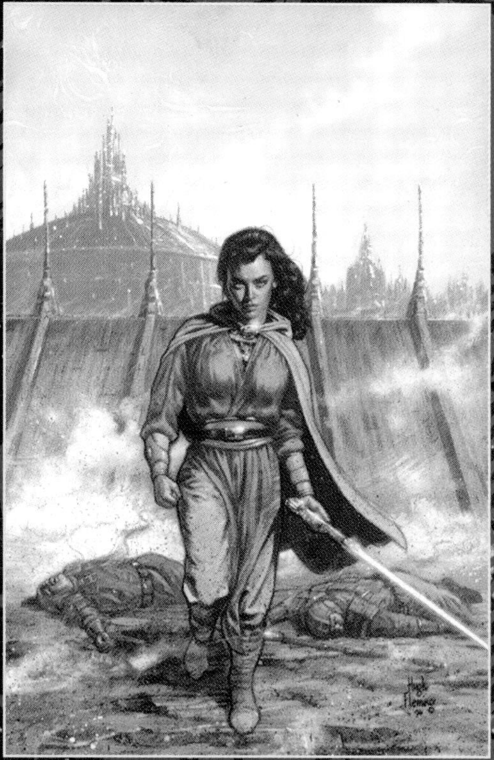

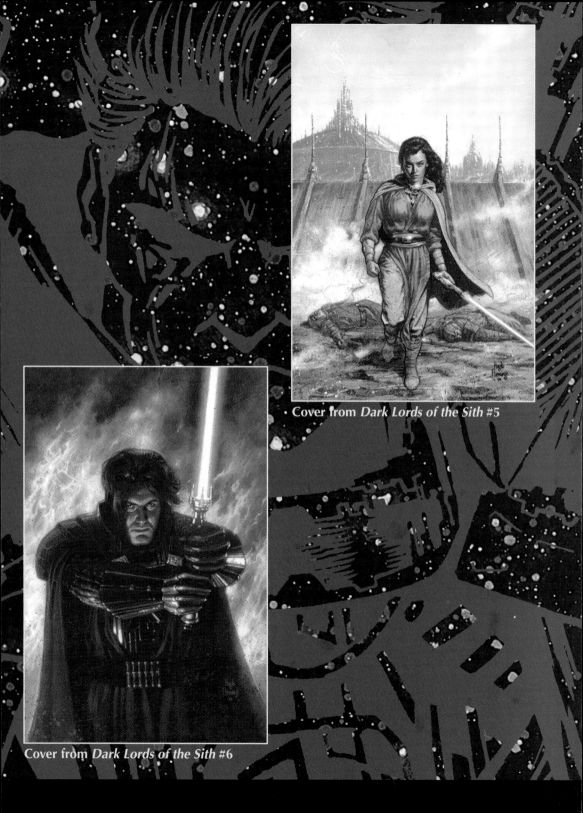

Cover from *Dark Lords of the Sith* #5

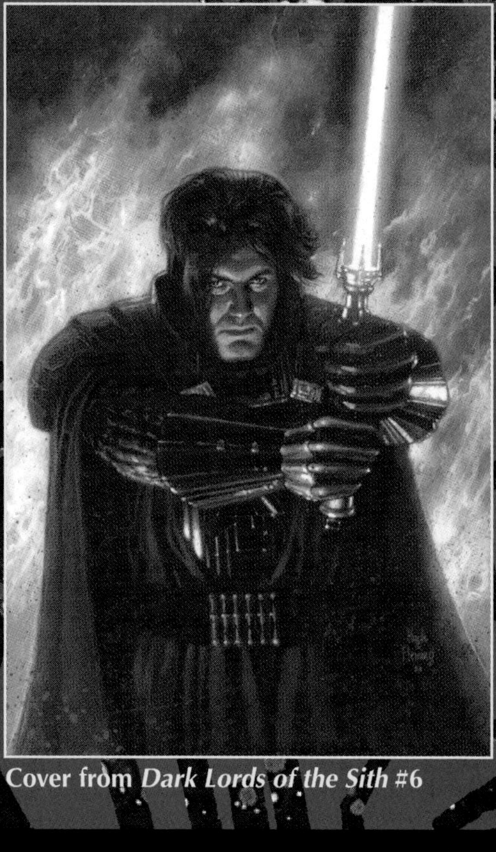

Cover from *Dark Lords of the Sith* #6

Dark Horse Comics: **Mike Richardson** *publisher* • **Neil Hankerson** *executive vice president* • **Andy Karabatsos** *vice president of finance* • **Randy Stradley** *vice president of publishing* • **Cindy Marks** *director of production & design* • **Mark Cox** *art director* • **Sean Tierney** *computer graphics director* • **Michael Martens** *vice president of marketing* • **Tod Borleske** *vice president of sales & licensing* • **David Scroggy** *vice president of product development* • **Dale LaFountain** *director of m.i.s.* • **Kim Haines** *director of human resources* • **Ken Lizzi** *general counsel*